A Soldier's World War II Diary

———— 1943–45 ————

BETWEEN
TEDIUM
AND
TERROR

Sy M. Kahn

Foreword by Ronald Spector

UNIVERSITY OF ILLINOIS PRESS

Urbana and Chicago

This book is printed on acid-free paper.

Library of Congress Cataloging-in-Publication Data

Kahn, Sy Myron, 1924–
    Between tedium and terror : a soldier's World War II diary,
1943–45 / Sy M. Kahn : foreword by Ronald Spector.
        p.   cm.
    Includes index.
    ISBN 0-252-01858-3 (alk. paper)
    1. Kahn, Sy Myron, 1924–   . 2. World War, 1939–1945—Campaigns—
Pacific Area.   3. World War, 1939–1945—Personal narratives,
American.   4. Soldiers—United States—Diaries.   5. United States.
Army—Biography.   I. Title.
D811.5.K2913   1993
940.54′25′092—dc20
    [B]   92-22934
                                                                           CIP

BETWEEN TEDIUM AND TERROR

Private Sy M. Kahn, age eighteen, Long Beach, Calif., June 1943.

To Janet

*For faith unshakable, for labor unflagging,
and for love immeasurable*

Contents

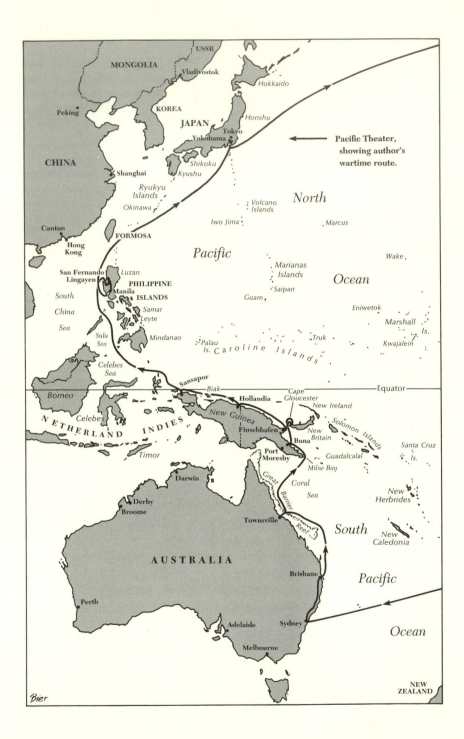

Pacific Theater, showing author's wartime route.

MONGOLIA
USSR
Vladivostok
Peking
KOREA
Hokkaido
JAPAN
Honshu
Tokyo
Yokohama
CHINA
Shanghai
Shikoku
Kyushu
Ryukyu Islands
Okinawa
Canton
FORMOSA
Hong Kong
San Fernando
Lingayen
Luzan
PHILIPPINE
Manila
ISLANDS
South China Sea
Samar
Leyte
Sulu Sea
Mindanao
Celebes Sea
Borneo
Sansapor
Biak
NETHERLAND INDIES
Celebes
Timor
Darwin
Derby
Broome

North Pacific Ocean

Volcano Islands
Iwo Jima
Marcus
Marianas Islands
Saipan
Guam
Eniwetok
Marshall Is.
Kwajalein
Truk
Palau Is.
Caroline Islands
Wake

Equator

Hollandia
Cape Gloucester
New Ireland
New Guinea
Finschhafen
New Britain
Solomon Islands
Buna
Port Moresby
Milne Bay
Guadalcalal
Santa Cruz Is.
Great Barrier Reef
Coral Sea
New Herbrides
Townsville
South Pacific
New Caledonia

AUSTRALIA

Brisbane

Perth

Adelaide
Sydney
Ocean
Melbourne

NEW ZEALAND

Bier

Foreword

Ronald Spector

Over 16 million Americans served in the armed forces in World War II. One of them was Corporal Sy M. Kahn of New York City. During his two years of service in the Southwest Pacific theater, Kahn kept a diary. It is a valuable and possibly unique contribution to the records of the war against Japan. In the five decades since the end of World War II, veterans have published collections of their letters and written a number of fine memoirs, yet few other complete contemporary diaries have been published.

Of all the theaters of war in which Americans served during World War II, the Southwest Pacific is probably among the least publicized and least remembered. To most Americans, even those with a little knowledge of history, names such as Midway, Tarawa, and Iwo Jima spark vague feelings of familiarity but few indeed have ever heard of Cape Gloucester, Biak, or Hollandia. These points along the north coast of New Guinea and its nearby islands were the scene of General Douglas MacArthur's 2,000-mile advance from Australia north and west toward the Philippines and Japan—"our jungle road to Tokyo," as one of his generals later phrased it. Even today this area is among the most remote, inaccessible, and unhealthy in the world. While thousands of veterans return each year to Normandy, the Ardennes, and Italy to revisit the scenes of their World War II service, far fewer have managed to return to Papua New Guinea or Irian Jaya.

Kahn served in the 244th Port Company, 495th Port Battalion of the Army Transportation Corps, part of what were then called the Army Service Forces. The primary mission of a port company, as the name suggests, was to load and unload ships. Logistical support was important in all theaters but in the Southwest Pacific it was especially critical. Outside of Australia and New Zealand, port facilities did not exist. Ships were unloaded by lighter or in landing craft, and as one of MacArthur's logistics officers recalled, it "seemed to take a year to get the stuff from the ship to the shore."

Not only was there a shortage of port facilities but throughout the war in the Pacific there was also a shortage of port troops like Kahn's battalion. American generals were reluctant to use their limited shipping space to transport service troops across the Pacific in place of combat troops. Kahn and his fellow soldiers in the 244th may not have been as glamorous as the Marines or the fighter pilots, but they were a far scarcer resource. As a consequence they were worked incessantly throughout the war.

The experience of the 244th, which received no periods of stand-down and practically no furloughs for the entire period it was deployed, is not unrepresentative of other Army service troops in the Southwest Pacific. The African-American 810th Engineer Aviation Battalion, for example, arrived in the Southwest Pacific early in 1942, served in Guadalcanal, Espiritu Santo, Biak, and the Philippines, and finally returned home four months after V-J Day.

Kahn and his company arrived in New Guinea at a time when the entire pace of the Pacific war was gathering momentum. Marines and soldiers had just landed on Tarawa and Makin in the Gilbert Islands, inaugurating the Allied drive across the central Pacific. MacArthur's forces in New Guinea and Admiral William F. Halsey's forces in the Solomons were completing their encirclement of Rabaul, the major Japanese base in the South Pacific, located on the island of New Britain. The 244th Port Company's first combat assignment was to provide support for the 1st Marine Division on Cape Gloucester at the extreme western tip of New Britain. The seizure of Cape Gloucester with its airfield was among the final moves in the encirclement of Rabaul. (Among the Marines for whom the 244th provided supplies and ammunition was a young battalion commander named Lewis Walt who twenty years later would command the Marine forces in Vietnam.)

While the 244th was at Cape Gloucester, other elements of Mac-Arthur's forces seized the Admiralty Islands in a risky surprise landing, closing the last link in the chain around Rabaul. By that time, MacArthur and his staff were already planning an audacious leap of 580 miles to Hollandia in Dutch New Guinea, bypassing some 40,000 Japanese troops along the New Guinea coast. Aided by knowledge of the Japanese codes and ciphers, MacArthur's forces achieved complete surprise at Hollandia and quickly seized all three nearby airfields. Kahn and the 244th landed at Hollandia on D + 12 and remained for about one month before proceeding to their third and most difficult assignment on the small island of Biak in the Shoutens off the northwest coast of New Guinea.

The fight for Biak, which the Americans needed as a heavy bomber base to support MacArthur's drive toward the Philippines and Nimitz's operations in the Mariannas and Palaus, developed into one of the toughest campaigns of the Pacific war. The Japanese held out for weeks in caves dug into the steep coral cliffs bordering the airfield in which they carefully emplaced artillery mortars and automatic weapons. The heat, disease, and lack of water proved almost as bad an enemy as the Japanese.

By the time the 244th left Biak in December 1944, American forces had returned to the Philippines with the invasion of Leyte. In January 1945, Kahn and his fellow GIs made their final landing of the war, part of the 175,000-man American invasion force which landed at Lingayen Gulf on Luzon.

"Whatever it means to be a civilian from the ages of eighteen to twenty-one was closed to me," Kahn notes in his introduction. To Kahn and to the millions of other Americans who came of age in the early 1940s, the war was a defining experience, one they could never forget but one which they could never completely explain. This diary is a rare window into that experience, into the world of young men suddenly transported from the everyday world of jobs, school, and family into a world impossibly strange and remote—a world in which youthful mistakes often resulted in death or horrible injuries, a world where the possibilities of escape seemed distant and uncertain. "We were simply enclaves of soldiers in the midst of remote jungles, our energies centered on hard labor and survival." Any reader wishing to know how these young men not only survived but retained the resourcefulness and determination to emerge successfully from war in a pitiless environment against an implacable enemy will profit from reading this book.

Acknowledgments

Above all, I am indebted to Janet Baker Black, the first and only reader in 1985 of the holograph diary, who urged me toward its publication. Little did we guess the book would require a labor of years, pursued not only in the United States but at various times and places in Portugal, Wales, Yugoslavia, and Germany—and in spite of the demise of two portable computers. Courageous counselor and companion, Jan was scrupulous in holding me to the accuracy of the handwritten manuscript, and unstinting in her encouragement of my attempts to shape the book from what sometimes seemed massive and exasperatingly intractable material.

I am also grateful to my son, David, the only other reader of the complete manuscript in its unlovely and miniscule scrawl, albeit in a photocopy. A professor of drama (San Jose State University), David offered keenly critical responses to his reading and helped me select my strategies for cutting the original materials in my search for, as it were, the figure in the stone. When David first read the diary, he was in his early thirties, more than ten years older than his father when he wrote it. I was amused when he observed: "I learned some things about you, Dad, that I didn't know." More than amused, I was rewarded by his enthusiasm for the book he saw embedded in the bulk of the manuscript and by his solid encouragement then and afterwards.

Special friends came to my aid in reviewing manuscript drafts, and it gives me great pleasure to acknowledge them here. Robert H. Fossum and his wife Virginia ("Gigi") closely read the work in progress, corrected various errors, and made valuable suggestions. Bob Fossum, retired professor of English at Claremont-McKenna College, a friend for close to forty years, has provided me with expert criticism of my work, beginning with his review of my doctoral dissertation. Carolyn G. Heilbrun, retired professor of English at Columbia University, and virtually a lifelong friend, read an early draft of the diary and offered suggestions, help, and encouragement in advancing the book toward publication. I am indebted also to Doris Hand, a special education teacher and especial friend, for giving many hours to proofreading various drafts, and for her ongoing enthusiasm for the book. During these past years Helene Williams, a librarian at Michigan State University, has proofread portions of the manuscript and has helped in matters of research. For aid in obtaining my unit's military history and rosters from the National Archives, I am indebted to Barbara Kahn Mayes, Arthur Sachs, and Maria Hakspiel. These persons, along with other family members and friends, sustained and rewarded my efforts while I developed and prepared the manuscript.

I want to thank Karen Hewitt, my acquiring editor, who responded positively to my submitted manuscript and who was the first to inform me of the book's acceptance for publication. She provided guidance in my work toward the final draft, as has, more lately, Patricia Hollahan, who copyedited the manuscript.

Finally, and at last, I want to acknowledge those wartime comrades, whether alive or dead, and wherever they may be, who were special to me then, and remain in vivid recollection: George "Pappy" Milligan, my "foxhole buddy," and twenty years my senior, friend and mentor to me in my youth; Andrew "Norm" Denison, a friend who lightened the travail and terror of those war years, and was also responsible for the original development of many of the photographs that came to be in this book; and Charles "Bud" Herbeck, a solid friend through those years. Of course there were many others of the 244th Port Company who were friends, as a reader can discover in the diary, and who remain clear in my memory, but the three men cited above were the kind of friends who help sustain life. I especially thank them.

Introduction

I had just turned nineteen when my unit, the 244th Port Company, 495th Battalion, sailed under the Golden Gate Bridge in September 1943. It was the beginning of a wartime odyssey that would take me to Australia, to New Guinea, to various other islands in the South Pacific, eventually to a D-day landing in Luzon in the Philippines, and finally to Yokohama in Japan, shortly after two atomic bombs dropped on that country ended the war. Camped in the center of that broken city I turned twenty-one. Several months later, in November 1945, debilitated by jaundice, malaria-ridden, scarred by metal and coral, my ears ringing, as they would forevermore from the sounds of explosions, I returned home, a veteran of various invasions, campaigns, and over three hundred bombings. I did not know then that just as I would never be able to hear silence again— in fact, silence makes the ringing in my ears seem louder—neither would I ever be free of the faces and events of those years that vividly haunted my dreams and memories during the following decades.

When I returned home to Manhattan in New York City, where I was born and grew up, I carried with me the journal I had kept from the time I went overseas until I was discharged. It was wrapped in the remnants of a worn-out poncho, its olive-green color faded and mold-marked, and tied up with an old brown shoelace, as the manuscript still is forty-seven years after I was greeted by my parents and sister at Pennsylvania Station. The journal was compiled from various kinds of paper stapled together into makeshift notebooks. Although the staples have rusted, the paper and ink have remained surprisingly intact. I had kept this journal even though army regulations prohibited such records because they might fall into enemy hands. It was no secret to many of the men and officers in my company that I kept notebooks. In fact, I was forever writing: journal entries, letters more numerous and voluminous than anyone else's, poems, and occasional essays and stories. Writing and reading were for me sane centers in an often lonely, dangerous, insecure, and violent world. However, when I began the journal I was motivated by two clear intentions: first, I knew I was participating in one of the important events of our century, and I wanted to record my part of it;

and second, I felt I would not survive the war, and I wanted to leave a record that perhaps might reach my family and friends after my death.

My preinduction pessimism was not at all relieved by my early army circumstances and experiences. At eighteen I was not particularly strong or athletic; I was infinitely more comfortable with a book or violin in my hands than I was with a rifle, or any other weapon or tool I eventually learned to use. Without glasses I could scarcely identify the giant E on the first line of the eye chart or distinguish a face across a room. Consequently all during my time overseas I carried several pair of spare glasses with me, including an additional pair inside my gas mask. I found myself in a company of men all older than I and drawn largely from the rural and small-town South and Southwest, men with physical skills, stamina, and strength, men with weapon and hunting experience, by comparison to whom I felt ill-equipped to cope with the army and the war. Although I wanted to be where I was (I had memorized the eye chart during my induction exam), I believed even more strongly than before it would be the death of me. However, after some months in the army, I slowly discovered a surprising physical and emotional resilience, and an unsurprising desire to survive underlying my bleak and pessimistic assumptions. I did not share, to be sure, that sense of invulnerability characteristic of youth, nor did I find God in foxholes, but I learned quickly to take reasonable precautions against danger and to speculate that with luck I might survive. I saw targets clearly enough if I squinted, and I handled my Springfield rifle adroitly enough to become, to my amazement, a "marksman." That accomplishment saddled me with that long and heavy weapon for several years, while poorer shots eventually carried shorter rapid-firing carbines of half the weight. I learned as much as I could as fast as I could—perhaps one successful semester in college helped—and I became stronger and abler. Nevertheless I counted each day as provisional. Once I knew I was going overseas, I kept to a routine of journal entries as my mark against oblivion.

My packet of notebooks, written in a minuscule hand to save space and spare weight, grew. At times during my army travels I had to store the journal in a barracks bag that followed us days or weeks later. When we reclaimed our canvas bags we sometimes found them soaked from rain or seawater. I agonized over the journal when circumstances forced me to relinquish it, as during the time, for example, when I was confined to a field hospital. One of the men in my squad with the chore of packing my gear carelessly stuffed the journal into a bag to be shipped out. I knew from my own experience in working the ships how roughly these bags were handled, and how when they were torn they were often pillaged. I had seen packets of letters scattered to wind and water. Con-

Sy Kahn and his mother, Sophie Wagner Kahn, Inwood Park, Manhattan, New York City, 1943. Grandmother, Fanny Ring Wagner, in background.

Sy Kahn and his sister, Barbara, Inwood Park, Manhattan, New York City, 1943.

sequently, as much as I could, I kept the journal with me, carried in a field-telephone cover slung at my side.

After my discharge from the army, years passed before I undid the knotted shoelace and unfolded the stiff skin of the poncho to look at the journal again. On rare occasions, during the decades after the war, I read only a few random pages. Before 1985 only a very few people had read or heard small portions of the journal, and not until then had anyone, including myself, read the entire manuscript. However, I had not forgotten about those pages written on board ships, in tents by candlelight, in foxholes under a blazing moon, even under fire—and sometimes in luxurious leisure on a smooth South Pacific beach. The old packet remained among the files that accumulate with graduate degrees and professional academic life in literature and drama. After thirty-seven years of teaching, the time came around at last to read that record of the past.

Since 1945 many books have been written about World War II in the South Pacific: novels, memoirs, histories, and biographies offer various reconstructions of that time and place. My journal differs from those works in that the events, observations, reactions, and feelings revealed here are the immediate eyewitness accounts of a young soldier engaged in war against the most alien of our Axis enemies. I wrote of my experiences quite close to the time of the events themselves, generally within hours, or a day or two. On occasion I was able to write during an unfolding action. The journal is a ground-level view of the war such as foxholes blasted out of the tough terrain of the Pacific islands permit. It reveals the narrow and swift visions of immediate experience, and it is a record of army life during those long years overseas in places that not one in ten thousand of us would ever have seen as civilians.

The journal also reveals, without my conscious intention, the changes and growth of a young soldier moving toward maturity. The shedding of civilian clothes and the donning of military garb is an important moment of transition, symbolizing a rite of passage and the beginning of a journey. Suddenly one is transported from home, reoutfitted, has weapons thrust into one's hands, and is subject to new rules and new figures of authority. The shock of transformation is great, but underneath the confusions and anxieties there is the sense that one has undertaken an adventure, even an unknown quest. I probably did not know then, as I believe now, that adventures and quests are ultimately explorations of new dimensions of self, of unexplored inner space, if you will. However, I think I had some instinctive notion of that, which in part explains the sometimes inward and quizzically self-examining passages of the journal. I also felt that "time's wingèd chariot" was at my back, spurring the private speculations of a young man who did not know if he had much time to find out who he was before he disappeared.

Ordinarily youths of eighteen to twenty-one spend those years finding their way toward their trades, or through college, slowly establishing their independence and beginning to create their private lives and personal world. In college a young man launches into a world of intellectual insights and important new relationships. In any case, whatever it means to be a civilian from the ages of eighteen to twenty-one was closed to me. An eclectic series of books did pass through my hands, and I noted them in the journal, but rare was the person or the occasion that permitted discussion of them. We were simply enclaves of soldiers in the midst of remote jungles, our energies centered on hard labor and survival. It was also, of course, a womanless world. We were cut off from the women who under other circumstances would be involved in our lives, would share in our growth and maturity, as we might in theirs. In those days, perhaps more so than now, men were wary about what they shared or revealed to another man. Feelings were taken as signs of weakness; ideas, more often than not, were ridiculed or dismissed. In such a world a bookish man, the youngest in his company, and not very worldly, sometimes turned to his journal to seek what answers, solace, and insights he might puzzle out. In later years it became an ongoing irony of my life that I, who spent those youthful years so strangely, should spend most of my life teaching college students who were usually between the ages of eighteen and twenty-one.

Soldiers in the South Pacific, as the journal makes clear, spent much of these war years in the tedium of relentless, repetitive work, or in the tedium of waiting to do that work. Part of the Army Transportation Corps, a port company is trained primarily to load and unload ships. We had received basic infantry training, and could be, and were on occasion, used as infantry troops, but our main function was to move supplies from off ships to the frontlines. Usually a port company could expect to be in a city, as were port companies in Europe, but in the South Pacific there was scarcely anything that resembled port facilities. In the areas where we found ourselves during 1943 and 1944, after we left Australia, there was not a single deep-water pier. Ordinarily ships were anchored offshore, out "in the stream," and their cargoes unloaded into amphibious craft or lighters. The work was backbreaking, especially in the deep holds of ships where the high heat and humidity of the region were intensified. Sometimes our work was delayed by a shortage of landing craft, which by turns permitted us welcome respite from our labor or more unwelcome tedium. Such interludes gave me opportunities to write, even, on certain memorable occasions, in the luxury of a ship's galley.

While working the ships, we were frequently bombed and occasionally strafed, and several times even torpedoed by attacking planes. These ships anchored offshore, or any nearby airstrips, were the usual primary targets for the Japanese fliers. From late 1943, when we arrived in New Guinea, until the end of the war, the 244th Port Company endured between three and four hundred air attacks. In addition to the casualties we suffered from these bombings, working as we did on the very bull's-eye of a major target, we also came under fire in attacks on the shorelines where an outfit such as ours inevitably made camp. Over the years our frustrations increased in that we were rarely in a position or had the weapons to fire on hostile aircraft; we could only take cover, curse, and depend on antiaircraft crews to respond for us. Thus we alternated between tedium and terror. However, we took solace in moving thousands of tons of bombs, ammunition, and weapons (not to mention general supplies), which we knew would eventually take their toll in enemy casualties, and in much greater numbers than our own.

Among us, it was not enemy action that caused the greatest number of our casualties but rather the harsh conditions under which we lived and worked. The war in the Pacific was fought mainly in the tropics. We lived in high temperatures by day and often chilly temperatures by night. Rain was frequent, even torrential. Heat, humidity, and rain rotted or rusted every sort of material. Our very skins were infected by a variety of "jungle rots," as we called them, fungus that corrupted the skin between fingers and toes, grew on the inside of ears, and in severe cases leprously wasted the skin to the bone. Adding to our woes, insects, known and unknown, bit and stung us constantly. Malaria and other fevers were endemic. No one escaped discomfort or disease, and these regularly decimated our ranks. Additionally, our work as stevedores handling heavy cargo took its toll. Because we were often exhausted, or ill, or listless with heat and depression, we became careless, and accidents occurred.

During the war years in the South Pacific the primitive living conditions, tropical heat, and hard work sometimes generated among us a general malaise and aching sense of isolation and loneliness. It was not so much the air attacks or occasional brushes with combat that were dispiriting but the common hardships that could, at times, seem even more terrible. There was little relief by way of recreational facilities, little diversion, and little chance of a furlough. During our service in the South Pacific, only two men from our company were sent to Australia for rest and recreation. Anything less than a furlough, such as an overnight pass or weekend leave, was meaningless; there was simply no place to go in New Guinea or on a tropical island. Only severe wounding, or serious mental or physical debilitation, qualified for a ticket home. Some men did eventually run amok, attacking others or wounding themselves, and as time went on these psychotic episodes and emotional breakdowns, though always alarming, were never surprising. All of us had felt the pressures. For thousands of miles around us there were no cities or towns, and little that resembled civilization as we had known it. As we pressed onward to the north and west, up the New Guinea coast, and from one island campaign to another (New Britain, Biak), we moved further away from Australia and deeper into remote jungle regions. When from time to time it fell to me to dig a grave for an American soldier in sand that few, if any, foreigners had trod before, the burial was for me the quintessential expression of our awesome isolation. It was a ceremony without tears or intimacy, its only litany the sibilant sound of sand sliding from the shovel, while a fierce sun cast the fleeting shadows of one gravedigger and one corpse.

Because there was a deficiency of service troops in the South Pacific, and because we became toughened soldiers who did our work well, the 244th Port was often at the cutting edge of our general advances. Although our frequent moves forward gave us a sense of helping to end the war, they also widened the distance of the vast seas and jungles separating us from our fading and increasingly unreal former civilan lives. As months became years, as our casualties increased and familiar faces disappeared, even the letters from family and friends became a chorus of diminished voices, speaking to us as from another world. By the end of the war, because of accidents, breakdowns, disease, wounding, and death, about 50 percent of the original troops had vanished. The journal I kept is a record of this attrition, of the daily cost of war.

Yet, despite the long and sometimes heavyhearted months, the illnesses (jaundice and malaria hospitalized me), the general threats to life and limb occasioned by our circumstances and the war itself, I was sustained by the wonder and adventure of finding myself in exotic lands. I found pleasure in exploring those distant and empty beaches, in swimming among the tropical fish that bejeweled the sea, in discovering strange animals, insects, and plants, and occasionally encountering native islanders. One of these I befriended in New Guinea, and during some weeks we periodically met to learn words of each other's language, and to exchange gifts. For a time, I recall, I owned a crude three-pronged spear for catching fish. On one occasion he took me by canoe up a river, made invisible by the jungle that overgrew it, to his inland village. I spent an afternoon there among Melanesians who had never seen a creature such as I. In turn, I was so fascinated by them that it was not until several hours later that I remembered that I could have been butchered, cooked, and eaten. New Guinea had such tribes. Unaccountably, although the experience in the jungle village is vivid to me, my journal contains no record of it. It does, however, reveal many discoveries of the external and internal worlds I experienced, which relieved many otherwise bleak and brutal days.

I was also sustained by letters, particularly those by two young women whose importance to me was doubtless considerably greater than each realized. One was the "Carolyn" of the journals, destined to have a distinguished career as a scholar and teacher, popularity as an author of mystery novels under the pen name of "Amanda Cross," and recognition as a leader in the postwar feminist movement. I was eighteen when Carolyn and her parents took me to a farewell dinner at the St. Regis in New York City early in 1943. I had already decided, privately and independently, that there would be no commitment between me and that remarkable young woman—even were she of a mind to agree to one. Fairly convinced that I would be killed, or possibly maimed, either fate seemed to me terrible to impose on another. In addition, I was sure that we were both too young, too unknown to each other to harbor serious expectations; I felt that I, surely, was still too unshaped, too much a mystery to myself to offer dependable promises. Nevertheless, my admiration for Carolyn Gold Heilbrun was boundless. During my years of service she was for me both a womanly and a human ideal.

The other young woman was the "Dale" of the journals, Dale Whitehead, whom I met in Sydney, Australia, during my eighteen days there. Our subsequent letters through the war years reveal that both of us increasingly felt, on the basis of perhaps half-a-dozen brief meetings and the correspondence that followed, that the seeds of a possible love relationship had been sown—but they were not destined to flourish. Once out of Sydney, I was never able to return during the war, and afterwards, half a world away, I was swept up into postwar life. Still, all during the war years the hope I held of returning to Australia, shared by Dale (now Dale Whitehead Cook), cheered many a lonely hour—forlorn as that hope proved to be.

By the spring of 1945, we had survived our campaigns in the South Pacific, the kamikaze attacks on our convoy to the Philippines, and our D-day landing on Luzon. Once Germany surrendered we knew Japan's defeat had been hastened. I began to think that I might survive the war. However, during that spring a rumor circulated among us that we were scheduled to invade Japan. Unbeknownst to us there was an actual plan at the time (code name "Olympic") to invade the southernmost island of the Japanese homeland, Kyushu, in November 1945. Strategists anticipated an invasion force of about 750,000 men, and high casualties of about 35 percent—about a quarter of a million. Had we knowledge of these plans and calculations, they would have verified our rumor-fed suspicions that our ordeal was not yet over, and would have confirmed my specualtion that I was probably living the last year of my life. There were those among us who darkly predicted that, after we defeated Japan, survivors would march against Russia as part of an endless war that would never permit our repatriation.

Then during the summer of 1945 we learned that indeed the 244th Port Company was already selected to participate in the invasion of Japan. We had by that time sufficient experience with Japanese tenacity, bravery, toughness, and fanaticism to imagine how costly this attack would be to us. I was not alone any longer in my pessimism. By then all of us who had survived the long trek from Sydney to Luzon wondered if our luck had run out.

In July white-scarved fliers from nearby airstrips brought a new rumor to our ears. The war, they said (and would wager on it), would end in a matter of weeks—a few months at the most. A new weapon, they said, would accelerate our victory; we would be home by Christmas. We dismissed all this as still another wild rumor among the many that constantly circulated. Of course the fliers were right.

My journal records the excitement I felt at the sudden and swift conclusion of the war a month later after two atomic bombs were dropped on Japan. My unrecorded initial reaction was quite different. Someone woke me to tell me that the war was over, and I remember that I felt a strange calm. I simply said, "That's good," and rolled over to try and sleep again. I didn't sleep. I lay there and permitted the icy sheath of cold resignation in which I had encased myself against my death to thaw and melt. Exuberance came later.

I did not feel that in dropping the two atomic bombs we had perpetrated a monstrous act. Admittedly the weapon was awesome, but I measured its destructiveness against the thousands of casualties on both sides that were spared by our not having to invade Japan. I don't recall that any soldier in the field objected to the weapon or its use. On the other hand, I realized that we had invented a device that could lead to world destruction. But above all, at the end of that long travail, I felt my life had been spared, and that I would live to be twenty-one after all.

I believe several other matters germane to this journal of almost half a century ago require commentary. In my references to African Americans, I refer to them as "Negroes" or "colored." As I hope the context makes clear, these terms were not intended as racial slurs; they were the common and accepted terms of the times. Had denigration been my intention, other terms would have been chosen. I also, on occasion, refer to Filipinos as "Flippos," a term generally used by American troops at the time, and not meant as derisive. Rather it is a typical example of the American tendency to streamline a word requiring too much time and effort to pronounce. Furthermore, my journal almost consistently refers to our enemies in the Pacific as "Japs," as did virtually all Americans after Pearl Harbor. Actually this was the mildest of the epithets used at the time to castigate an adversary we were meant to look upon as diabolical and subhuman.

Of course there was plenty of racial and religious prejudice among our ranks. I was particularly pained when I heard anti-Semitic slurs, although they were rarely aimed at me specifically, and they were reduced to the point of disappearance by the end of the war. I made no attempt either to hide or to deny that I was a Jew, but neither did I make a banner or cause of it. Within myself I was comfortable with my heritage and religion, though relaxed in its practice, and I was pleased to have H indented on my dogtags (for "Hebrew," considered a more delicate designation in those days). Nevertheless, I was keenly sensitive to the common anti-Semitic assumptions that Jews could not be good soldiers or stomach hard physical work. I was determined to give the lie to these opinions. The pain I felt in encountering anti-Semitism is nowhere directly noted in the journal. Even in so private a record I could not bring myself to deal with my anger, fear, and bewilderment, or a curious sense of shame for the perpetrators of prejudice, when I encountered anti-Semitism, whereas no other subject was sacrosanct. These suppressed feelings, though, were sometimes the cause of my explosive criticism of the men around me, particularly when I refer to them as "crude" or obnoxiously loud, or narrow-minded and insensitive. These, on some occasions, were the metaphors with which I castigated their prejudices, and particularly the anti-Semitism I detested so deeply that I could not call it by its name.

The journal has been edited for the purpose of eliminating the verbiage, repetitions, and annoying errors resulting from pressured writing and youthful awkwardness and ignorance. Occasionally I have reordered passages within an entry to clarify the chronology of events. Several hundred pages of the holograph diary have been omitted, generally dealing with my record of books read, letters received, European war news, and repetitive descriptions of work. Names have been changed on a few occasions to spare the feelings of those men I refer to, if they are still alive, or their families. Nothing of the tone, mood, or content has been altered, tempting as it is to spare myself and the reader evidence of my glaring immaturity, as, for example, my naive references to homosexuals. Although I am sometimes abashed by the image of that youthful soldier, I stand revealed in these pages as I was. I am unapologetic; I was what I was.

Glimpses of some of us during the war years are provided by the photographs in this book. They were taken with a simple and battered box camera. Family and friends at home sometimes sent rolls of film, and these we encased for protection and mailing inside army issue condoms. It took months for film to be developed abroad and pictures returned to us. Therefore, when we could, we begged, borrowed, and bartered for the photopaper and chemicals needed to develop our snapshots. In a stifling tent converted to a darkroom, we rejoiced in the often grainy, over- or underexposed pictures we produced. Although some photos have faded to ghostly impressions, most retain their images, like my memories of the war itself.

I will add this: Long ago I closed the book on the war and kept much of it as wrapped up in my mind as were the journals in their poncho. But I never forgot. For both better and worse I was changed by the war, haunted in dreams and memory, rendered restless, and sometimes alienated, sometimes more at home abroad than in the United States, sometimes a stranger everywhere, and in mysterious ways beyond my knowing, perhaps a casualty. Not long ago I was traveling on a local road that lies between Pittsburg, California, and the area where Camp Stoneman once existed. The place now called the Marina in Pittsburg was probably where the 244th Port Company once boarded a small ship to transport us to the large troop carrier docked in San Francisco. Camp Stoneman, which operated from 1942 to 1954, was then a staging area for troops bound overseas. We stopped, Janet Black and I, after she drove us to the only remnant of that once large camp, its white clapboard chapel. Around us were shopping malls, condominium complexes, and chain restaurants typical of urban California—and nearby even a small carnival. As we read the plaque on the church dedicated to the memory of those who served and fell during 1942–54, one could hear the screaming young people on the gyrating carnival rides.

I looked at the golden hills where I had once marched with full field pack, and I could visualize the camp spread around me between the chapel and the hills. I remembered again those I have never forgotten, especially those of the 244th, and friends who had served elsewhere during World War II, who had not returned. The war years came whirling back like a huge kaleidoscope of faces and events, so large as to make of the carnival Ferris wheel a poor miniature of that turning wheel of memory. That memory is informed by all that follows in these pages.

Chronology

September 5, 1943   Arrived Camp Stoneman, near Pittsburg, California

September 25, 1943   Left the United States aboard the USS *West Point* from San Francisco, California; destination unknown

October 10, 1943   Landed Sydney, Australia; proceeded to Warwick Farms

October 29, 1943   Arrived Brisbane, Australia, by train (Camp Doomben)

November 14, 1943   Left Brisbane aboard the USS *John Jacob Astor;* destination unknown

November 23, 1943   Arrived Milne Bay, New Guinea (Camp Ahioma)

December 16, 1943   Left Camp Gama-Dodo aboard the USS *Dodge;* destination Oro Bay, New Guinea; shipwrecked on Colingswood Reef; transferred to destroyer USS *Smith*

January 30, 1944   Left Cape Sudest, New Guinea, aboard *LST 475;* destination New Britain

February 1, 1944
D + 35 days   Landed Cape Gloucester, New Britain

April 8, 1944   Left Cape Gloucester aboard the British cargo ship *Annui;* arrived Finschhafen, New Guinea

April 30, 1944   Left Finschhafen aboard *LST 41;* destination unknown

May 4, 1944
D + 12 days   Landed Hollandia, Dutch New Guinea

June 3, 1944   Left Hollandia aboard *LST 469;* destination Biak

June 5, 1944
D + 9 days   Landed Biak Island, Ewick Bay

December 22, 1944	Left Biak aboard the *John Marshall;* destination unknown
December 23, 1944	Landed Sansapor, New Guinea; left aboard the *APA LaSalle* on December 30, 1944; destination Luzon
January 9, 1945 *D day*	Landed on Luzon at Lingayen Gulf in the Philippine Islands
August 20, 1945	Left San Fernando by train; destination Manila
September 4, 1945	Left Manila aboard the *APA Okaloosa;* destination Japan
September 13, 1945	Arrived Yokohama, Japan
November 4, 1945	Left Yokohama, Japan, aboard the *Sea Runner;* destination the United States
November 15, 1945	Arrived Portland, Oregon; proceeded to Vancouver Barracks, Washington
November 20, 1945	Left Vancouver by train; destination Fort Dix, New Jersey
November 25, 1945	Arrived Fort Dix, New Jersey; discharged from the U.S. Army on November 28, 1945

BETWEEN TEDIUM AND TERROR

1

From California to New Guinea

———————— Sept. 15–Nov. 21, 1943 ————————

September 15

Camp Stoneman   Pittsburg, California

Today I am nineteen.

Here, in the army, as Private Sy M. Kahn, ASN 32818087, I am learning much, not so much in a technical sense as I am about myself, people and ideas, and life itself. I want to remember as much as I am able.

For the sake of the record, I was inducted into the army February 27, 1943. On March 6 I was sent to Fort Dix and 10 days later to Indiantown Gap Military Reservation for basic training. During that time I have experienced some mental and physical shocks, having been drafted from the physically soft life of college. During basic training I spent 10 days in the hospital with a painful strep throat. As the first six months of training passed, I became hardened, or should I say "processed." Also I am beginning to find myself and to face myself honestly, no longer making excuses for my weaknesses but admitting them to myself and trying as best I can to cope and overcome them. These weaknesses shall probably make themselves known as I write.

The year as a whole has proven interesting and educational. My semester of college followed by the quick contrast of the army makes me only more convinced of the value of education.

Two days ago, while we were pitching pup tents, the Captain approached me. He informed me that my application for ASTP was marked ineligible because our organization probably will soon go overseas. [*The Army Special Training Program was established to meet the army's need for various specialists. The men who were selected were trained at colleges and universities.*] As the Captain put it, our "dry run" days are over. My disappointment is great. I've been waiting for four months, and it is heartbreaking to be eliminated by our present circumstances from this chance to study. There goes my last hope to further my education.

Yesterday we went on a 12-mile hike. I was quite sore, as we all were, not having taken a hike for quite awhile. One fellow passed out. I've wanted to explore these "golden hills" that stretch behind our barracks ever since we got here. The hills were as beautiful as I pictured them. Some rose at sharp angles or nearly straight up for hundreds of feet. Here and there beef cattle spotted the landscape. There were deep gullies, too. All in all, these were the most unusual hills I've ever seen. We climbed a few. Short hike today.

September 17

When I was on the range today, firing a carbine for the first time (score 29 out of 40), the Captain asked me if I knew anything about checking. He told me that there was a possibility of an opening and to learn all I can about it. I already have learned some elementary things from Flynn, who is a checker, while I cleaned his carbine after I used his rifle on the range. [*The checker's job was to keep a record, a "manifest," of all cargo either loaded into or unloaded from a particular hatch of the ship during a work shift.*] Naturally I feel elated at this encouragement. I've received encouragement from Lt. Wenz and the Captain on several occasions, but perhaps nothing will come of it. I am sure that responsibility would balance me and make a remarkable change. It did today in my whole attitude toward the army when I took Sgt. Herbeck's place as section leader while he was out on detail. I shall work hard and hope for an advancement which I feel I can attain. I shall be happier if I can feel a greater part of things. And I'm tired of being a buck private.

We are due for a move soon, although we are not as yet alerted. We are in a staging area and an overseas move seems imminent. Some of us are anxious to go overseas. I am and am not. Perhaps I would be if I could see my family and home once more. We will soon know our future for the next couple of months. We have not been thoroughly staged, and our future remains hazy. Ordered to pack bags tonight with special equipment and clothing in each bag. Order rescinded a couple hours later, as I suspected it would be. Glad I did not start to pack early.

September 21

The time draws close for our departure. It sure gives me an unusual feeling. This morning our "B" bags left and we should soon follow them.

27 August 1943

This letter was received by me and I am sure that all men in the battalion woul like to have a copy of it.

LESTER R. DORFMAN,
Warrant Officer (jg), USA,
Special Services Officer.

UNSUNG HEROES
by
Pfc. Thomas Haynes
245th Port Co.

Out of this war-torn nation comes an outfit whose future destiny may challenge the chapters of history in ages to come. This outfit, still in its infancy, is know as the Port Battalion.

When this great nation of ours was confronted with the task of defending globa peace, she also was forced to place able-bodied manpower on foreign soil. This in turn led to one dynamic answer—war. When war did strike its deadly blow, men and materials were sent to the defense of helpless, unprepared allies.

Today, as the conflict is at its climax, more materials have to be sent every day to far-flung corners of the world. This is where Port Battalions play their most important role. Men from all walks of life start their new vocation with vigorous effort to first, become soldiers and second, to become skilled and capable of loadir and discharging ships loaded with vital materials at ports abroad.

These same men are taught the Army's Ten Commandments in addition to their tech nical fields. Hard hours of drilling, hiking, and learning to defend themselves, is but a minor detail compared to future accomplishments. Hence, when basic training ir completed the men of the Port Battalion are taken to a port where they learn winch operating, longshoremanship, and in general the complete fundamentals of loading a ship properly.

A great majority of the American public knows little of the enterprises that are a constant burden to these men. Unsung in their acts of patriotism and glory their slogan is cherished among their outfits, namely, "The Supplies Must Got Thru Regardless of How or What the Cost of Human Annihilation." Oftimes they are sent to foreign outposts unaware of what difficulties and obstacles are ahead of them, but i true American fashion they land as pioneers, and work day and night until their des-tined port is their home. Here happy and content they feed the life-line of the Arm-ies. This same life-line that brought devastation and humility to great nations and world conquerors. This life-line is based on one title and one title alone,- Supply. Without supplies the power of a mighty nation could, and would collapse in a short time.

But then the inevitable question arises. "Who are those men? Are they trained to do this work, or has it been their life's occupation?"

No, they were men who were formerly clerks, salesmen, students, businessman, of laborers. But by constant training they were taught how to handle cargo with the utmost facility.

Prior to the inauguration of the Port Battalion men who were unskilled and inca handled the cargo, and most times there were casualties and heavy losses of equipme Today though, by the great genius of far superior brains, there came forth the Port Battalions to meet and correct the errors of their forbears. Hence, when ships are to be loaded or discharged today, there is a skill and workmanship uncompared to fo mer times. We do not condemn or criticize these men before us, because we understan the fact that they were not trained in that line. The training and connection with a Port Battalion leaves us no alternative, but to believe that it is one of the greatest ideas of modern warfare and rapid transit service.

-4-

Letter, Unsung Heroes, distributed Aug. 27, 1943, before the 495th Port Battalion went overseas.

The urge to call home is strong, and I have to fight it to keep from telling them.

I've found a friend in Denison. He left college about the same time I did; thinks along the same lines I do. Even one year in college is important! It makes or breaks a person, not only shaping his character but determining his future life and the right way to live.

I have had the advantage of friends like Carolyn, Enid, Dick and Ginger who have influenced me not a little in what I believe is the way to live. Wonderful Carolyn—she haunts me all the time and I am continually drawing comparisons with her—and of course disappointed in others as a result.

September 23

The order came through a short time ago to pack our "A" bags. This is probably our last night on these shores. The news was greeted with much boisterous enthusiasm. It gives me a strange feeling that I am going overseas. I wish I could communicate with my family who will probably not receive any word from me for about a month, I imagine. Of course we do not know exactly where we are going, but we shall probably go a great distance. Anyway, I'm going to see a part of the world. I remember now, rather ironically, the nights I used to sink into my battered armchair at college and dream of far-off places. It looks like my dreams are going to be soon realized. I'm lying on a top bunk, surrounded by men who are preparing for tomorrow—or just thinking.

I am especially concerned about my mother who will take this move very hard. When she doesn't hear from me for about a week I hope she will realize what has happened. This move will surely shock a lot of people and perhaps bring home the realization that there is a war and we are definitely in it. It is a thrill to know that we are "going over." I look forward to it with excitement and anticipation. However, I wish I were rereading this in one of the easy chairs at home. I have no doubt there is going to be plenty of hell over there.

I wish I could write more; there are volumes to write at a time like this, but there are things yet to do, and I am very tired because I've been up since 3:45 this morning.

September 26

I am now one day out to sea from San Francisco aboard the *U.S.S. West Point*. The events of the past few days have run as follows: On the morning of the 24th we made final preparations to leave. In the afternoon we marched a few miles into Pittsburg and awaited the boarding of ships that resembled the excursion boats on the Hudson. They had big paddles on the back. While waiting to board her (there were several of them and quite a large number of soldiers), I saw many girls around at various points, some of them the wives of men who were leaving, including some in our outfit. I was thinking what a thrill it would be if my family and some others I knew could see me at this moment in full regalia—full field pack, belt, rifle, gas mask, OD [*olive drab uniform*], leggings. At this point we began to move slowly toward the ships, and women, who had been gay heretofore, suddenly burst into tears. I was glad then— very glad—that nobody was there to see me off. Just seeing these women cry was heartbreaking enough—but my own family would have been horrible.

We boarded ship after picking up our A bags which were on the dock. Mine was not easy to handle along with all our other equipment. We were placed in the enclosed lower part of the ship, crammed together like cattle. One could hardly tell men from equipment. We figured the men who had drawn the outside positions were lucky—but as the day wore on and grew colder on the water, we were more fortunate. Many dice games started, and hundreds of dollars exchanged hands. Some men winning and losing two, three and four hundred dollars! We sat on our barracks bags and were served a box lunch. Cigarettes were distributed, but I've enough of those God knows—nearly two cartons. I spent the five-hour trip sitting there, standing near the railing, or sleeping among the barracks bags. We were nearly docked in San Francisco when we began to put on our equipment.

We then waited for an hour and a quarter with all that on and in foul air and terribly uncomfortable heat. Being in wool and all those straps pressing hard into the body was not comfortable. You could not take a step without stepping on something or somebody. I tried to protect my gas mask as much as possible. We were all terribly tired at this time. The scene of men and equipment spread all over the floor, the men tired and sweaty, and the nauseating heat reminded me of the pictures I have seen and stories read about transporting slaves in the holds of ships.

We finally disembarked, each in his assigned number, Joslyn in front, Pappy King in back. I was and am No. 172. The barracks bag was twice as heavy, it seemed, and I was twice as tired. We quickly were marched in single file through a fairly large warehouse, handed a card by an officer, and checked just before putting our foot on the gangplank and leaving the U.S. The Captain was there calling the last names, we hollered the first and up we went. I didn't get a look at the ship, nor much of anything else because I was well occupied in keeping my equipment balanced.

The gangplank went up at a sharp angle and seemed interminable. One had to be careful because one slip and into the water would go irreplaceable equipment. I was finally aboard after the arduous climb and followed in single file into the interior of the ship.

I was able, during a brief stop, to glance at the card which indicated that our outfit was assigned to the main deck. This I knew to be a favorable position. We were assigned to a section located amidships on the starboard side, where we are at this moment. I chose an upper four bunk. With some effort I got the barracks bag up there, pack, rifle, gas mask *et al.* On each bunk was a life preserver. I sank back against it, looked to my left to find Heffle sleeping soundly there. I intended to take a few minutes rest and fell into a deep sleep amidst all the equipment, the rifle lying alongside of me, the other stuff at the foot, life preserver as a pillow, and me crammed in the middle of it all. We all fell asleep as soon as we lay down—in full uniform including leggings.

The next morning I set about getting my stuff in some semblance of order and trying to be as comfortable as possible. It is quite impossible to be really comfortable with all your equipment in bed with you and in very cramped quarters. However, I was able to string my helmet and rifle up after some maneuvering and figuring.

I thought I would awake to find us well out to sea, but much to everyone's disappointment we were still docked. While maneuvering equipment, I took stock of my position. I am a good 12 feet from the floor but with nobody above me. This advantage only upper fours enjoy. The ceiling is about a yard from my bed. Right next to Heffle's bed and slightly below is a porthole which can be kept open during the day. Having a porthole so close makes me indeed fortunate. I also have the advantage of a light at my left shoulder which is allowing me to write at this moment. The deck is a favorable one. All in all, I could have done much worse. I like it up here the best though, because I'm up away from as many people as possible. From my bed position I can see the sea rush by us, though not the horizon. (Have to keep changing positions to write.)

Our first meal aboard was a nightmare. We were crushed, shoved, pushed from chow line to dining room (a room in which one stands at chest-high tables and consumes his meal). The food is as one might expect aboard a transport with so many soldiers. We receive only two meals a day, 8:30 A.M. and 4:30 P.M. roughly. Subsequent meals have been more organized. After the meal and getting settled as much as possible, Hale and I walked around the ship. There are a great many soldiers and various outfits aboard. The transport is a large one—nearly 900 feet long. From the railing we got a glimpse at San Francisco and the Golden Gate Bridge—something I've always wanted to see. I regret not getting to see San Francisco intimately.

The officers' quarters are beautiful, and for them the trip is a great deal more pleasant. There are also quite a few women's organizations, WACs [*Women's Army Corps*], a contingent of nurses, etc. The men cannot mix with them, and that doesn't bother me at all. However it is pleasant for the officers who can. This move must be a great deal like a pleasure cruise for them with fairly comfortable quarters, dining room, and pleasant company of both sexes. My company is not always so pleasant. Anyway, we don't have to get up until 7:15 A.M. and hit the hay at 9:00 P.M.—with closed portholes. The air circulation is good, however.

I am leaving the U.S.A. quite girl-less and do not regret it. I shall be away for a long time, and a girl on my mind would not help matters. It is easier this way. Missing my family and home is quite enough to take.

I shall never forget this bed. It is seven feet long, 2½ feet wide. It has a pipe frame and stretched to it by ropes is a canvas mattress. As Al [Kaplan] would say, "And that's all brother!" One blanket serves as cover or mattress, as one chooses. It is not comfortable, as last night proved.

Vierschilling got a wire a few hours before we pulled out, informing him that he is the father of a baby boy. It sure was a dramatic time to find out, but he was lucky in finding out then before we left. He sure was happy. Looked like he was going to cry for a moment when I saw him. I congratulated him.

We began to move at about 5:00 P.M. last night. We all crowded to the portholes to get a last look at the U.S. We also passed under the Golden Gate Bridge. As the last hills began to fall from sight, I thought fondly of my family who seemed to be cut from me by that growing expanse of water. I wondered when I should again behold the shores of the United States. I could not help but feel sad at the departure. However, in the company I am in one does not hold a mood long, and that is good for all of us.

I imagine, if all goes well and I do not meet any misadventure, that it will be at least a year before I again see home. It is not going to be easy, that I realize, but I am anxious to get there and be a part of the telling blow that shall smash the enemy and forever end war.

I have no fear. Though we are now liable to torpedoing at any time, it does not seem to bother me. We are all, for the most part, in good spirits in spite of our cramped quarters. We regard torpedoes philosophically—if they come, they come. One cannot worry about it. The sea is calm, nobody's ill yet. In fact, nothing looks very menacing at this moment, and the sound of the sea is pleasant.

We just had lifeboat drill a few moments ago and it was quite simple. I suppose it will be a regular occurrence from now on. Equipment for drill is belt, canteen, helmet, preserver.

September 27

Today I've been in the army seven months, and it sure has taken me places. Here I am a couple of thousand miles out to sea, heading into the South Pacific (a sea I've always wanted to see and travel on), and destination unknown. The sea has turned a beautiful blue, and this morning the swells are quite heavy causing a rather heavy roll. Very, very few of us are sick, although I understand it's worse in the hold. I feel quite well. While on deck last night I listened with interest to the stories of torpedoing one of the sailors was relating. They were fascinating—but not pleasant.

September 28

Every meal is a trial. It means sweating profusely, being jostled and cramped, and emerging from that hold drenched and feeling weak. The stench of crowded humanity is beginning to be quite disagreeable. Washing facilities are limited. Although in rather a poor mood this morning, four hours on the open deck, reading, watching the sea, and breathing good clean air has put me in much better humor. If only I'm left alone for the remainder of the trip, I shall manage nicely.

September 29

Because we sweat continuously, the stench in the sleeping quarters has become almost unbearable. I now spend the majority of the waking hours reading on the open deck. I would even sleep here if I could. The living conditions are bad enough to test one's sense of humor, which I've been able to maintain desperately. It's strange, but when hardships are faced and I manage to joke my way through them, I always think of Carolyn. That is her style, and I probably learned it from her. She would be proud of me. How I wish she could catch a glimpse of me for only a minute.

I was lucky enough to see some gunnery practice during the practice alarm to abandon ship. They fired flares into the air, and the gunners shot at them. I could not see the guns, but they sounded like 50-caliber machine guns. I could see the tracers, and it was fascinating to watch them whizzing away over the sea into the horizon. Just sparks of light travelling at a terrific rate of speed. You could not even observe where they fell. Descending to our quarters, I could hear the staccato of the guns above. It's both a menacing and reassuring sound.

October 2

I think this is the right date. We either have passed the international date line, or we shall soon. Sometime yesterday we passed the equator. There was an initiation for sailors who were crossing it for the first time. They were dressed as buccaneers and were put through some sort of ceremony. I would have liked to have seen it, but was too lazy to follow it up. Besides, I was engaged in good conversation with Blanco, which continued off and on throughout the day and evening.

Yesterday it was rumored that we passed quite close to a Jap destroyer and that we were forced to change course. Also, that we were 500 miles from a Jap airbase. This came from the officers. I have learned that this ship was strafed near Singapore, but that the large amount of fire power that this ship can muster drove them off. Also that it has had torpedoes fired at her but has never been hit. Oh well, one worries about torpedoes when they hit you. It's a waste of time otherwise.

The nights are quite difficult, being hot, smelly and generally unpleasant. The weather deck is always jammed from bow to stern, and one has to be quite lucky or fast on his feet to attain a decent position.

It is odd that one lives through dramatic moments hardly ever realizing them. Whereas I used to have to dramatize everything, I no longer have to, for so much drama is at hand. I think I have quite outgrown that. As I consider it in the long run, it caused me more trouble than it was worth. Now on a ship headed for "somewhere," liable to attack at any moment, men constantly on the alert at the various guns on board, the radar spinning from the mainmast, here is drama, and one hardly realizes it.

October 5

There is now seven hours difference between me and NYC. We have been progressing along steadily and should reach our destination sometime the end of this week. It will probably be somewhere in Australia. We have been given guidebooks to both Australia and New Guinea. I don't believe it would be bad at all to be stationed somewhere in Australia, but New Guinea does not sound particularly inviting. It's going to be tough enough being away for what looks like a year (or even more) without being stationed on some South Seas island. Of course, I have always wanted to visit and see them. Anyway, in spite of every minute taking me further away, I cannot help but anticipate the future with interest and excitement. It is really great adventure to be going to foreign lands.

October 11

We landed in Australia, at Sydney, yesterday morning at about 10:00 A.M. I wanted to get a good look at the ship we came across on, but I was so occupied with balancing myself and the equipment down the gangplank that I never did get a chance.

We disembarked, threw our bags into a truck, and boarded a bus. The bus took us through Sydney, and that was exciting and fascinating. We saw some Australian soldiers about, and the part of the city we did see, while not the best part, it seemed, was much like any large American city. Women looked interesting too. Other than the names and signs one saw, there wasn't too striking a difference, except for a certain strangeness and excitement which I imagine was more within myself than in my surroundings. We rode for about 15 minutes and got off the trucks at the railroad depot. I spotted Churchill's sayings on the walls, much like billboards, and the people around here gesture "thumbs up" from children to old women.

The steam engines are small, those I saw, and the passenger cars have spoked wheels. There are compartments which hold eight people, four facing four. The whole effect made one feel that Jesse James would hold up the train any moment, or, at least, it was the kind he did hold up. Although there were electric facilities, the compartment had a gas lamp in it, but neither was working. There was a sign reading "Non-smoking," which we all disobeyed, and another sign stating that a five-pound note was the penalty for throwing things out the window. A bulletin about air raids completed the reading material. A washroom adjoined the compartment. Civilian passengers soon become chummy in such trains.

We arrived at our present camp last night at 4:50, approximately 25 miles out of Sydney. Although the trains on which we travelled looked antiquated, they could move along. Naturally, we were all terribly hungry, having subsisted for 14 days on two meals, and not good ones at that, and then not having eaten since 8:00 that morning. We got off the trains, lugged our stuff across the tracks and into camp. It was a cloudy day, and rained a bit and was chilly. (Still cloudy today.)

We moved into tents, six men to a tent, drew army cots, and there we were, Gillis, King, Hellman, Grant, Blanco and me. It turned cold, so after getting settled we all stretched out on our cots. It was good to stretch out full-length again and not have anybody too near. It was 8:00 P.M. before we lined up for chow last night, and every man was starved!!

Just before chow, the Captain told us that we've been alerted the same afternoon for further movement and to enjoy the land under our feet while we could. (Cheerful!!)

The meal consisted of one tablespoon of salmon, one medium-sized potato, ½ tablespoon of marmalade, two slices of bread and one gulp of coffee. Also ½ cup of soup. The coffee, as usual, was terrible. There is nothing worse than GI coffee. We drew an extra blanket, and I hit the cot. It was a really cold night. Quite different from the equator.

This morning we got reorganized into tents, and I was definitely assigned to 2nd platoon, 2nd section, as assistant checker. Now that we are over, everyone is able to make a rating, and I'm really going to try to make one. I'm tired of being a buck private!

I've just come back from a company meeting, and the Captain told us this: we are slated for further movement along with another company. It's going to be on a ship, and it's going to be a long trip. The place is "not nice," and there will be hardships. There have been two port battalions there before us. When the first one was relieved, it had 300 men left. [*A full port battalion complement was approximately 800 men.*] The future looks black! The present is interesting, however.

October 12

This camp is very pleasant. It is set among trees and gentle slopes. The grass is green, the sky is blue, the sun friendly. There are familiar clouds, and tonight is especially agreeable.

Tonight I went to see a movie. I was surprised to find only a short distance from the camp a huge and still well-kept racetrack. Of course it has been converted to army needs, great sections of it now a tenting area. However the grandstands, which incidentally served as seats for us to view the movie, the buildings and drinking fountains, and the black letters against the clean brown buildings stating "Bar," "Cloakroom," "Restaurant," etc., reminded one of the probable scenes that have taken place on this spot not too long ago. War has caused many changes. The loudspeaker, stands, open grassy grounds, and environment in general of a race track seemed like a spectre coming to haunt the present out of a gay and frivolous past.

This afternoon I was happy. Tonight it feels good to be alive and well. I feel that sometimes, a certain vitality, a certain thankfulness in living. But, this has its shadow. Sometimes I think it would not be unpleasant to be dead—but this is rare and usually provoked by something.

The army has taught me one great lesson. It is being honest with myself. Carolyn tried to teach me this, and she is, I do not doubt, the impetus behind my learning it. I have fooled myself a great deal in the past.

I also have a cold nature, but it is latent. I don't fully understand it, nor do I know its cause. It seems I am hard, cold, unfeeling when I should be the most sympathetic. I fear this a little, but it has served me well in trying situations all through my life. The more trying, the harder I am. It has perhaps served me well then, protecting the person that I normally am, the person that I also happily want to be. The other must not become dominant. This hardness surprises me and yet is always there when needed. It is a good thing to have during a war; it will carry me through difficult experiences, such as seeing fellow soldiers die, perhaps facing death myself. Perhaps dying. I believe more and more that we are near death. I am not as sure as other men seem to be of themselves that I will survive if we do face battle or disease. I do not have much fear of dying.

If ever this is read by my family, I want you to know that these are the words and thoughts honestly set down of a mature person—or, at least, of a much more adult one than left you. I hope someday we may laugh over this night's writings as those of an over-dramatic youth, influenced by the war, a foreign country, the night, and his emotions.

October 14

Yesterday all our woolen clothes were collected. I kept my OD hat and knit cap. I like them too much to hand in. We are told that we are going to a place near the equator—and it will be hot. That may be true in more ways than one. I feel we may be here for a week or two, but we will soon be on our way.

October 17

Ratings came out yesterday, and I was not on them. I know that I have been a good enough soldier in the past months to deserve that first stripe. I see others getting it who I know don't deserve it. I don't begrudge them the advancement. But, I know I really deserve it. In fact, I really have been trying for it for four months. True, I am now listed as assistant checker—but what the devil does that mean? I do not play favorites among the NCO [*noncommissioned officer*]—in fact, I avoid most of them as much as possible except for Herbeck. I know favoritism has played some part, and that is sickening.

Yesterday I was sick with rage and disappointment. The only person

I disclosed my feelings to was Denison. I shall keep trying, but this has been a damaging blow. Some time ago the Captain said action would be taken because of my good work, and Lt. Wenz kept paying me all kinds of compliments. What kind of a game is this—I feel that I'm being thrown bones while the meat dangles out of reach. In order for me to be happy, I have to feel some sort of accomplishment. If only I knew why I am not getting anywhere.

Everything, including this organization is just a lot of noise and talk. It's appalling to have to write this—and I regret it—but we have done *absolutely nothing* toward the winning of this war. *Nothing!!* We have spent thousands upon thousands in food, equipment, transportation. We are literally burning the country's money, and there is not one day to balance the books. I can only feel at this time that the whole situation is a huge joke, and I am the hugest joker of it all. I again feel these months slipping away, the best years for studying spent meaninglessly. It strikes a coldness in my brain, causes sarcasm in my speech and a bitter feeling. It would be easier to take if there was some sense of accomplishment, some sense of our helping terminate the war.

October 21

Night before last Pat and I, and Denison and Dale attended an enjoyable play, *George Washington Slept Here,* at the Minerva in Sydney. [*Pat and Dale were young Australian women we had met at dances several nights earlier.*] Pat is a sweet person, kind—but definitely young. I especially noticed Dale that night and decided I would like to see her. She is a more mature person than Pat, and much older for her 19 years. In fact, I've met nobody either in this country or my own who surpasses her.

So last night I saw Dale. Denison thought Dale was a little too intel-lectual—but he is looking for sex more than anything. The brunette I introduced him to should serve nicely. I do not find Dale intellectually threatening in any way. If I had met her in the U.S., she would be my main female interest.

Dale is slim, tallish, with brown hair. Her face might be described as pleasing; it is neither pretty nor beautiful. However, in repose or in shadow, her strong points are accentuated, and she borders on beauty. Her mouth seems to me a strong feature. I recall this best now that I think about it. It is odd-shaped, wide, like two gentle arms meeting each other in the center. They terminate in sharp corners. Her smile is very pleasant, hands delicate. She is everything I would want in a person, judging from these early meetings.

While killing time yesterday afternoon, I played ping-pong at the American Red Cross. After playing with a particularly handsome-looking fellow, and a good player, we got to talking. He had been in New Guinea for 19 months. Told him I was in a port battalion. Then he mentioned the 491st, whose training preceded ours by a few months. We saw them march out of the Gap to California. This is what he told me:

> Two days after landing in New Guinea directly from the States they were bombed. Being green troops they did not know the air-raid signal and took no precautions. The Japs came over and dropped six bombs in the midst of the area, killing 45 men outright, with more wounded.

This struck me like a hammer blow. That hits close to home. It makes me think this about the Yanks, "The poor devils," and this about the Japs, "The dirty bastards." It was quite a shock, and I couldn't get over it for several hours. War is horrible. What right has any man to take another's life, to maim and cripple and cause such profound grief? War is stupid, and yet it appeals to an undeniably savage instinct, a lust. The world must be educated.

What is the solution to ending future wars? It will be terrible if I see men of this organization killed, every one of whom I now know. Forty-five dead multiplied by the grief those deaths will cause. What kind of a stupid world is this that wants men to slay each other, that lets people starve? But I know it is easy for events to slip off the shelf of one's memory when one is not affected to any degree. It is the truly great and remarkable person that can concern himself honestly, and not superficially, with human problems when he is outside their influence. How selfish people are, how stupid, and yet I would not have realized this myself if I wasn't close to these events. At college I would have remained more or less oblivious. The majority of humans are small-minded, thick, subject to lustful emotion, selfish to a degree that is appalling. I never had a great love for "people," and yet I would like to lead them. I would be a good leader. I know this. What a paradox it is that in order to realize wrongs, some people have to die to show intelligent ones the intelligent way. How easy it is to be unconcerned when one is untouched by wrongs, how easy to overlook them; and the worse crime is when you know the wrong is there. War! What a sad joke the whole thing is. What a complete waste. What clever man was it who wrote, "When ignorant armies clash by night"? I feel like I'm shriveling up inside amidst all this daily crudeness, a dehydration of my spirit.

October 25

Been having a pleasant time going to town almost every night. Saw Dale again a couple of days ago. Went back to camp on the last train. Didn't get to bed until after three this morning. As a result am quite tired.

The soldiers coming back on the train at that hour are asleep on their feet. They lie in the aisles, on benches, and grasp tiny morsels of sleep on each other's shoulders. Red-eyed, drunk, with disheveled uniforms and the perpetual cigarette, they make a mixed picture of wry humor and sadness.

The soldiers of the Australian army have been in the army and fighting a long time—some, three and four years. Sometimes I see them come in with equipment on their backs. Their uniforms are always rumpled. Yesterday, while watching a parade, I met one who was quite drunk, with a mean-looking Aussie rifle slung across his back. Drunks have become common in my life.

Yesterday I watched a parade of kids dressed in blue uniforms. They ranged from about six to sixteen. They were some sort of Air Corps auxiliary. They sure do start young. I personally couldn't get enthusiastic watching 1,000 youngsters marching and swinging their arms in true Aussie style, in time with drums and bugles. It reminds me of the pictures I've seen of Nazi-trained youth. I hope the war will not be long enough for the children I saw marching to become soldiers.

October 27

Eight months in the army today. We were supposed to leave today, but it has been postponed with nothing definite when we shall move.

Had a date with Dale. Secured best tickets for the concert last night from a Red Cross worker, an extraordinary piece of luck for a change. Met Dale, who made special efforts to get away, so she informed me, and proceeded to the concert.

I was surprised at the beauty of the hall, which resembles Carnegie Hall. I was thrilled to listen to the music of Franck, Wagner, Berlioz, etc. As I mentioned to Dale, I felt rehabilitated afterwards. We went for a walk, in the park as usual, both of us thinking this was my last night in Sydney. She'd be the girl I'd have, if I had time. She is amazed that I'm only 19. She is nearly that. I keep being taken for 21 to 25.

The conversation just before the train came is worth putting down in case I forget, though I shall probably not. I asked, demanding a frank rather than a kind answer, whether we should write or forget the whole thing. "We shall write," she said. I hope that was frank. I believe it was. A short time later she was gone.

October 28

We leave tonight, destination unknown as usual. I am hoping for Melbourne, but it will probably be Brisbane, a sort of jumping off place for New Guinea. Possibly Darwin. Company A has left for Darwin, supposedly. Company B and a platoon of D remain here—the lucky dogs. We are ready to move with full field equipment, everything in order. Got new clothes today—everything goes in one barracks bag, and it weighs plenty. Everything I own in the world at present is spread before me, and it all can be carried on the back.

Being able to go to Sydney last night was a terrific piece of luck. But I have that old gnawing feeling in the pit of my stomach, which always indicates that I'm going to miss somebody. Understandable after last night.

I was hesitant about calling Dale, and telling her I was still here. But she greeted my voice so enthusiastically that my spirits soared, and I practically skipped up the stairs of the Town Hall Station after making a date for eight o'clock at the usual place.

We decided to take a ferry to Manley Beach. It reminded me of the rides at home on the Dyckman Street Ferry, across the Hudson River. After getting out of the harbor a bit, the ship dimmed its lights. The sea became alarmingly heavy. The boat was small and pitched when the strong current hit us crosswise. It was good to feel the breeze against my face, the dark ship, the shoreline indistinct, and Dale in my arms, huddled against me, with the scent of her hair and the sea, with the wind brushing wisps of hair against my face. Who could want to spend one's last two evenings in civilization more satisfactorily than I have! I have been fortunate, doing what I enjoy with a wonderful girl. The harbor, I learned, is full of sharks.

After getting to Manley, which was as lit up as a graveyard at midnight, we walked to the shore that's bathed by the Pacific. We passed the dormant, darkened amusements that were mute testimonies to gayer times but now seemed sad and forlorn. The beach was just like the scene I used to watch often in California at Long Beach, only more resounding, more powerful and more exciting. We started back from this beautiful spot that was protected by barbed wire, keeping us from the beach.

We walked back after talking, but the boat for the return trip had not yet arrived. There was a very narrow bridge extending far out into the ocean. We walked out there, and the wind was blowing violently, the sea roaring.

She strained toward me; there was tenderness in the way she lay her head on my chest. Going back on the boat I was happy and content for the first time in many months. I've always wanted to kiss a girl on a darkened boat in a roaring sea. I did that frequently, long and satisfactorily. I loved the way she strained toward me; it was something I needed and who could have picked a better time. She is worth the waiting and discriminating. Oh, for only another week, another evening.

Dale was positive that we would leave today, not yesterday. Women's intuition, I guess. She was going to see me tonight—and I would tear walls down to get there. I feel like I'm being teased by fate. Yes, we would go well together, and now the chances are that I shall never see her again, and she will fade into the dusty storeroom of fond memories. Perhaps we shall meet again—who knows!

October 29

Called Dale a few hours before leaving. A very quiet goodbye in which we both sincerely, I believe, regretted not being able to see each other again. This was gratifying after last night. A few more nights would have proven fascinating. Anyway, I shall write her.

We left at about 7:30 P.M. The train cars are old and small. Curled up on a seat three-and-one-half feet long and two feet wide is not comfortable for a six-foot long body. (At this point interrupted for dinner. Continued in Brisbane camp next morning.)

October 30

Chilly in a drafty car, I woke up every hour or so and walked around a bit to keep circulation going. It was a long, uncomfortable night. On the way we passed a train going south that had a load of Jap prisoners aboard. I did not see them because they passed our car too quickly, but some of the other fellows did. They claim that the majority of them were small, but there were some big ones.

We arrived in Brisbane about 9:30 last night and piled into trucks. We were all dead tired, of course, the previous night not being restful for anyone. However, all in good spirits.

November 1

We have been here several days, and my liking of this place has not improved. The food is terrible, and the camp crowded. I've been cutting two meals a day, but I've had plenty of sleep. I've been in bed by 8:00 last two nights. That garbage detail didn't help my attitude any yesterday.

Company A was flown out of here a few days ago, presumably to New Guinea. We are supposed to go by plane, too, it is rumored. The war is getting closer all the time.

November 6

Days have been filled with tedious details that have left me quite tired. Same old thing.

Have visited Brisbane three times, and it is not as impressive as Sydney. Haven't enjoyed it at all. Received letter from Mom today, first one that contains realization that I am overseas. Days have been moving along with an occasional sprint of interest. Saw Jap Zero at the airport here. Also met a driver who nearly ran over MacArthur day before. Haven't seen the old boy as yet, but this is supposedly his headquarters.

The mosquitoes are terrible, and tonight we all put up mosquito nets. Swung sledge all day today, dug gravel all day yesterday, tossed 80 pound boxes and 150 pound flour sacks around day before. Being out of condition, I am tired.

November 13

We are getting ready for a showdown inspection [*unannounced display of all equipment*] now having gone through the usual venereal disease inspection earlier this morning. Speculation vacillates about our next destination. Up to now it has been N.G.—mainly Milne Bay and Port Moresby. Now it includes the Fijis. Worked as garbageman two days ago; worked in warehouse yesterday shipping and receiving medical supplies. Many interesting pieces of material were there, along with morbid olive-drab GI coffins with army insignia. We should leave shortly, probably tomorrow. I am anxious to get started on our job at last and help shorten this damnable war.

A big break has come my way. When I was returning from washing clothes a few days ago, Sgt. Stahl approached me. He asked me if I would like to come back to the 3rd platoon because his section, the 1st, is without a head checker—Klein was transferred to the service section. He asked me if I was rated yet, and of course the answer was obvious. The job would be head checker of the section and a T-5 goes with it. I told him I was not too familiar with all the angles of the job, but I thought myself capable of handling it. To this he said, "I would not have asked you if I did not think so." I would much rather be back under S/Sgt.

Eriksen, but Sgt. Stahl is at least an intelligent person. He told me to ask Eriksen, which I did. Eriksen said he would see what he could do, after asking what function I held at present, which is, of course, assistant checker to Majewski in Russell's section. It is the break I've been waiting for, and I'm keeping my fingers crossed that I get it. I think I've an excellent chance.

November 14

We boarded the ship at about 6:00 A.M. This morning at 1:45 A.M. we were awakened and made ready for leaving Doomben. No one was particularly sorry. Had breakfast at 3:00, which was unusually good for a change. (Sort of being fattened for the kill.)

We boarded easily, although the rain made underfooting hazardous. This time, unlike my boarding of the *West Point*, I got a good look at the ship. It is the usual liberty ship that we became acquainted with at Wilmington [*California*]. Of course, a liberty is not big, which in troop movements seems to me advantageous. She is only a fraction of the size of the *West Point*.

Our company was assigned to No. 4 hatch, where we are all now situated 'tween decks. There we live, and to see this scene would appall most people and us as well several months ago. Now, however, we are hardened to everything. As usual, our equipment is hung on every available hook, or in every nook and cranny, but most of it is alongside of us on the deck. Our "beds" are nothing more than sheets of plywood, ⅝ths of an inch thick, which are laid on top of the iron hatch. Needless to say, there's no give. It's every man for himself, and so each used his own ingenuity to make himself as comfortable as possible. Already two makeshift hammocks of blankets have been slung from the "ceiling." We are crowded, but I'm lucky enough to have a whole sheet of plywood to myself. It is six feet long and four wide. I am fairly well-arranged, system being one of my virtues. I've managed to get over four hours sleep today already. We got conditioned to sleeping on the decks of ships at Wilmington. The lighting is fair, and I know that we shall all be more comfortable and have more privileges than we did on our last trip, which was rather disagreeable. There is much more air available; we are only about 12 feet from the open deck.

November 15

Yesterday we sailed slowly out of Brisbane harbor, and along the way a large convoy formed. I have easily counted 13 cargo ships, and there are undoubtedly more, some impossible to see over the horizon. Indeed, some hang right on the horizon line. There must also be a number of fighting ships. It is an impressive sight to see the convoy forming, with ships steaming in from different quarters and dramatically moving into position.

I got some uncomfortable sleep last night and awoke to go on deck just in time to see the last of Australia. It seemed like the closing of a chapter in a book and the starting of another. I liked Australia, especially Sydney and Dale. I got a letter from Dale, which I much enjoyed and answered just before the deadline on mail. Also, sent one home. I think I struck Dale favorably. Anyway, she claimed that both my letter and love-making were "polished and successful." I know where I shall go in event of a furlough.

Slept on deck last night on top of the hatch cover with Ron, Herbeck and Heffle. We pulled a tarpaulin over us which was as heavy as elephant hide and quite warm. It was beautiful watching the yardarm swing from side to side like a giant pendulum and hearing the quiet hush of the water. As it grew dark, one could hardly make out the huge dark hull of the nearest ship. The blackout is pretty effective. The whole mass of stars seems to swing in the sky, making them all look like shooting stars. Later, the moon climbed out of the sea, first lighting up a dark blue cloud which looked like a velvet cloak with yellow lining. It was a bright yellow moon. I felt rather contented. I used to daydream about such scenes at college—and here it had come true.

We had a company meeting this morning, covering emergency drills, atabrine, which we start to take today as an aid in preventing malaria, and it was announced that we are going to New Guinea! At present, we are only six miles off the Australian shore and in comparatively safe waters. Before we get to our destination, we shall have passed through a comparatively dangerous area, in which we will be subject to attack from both air and sea. I have no fear. Most of us haven't. However, we are headed for an island that is one of the main fronts of the war and is half-occupied by the Japs. Just as potent an enemy as Jap shells will be the numerous tropical diseases, mainly malaria. As a result, a detail known as the Malaria Control Detail has been composed consisting of Sgt. Havron, Cpl. Brothers and me. It will be our job to keep the possibilities of malaria in check and to learn about it during this trip. This afternoon we are going to a lecture by the ship's surgeon on malaria control. This work, of course, to me is fascinating. In Brisbane I tried to secure a book on tropical diseases but stores close on Saturdays. It is my plan to ask the surgeon for a book on tropical diseases that I can borrow during this trip.

I don't know what lies in front of us in New Guinea—if we get there. There will surely be much hardship and adventure and, of course, danger. My only fear, as it has always been since leaving home, is that mishap will have its more terrible effects at home. After all, if a bomb gets us or a bullet, we never feel it if it hits us right, but a telegram home in the "We regret to inform you" vein I dread to think about. To think of Mother reading that, I would rather cut off my right arm. I trust, for her sake, that I shall be in condition to return home in a few years. Of course I'm homesick, and of course I miss family and friends and comfort, but is this not adventure, bordering on further adventure? It is what I've always dreamed about since the first adventure story I ever read. Perhaps I don't appear like the adventurous type, but essentially I am.

We shall be close to the equator and are heading toward it every hour. It shall be hot as blazes. Anyway, life gets more interesting every day and is beginning to break in my favor. I want to write to Carolyn, but I am reluctant until I can sign "Corporal" in front of my name.

November 17

We are all dirty and unshaven because we lack good washing facilities aboard the *U.S.S. John Jacob Astor*. We are hugging the Australian coast and passing close to the well-known Great Barrier Reef.

About a day and a half ago the convoy broke formation, and we are continuing up the coast alone as fast as possible. This ship now leads the convoy, and we've seen no other ship since passing the others except one, which hangs on quite a distance behind us. That makes us the fastest ship.

Because we are approaching the equator again, it is becoming beastly hot. We did not feel the terrific heat till yesterday noon. By 9:00 A.M. any exertion produced a sweat. Every man has his shirt off and is sunburned. I have a fine tan already. We have become quite friendly with the Australians on board, especially the one who spends the evenings talking with us. Last night I found out that he was from Tasmania and learned a little about that island.

November 18

We have been anchored off Townsville ever since yesterday morning at 10:30. It appears from the ship to be an outpost, caught between the vast, heavily vegetated land and vast ocean. I understand Townsville to be a town of 30,000. It surely looks forlorn and cut away from civilization, as does most of the surrounding country. This is a stopping place for ships to take on additional supplies on the way to N.G. I've counted 13 ships anchored here, and there are more. All are freighters, some carrying small numbers of troops. Saw a sub out in the bay, ours of course, and tonight while shaving I saw some huge sharks swimming off the port bow. Ugly looking creatures. They swam leisurely and playfully, seeming to enjoy their life in the calm and warm Pacific.

Last night was unusual. Because we were at anchor and in a safe bay, we were allowed to smoke on deck and in the hold until 9:30. Under a bright spotlight a five-piece band assembled, a sax, clarinet, two guitars and a drum. They were excellent, and some of the musicians were professionals before the war with Johnny Terry. Many of the pieces they played brought back distinct memories. For instance: "Black Magic"—Carolyn; "Beer Barrel Polka"—my first weeks at college.

The running lights of the ship were lit all night. The whole throng seem to relax last night, dancing with one another, laughing, joking, much hubbub and smoking. It was good to feel this sudden relief, like a huge sigh after having held one's breath for a long time. I enjoyed this mood immensely. Later, in the comparative quiet, I lay looking at the always-friendly stars, or so they seem to me, and thought that here I was lying on a ship bound for foreign and unknown places in the South Pacific. I have hardly any responsibility, and my death would only directly affect my small family. Life ahead is adventurous, exciting and unknown. The night was perfect, languid, warm and full of euphonious sounds of the sea and ship. Surely it was what I always wanted—and here I was doing all that I had dreamed about. I suddenly realized that I had gotten my wish. To complain would be hypocritical. The weather, though terribly hot during the day, is most beautiful at night. However, it will get hotter.

November 20

We left Townsville last night at about 6:30 P.M. in convoy formation. This morning we are sailing along at about seven knots with the Australian mainland plainly in sight off the port bow. We have a few additions to our convoy; two hard-hitting PT boats tail us. [*These were small, fast motor torpedo boats, of the type used in General MacArthur's escape from the island of Corregidor in 1942, and later in the war commanded by then navy Lieutenant (junior grade) John F. Kennedy.*] The ocean is like a lake this morning, hardly a ripple.

The Captain told us that we are going to N.G., to Milne Bay, and we will work there. Milne Bay is at the very tip of New Guinea, at the south end, and about 400 miles behind the front lines.

Sure am curious to know how the war in Europe is progressing.

There has been a lot of stealing aboard ship. I think there is nothing lower than a fellow who will steal from a soldier, especially when equipment can't be replaced easily and the loss of some of it can result in the loss of life. Thieves deserve the vilest names and the direst end.

I blew up at one of the fellows yesterday who was yelling for seconds before the whole company had gone through the chow line once. I told him off. His attitude was typical of so many other fellows and so much of the world: "The hell with you, just as long as I get my belly full and my needs satisfied." I vehemently detest that attitude and those that practice it. Of course that is dangerous because I may have to fight alongside these fellows—and they can mistake me for an enemy as like as not. Here an individual's life has lost its importance. But I am sick of the inconsideration of men for other men.

November 21

Today has been exciting. At about 2:30 P.M. we heard a dull boom and two sharp blasts from the deep-sounding horn brought us all on deck. Upon getting on deck I found all the men lining the rails and looking back. All the ships of the convoy were changing course and darting around, making radical changes in direction. One of the corvettes accompanying us had dropped a depth charge, and some of the fellows saw the shower of water it produced. Another corvette set out in the direction of the former. Meanwhile ships kept changing signal flags furiously, accompanying each change with two deep blasts, all the while holding a zig-zag course. After half-an-hour the two corvettes were dimming on the horizon and all seemed well. This submarine scare is probably connected to the fact that four Jap planes were spotted early yesterday morning.

The whole watery world seems so much at peace that death lurks underneath this gentle ocean seems inconceivable and a paradox. None of us is apprehensive—but we are keeping our canteens full and life jackets handy.

This morning while sitting on top the hatch eating breakfast with Herbeck, he said that last night he, Ron and Heffle were talking about the various men in the outfit, and they decided that I was the happiest man in the organization. Of course, I am miserable sometimes and torn with loneliness for the least bit of affection, for a kind word. I have been as kind to my fellow soldiers as their individual characters will allow. About half of them act like animals. However, for them to think of me as happy shows that I've conquered a great fault, acquired an admirable covering for emotions and feelings easily damaged. They also said I seemed to say what I think, which is true. I'll never be subservient to anyone except for the common good, nor can I ever be a hypocrite. One of the main rifts between Carolyn and me was my frequently morose moods. I must have caused that wonderful person many trying moments.

2

New Guinea

──────── Nov. 25, 1943–Jan. 31, 1944 ────────

November 25

Thanksgiving Day in New Guinea. Gad!! Tonight we shall have turkey. What a sad comparison this day is with past Thanksgivings. We've been kept so busy since landing on this island that I've barely had time to write. My time for writing will be much decreased from now on, I imagine. Anyway, I shall give a synopsis of what has occurred since landing on November 23, at 2:30 P.M.

When I awoke the morning of the 23rd, land was in sight. It was a vast mountainous country, bathed in mist, and luxuriously green. As we entered Milne Bay and got a close look at the shore it looked inviting, and like the typical tropical islands that one has seen pictures of, read about, or imagined. I was excited about landing on a tropical island and was anxious to go ashore, which we shortly did. We disembarked and I was happy to see the last of that ship. We walked about a mile-and-a-half, and the heat was terrific—and has been. The growth here is thick. In fact, I've never seen anything quite like it. Coconut trees are abundant.

We arrived at our present camp to find it filthy and dilapidated. We have done much to improve it, digging ditches, filling in holes. The tents are kept open on all sides. The weather has ranged from warm to hot. It rains often—all day today, and so our company street is a sea of mud up to our ankles. A little cooler when it rains, and it also cools off at night so that sleeping is pleasant and comfortable. I never appreciated an army cot as much as I did that first night here—and all mine too. They are really comfortable—after the hold of a ship. There is a stream right in back of our area which serves as washroom both for body and clothes. It was a treat to bathe in that stream and get really clean. Also clothes. Water for drinking is chlorinated, atabrine and salt tablets a steady diet. Since arriving we have had three meals of C rations.

That first night six of us gathered around a candle, chasing the lizards, bugs and snakes out of our tent—including the myriad kinds of insects that inhabit this place—that play with C-ration cans. Last night from 8:00 to 2:00 A.M., I worked as checker down at the docks, which was long, but I enjoyed doing it. I learned much about the area, Jap activity here, and about New Guinea in general. The 489th is stationed here, and they are a tired-looking lot. They have had five cases of malaria, a number of accidents on the ships—one resulting in amputation—and various cases of jungle rot! Milne Bay is now the biggest base in the South West Pacific.

The Captain, who recently is getting himself thoroughly disliked for various reasons, informed us that we are attached to the 6th Army and to the 5th Marines, who now are on maneuvers, for a probable invasion of New Britain in order to take Rabaul. We may see action.

November 26

Worked today making a rock dock for transportation of garbage. Same old details. We were all pretty disgusted. Have, and had all day, a terrific headache which throbs at every move. Only relief is to remain absolutely still. Every time I bent to lift a rock, I felt the top of my head was coming off.

Saw show last night which for the most part was amateurish and rotten. However, anything is appreciated in New Guinea. Lanny Ross was there. He has been in N.G. for several weeks in special service. Band was very good—but made us all the more homesick.

The letter I got from Enid yesterday—Thanksgiving Day and also her birthday—was as interesting as ever. It proved that much more interesting in that it contained a message from Carolyn about corresponding with her. I read those few lines at least 20 times. If I were capable of crying, I might have done so. At any rate, something seemed to be crying in me. After much deliberation, I've decided to write to her tonight and frankly tell her how much she has meant to me. It's sure been a long time, but it will not seem strange to write "Dear Carolyn," when I've composed so many mental letters to her. I could safely say I love Carolyn and not be far wrong. The meaning of the word "love" has become more clearly defined for me in the last months. Her name is like a breath of cool air in this damned land.

November 27

Just had long talk with Denison which, incidentally, has kept me from writing Enid. So now dark and am writing by the aid of two candles. We talked of marriage and what we wanted in wives. It amazed me to find how much my ideas have changed from those of a year ago. They are more realistic and less romantic now.

Sure felt funny to take a bath in the creek with those three natives watching me.

November 29

Last night we had one of our famous company meetings, and after the Captain went through the customary motions, he gave us the best news we have heard in many moons. We are moving out of this area on Wednesday. It's a place across the bay that needs us badly and is completely occupied by navy personnel. The privileges will be many, the food excellent, we shall have access to ships' stores, and the work will not be heavy because they have not the facilities to handle the tonnage. They are going to put tents up for us, with *floors*. Also, electric lights and running water. It sounds too good, and I'll believe it when I see it.

Sgt. Putt seems to be having a tough time with the heat. Perhaps our new area will be better suited for him. He's an old man, 28 years a soldier. That's about 26 years more than I want to be one. Visited N.G. Red Cross last night.

Have changed tents and am back with old 3rd platoon. Tentmates are Gillis, Adams, Hellman, Howe—all easy to get along with.

December 2

A few days ago an order came out, raising and lowering men in rank. On this order I was made Pfc. T/Sgt. Kowalczyk was lowered to buck, along with other lowerings of long-established staffs and techs. The chief victims were Pietrangelo, McNutty, Kowalczyk, and Milewicz who turned in all their stripes. Others threatened to do so. Finally, they all met in the Captain's tent, not taking any of his offered cigarettes and acting cold in general. Shortly after, they all went down to the creek bank minus the Captain, who, I observed, smoking and agitated, watched them from above. Sgt. Putt talked to them, and when it began to rain, as it frequently does here, they adjourned to a nearby tent. I was on KP that day. The final outcome of that blow-off was that the whole order was rescinded and, thus, my Pfc. The entire camp was aroused, and all were interested in what the outcome would be. However, all this was forgotten for the moment in the excitement of moving.

Yesterday we packed our bags, rifles, gas masks, all our equipment onto trucks, and were driven to the edge of the bay where we boarded a fleet of barges. These were the famous landing craft for marine invasions. The trip lasted about 1½ hours. The heavy vibrating and rolling of the barges, along with the intense heat, gave me a severe headache, and I was slightly ill. I felt better when we landed and after the rain soaked us. We then unloaded our equipment, during intermittent heavy rain which soaked everything, especially our barracks bags. Quite a few bags went into the ocean or were saturated by the puddles forming in the barges. They also were roughly handled. We all paid for this stupidity later.

Our equipment was taken to large tin warehouses, which are now serving as our temporary homes. They are rounded affairs, having a half-arc for a doorway. They have concrete floors, are dry and airy. So after cleaning them out, setting bunks up, putting up mosquito netting by light of gas lamps, it isn't bad. Each platoon has one to itself.

I got my bags last night, one dry, one wet. I got into bed and was going to settle into a much-needed sleep when Sgt. Eriksen called a platoon meeting. Eriksen informed the platoon that it would have to follow the new T.O. [*table of organization*] and that men would be both raised and reduced to fill it as quickly as possible. Sgt. Mishalanie spoke up, saying that the T.O. issue had developed into a fight between officers and enlisted men. The result, to sum it up, is that the whole outfit is, to some extent, disorganized.

Eriksen said that the Captain wanted a military outfit, and that the laxness that exists between officers and men would cease. That is foolishness, because it hardly ever existed. Who thought he was going to crack down on little things, like wearing dog tags, socks, shoes laced, etc., all the time. In other words, he is cracking down on us to put us in our place and to show his authority. Anyway, I'm still with him. We can't win a war with disorganization. The army must be a dictatorship, not a democracy. I don't like it, no intelligent man does—but it is a necessary evil in wartime.

Well I hit the bunk again and was about to fall asleep when in pops Eriksen to rouse the whole platoon into an uproar by announcing that we were *alerted* for further movement (which still stands). After this, Denison and I had a talk about all that has happened in the past few days. We finally did get to sleep.

I am assistant checker and am going to get Pfc. Of course I was after T-5, which was given to Thomas as checker. He has seniority in the section. Fair enough. However, I was brought into the section by Stahl with the understanding I was to be full checker, so I had a legitimate bitch. He agreed that I was getting the short end, but he did not reckon with the opposition he would receive in not appointing Thomas. The main reason for appointing Thomas is not his seniority, but that he is a Southerner, as is almost everyone in the section, and I am not close with any of them and maintain my distance. My independence is worth all their stripes. Of course I got the old slush about "if Thomas messes up the job" I shall get it. However, once a man gets a rating now, he's got it. Stahl said I was liked in the section and recommended that I stay. The only advantage in doing so is that Stahl likes and favors me. The main bitch is that this is the third time I've been changed, and each time it has taken several months of hard work to establish that I am as good a soldier as any of them. There is no doubt in my mind, or anyone else's, that I got the short end, but at present there is nothing I can do. So I decided to stand my ground and at least get the Pfc—long overdue. Also informed Stahl that I want consideration in the event that Watts fails as assistant section leader, which holds a buck corporal rating and makes one a NCO. He said he would. I would like that as I think I would make a good NCO. At present the chance is slight.

At present everybody is handled with kid gloves, and not a move is made between a NCO and the rest of the men until all are consulted. This past day the men have been more human toward one another than I have ever seen them before. Many are fed up with the outfit and are going to petition to be transferred into the infantry. Doubt if it will come off.

Rumor has us slated for Goodenough Island. Just had rifle inspection and pep talk by Lt. Wenz—new platoon leader. We go to work tomorrow on the ships at last. There is high tension. Perhaps it shall be smoothed over under the brunt of the heavy work we will do.

December 4

I've been the first man in our organization to be hit by a bullet. Some fellows were firing out in the jungle. I was standing in the doorway of our warehouse with just half my body exposed, rubbing off the pieces of paper stuck to Mother's picture (caused by the rain), when I felt a sharp blow in the right leg, just below the knee. It felt like somebody had kicked me with all his might. I was about to turn and howl at somebody, when someone picked up the bullet that had hit me. It was a ricochet, as one could easily see from its distorted shape. Luckily, it hit me sideways, not point first, or else it might have caused a wound. As it was, it did break the skin a little. Also lucky that the bullet was pretty much spent when it hit. Of course everybody in the platoon wanted to see the scratch. And by that evening, several hours later, everyone in the company knew about it and asked me about it. Some heard I was severely wounded. Now everybody has been kidding me about getting the Purple Heart. I was amazed how fast the news travelled. Even the Captain was looking for me for two days, but gave up, I suppose, when he found out it wasn't serious.

I have had several close calls during the past few days. Our first morning at work, waiting for the barge to take us out to the ships, I was sitting on a bunch of heavy girders when one gave way and narrowly missed catching my leg. That also stung and broke the skin a bit. Then today while holding the guy line, which had a single turn around the cathead, Sgt. Eriksen turned the winch the wrong way and I narrowly escaped severely hurting my right arm. It did get skinned and hurt a little. These incidents have been too close for comfort.

Because we work with machinery, heavy materials, ropes and cables, one can easily get hurt. For example, Fitch has a slight leg fracture. Furthermore, this climate raises havoc with any break in the skin, causing infection. Many of the fellows have odd rashes (Kaz still in hospital with one) and various other skin diseases. House had a swollen eye tonight. Stewart has a broken wrist, Glasgow a cut hand, etc. So far I have been lucky.

We have been working for two days now on our own. I am checker in Cpl. Watts' crew, working on the *Anthony Ravalli*. We have been unloading pilings weighing about a ton each and covered with creosote. This stuff burns, but I have escaped it. My job is easy because the checking of this material is simple. I work with the gang when the urge moves me, which was not too often today. Yesterday we unloaded 20 tons. Today we unloaded 30. It's difficult stuff to handle. The fellows, some of them, have to work in the water with all the creosote floating around. Half the time they are in the water or in the small dinghy.

Yesterday I decided to help the gang in the water, so in fatigues I went over the side and swam around the ship to reach them. This was my first real swim in the ocean, only having fooled around a bit offshore. It was a rough ocean, and I found the swim tiring. I wrestled with logs for about an hour-and-a-half and decided to swim back around the ship and board. I was quite tired. Swimming in a rough sea, pursuing the logs, not to mention swimming with heavy fatigues, is no joke. I got half-way back and around to the other side of the ship, where the sea was much rougher than the port side. Huge swells broke near me. About a quarter of the way toward the gangplank I felt so fatigued swimming against the swells that I knew that I might not make it. I headed for a dangling sea ladder hanging off the end of the ship about 30 feet away. I reached it, gratefully. A navy boat, chasing a log that got away, hauled me aboard. Then I went up the ladder, which was a job in my condition. To add to this, one of the sailors told me that barracuda were sighted near the ship the day before. Oh well, all in a day's work.

The atabrine is beginning to show effects. My skin is taking on a decidedly yellow color. My beard is coming along nicely and looks rather good—no matter what the others say.

I am going to put in an application for OCS [*officer candidate school*], which is now open.

We got a voucher tonight, allowing us one bottle of beer this week. If one is not a coffee or beer drinker, or heavy smoker, or user of foul language, he will eventually come to these in the army. Think that I've held out the longest, especially against the latter, although of late I've been a little lax. I hate the foul language I have to hear all day, but I've become used to it. I still dislike coffee, but sometimes it is all we can get. Smoking is one of our main pleasures and relaxations. Although I am smoking more cigarettes in the past few weeks (about 10 to 17 a day), this is light compared to others.

December 5

Today is Sunday. We worked half a day this morning. We had dinner on the *Ravalli,* and it was the closest thing to a Sunday dinner I've experienced in six months. In the afternoon we were entertained by Gary Cooper, Una Merkel, and Phyllis Brooks. The most impressive part of the program was the speech by Lou Gehrig, as given in *Pride of the Yankees.* I remember first hearing it when I saw the picture last Thanksgiving. Little did I imagine that I would hear Cooper in person say it on the shores of New Guinea.

An outstanding thing happened tonight when Denison and I were walking back to our warehouses from the library. I was expressing my enthusiasm about the various books. He said, "You know, I hardly can realize that you wanted to become a veterinarian, for you hardly ever speak of it. Whenever you show enthusiasm it is about music and literature, and, in general, the liberal arts." Perhaps he is right that my interest, though perhaps not my talent, lies mainly in that field. I may someday prove I can write. However, it is important to realize that I still do not know nor am definite where my field lies.

December 8

Been working hard last couple of days. We've got the hang of things, and we are putting the cargo out. Was signal man today and enjoyed that. Last night brute Rouse and Hollenback had a little tussle. Rouse, after breaking a hold and pummeling Holly, said, "Get up, I'm going to knock the hell out of you." Holly stayed put, breathing hard, and wisely so for Rouse is a bull of a man.

Handled ammunition today on Aussie boat, and it was no fun. Bombs weighed 108 pounds, and it was hot. Besides you can never trust them, and we were all jumpy. Perhaps they'll make the Japs jump more. Faz came pretty close to losing a leg when a ton piling crushed him up against the cabins. It burned him a bit, but he was lucky. Jack Harris in hospital with malaria symptoms. My hands acting strangely, burning and itching. Right now both. Very annoying. Skin turning yellow from atabrine.

December 10

We are now moved into the six-men tents, the closest thing we have had to a home in many months. I'm pretty well set. Tentmates are Watts, Rice, Fazekas, Morales, and Overstreet.

I nearly made T-5 again. They needed a hatch tender who had to be one of the Pfcs. Stahl told me I am a Pfc, although it is not yet official. They voted, and I came out second, which surprised me as I've only been in the section two weeks. I know that my being placed in the section was not heralded with delight. However, I have gotten to be pretty well-liked, as I have always managed to be among all kinds and classes of men. Sixteen of twenty-one of our section are Southerners, and most of them of the thick variety. It is difficult to keep my temper. Watts and Pappy Milligan have become my good friends, and Stahl is always friendly. When I found I had come so close again to making corporal, I was disappointed, especially when I learned that two men who would have voted for me were absent from the voting. Then I would have gotten a tie.

To add to my ill luck, last night I smashed my watch, and the top part of my pen got lost during the short move. This sort of topped my day off beautifully, seeing these are my most sentimental and dearest articles. The watch was a present from my father for graduation. The pen I carried through my last year of high school and my brief time at college. It's written many a theme, letter and exam. As I remarked to Cpl. Watts, all I need now is to break a leg and have Carolyn marry somebody!!!!

My application for OCS has gone through the Captain's hands—now all I have to do is wait. Watts and Rice told me tonight that they hope I make it and were sure I would if I can get to the school. So do I!!

The Colonel has now joined our unit, and, as far as I know, the whole 495th is in New Guinea. We caught the Captain smiling with the Colonel yesterday. Holy mackerel! The Captain certainly has made himself thoroughly disliked, and I have no sympathy for him since he has brought it all on himself. I understand that he has applied for a transfer, because he cannot maintain discipline and because he has received no cooperation. I doubt if he actually gave these reasons; he would only be hurting himself. However, it is possible. I sort of hope he is stuck with us, because he has not allowed one man in the entire organization to leave for OCS or ASTP.

There has been an awful lot of stealing going on. Today all of the fellows ravaged the supplies, taking everything they could get away with in spite of armed guards. Such things as head flashlights, knives, mess kits, paper, bed rolls, clothing and what not. Much beer has been stolen. I have five mess kit knives, one which I badly needed, the rest for trading either with soldiers or natives. (This coconut is good Watts just gave me.) The whole company is on a stealing rampage; something is going to blow.

That alert the other day was no joke; one Jap recon plane dropped two bombs. Bad aiming, no damage done. Plane 500 feet above nearest anti-aircraft guns. We just recently moved out of that area. Needless to say what would happen if a bomb hit one of the ammunition ships we've been working on.

Gene Tunney here and refereed a couple of fights last night. Was not interested enough to go. A lot of fellows are beginning to show strain. Morales claims he cannot sleep at night.

December 13

Yesterday, Sunday, I was in for a surprise when we were awakened and told that we were to work on the *West Point*! Although I came across on her, I never did get a good look at her. She's a big ship, painted with camouflage colors, great splotches of gray and white. She looked trim. We came alongside her huge sides with our LCM [*landing craft mechanized*] and boarded. There were many soldiers aboard, for she had been back to S.F. and brought another load over. I felt sorry for the poor devils, for I remember the trial it was for me. As soon as I set foot on her, all the old repugnance of those stench-filled, starvation, crowded days returned and I nearly visibly shuddered. I went through the mess hall where I had stood so many times stripped to the waist, with my life belt slung around me, and every man looking as if he were a waterfall. And that first disorganized meal, when many men nearly fainted trying to get out. I saw the water-cooler that I used to go to during the stifling nights to find only a tiny trickle. And I saw the "bed" in which I slept. I did not linger long there. For me, ships and inanimate things have a personality, and I felt that we, both the ship and I, thoroughly disliked each other.

We were assigned to work in the coolers, and how nice it was to be cold again. It was probably the same temperature in there as it is at home now. We all remembered those starvation days, and we got even with the old ship. We were to unload foodstuffs!! Need I mention the consequences of this bit of luck. The first thing we took out were apples, and we each polished off three or four of those pretty quick. Most of us had not had breakfast, so there was plenty of room for what was to follow. In that same cooler were lemons and grapefruit, but they were not so popular. What a treat it was to have our fill of fruit—and ice cold. In our rummaging, between passing out 60 tons of apples, we found a 28-pound box of grapes, and that was devoured in no time flat. Being a grape addict, I took some! There, of all things, was a whole box of small candies. We all dipped big fists into that and stuffed pockets. We learned that it was candy for the crew for Christmas. Yes, we felt so sorry for the crew—who get back to the U.S. every couple of months. Then Rouse found a cold gallon of pineapple juice, and we made short work of that. I remember bursting out laughing and thinking that we were a flock of locusts descending upon the ripe fields. We moved out boxed chicken, a large liverwurst, salami, and a couple of large pieces of meat which we sent back because they were useless. We took what we could eat, and that's all.

It was funny, really funny, to stand in line and wait to see what would come out next. Then, all of a sudden out came a box of frozen strawberries! Can you imagine having frozen strawberries in New Guinea? They were delicious, and our stomachs had a treat that had been foreign to them for a long time. Never did anything taste as good as those strawberries. To add to all that we got during the day, there was a box of cheese, the one thing I did not get my share of. Also, somebody had a case of K-ration chocolate, so we polished that off. Later came ice-cold oranges. The sailors were moving them on their shoulders, a crate each. One of us suggested that one of the sailors could accidentally trip. One obliged, heaving the crate to the floor, smashing it, and spilling those beautiful oranges out. We all had from two to six apiece. Well, that took care of what we consumed, which was plenty of poundage.

December 15

As soon as we stepped off the boat for our midnight dinner, we were informed that we were going to move again! This was greeted with surprise, because we had counted on remaining here for some time, the only civilized place in N.G. Well, after the first hubbub, we climbed into trucks which carried us to the mess hall. "Fuck them all, fuck them all, we're going to Rabaul," we yelled. Our spirit was high, as always, in anticipation of another move. We have not been in any one spot for three weeks since leaving the U.S. Here we have built a new area, tents that we dreamed of having—a certain amount of permanence—all gone. The speculation runs that our destination is Finschhafen or Oro Bay or Good-enough Island, where we were originally rumored to go—or, more fantastically, Samoa. If we went to Samoa, it would be a dream realized; I've always wanted to see it since I was a boy.

We went back on the ship that night only to run into an air alarm. The men scampered out of the hold, and the barge pulled away from the ship. Little by little the bay became dark. I heard the ominous click of the shells going into the machine guns and ack-ack guns. Gun crews scurried about. We waited under a bright moon. It would not have surprised me if planes came over because there was recent reconnaissance. The place is loaded with vital supplies and ships. After awhile we heard some distant rumbling explosions. The bay is well-fortified. The raid passed. Just before dropping off to sleep on my cot at about 4:00 A.M., I heard a few more rumblings. With this, I rolled over and fell into a heavy sleep.

I went to the library and got a book of poetry that I've had my eye on. I stole it, but I have no qualms about it because it was hardly read. This excellent collection contains not only comments on the poems, but information about poetry, metre and copies of original manuscripts! I could not leave it to the dusty shelves. So I managed to get it into my bag, which happily had not left, along with my other books. It is exactly what I've been looking for. Also have in my possession *Berlin Diary.* Will somehow take it along in my pack if I cannot finish it. Denison stole a calculus book via the "under-the-shirt" method.

Berlin Diary is fascinating and enlightening on Germany and pre-war intrigue. I am learning a lot about the politics, the game played by the democracies and their stupidity before the war. There were innumerable possibilities for nipping the war in the bud. At times I become exasperated at what I read. If all is true, it is difficult not to become cynical about this war.

While reading last night alongside the hatch waiting to go to work, I was paid a rather high compliment from the men of this section. I heard them say, "Kahn would make a good lieutenant." I looked around to find about 10 of them smiling at me. I think so too, but I just smiled back and went back to my book. This move will probably mess up my OCS application.

So we are going north, perhaps into battle. It seems a natural sequence in our lives now. Everything else has become so "dreamified" except the army, the war and discomfort. Each move takes us closer and closer. If I could only see my family once again. Next to them, I should like to see Carolyn once more—but what is the use of torturing oneself with these thoughts? It is sometimes a battle to maintain one's sanity. So on we go, time moving on, and the past becoming distant and unreal.

December 16

Am at present aboard the *U.S.S. Henry Dodge.* Events as follows: Awakened at 4:45 A.M. The usual procedure of packing and clearing out, efficiently done from long and frequent practice. Marched out at 7:30 A.M., in formation with full equipment, down to the shore at Gama Dodo. Because this is a naval base, we were a novel sight to the sailors.

There we boarded barges (LCMs) which again took us across the bay to Ahioma. I secured a bad spot and had to stand the whole way with full equipment. After landing, we waited two hours for the *Dodge* to finish loading. I was glad to have *Berlin Diary* along. Am a hell of a soldier—always carrying books.

We boarded about noon in the usual single file, yelling our names as we passed by rank. Incidentally, yesterday afternoon I officially became private first class, long overdue. Two men have dropped out due to sickness. Pappy King has not rejoined us, an irreparable loss, a swell old fellow. Poor Gillis will be lost without King riding him. Herndon, ill for several days, was carted away with malaria symptoms.

Shortly after boarding we drew a fair-sized box, rations for our voyage which Gillis and I shared, since there is one for every two men. Incidentally, poor Ray lost his helmet and liner because of Hollenback. It went over the side of the barge and sank immediately. A loss of such equipment at this time is disastrous. It is difficult to replace, and the loss reduces the chances for survival. The box contained an amazing assortment of good and well-packed foods, mostly condensed or dried: powdered milk, dried apricots and peaches, box of raisins, gum, salt tablets, sugar, cigarettes (Fleetwoods!!), cans of meat, peanuts, cereal, cheese, candy, coffee, lemon flavoring, cocoa, biscuits, etc. All of this in great quantities. We are not hungry.

(At present the fellow standing at the rail next to me has called his wife a "god-damned old whore" for neglecting to write him the sex of their newborn baby after not having heard from her in a month. Oh well!!)

This trip is dangerous. We are subject to air and sea raid at any moment. Light protection. We are all a little jumpy. Getting used to that, too. Harris worried, poor fellow, flared up at me this afternoon. Told him off, as I was in no mood myself to soothe people. Later reprimanded him when he interrupted Blanco and me talking. Many do this and I dislike it. Gave him a lesson on manners. Manners *now*—maybe I'm crazy. Life is hard enough, it doesn't have to be crude. But it always is.

It looks like we are going to see some action. No fear, half anticipation. Denison and Hillsberg, the same way. Seth Hillsberg is quiet, unassuming, cool, slightly built and meek-looking. He is one of only four Jewish fellows in the company out of 225 men! Of the three (the others are Klein and Brummer), I like Seth best.

Heard a fascinating story today from a sailor in the merchant marine. On a trip over, he saw an officer jump overboard. The officer came out of the deck latrine, flipped away a cigarette, and over he went. The sailor tossed him a preserver within easy reach, but he ignored it purposely. He raised himself out of the water slightly, waved a final farewell, and plunged into the next wave. The ship, of course, could not stop. It circled once, did not see him again, and continued on its way. Quite a story!

Who knows what adventure tomorrow brings, or if there will be a tomorrow? It's almost dark.

December 17

Am sitting in the bow, practically at the tip of the destroyer *U.S.S. Smith!* Did I write that this life is fantastic, full of adventure! Let me describe what the unknown tomorrow has brought.

Suddenly, at about 10:00 this morning there was a shudder, the booms rattled and the sea churned. We had run atop of a reef!! For an hour the huge prop thrashed the water into furious spray—we did not budge. They tried shifting the weight of the troops (I had thought of that an hour before), but to no avail. More churning. After a time small boats began to circle around us. From a motor-launch off our starboard stern a diver went down to investigate. The diving equipment consisted of an air-fed mask and weighted belt. Guns ready for sharks. He came up frequently. It was fascinating to watch the huge bubbles coming up, and the water was so clear that you could easily see his every move. He went 15 feet down to the coral bed. When the ship was not churning the sea, I could make out the reef, a great stretch of it, white with various shades of green splotches, hazy and vascillating under the green sea. The diver reported disgustedly that we were well up on the reef. I could easily see that. The launch left.

Two destroyers turned up and hove to about ½ mile off the port bow. Rumors started: engine damaged, hole in the bottom, leaks. We made a fine stationary target on the reef. After their initial excitement, the men settled down to reading, cards, and watching over the side. Water not plentiful, food running low. After several hours of broiling in the hot sun, an order came through. Tear down packs, take blanket, mosquito bar, mess kit, rifle, cartridge belt, canteen, gas mask. Then no gas mask, then take it, then don't, don't take helmet!! A general confusion started, men getting prescribed equipment, filling their pockets with what food we had. Trying to get water. Me too, I was out. Just when you need officers the most, they are not there. I salvaged some candy, some cigarettes and, more importantly, salt tablets, which proved of value later. Then, more waiting. You're always in a hurry to wait in the army. I managed to get half a canteen of scummy water, but one cannot see it when he drinks it from the canteen. Have ¼ canteen left.

Two motor launches and a small schooner were taking the troops off to two destroyers. Blanco ill from the heat (heat and Blanco don't go well together). We lined up and were carried to the destroyers. On way to schooner was able to fortify myself with full cup of water, which I badly needed, and it has carried me through the afternoon. The boat swayed considerably. Milligan said something funny. He was sitting directly across from me. "I've been a seaman seven years, and I had to come into the army to be shipwrecked."

On getting off the *Dodge,* the ladder leading to the deck of the schooner was almost vertical. My rifle, the piece of equipment that is always most cumbersome to me, was slung over my shoulders and kept entangling in the ropes. I threw my blanket, net, mess gear, one book, all tied together, to the deck. Maneuvered easily after that. Fellows with carbines are lucky when it comes to moving about. The *Dodge* looked sad, sitting on the reef, deserted. A crippled ship is a pathetic sight. The crew remained aboard. Denison, the bad-off Blanco and I settled on the *Smith* in an exclusive little corner in the bow. The heat was terrific, accentuated by the steel plates of the deck. We strung Denison's blanket from the railing to the base of a huge canon for much-needed shade. I distributed salt tablets, which helped. Looking back at the *Dodge,* she was listing, stranded on the rocks, a huge helpless hulk. The destroyer started.

Destroyers go very fast, and I watched the water literally race by. Huge waves knifed out of the sea by the pointed bow. Thought: My journal is in one of my bags. It's an irreplaceable piece of writing and, for the moment, abandoned with everything else. Also pack of letters. The hell with the rest! To lose the journal would be like taking a piece of me away.

December 18

Landed in Oro Bay, 25 miles below Buna, once held by Japs. We are further south that I thought, Buna being pretty safe. When we arrived here by means of ducks [*amphibious craft*], we saw a sign with a bathing beauty on it which read "Soupac Seaview Hotel, 1,000 rooms, hot and running water." Yeah!! Humor in N.G. Code name for this hole is Sumak.

When we arrived at this camp, situated about 100 yards back from the shoreline, it was a discouraging sight. Funny how we drove right out of the ocean and into camp. The camp is a huge mud hole. Tents were up. Ground very wet, huge puddles and swamps about. Some of the tents couldn't be used, filled with water. Everything looks dilapidated and rickety. Conditions crude. Water is heavily chlorinated so that it puckers your mouth when you drink it. It must rain a great deal here. Directly to my left there is a small swamp filled with frogs. They make a continual racket, really an amazing amount of noise—which continued all night and, more surprisingly, all day so far. (Later found they croaked only when it was raining.)

For awhile we thought we would have to sleep on the ground, but we were issued cots from a nearby building. Strung mosquito net up and hit the bed. We built a small fire last night which provided light. Gosh knows it was hot enough. The night cooled, and I fell into a heavy sleep.

December 21

Saw the "fabulous" 491st, who have been here all the time except for their C Company which is at Lae. They have lost two men: one died of typhus, the other got killed working on the ships. One man was shot in the derriere at Lae and is now here. The Jap sniper must have had a sense of humor. The 491st has experienced a few bombings, one shell-shock case. A few men sent home.

The reef we got hung up on is known as Colingswood Reef.

The plans for this organization are as follows. We will proceed to Buna, 25 miles north of here. We shall remain in N.G. until Christmas at the very least. Hurray!! That gives us four days. We shall probably be in the invasion of New Britain. The plan has us following in the marines, to whom we are attached, by about six days. Something will probably upset these plans, something always does. It's probably going to be hell and we'll have casualties.

Our ship came in yesterday with packs, gas masks, helmets and shelter-halves. They were all dumped on the ground, and what a mess finding one's stuff. I was lucky; I eventually found all mine.

Last night I went to bed early, but an Aussie soldier came into the tent. He stuttered so badly that I was curious about him. I climbed out of my mosquito net to see him. Over cigarettes and candlelight we had an interesting talk. He's been a soldier for four-and-a-half years. (Makes my 10 months look anemic.) Fought in Greece, Crete, Tobruk, the Baltic, and was in Coventry during the heavy raids. Saw much action, hand-to-hand combat, and saw many "cobbers" killed. His force of 18,000 was reduced to 9,000 by the time it came back. Wounded by a bomb burst which badly fractured his skull, he was shelved in Australia for awhile. He also had a bayonet wound in the forearm. He was a nervous wreck for a time, and his present speech impediment is a result of shock. He was tall, heavy-set, nearly bald but moustached, moonfaced, and pleasant but rather serious. He leaves here this morning by plane for further movement north. He volunteered to come to the islands to fight the Jap after all he went through. Guts! He said he was 28—he looked 40.

He said war was especially rough on the young fellows. Doesn't speak well for me—but I don't feel 19, rather 25. When I think I'm only 19 it surprises me. He said, "Man was never made for bombs." He told me about the effects of concussion, how it makes your nose and ears bleed, and about the terrible tension. Sounds theatrical, story-book stuff, but it's horrible when it's true. How horrible war is. I know its discomforts and pangs—soon I shall probably know its terror and horror. I had to listen closely to catch all he said. His speech was nervous, but he was calm. I felt honored to shake hands over the candle when we parted.

December 23

It looks like we are going into New Britain. We've had several company meetings, and this is the way the information goes. We are going to follow the marines in after they make a beachhead, probably two to six days afterwards. The place we are going to land is called Cape Gloucester which is in direct defense of Rabaul. It should be a tough fight. Cape Gloucester and Rabaul have been bombed for nearly a month now, some of the heaviest raids of the S.W. Pacific, raining down tons of bombs. It is rumored that the Japs have a force of 20,000 defending the island.

[*Actually, almost 100,000 Japanese, with artillery and tanks, defended Rabaul. Contrary to General MacArthur's earlier intention, we were sent to New Britain to isolate rather than attack the base at Rabaul. According to Samuel Eliot Morison in* Breaking the Bismarck Barrier, *"Tarawa, Iwo Jima and Okinawa would have faded to pale pink in comparison with the blood that would have flowed if the Allies had attempted an assault on fortress Rabaul."*] Every day and night we hear the bombers going over and coming back from raids, softening up the defenses. We have been read the rules on captured enemy equipment, what we can and cannot keep, and what must be turned in to intelligence.

We will be well-fitted out for this expedition. In the past few days we've received jungle boots and socks, rubber band for helmet for holding camouflage, green dye for hands and face, jungle pack, jungle hammock—which I spent part of the day washing to get the preservative out of it. Also small and medium rubberized "barracks" bags, an inflatable rubber pillow, a shovel, with a cover for it, to dig foxholes, a fine first-aid kit containing bandages, iodine, atabrine, salt tablets, water-purifier tablets, athlete's foot solution. Everything is green. The hammock is really a fine piece of equipment. In addition we received an emergency candle, carton of cigarettes, poncho and a small single-battery "jungle" flashlight. We shall soon be issued emergency rations and ammunition, about 300 rounds.

The invasion may be hell, it may be not so bad. Sometimes all this seems fantastic. Is this Sy Kahn going into battle, to fight the Japs? He has some vague ideas what it is all about. Sy Kahn, soldier, might have to kill men, he might be killed. Perhaps the former is worse than the latter. Sometimes it all seems like a bad dream. It's going to be a pathetic Christmas, and we'll probably spend New Year's Eve in a foxhole!

Tonight we had an excellent talk on malaria prevention. It is good to meet an officer with a sense of humor. Humor is one of the most valuable qualities a man can possess. We are going to be highly exposed to malaria, denque fever, elephantiasis, typhus and various skin diseases. Aside from these, said the officer, it's fairly clean! Our present area is considered sanitary. Malaria has been reduced from 700 to 380 cases out of every 1,000 men. On Gloucester we will be limited to one canteen of water for a couple of days. There will be a tank coming in for us containing about 500 gallons. If a bomb hits it, it's going to be tough going.

The company is cracking down on the men. S/Sgt. Mishalanie and Cpl. Eaton were broken for gambling with the men. Tough for Mish with a wife and baby. Also T/Sgt. Mira was broken, the loud little man, and Pfcs. Illes, Rosenberg and Basil Jones! It's easy to lose your rank now.

We have been issued hunting knives, and section and assistant section leaders will be issued machetes. Two more men have dropped out. Dumas fractured his neck. This is a bad loss. Although a private, he is one of the few men of this organization that has seen action. Billy Dixon suddenly got a case of high blood pressure. The fellows talk continually about the coming move, anticipating, planning, speculating, and fearing, a little.

Last night some of the fellows "acquired" six bottles of vanilla extract, 85% alcohol. I took a little of it straight, and it was liquid fire! It made you tingle. It's famous for its use in place of alcohol. I had a little more later in the evening cut with my can of orange juice. It really is powerful stuff. The whole section was drinking the stuff. Cpl. Watts, Sgt. Stahl, Rouse, Redwine, Davis, Hudaick, Rice, Fazekas, and even Wingfield had a couple of slugs. Some of the fellows really got lit. Hudaick, Rice, and Rouse were the worst. Fazekas really could hold the stuff. He was sober as a judge and disgusted with the other fellows. He even cooked some ham, and we had ham sandwiches. Hudaick, Rice and Rouse were raising hell. Kelly wanted to fight everybody in the company. Knives were brandished, and for awhile it looked like somebody was going to get cut. Kelly ordinarily is a top fellow. A couple of guys got socked, including Rice. Hudaick was calling them all a bunch of names. They finally had to drag Kelly to bed.

This morning Hudaick polished off another bottle and was still drunk. He dug about 10 holes in the tent floor, yelling because no one would help him, and then telling everybody how pretty it was, and to come and see it. Kelly was a wreck when I saw him at noon. He said he was spitting blood all morning. He had been unfortunate enough to draw a detail. They had to give him the afternoon off. He came in, laid on the ground and slept most of the afternoon. Redwine hardly budged all day. Last night Davis was also well-oiled and had a skin-full. He was draped over the bed and mumbling something about six inches of cold steel between the ribs. Later he was sick. Could hear him retching. The stuff gave me a dull headache. I slept like a log and didn't even hear first whistle, a rarity for me. When Fazek jokingly offered the souses a drink this afternoon, it was funny to see their faces. Last night when the fellows were half-lit and throwing compliments around freely, they told me that I should really have rated the checker rating, and that they all thought I was a good guy, but Thomas was "one of the boys." That was no secret to me. I'm in line for the next rating, if there is an opening. It was quite a night all in all.

December 25

Christmas night, and the "perspiration is rolling off me like sweat." It is also washing off my mosquito repellent. Redwine is doing his usual bitching, and I am again writing by candlelight.

Last night, Christmas Eve, the boys got well-lit on vanilla extract again. We all had a wonderful time, though, singing, joking. By luck I found the correct ingredients to make a smooth drink, and it went down like soda. For most of the evening I was kept busy mixing half-pint after half-pint. The compliments were frequent on my mixture. Just for the sake of the record, the mixture was a little less than ¼ of canteen cup of extract, two tablespoons of sugar, one tablespoon lemon-flavoring powder, and fill with water. The result of this "jungle juice" was that Milligan and Fazek got a skin-full. Just for the hell of it, I poured a little on a candle flame, and the flames nearly reached the tent top! Gad. Rouse produced good cigars, I produced a hoarded large can of apricots, we heated a can of hash, and Stahl produced crackers; Fazek made a batch of the good coffee he is becoming famous for. We sang everything from Christmas carols to bawdy army songs. This was our Christmas celebration. I spent the day packing my jungle pack. It makes a heavy load.

As luck would have it, I pulled guard duty on Christmas Eve and had to leave the party at 10:00 P.M. It was a warm, starlit night. The stuff that had to be guarded was ammunition. It was out of the area in the middle of a field of mud and ruts, with the jungle starting at the edge of the field. There were many sounds, and sometimes I'd hear the cracking of twigs which made me a little uneasy. I had my ammunition-less rifle with me and a small jackknife which I shifted to an available pocket. A few times I sat up and listened. It's awfully lonesome and dark out there. After the first half-hour my nerves quieted. I was surprised to find myself so jumpy. I had Beal's watch and jungle light. I lay on top of the ammunition, rifle alongside, head on my helmet, and watched the stars shoot, and thought of home, and Carolyn and Sue a bit, and of other people I know.

The advance detail left. In cleaning up the mess of our tent, caused by numerous midnight snacks, I found a GI knife, and I took the machete I found the other day, which I intend to hang on the wall of my room some day. Spent the morning listening to Hyer, who felt like talking about himself and family. Often I listen to some soldier who gets a talking jag. One learns a little, and I am an easy listener. It does the fellows good. Once in awhile I feel like getting a load off my mind, but there are few I can talk to.

Trucks took us to an area just evacuated by the marines going to New Britain. We will follow them in a few days. We are fully equipped and ready. The fellows have been discussing it quite a bit. The bombers have been going over continually day and night. They make a beautiful sight, those big birds roaring in formation. We're going to be in on the most important invasion of the S.W. Pacific so far. Would not be surprised to find myself in a foxhole on New Year's Eve.

We have been investigating the evacuated marine areas, and Milligan came back with ammunition and a good bayonet, the lucky dog. We are not issued a bayonet. He also found a can opener, more ammunition and a large stand that we carried back. A few minutes ago Milligan and Fazek brought back a lantern, coffee pot, knife sharpener and some canned food! Redwine "acquired" some 200 rounds. We ought to have a jolly time firing the stuff. I figure this tent has about 2,000 rounds right now. There is much looting and waste in this war.

December 28

Last night Putt put me on detail. I tried to explain that I'd been working six hours on six hours off for three shifts and was tired. We've had to find our own transportation to boot, and it's 15 miles to camp. Also missed quite a few meals. All this taken in stride, except I "blew my top" when he ordered me on this detail. The only reason I got out of bed was for mail call. Explained to Lt. Reinhardt who let me off. When I told Putt he got really mad, and I found myself on another detail till 10:30 last night after working practically 24 hours previously. I figured he had his little revenge, and it was done. This morning, with all the rest of our crew off, I was called out to help rake the area. With this I went to Sgt. Eriksen who finally gave me the time off I deserve.

To demonstrate the efficiency of the army, we are now working about a mile from SowPac; when we were at SowPac we worked about a mile from here. And you can't argue with a superior in the army, even if he's dead wrong. There was so little I could do last evening that I had tears of rage in my eyes.

Yesterday afternoon in the first few hours I had off, I went out and fired about 20 rounds. The rifle fires all right, but it has a tremendous kick. It left me nearly deaf for the rest of the day, and my ears are still ringing this morning. Also fired a Thompson submachine gun, and that's a really smooth and deadly weapon.

The Captain gave us one of his delightful talks last night, which made him more disliked, if possible. Everyone would like to get rid of him. He's ruining the whole outfit.

The marines have run into opposition on New Britain. Several ships have been sunk. The wounded have been filtering back, and the hospital here was full of activity last night. I understand there is a hospital ship laying up there, taking care of some of them. Seven dead sailors were brought in yesterday. War is great.

December 30

Hoffman has gone off his head. He is the first of many that are borderline cases now. At present our main cause of casualty looks like nervous breakdown. We are woken up and kept up at all hours. One is not sure what he will do from one moment to the next. We are doing every imaginable physical job and sometimes for more than 24 hours with only a few hours sleep. The men are beginning to show it. Our morale is seriously low. Men are snapping at one another, and they complain all the time. The Captain is hated by both the men and his officers. He drives us like a labor gang of morons, and everywhere you see the men talking about him. The men are beginning to look old. Some are getting gaunt. Alexander recently came out of the hospital after a malaria attack. No furloughs for at least four more months—and probably not then, according to Lt. Wenz.

I've been doing a rated man's work the past few days, but the hell with it. As long as I can do something aboard the ships to aid getting the supplies along, I feel happy. There is a terrific amount of looting going on, and the inefficiency of the army seems more apparent every day. We have been called a valuable organization. True enough. No other outfit does the dirty jobs we have and are doing.

Wounded and dead marines are dribbling back from "the front."

January 1, 1944

A new year, and the last one of the war, I hope. One hardly realized it was New Year's Eve last night because of the bombshell thrown into our company. The old year has gone out and so might our captain who has made himself increasingly disliked ever since the first day in the States when he stood before us, helmet low over his heavy eyebrows, and said, "My name is Drown, and I can drown any man in this company." Ever since then we have had periodic speeches berating us, or warning us of future dire conditions and death, all of which have proven exaggerated.

Yesterday some of the fellows called me in to their meeting and asked me to write a petition for them to get the Captain out of the company. I told them I would write it, but that I would not sign it because of my chances for OCS. (Sgt. Tipple has recently called Denison and me in again to ask for our three choices of service organizations.) The fellows agreed that this was all right with them, and Cpl. Watts said he wouldn't want to jeopardize my chance. They all want to see me go.

So I wrote a rough copy in about 20 minutes and read it to them. They all thought it was excellent and contained everything they wanted to say. I wrote it in plain language, essentially stating that we were willing to continue under the command of the C.O. but that we wanted a change of attitude toward the men, that he has unnecessarily berated and frightened us, causing low morale, that we want the respect due to men no matter of what rank, and that we be told the truth. The writing got excellent comment, except from Flynn who thought it poor. (Ron had signed and then, after talking to Heffle and Herbeck, crossed his name off.)

Later that night we had a meeting, and all the fellows decided that we should have about 180 names before submitting it. I was emphatic on this point. I said, "We hang together or we will hang separately." Mish was dead set against it; he claimed that if we waited it would not go in. We said not to send it in until we had more support, but he told us he had already sent it into military channels. Fazek and Mish had it typed in another company, with the help of some lieutenants, and put it in a special blue envelope (not to be opened by any of our officers) and impetuously mailed it last night to the base commander. We were told it had 110 signatures, slightly better than 50%. However, only four non-coms signed, all corporals. About 40 men are out in the stream working the ships and don't even know about it. The die is cast. I realized that in sending the petition in without consulting the men, Mish is acting more for himself than for the company, and fanatically for revenge against the Captain for taking away his s/sgt. stripes. I didn't like this. My position is dangerous in this mess, and I really don't want to see anything drastic happen to the Captain.

Only seven or eight men know I wrote most of the petition, and they have not breathed a word. Cpl. Watts has covered me well. But still it doesn't sit right with me, and all day today it gnawed at me. There will probably be an investigation, and either the Captain or the company will pay. If ever he gets the list of names, or learns who wrote it, there may be dire consequences. I can't feel right about it, even though we have had some raw deals and rotten talks from him.

Today all the officers seemed especially nice to the men, and this afternoon the Captain was patronizing all the men. (I hate the way Mish has been patronizing me, practically groveling at my feet.)

Really worked hard this afternoon loading a LST [*landing ship tank, a 300-foot seagoing vessel that could carry over 2000 tons of cargo; shallow draft; also known as "large stationary target"*] taking supplies to New Britain. I was in charge of my first detail, and I found that I worked extra hard because I was the leader. I can work best when I lead, I have found. The Captain told me what to do, what supplies to load. I told him that because they were going to N.B. that we wouldn't mind working hard. To this he said we would probably be up there in a few weeks. He was so pleasant for a change that I winced to think of what had happened. This can be a damaging blow to a man, this petition.

Later: This evening, while I was bathing in the creek, Havron joined me and told me that this morning the Captain asked him if he signed anything. To this he answered no. The Captain replied, "Don't, don't make a fool of yourself." Some of us had an idea that Sgt. Putt and the officers already knew of the petition. Coming off detail tonight we saw they had their heads together over the Army Regulations. Sure enough, there was a notice on the board stating that the Captain knew a petition had been filed, and calling officers' and men's attention to the 66th Article of War which concerns mutiny. This is foolish, because there is no mutiny and nothing written that can be interpreted as mutinous. The Captain was seen talking to MP officers tonight. We have a regular grapevine. The petition has been a constant topic of discussion for nearly two days now, and everybody is aroused. Some of my best friends in the company don't know my part in this; it would greatly surprise them if they did. I feel like an intriguer.

It was probably 1st Sgt. Putt who got wind of the paper and reported it to the Captain—or one of his stooges, who are thought to be Klein and Hennel. Possible, very possible. Anyway the fat's in the fire, and somebody is going to fry in it. When I went to fill my canteen a little while ago, I noticed that the orderly tent was all lit up. The C.O., Putt and Sgt. Pietrangelo were there. I believe they were discussing the petition, but they all seemed in good spirits. The Captain was laughing a great deal, and undoubtedly he has something up his sleeve. I plainly heard Pete say, "You wouldn't do that, would you?" Shortly something will pop. The situation is confusing, and I don't like it. However, the guys seem determined to stick together. But "the guys" are not always very clever. I am in a disturbed state of mind and in a ticklish position.

Latest rumors have us flying to N.B. soon. Very possible. We took a New Britain airport yesterday. A few Jap prisoners have been brought back here. A strong, fantastic rumor has been circulating for the last five days. Supposedly we are going home in March to be broken up into cadres to train other troops.

The next few days should be bombshells. Watts and I have become thick. Tired tonight. What a mess.

January 6

It seems almost fateful that I should terminate this notebook with the events of the past five days. It marks, I sincerely believe, and closes forever a certain phase of my life. Though I have a tremendous lot to learn, the experiences of these last days have been the most invaluable of my life.

A mess was created, one I helped create through my own lack of thought, my stupidity and the worst judgment I have ever used. I wish I could write all the details, all the psychological effects, and all about the new spirit among the men that has been born. The details may be written here only in part, but they will always remind me of events I will never forget.

I knew even before the announcement was posted concerning the 66th Article of War that eventually I was going to have to straighten the mess out and talk to the C.O. It took three hellish days and nights to form my plan. I watched events slowly gather like storm clouds before all hell broke loose. Those men who knew of my part in the petition advised me to keep out of it, that I was clear, that I would jeopardize my OCS application for which I have hoped and worked.

Having made a mistake, I was not about to be swayed by foolish advice, or by any spur-of-the-moment feeling, not use my own head and judgment. Sometimes it seems easier to let another do your thinking and planning, but I have learned the lesson well and the hard way that it is best to make one's own decisions.

I began to figure out how to straighten out the mess and how to straighten out me with me.

January 7

On January 3rd the original typed petition with all the names of the men who signed was posted. A bombshell. The Colonel and some other high-ranking officers (the Colonel happened to be visiting the company at the time) did not appear to be taking the petition too seriously, but I still thought there could be dire consequences.

For three days nobody talked about anything except the petition. For those three days I went through mental hell. I slept and ate little. Slowly I worked out a plan. I knew that I had not written the petition out of malice but with the feeling that I was doing something good. I was not out to get anyone. My intention was to change the Captain's attitude toward the men. Now, I also felt that I had to right a wrong against a man whom I may not have understood.

During the afternoon of Jan. 3rd, Lt. Wenz called a platoon meeting and explained that he considered the instigators of the petition dangerous people. It seemed to me I was in a serious personal situation in that I had written almost every word of the petition, but had not signed it. I could easily be considered a saboteur, even more dangerous than the "instigators." To disrupt an organization such as ours about to play an important part in the invasion of New Britain might indeed seem a smart enemy move, if it were true.

At the time of this meeting I thought I knew as much about the petition as anyone, having been called in at its birth. I was wrong. Only later did I learn that the scheme to attack the Captain had been hatched days before. I had been used for my ability to write. Neatly sucked in.

That night, after the platoon meeting with Lt. Wenz, every man was called into the Captain's tent and read the punishment for mutiny. In wartime that can be death, and enforceable if the petition were interpreted to have traitorous motives. Most of the men who had signed were simply bulldozed into it by the instigators—demoted noncoms. Some men had not read what they signed. Some were tired, having worked long hours, others had an out-and-out dislike of the Captain, a few signed for revenge of some supposed wrong. Only a few signed out of their sense of injustice to the company as a whole. Most of the men went into it unwittingly because they, like I, did not know of the personal maliciousness behind the petition. For these men I felt wholly responsible. For the rest I also felt partially to blame.

So, the next day I decided to see the C.O. After work I went down to the creek and smoked that old pipe I have smoked through many trials, tribulations and joys. The only man who saw me there was Johnson, who came to wash some clothes. I told him, in broad terms, the situation. He was the first to know of my part in the affair, aside from the small group of men who had requested that I write the petition. I told Johnson mainly to hear the words worked out mentally. Of course he was taken aback to learn that I had even a finger in the mess, much less a whole arm!

Later that evening I went to the Captain's tent, but he was not there. I ran into Lt. Wenz, to whom I also revealed my involvement. I felt he was entitled to an explanation because he was our platoon leader, and because half the men that had signed were in the 3rd platoon. Altogether seven NCOs had signed.

Anyway, I sat down in front of the Captain's tent intending to wait till any hour to see him. At about 10:00 P.M. he drove up in his jeep with the Colonel. He invited me into the tent after I requested to speak with him. We sat. I saw a softness in his face and an expression in his eyes that had been foreign to me these past 10½ months. And he seemed exceptionally kind.

I began by telling him the part I had played in the petition, and that I now felt I had made a mistake. Already he had broken every man who had signed the petition and had given each man 18 extra duty hours that had to be worked out in his spare time. We are working very hard, and these extra hours are a burden on the men. Because my name was not on the petition, I got neither the punishment nor was broken. How could any man who has any respect for himself stand by and watch other men pay for what has been his error, unwittingly or not? I offered to take a court martial and the entire blame if the ratings could be restored to the men who had worked so many months for them, and that I would do all the extra hours for every man who had signed. Actually this amounted to 62 men. Mish had misinformed me earlier that 110 to 120 men had signed the petition, which is over 50% of the men. Actually about 25% had signed. This lie led me to the conclusion that I had been used—but that did not vindicate me in my own mind. The Captain refused to do what I suggested. First, he said, he knew all along that I was not really responsible for what had happened and intended no court martial. He stated he would not restore those men broken in rank and given extra work. They must learn an invaluable lesson for what he felt was their stupidity.

January 9

To continue catching up on events: in our talk of several nights ago the Captain said he would not break me or even give me extra duty, claiming that by not doing so my punishment would be the greater. That is true, for I have to watch these men take punishment about which I can do nothing, or even share. Even more ironic, Sgt. Stahl has been considering me for assistant section leader, which is corporal! I have to laugh. I have discovered, to my satisfaction, that despite my being in one of the most serious situations of my life—even facing death had my motives been misunderstood—my sense of humor never for a moment abated. I believe I will die laughing at something.

But to continue, my talk with the Captain was one of the most interesting of my life. We were in his tent with no light but the moon. After we discussed the petition and its consequences, he told me a little about himself. I now realize that he is one of the strangest men that I have met. He told me that early in life he was greatly wronged, and that only two people in the world understand him, his wife and a friend of 20 years. Then he said he now was going to tell me something intimate about himself. I seem to have this effect on many people, and I would like to know why.

Anyway, he said that he loved nothing better than to trap men, to play against them as one plays a game of chess, and to crack down after he had outmaneuvered them. Such a man seems dangerous to me, especially after he also told me that he sleeps with a loaded revolver under his pillow. Perhaps these words seem storyish, but I was impressed by his intensity, and by the atmosphere in which this oratory was delivered. As fate would have it, it began to rain and lightning. Because there was no light in the tent, the flashing, crashing lightning threw wild white streaks on his strong-featured face. He has features that spell power. The rain made a staccato sound on the tent. His voice took on a fanatical, gleeful tone. He spoke in a half-whisper. With this symphony of sound bursting from the heavens and the emotional voice flowing from the man, I found myself, to my amazement, on the verge of hypnosis. However, I snapped out of it. The experience was fascinating and terrifying.

Suddenly he seemed a more normal man, after those indelible 10 minutes during which I was mesmerized by his revelations, the special quirks of a mature mind.

The Captain had to go on duty, so he invited me to go with him. He tossed me a poncho, and we piled into his jeep. It sure is weird, riding around in the middle of the night with one's C.O. The mood changed. Now we had a sort of father-and-son talk, and it felt strange and, damn it all, good to be called "son" and "my boy" instead of "soldier" or "son-of-a-bitch."

I learned much that night about the army, about men, and about myself. We discussed many subjects. I have learned more in the last five days than a year of college could have given me. This is when I fear death, because every day I am beginning to learn more about life. Though I have been miserable during these torturous days, I would not have missed them. They have been worth the discomfort. Most important, I feel that I possess the potentialities of being a man, an intelligent man—and incidentally a soldier. When we got back we had coffee together, talked some more and then said goodnight at about 1:30 A.M. With reveille at 5:00 and with three previous nights of little sleep, I was exhausted, but I hardly noticed it till last night when I slept nine hours without changing position.

During the days that followed my talk with the Captain, a training schedule was initiated. Reveille is at 5:00 A.M. and retreat at 5:00 P.M., with inspection of rifles. Our heretofore free time is now occupied by infantry drill, hacking jungle, digging machine-gun emplacements, foxholes, slit trenches, wells. On top of the regular physical work, the extra work at night has been hard on the men. It comes to 18 to 20 hours a day and takes its toll. There were 15 sick men last night, eight of whom are in the hospital being treated for malaria. Some bad food has made everyone ill and given many the GIs [*diarrhea*].

I put the rest of my plan into action. I called all the fellows in camp at the time to a meeting and made a powerful speech. I spoke for nearly an hour, and not a man budged or spoke. I explained my part in the mess which, of course, surprised nearly everybody. I explained that I had talked with the Captain. I told them that any man who would feel better by physically punishing me, I was ready for each one and hoped he would do it. I would make no attempt at defense. (I would have stood under an unmerciful beating if necessary. Happily nobody did so.) I told the men that the only way they could avoid further serious consequences was by each going into the C.O. and admitting his part and stating he had made a mistake and was sorry. Most of them were.

With regard to the men, my faith in human nature was greatly restored by events which followed. My speech accomplished its purpose. Because of the speech and the events which followed, I won the respect of many men. Having the respect of other men is a great feeling, especially when they number in the hundreds. The information spread like wild-fire through the company, and all that day I spent talking to men and being greeted with smiles, respect, and slaps on the back.

I was beginning to feel vindicated—but not completely. I had also directed the speech to the instigators, but I found they were determined to hold out. This was the remaining problem, and here I had to use psychology. The seriousness of their not going in to talk to the Captain I could not emphasize too greatly. In spite of the success I had, Fazekas and Mishalanie held out. Here was the problem: Fazekas is an experienced guardhouse lawyer and felt he could beat the rap. Even more difficult was Mish, who felt that he had been wronged, that his wife and baby were cheated out of necessary money because he had been unjustly broken from staff sergeant. He wanted revenge.

That night following my speech I sat in the dark and watched the men waiting in line in front of the Captain's tent and going in one at a time to talk to him. I guess the conversations were calm; every man came out satisfied. It felt strange to have advised men many years older than I. So far, 60 men had followed my advice to the letter.

A new spirit is growing in the organization. Until 1:00 in the morning, and after a terrifically hard day, with reveille a few hours away, the men waited, sometimes kicking one another and laughing hard. Hollenback

George "Pap" Milligan at thirty-eight, a close friend and foxhole buddy, New Guinea, 1943.

Sy Kahn clearing jungle with a machete, New Guinea, 1943.

From left to right, Sy Kahn, Seth Hillsberg, Ray Blanco, and Sol Miller, New Guinea, 1943.

From left to right, Horace Grant, George Milligan, Rafael Sanchez, and Michael Hudaick, New Guinea, 1943.

insisted on kicking me, which I obliged. The men have worked harder than ever before despite the tremendous strain and additional work. (Here comes Morales in good spirits after digging a hole.) But one sees only a marvelous spirit, whistling, singing, joking—and no complaining. However, the strain is visible, and men *are* in the hospital.

After all the men had seen the Captain, he saw me and came out of the tent. We walked around the ballfield in the dark, again in the middle of the night, and talked. He quoted from the Bible freely, and he talked about guidance. Tonight the Captain was deeply religious, revealing another facet of himself. I simply said to him that I thought religion was nothing more than a set of morals, and let it go at that.

I asked him for a little more time for the ringleaders to come in. This was granted, but he made it clear that he would not wait much longer. This remained my last problem before I felt that I had vindicated myself. During these days a stockade had been built, but it will remain empty now.

We then discussed if I was officer material. The possibility of officer training was still on my mind. He told me the requisites, the code of an officer, and that I had much to learn, but that I probably would make a good one. There are few things I am sure of, but one of them is that I would make a good officer. He told me there is a surplus of 60,000 officers and that enlisted men are now the most valuable and needed. This makes sense. Although I have my formal application in my tent, I may not turn it in. The war may be over soon, it looks that way, and if I spend four months in OCS, and more getting a command, I might be of no value to the army and the war. I have not yet absolutely decided, but I may decide simply to remain an enlisted man.

Jack Harris has proven himself a pretty good fellow and is now in our section, which has become a damn good one. Jack tried to take the entire blame for the petition when he was not in the least responsible. I used this fact with Mish, working on his conscience, guessing he would not let another man take his place for blame. This, along with the help of men I told to keep after Mish, finally broke him down. I don't know exactly how Fazek squared himself, but at present the whole stinking mess is finished, and I have done all that I set out to do. The sleep I had last night was good and deep. Later Mish came to me and told me that the Captain gave him both barrels. He got 96 hours extra duty, which is stiff—but light in comparison to a death sentence.

The Captain and the Colonel delivered speeches to the men last night, which cheered the men. I was surprised and pleased when the Captain used phrases that had been mine during our recent talks. So out of the mess has come a new unity. And I learned a lot. Maybe Captain Drown did too.

I have decided that I would not take the rating of any man in the organization who lost it through this mess. However, there is an opening in the section unrelated to these demotions for which I have a good chance. At the same time I shall help each man regain his rating, if I can. Most will.

The Captain told me today he is going to be a major. Some time in the future we will get a new C.O., but not because of the petition. In the meantime he intends to go to New Britain with us. I said his leaving would be a personal loss for me, and that I thought him a clever man. He put his hand on my shoulder and said I had given him one of the best compliments he has ever received. I know I shall never forget him. I still disagree with some of his attitudes and ideas, but I think I understand them.

In the past few days I've seen terrible things. I've seen the wounded and shellshocked come back from New Britain, and if this sight could be seen by the people at home, it would shorten the war by many months. It's not very pretty to see what war does to men. The most horrible event I have ever witnessed was when I recently saw a soldier burn to death at my feet. I was in charge of a detail when an explosion occurred about 60 yards in front of me. A huge sheet of flame burst forth, and for a moment I thought a barrel of gas exploded. Then suddenly out of the flames came a man, a human torch. He ran about 20 yards and disappeared behind some boxes. For a moment I was stunned, then I remember saying, "My God, the man's burning alive." I ran toward the man. When I got there he was lying face down in the sand. As I knelt down I could just hear his voice in an agonizing whisper saying, "Help, help." He was a MP. Another man was there before Morales and I. It was horrible. His whole body was smoking, smoke coming even from his eyes. All his hair burned off. His face had screwed into a supreme agony and burned livid white and red. I began to cover him with sand to shut off the oxygen, but the smoking could not be stopped. The pain and his still-burning body were cracking his mind. He made little sound.

Soon there was a crowd and in a few moments a doctor and ambulance. When the doctor got there I stepped back. They rolled him over, and as soon as the air hit the front of his body, he burst into flames again. Because an incendiary grenade, that he had been fooling with, exploded in his hands, the chemical splattered his entire body and made of it a human torch. This chemical was nearly impossible to extinguish. When they rolled him over to get him on the stretcher, his stomach, testicles and penis were afire. Flames were licking around his body, and his boots began to burn. God, it was horrible, the smell of burning flesh and seeing it burn. Luckily I had stepped back when they rolled him over, or I would have been burned as were several of the men helping. The doctor's arms were burned also, but he stayed right in there, yelling for blankets and more blankets to wrap the burning man. The blankets began to burn. Finally the flames were smothered, but the blob of a near-corpse continued to smoke. The burning mass was lost in a confusion of thick smoke, flames and scampering men. The doctor stayed right in there. They finally got the flames out and cut off his clothes.

I knew he was dying. They got him in the ambulance and took him away. The stench and, on the ground, his still-burning clothes and blankets remained. I turned away much unnerved by seeing a man burn to death within arms' reach and able to do so little in this hopeless situation. His pain must have been indescribable, though probably he was now unconscious. He died that night.

And men use these grenades against one another in wartime—and flame throwers. Civilized world! For the rest of the afternoon I was physically ill and shaken. This man had come to New Guinea to meet a horrible death. I never want to see such a sight or such a face. They haunt me. Now, whenever I smell burning clothes or rags, it makes me ill. However, in the past few days I have been able to harden myself to the memory. It is the first time I have seen a man meet death violently and terribly in front of my eyes. The clothes on the ground had burnt skin stuck to them. I'm afraid that sight and the smell of burning clothes will continue to haunt me. (Good, it is raining.) Perhaps this is only the beginning of what I shall soon see.

We should be in New Britain within a few days. The 1st platoon has received its rations and will leave tomorrow for the front. I believe we will follow in about a week. Well, here it comes. Perhaps death and fate wait there for many men. I don't know how many sights as I have seen I can weather, especially when the casualties might be men in our organization, and I personally know nearly every man in it. There are many who believe that few of the 244th will see home. I hope they are wrong. Damn it, I have learned too much of life to lose it now. And the job now facing this outfit is important.

Incidentally, at present there is only one buck sergeant, Milligan T-4, and two Pfcs, Norvell and me, which makes me third in command in the squad. However Cpl. Watts will eventually get his position back.

Besides the events of the past week, we are hard at work loading LSTs for New Britain. We are still attached to and in support of the 5th Marines, which is a distinction and who, at present, are fighting and dying in N.B. Several Jap prisoners have been brought back here. Have not seen them though. Have talked to men who have been there. The campaign is only two weeks old.

Received today the poetry book written by Miss Wrinn sent to me by Miss Sophian [*my high school English teacher*]. I noticed it was sent the same day I left the U.S. It has finally caught up in surprisingly good condition. Today many packages came through, a pathetic mixture of battered cakes and foods—all uneatable. Really sad to see them go into the ash can, and then the fellows write home how much they were enjoyed. Have to keep up the civilians' morale.

Currently we have men in the hospital, and three men have had their lives threatened by some man or men in the organization. If the Captain finds them it will go hard with them. I knew Klein was scared; most of the men think him an informer. He has been transferred to the 491st. Rybicki and Demers are the other two under threat. The Captain informed me of all this several days before announcing it to the company. He carries his knife always and has told me he also fears for his own life. No need to now, I believe. Enough for tonight. Whew!

January 13

The 1st platoon left for New Britain two days ago. It was anticipated for a week. They really looked like soldiers, combat soldiers, too, when they pulled out under Lt. Reinhardt. They are probably ashore by now, travelling by LST. The rest of the company should leave soon, about the 16th or 17th. I have everything in readiness. We have been issued 40 rounds of ammunition. It is the first actual ammunition, besides for guarding prisoners, that we've been issued for the purpose of self-protection and killing Japs. Gives you a funny twist to see those neat, shiny bullets gleam menacingly in the clips. Yesterday when Redwine fell out for retreat with 100 rounds, the Captain didn't like it.

There are casualties coming back from New Britain with nearly every LST. The resistance is sharp at Cape Gloucester, especially Hill 660 where the enemy is strongly fortified. The marines bring back stories, souvenirs and wounds. They report hard fighting, and at times they have had to call in auxiliary organizations. Some of the stories are as follows: finding marines tied to trees and bayoneted; surrounding a contingent of Japs, including a group of Jap nurses who came running toward U.S. lines nearly nude to show they were females. The marines cut them down unmercifully, claiming revenge for Bataan. Three Japs were surrounded when one came out who spoke English and wanted to surrender. He explained that he had a wife and three children. A marine shot him and quietly said, "Now he has a widow and three orphans." Stories of bombings and wounds and of fighting up to the chest in water. I have some Jap writing paper brought back by marines and have seen scraps of Jap books and magazines, and bullets.

Eriksen, Johnson, Denison, Sweeney and I spent a good part of yesterday planning the loading of the LST that shall carry us and our equipment to N.B.

Although the mess about the petition has nearly died down, and the training schedule has slacked off, the extra work continues. It was difficult. Men were working hard all hours of the day and night, then having to drill, do calisthenics, and dig under the sun. It weakened the resistance of many, and as a result we have about 18 men in the hospital, mainly for overwork. The 1st platoon had to draw eight men from our platoon. Most of them poor soldiers. Though many men volunteered to go, some of the eight were selected. Mishalanie and Fazekas both volunteered to go. Both went, and Mish was all smiles. Honold and Hennel are down with typhus, bad cases. Alexander down with another attack of malaria. Ray Miller in bed with something. The others are fairly well, it's reported. It will be a good rest for them.

That petition seems to have had an effect on the Captain. He is more friendly with the men, smiles more—even plays ball with us now. We've played some of the best ball games here in the last two nights, between the 3rd and 2nd platoons. First night 2nd platoon lost in the last inning 7–4. Last night I pitched, and we won 10–9, last inning. Lot of fun.

Hoffman has "blown his top" again and has been missing since last night. The longer I know "old man" Milligan, the better I like him. He's one of the best soldiers in this outfit and has a lot of common sense. We see eye to eye on many things. Not much mail this last week for me or company. Not much time to write either. I'm afraid many of the men who recently lost their ratings will never again get them back. There are a few for whom this is fateful justice, but there are some good men who worked hard but lost them through stupidity. I am trying, through NCOs, to get these men back as much as I can. There are still a lot of changes being made in the company. Norm Denison made buck corporal yesterday, and we've been riding him all day. Gone to his head slightly, but he'll be all right. We both got good recommendations from C.O. for OCS. I spent all of last night until taps making out application for OCS, finally deciding to do so. Have received supplementary papers and have to see the Captain. That ought to be fun!!

The rumor persists that we have strong chances of returning to the States around March or April with the marines. If we return we are entitled to almost immediate 30-day furloughs. Wow!

The 7th Cavalry across the road is a really traditional organization, although it's motorized and no longer transports itself by horses. It is an organization over 100 years old. Compared to it, the transportation corps is a baby. It has a fine tradition, the 7th Cavalry; it has lived though many of its men haven't. That's what makes a name go down in history and builds tradition—dying men, a fine job. This is the same organization that went into the Little Big Horn under General Custer and came out without a man! But the 7th lives on, and now it is across the road. The 244th has also built a good reputation for its short time. This anticipated mission will be a telling blow against the enemy. I hope we all live to tell about it.

Must get at rifle for retreat. We follow the war in Europe in the *Guinea Gold* like a bunch of vultures waiting for the kill. Every day seems to mark new and greater German defeats and Russian victories. The fall of Germany seems imminent. However, I believe I am still a long way from home in time.

January 14

Not much time to spend writing. Orders have us possibly moving tomorrow morning—probably next day though. Must pack all equipment tonight. Many in hospital still sick. Have been ill myself since last night with dysentery. Can't eat, weak, ache. Butler went to hospital last night with 104. Sgt. Russell, Merritt and I are pretty bad off. Some have light cases. If I feel this bad tomorrow am afraid will have to go on sick call for first time in nine months.

January 16

This afternoon Milligan and I went down to the beach and swam and slept. Morning was spent explaining the theory of evolution to some of the fellows who wanted to know about it.

We were supposed to leave for Cape Gloucester today. However, plans have changed, and it looks as if we may spend the next 10 days here, in spite of the fact that we have most of our equipment and rations packed and down near the beach. There are several possible reasons for this change of plan. One, they don't need us yet. Two, it is still too dangerous to move in an organization such as ours.

We have had the unofficial report that three of the seven LSTs that pulled out of here for N.B. (among which was the 1st platoon) have been sunk either by mines or torpedoes. It is further rumored that we lost 25% of the personnel of the 1st platoon! If we have, this will be tragic.

I know them all well. This rumor has shaken the men. It could have been any of us. However, it may be a false rumor. The army for enlisted men is one rumor after another. Every day Seth and I get together and discuss the rumor of the day and latest war news. Seth always reminds me of the dwarf "Dopey" with his droll face and slapped-on fatigue hat. He's a swell fellow.

January 21

No work for quite a few days now except an occasional detail. Went down with Sweeney, Denison and Eriksen yesterday to check on an incoming LST. It didn't show up and is not expected until tomorrow. Met t/sgt. from Headquarters who gave me whereabouts of our companies. Headquarters and Co. A at Lae. Co. B with one platoon of D at Finschhafen. Two platoons of D at Goodenough Island attached to marines. As for our company, we have one platoon in New Britain, we hope, and two platoons here below Buna. Incidentally, Co. A has given furloughs to its men, and they have 25 on furlough in Sydney. They flew down. I really could use one of those, but our position makes it impossible. Would like to see Dale again very much.

Have been reading a lot of poetry and marvel at the mastery of words. Poetry has interested me ever since I can remember, and I've tried my hand at it often. Some of the stuff I am satisfied with and, for the time being, that's all that's important. Have been thinking a bit about what my life shall be after the war. To go back to school to study seems to rate highest. I have definitely decided that there is nothing superior to a good education. But what shall I educate myself in? Whatever it may be, college life is not bad, and I could spend four or five years there without doing any harm, especially if I get back before I am 21. Ye Gods, 21 already. It worries me a little when I see Denison, for instance, wrapped in his physics and abstract theories. All I'm wrapped in now is poetry, literature and a damnable fatigue uniform. Boy, for a real clean set of clothes—with color and life and comfort. Am tired of smelling sweat, and dampness, and men. Anyway, there may not be any future for me, so I can't worry about it.

I have discovered in the army and in life that there are few "real people." Carolyn once said that to me. I guess I wasn't quite real enough to her. The trouble is that I have never been real enough to myself. I have avoided meeting this fellow Kahn for nearly 20 years, but I am managing to find out what makes him tick, slowly but surely. I learned a good attitude toward life from Carolyn, but I fear I shall never quite agree with all her points, though I have come to see many.

January 24

First platoon is said to have landed safely. Announced this morning that the 2nd platoon, service section and some of our headquarters are scheduled to leave January 26. We will probably follow in a few days. We will be the last of the company to go up. Because we have anticipated going to N.B. for quite awhile now, some of the excitement about it has cooled.

Denison and I go swimming regularly, after which we lounge on the beach and talk. We've discussed everything from sex to the machine age. We get along very well. He has a willing intelligence. However, we disagree on nearly everything. I am glad of this because there are few things I enjoy better than a good discussion, whether it is on the shores of New Guinea or in a living room off Central Park West. He is one of the very few with whom I ever discuss anything intellectual or disclose some of my ideas and theories.

Press has broken down, thus no news of the world in past three days.

January 26

Most wonderful thing happened: evening before last I received the long-awaited letter from Carolyn. It just felt good to hold it, which I did for some 20 minutes, just in anticipation of reading it. Carolyn is still Carolyn, thank goodness for that—and as marvelous a person as ever. It gives me a warm feeling to know that she exists and will exist for other people. I can't exactly pin down all the reasons, nor do I want to; she means much to me and that's all I care about at present. Doubly glad to receive that letter a few days before leaving for perhaps my greatest adventure.

Here are 10 words which nobody has been able to spell correctly in camp. I got them from *An American Doctor's Odyssey* [*by Victor Heiser*]. The average is two or three correct. A few five or six. Milligan seven. Milligan proves more fascinating every day. The words: inoculate, embarrass, harass, supersede, innuendo, rarefy, vilify, plaguey (must find out meaning), desiccate, picnicking, phlegm.

January 27

Orders slightly changed. Second platoon and accompanying men leave tomorrow instead of today. We are scheduled to leave the 29th. Lots of stories coming back about bombings, mines, strafing, killed men. We are about to be thrown into one of the major campaigns of the war here and our furthest advance north. "What does a soldier think of before going to meet the enemy?" I have a strange feeling, a little pessimistic, but a subdued sense that all will be well. My concern is for those at home, my mother, father, sister and grandmother. To think I may die in some lost, remote part of the world! What a crazy world. If I face hazard I hope I have courage. I believe I have. I'm not really afraid, just sort of in a turmoil. What is needed now is diversion, amusement. It's been one of those sullen, rainy days that I like. Can't write anymore tonight, just want to think.

January 30

At present am aboard *LST 475* headed for Finschhafen and then New Britain. Worked steadily, got little sleep in past three days except last night. My mosquito netting was packed and I got bit up. Think I have ringworm, and do have a heat rash. Most of us have these. Water we used for washing was foul. The other night I drank some of it that had been put in a water can. The night was dark, but I tasted the foulness at the first swallow. Expected to have consequences, but so far so good. Drinking impure water here is dangerous.

This morning we walked with full jungle equipment from camp over to the LST. Everything together weighs at least 100 pounds, probably more. We felt it. Although only a 15-to-20-minute walk, we were soaked with perspiration and tired after the short march. We soon boarded and found that the troop accommodations were the best we've had so far aboard a ship. Compartments run alongside hull of the ship, each for 18 men. The bunks are the same as on the *West Point* but more comfortable and roomy. There is a good air-conditioning system, but in spite of it I am in a heavy sweat. The ship is heavily loaded and rolls. I've never been badly seasick in the army, but this trip may break that record. Not bad now, but heavy pitching earlier. I understand that it gets rough further north, so we have been lashing down cargo and trucks all afternoon.

Spent an interesting afternoon talking with the sailors on board and listening to stories, some not very pretty. The Tarawa battle in the Gilberts was terrible. Everyone talks of furloughs, home, and war. Even the usually stolid Milligan mentioned to me at dinner that "We are really getting into it now." We hold, it is reported, 42-square-miles on N.B., which is not much. Food has been good on board. It is a real luxury to use a latrine with running water and no maggots, to take a good shower, although salt, and to have a real wash bowl! Would these were classified as necessitites!

Mostly soldiers aboard, smattering of marines. We are heading into dangerous waters. This LST has shot down two Jap planes at Lae, shown by the two Jap flags painted on the conning tower. Last trip up to N.B.

the LST was dive-bombed but no damage done. We should land Tuesday morning. It is now Sunday night. In N.B. we will be part of our foremost front against Japan in the S.W.P.A. [*Southwest Pacific area*]. We may get more action than we bargained for—I've seen the casualties come back. Nevertheless, we are all in good spirits. Butler remained behind in hospital.

January 31

Hot as the devil down here tonight. Incidentally, am writing this in the latrine (Hollenback and Milligan alongside), because it is the best lighted place.

A slate-gray sky and heavy, inky-blue sea. I've never seen the sea so rough, huge waves and angry foam and spray. Sometimes waves break over the bow of the ship, and, driven by the wind, they come winging back and drench everybody. We had a 50-mile gale blowing, and it made the sea pound the ship, and you could feel the ship shudder. (It is doing so now.) This disconcerted me for the first few hours. When she shudders, catching the waves under her uplifted hull, our bunks and the cargo rattle, and the whole ship feels like she will fall apart. She has been constantly pitching and swaying. (I'm sitting still, but the sweat is pouring off me.) We have been playing tag with the coast of N.G. all day, and we are scheduled to hit N.B. between seven and nine tomorrow morning, and to unload this ship upon arriving.

There are four LSTs and four destroyers hovering around us like anxious hens over their chicks. Gray day, high wind. A filmy mist shrouds N.G. and the sea, which makes everything eerie. From this distance, the destroyer in the low-hanging mist is like a ghost ship skimming silently and effortlessly through the frenzied sea. After getting used to the pounding, I immensely enjoyed feeling the spray, watching the sea drench the boats, and the boats pounding the sea into spray—like blacksmiths pounding metal into white fountains of sparks. The wind was so strong I had trouble walking against it, and it whipped food from my spoon and fork. Spaghetti flew about like confetti. I had a slice of bread go flapping away like a bird. I spent some time cleaning my rifle this morning and laid it under a nearby truck. An unusually large wave came over and thoroughly doused it with salt water. I used accepted army vernacular then!!

Later this afternoon I tried to read a small-type overseas edition of the *The New Yorker*. I enjoyed it, even though the reading was difficult by dim light. All of a sudden the lights began to fade, getting slowly darker and darker. Then complete blackness and the motors quit. I felt gripped in that sudden dark, everything and everybody silent and scared, with the sea pounding our hull. A sailor came crashing through yelling oaths at us to clear a passage. I thought we were in for it and began planning my moves. All remained silent and dark for about 30 seconds, and then slowly the props started and the lights came on. Strange how nobody spoke of the incident after, but the expressions on the faces told the story.

At dinner I met a marine (5th Division) whose name is Pvt. Palmer (Sandy) Fischer, resident of L.A., Calif. He popped out of a hatch in front of me as I was in the chow line. We got to talking and have spent most of the evening together. His is a motley life. His mother married four times; she is the model for the picture of the girl on the raisin boxes. She posed for it at 16 or 17. He joined marines at 16, has just turned 18, and has been overseas for nine months. He related his sexy adventures in Melbourne. He is returning to Gloucester, where he was wounded by mortar fire in hand, elbow and face. He said he had gone eight days with little sleep and was hoping to get hit. Now he's going back with a piece of shrapnel still in his elbow.

He told stories about marine combat, about his friend whose brains were splattered over his arms from a bullet in the head. We also talked about books, Southerners (he has a low opinion of them), and he mentioned that I talked "like a human being."

Sandy has been to Samoa and told us about the beauty of the Polynesians and the island. I envy him. I have always wanted to see Samoa and those famous South Sea islanders. The ship is making all kinds of noises tonight, chains rolling and knocking. Tomorrow we land. Shower and bed, it's after 10:00 and I'm tired.

3

Cape Gloucester, New Britain

——————— Feb. 1–Apr. 27, 1944 ———————

February 1

We landed yesterday morning, a gray slaty day. It was a rough trip but we were not attacked. Upon arriving I worked for three hours, checking. Said goodbye to Sandy; he didn't look very happy about rejoining his outfit. After being relieved I got a lift to camp which was situated about 1½ miles from the LST landing. I got a lunch of peanut butter and graham crackers, and then, still toting more than 100 pounds on my back, came across Denison bathing in the ocean. He saved a place for me to sling my hammock alongside his, and I tossed the rest of my equipment under a poncho. I got the fellows together who had slung hammocks in the same vicinity, and we scouted for a tent site. Finally found one, drew and dragged a tent from our supply dump and went to work with hand and hatchet to erect some sort of shelter. Langham, Denison, Kasprzyk, Sweeney and Hollenback and I made a fairly decent "home" after a few hours work.

Our camp living conditions are the most rugged we have experienced so far. Tents and all sorts of lean-to's are wedged at all angles between puddles and trees and foxholes, and these shelters are fortified by sandbags. We are situated right on the shoreline, and as I look up I can see huge breakers beating the beach, a flurry of white foam, and driving rain. The whole company is here now.

News as follows: A few light bombing raids, a few casualties, but fortunately nobody in our company hurt except Egan, who lost a toe when a 500-pound drum fell on it. We look like savages, dressed in all kinds of apparel, and half of us going around stark naked or with a pair of shorts. Shoes, in general, are not worn.

The ocean is beautiful, raging with huge breakers continually pounding the shore, rising ghost-like from the gloomy ocean. After getting the tent up and throwing our equipment on the ground, I proceeded to dig a foxhole. I came across an apparently abandoned one and, while deepening it, killed three lizards, two frogs and a very mean-looking crab. Later, I found the foxhole was owned by somebody, so Norm and I decided to dig a double one.

Just as we completed the foxhole, we heard a blessed sound—"Mail call!" Having received only six letters in the last month, I knew I would have some. I got 27, along with two long-awaited packages. After getting my mail, I slung my hammock, bathed in that wild ocean, and then settled down with my back against the tent pole to read my letters and open the packages. The only light I had was from a single cell flashlight, but it served.

I read the letters until midnight, fighting off the bugs. God, it was good reading. If only there had been one from Carolyn, it would have been a complete evening.

In the morning I found my shoes nearly covered and filled with water. The whole camp was one huge puddle. Most tents were swamped; we were fortunate to have 20 square feet of only damp ground. Soon everybody was up digging runways to let the water down to the shore. There are well over 300 inches of rainfall a year here. Our foxholes were little swimming pools, filled to the brim. I've never seen any place so wet. Glad I like rain and rainy days and the ocean. We finally got the water drained off, and we built sand bulwarks and runways. At present, we are fairly dry. We got palette wood and built a platform and table, so at least our equipment will be only damp.

An odd sight was coming across Lt. Wenz excreting in his helmet. Can't blame him for not wanting to use the latrines. There is a tree trunk in my corner of our tent, and it is useful to hang things on. We have a stick of dynamite holding up one corner of our tent. A live grenade sits on a log out in front of the tent. Sweeney is engaged in throwing knives into the tree, just below my hanging leggings. The fellows are arguing who is going to sleep on the table tonight—glad I've got my hammock up.

We are near famous Hill 660. The camp is situated right where the first landing was effected a little over a month ago. The Jap is on a peninsula up the coast that can be seen on a clear day. Last night Heffle told me he saw gun flashes and tracers, though I haven't seen them. We have a 50-caliber machine gun guarding our beach, with all the spare parts and ammo under water at the moment. We shall probably have some air raids here when the weather clears, which is seldom I understand. We are within 15 miles of our furthest line against the Jap. There are a number buried around here, which I understand could be smelled a few days ago. To add a macabre touch, one of the truck drivers has a Jap skull on the cab of his truck. Some of the fellows who were here earlier have Jap equipment and have seen piles of dead Japs. As yet I have seen neither dead or alive ones. We are close enough, however. Nobody is very visibly afraid.

February 4

This afternoon at mealtime I saw some of the marines who have been relieved from frontline duties. Having served five weeks, the length of this campaign, some of them hadn't eaten in several days. The food we shared with them disappeared in short order with gusto. Never saw such a bedraggled group of men, dirty beyond description, hair long, unshaven and clothes rotting off their bodies. They looked haggard, worn, eyes bloodshot, not too talkative. They claim that the Japs are in retreat. One marine gave me a wink and a gesture signifying that all was well. This N.B. weather turns the terrain into a quagmire and makes the fighting and support more difficult.

We've had air alerts during the past two nights, but no attacks. The alarm is sounded by the firing of three shots in quick succession by the coast guns. The warning is ominous. We can hear the warning repeated up and down the coast. Then we wait for the sound of planes, ready to head for our foxholes. The all-clear is a single blast. Hearing that, we roll over and go back to sleep. Popular opinion has it that "the" great battle that we shall have with Japan shall be in the Philippine Islands, which MacArthur has vowed to retake. The Japs by now, after two years, are no doubt well-established there, and I'm afraid that that eventual campaign shall be costly.

Last night while we swam among the breakers, Rouse informed me that he and J. Harris, Rice and Nelson had gone into Jap territory to see what they could see. They nearly got blown up by a booby trap, a cunning device which consists of a bomb on one tree, a few hand grenades on another with the pin attached to a wire. This wire runs along the ground about a foot high and is concealed by the dense undergrowth. When one walks between the two trees, he trips the wire. They discovered it just in time and cut the wire. Scouting around, they found discarded equipment everywhere.

They came across two dead Japs in a foxhole that the maggots were using for stamping grounds. Later they found another that was half-buried face down to the waist, with legs sticking up. They dug him up. Jack wanted a Jap skull, so he hacked away the head. Rouse drove a bayonet through the skull just for practice. The hacked head didn't come off cleanly, leaving the lower jaw torn off. The head smelled so badly that they discarded it after taking its three gold teeth.

I've got my bed arranged so that I can watch the sea roll in. I love the sea, especially when it's wild.

February 6

During the last three days we've had innumerable air alerts and some air attacks and bombing. I've been working on a two-hatch Australian ship out in the stream. This is the same ship that has been the objective of two attacks carried out by single planes dropping single bombs. Night before last, I got in at 6:00 A.M. At about 7:30 A.M., I was awakened by a series of machine gun bursts and shooting shore guns. By the time I got out, the action was over. It seems one Jap plane had followed a fleet of our bombers, wheeled about the bay, and then divebombed the small ship. First platoon was out there at the time. The bomb landed about 40 yards from the ship. We didn't even come close with our firing.

Last night we had three alerts. I was working the 6:00 to 12:00 shift, but didn't get in until 2:30 A.M. because of the alerts. After the third alert some Jap planes did come over. I was working on the same ship that was the target for the last raid. These planes headed for the airstrip, some few miles away. It was a very bright night, and everything was quite distinct in the moonlight. The machine guns started firing, every fourth bullet a tracer, making a dotted line of red into the night. Then many lines cut into the blue. One searchlight swept the sky with a seeking finger of light, and then the ack-ack let go, making small puffs of purple smoke which floated lazily across the sky. The tracers gave the appearance of floating gently through the air, while actually travelling at high speed. Then the heavy gun back in the hill let go, causing white flashes to mushroom over the hills. Not the target for tonight, we sat on deck and watched, as if we were at a 4th of July exhibition.

This morning we saw the wings and part of the fuselage of a Jap Zero. It was dragged in out of the sea. It had two large red circles on its wings and some bullet holes in it. The insides were a mass of twisted wire and apparatus. The pilot's seat seemed incredibly small, and the whole plane not very big.

February 7

About 9:30 last night the alert was sounded. We all rushed to the beach (15 yards away). Firing commenced nearly immediately. A searchlight picked up two bombers, and the night was pierced with dotted red lines.

When the tracers seemed to be hitting the planes, Norm and I and the others cheered as if we were at a college football game. The planes were quite high and each looked as big as a finger. They flew out of range, but further down the bay the searchlights picked them up again. Another barrage, this time 90 mm, winking on and off like fireflies. The bombers flew off; we stood around the beach for awhile, and then I went to bed. I've got to remember to take my helmet next time; shrapnel kills.

Sweeney has found a few Jap helmets, writings, cigarettes and a propaganda sheet which shows a Yank having intercourse with an Australian girl. The caption told the Aussies to take their time at the front because their women were being well taken care of by Americans. There was also a sheet showing an Australian raping a native. It was funny because all the faces in the drawings had a tendency to look Japanese, as did various designs, for instance on the curtains. The American flags bordering the intercourse picture had yellow stars on green fields.

February 9

Yesterday I passed the graveyard where those who died invading and taking the part of the island we now possess are buried, and others are being interred. There are just plain white crosses with names on them— not too many, a few rows—but one is too many. It gave me a lump in my throat to see those simple graves under the trees, men buried in the soil of New Britain. What a place to die! As Sgt. Stahl said in passing, "What a sacrifice."

Sometimes the whole world seems mad, or is it me? Why is it that the human race is so determined to exterminate itself? Is this how a man's life should end, in a grave in some remote part of the world? Is this the ironic answer to all our education? Perhaps we bear some blame for having been niggardly with Japan. But men die, "ignorant armies clashing." And yet, it would be better to be dead than to look forward only to a life in the army. The only thought that keeps many of us going is that someday, not too far away, the war will end. Perhaps if it were not for Russia as our ally, we might have to dedicate the rest of our lives to the army and war. What a prospect.

But if we die, we will not feel the effects of death. A bomb explodes, a bullet through the head, a grenade in your foxhole—and oblivion. Of course, not all die so easily. But the poor people at home. I'm sure for every man killed, there are three at least who know a living death. I dread to think of what would happen to my own family—the mere thought makes me shudder. Must keep alert.

When the sun does come out here, it is as hot as flame. The sea is blue and serene today, gently shaking the shore. It's a pleasant change.

February 13

Last night there were four alerts. Each time during the night when I was jolted out of sleep by the report of guns, the moon was in a different part of the sky. A bright night, a good night for bombing; and on the velvet water the beams of the moon sparkled like jewels on a velvet cushion. I heard the heavy guns shooting. Above flew death. During the last raid I could feel the jolt of bombs exploding. One landed behind camp and one in front, out in the bay. No damage was done in the immediate area.

This morning, because of the proximity of the explosions, everyone was out deepening neglected foxholes which have become shallow because of the rains. I noticed Lt. Wenz having some of the extra-duty men in our section digging a foxhole in his tent for him. After a few close ones, you dig deeper.

Yesterday afternoon we went on detail with Lt. Lake to pick up some cots from a Quartermaster colonel. We never found either, but the trip was interesting. It was the first time I had been out of the area between the LST landings and camp. There are now innumerable organizations lining the shore. The fields are packed with ack-ack and heavier guns, capable of putting up a heavy barrage. There is a lot of mud in these areas, and they are less developed than ours, although some of the camp settings are nicer and more spread out. Also, I got a close-up of that little island out in the bay. It looked as inviting as ever with its foam-washed, white-sanded shore. I also got a look at the old and new airstrips and saw some of the fighters and observation planes. A few bomb craters were visible, almost perfect circles of about 30 feet in diameter. Numerous radar stations are situated in the hills. In back of all this war activity that borders the island sits the volcano, nestled placidly among the green hills, its red lava-coated slopes sometimes visible on clear days from certain angles, with its lazily-drifting plume of smoke sometimes looking a little ominous.

Last night Maddox seems to have wanted to kill himself, but perhaps he is bucking for a "Section Eight" [*discharge because of mental distur-bance*]. I don't believe he has the guts, but a man can be driven to a keyed-up point when he will do most anything. He was broken from a Pfc and given a week's KP, which is laying it on heavily, and the men have been picking on him. All this might have gotten the better of him. But it might be sham. Last night he loaded his rifle and threatened to shoot himself. Demers got the gun away from him and emptied the shells. Maddox then got a knife and started hacking away at his arms, and cut himself up somewhat. Both men and officers were standing around the tent Maddox was in. When anyone came too near him, Maddox threatened to cut himself. One by one the officers went in and came out, all unsuccessful. Finally, somehow, the men overpowered him, and seven of them carried the struggling Maddox into a truck. Some of our most powerful men were holding him down: Gligo, Hancock, Pietrangelo, Henehan, etc. A few minutes after the truck left, an ambulance drove up. I have heard nothing since.

Denison, who has been ill these past few days, went to the hospital this morning. Might be malaria. Herbeck is in now, too, with either malaria or typhus. It seems most of the fellows have been in one time or another. So far I have been lucky.

It was announced that Capt. Drown is no longer our C.O. Lt. Reinhardt is the apparent successor although no official word on it yet. It looks like the petition-signers will get their wish after all.

February 14

All hell has broken loose. They've finally started hitting us. On February 12 at 4:00 A.M. we had an alert. We had a fairly heavy attack earlier, and then about a half-hour later, at 4:00, I heard the drone of a plane coming over the mountain. I listened, sat up. "Condition is red," I heard someone yell. Those words ring in my ears these days, those ominous words, "The condition is red." The drone got louder. I was the only one awake in the tent, Sweeney and Kasprzyk slept, Hollenback out, Denison still in the hospital. Suddenly a Z-Z-Z-Z sound cut the night. I acted instinctively. Just before this, I yelled to Sweeney and Kasprzyk, "Everybody out, there's a plane overhead!" They didn't get up. When the flash went off, I was near Kasprzyk, but heading for my foxhole. It lit up his face. I dove about six feet dressed in nothing but shorts and tumbled into the hole head first. No damage except a slightly bruised ankle, where I had hit a cot on my way out. I hit several things on the way out; it was dark in the tent. Outside a bright moon shone.

After the explosion, everybody was up. The plane continued out to sea. Sweeney and Kas came out of the tent. I climbed out of the foxhole. About 200 or 300 yards down the beach, opposite to where the boats are out in the stream, a fire was burning, figures silhouetted against the yellow light. The bomb hit only 200 to 300 yards down from our camp. S. and K. went toward the fire; I was tired and went back to bed. I suddenly found that I was highly tense, and when I relaxed it felt as if a

150-pound weight had been lifted off my back. When S. and K. came back they told me that an amphib was aflame, tents blown down, articles scattered all around, a great tree shattered, and six dead, many wounded. One fellow got a piece of shrapnel in his back, another through the abdomen, another had his foot blown off, another his leg. I went back to sleep. Ten minutes later in came Stewart. "KP, Kahn." The details go on in spite of hell and high water.

All that day we spoke only about the bombing. Not a shot had been fired against the plane which sneaked over the mountain. Final count, nine dead, ten wounded, and undoubtedly some of those have died. Hyer came in looking a little white and shaky. He had gone down to help, and somebody told him to jump in a foxhole and help lift this fellow out. He jumped in, the other fellow lifted the marine by the shoulders. Hyer looked up and found to his horror, nearly fainting, that the marine's head had been blown off across the collarbone. Most of the fellows over there did not get up during the attack, and six men in a tent were wiped out.

Few of us have been getting up for the alerts. They have become quite common, and when the planes rarely do come over, they have done no damage here, but go for the airport. I have learnt a lesson which I narrowly escaped ever learning.

More reports. There were six fellows in a foxhole, another rushed up and asked to get in, one yelled that there was no room. A moment later the bomb exploded; the fellow who had asked to get in was blown apart. The fellow who had yelled he couldn't come in is now in the hospital raving mad. Three fellows lived in a shack close by. One got up to urinate shortly before the attack. He was saved, the other two got it. Fate separates its victims by a hair. Milligan came by to inform me that the fellow with the red hair and well-kept red moustache, who only the day before had been driving an amphib that we were loading from the boats, had been killed. All of those killed were marines, the bombs landing where the marine amphibian unit was camped. The red-haired marine had been over 21 months, was soon to go home, and had survived Guadacanal. He's dead now. One day you talk to a man, the next day he's dead. He is the first man I've known who was killed by enemy fire. The reports, the continual talk, the dead red-head; it all began to work on me.

In comparison to these events, KP was a laugh; it was hot and I was greasy, tired and rattled. My foxhole was nothing more than an unprotected gap, offering little protection. The other fellows were digging better ones, reinforcing them. I was on KP and couldn't get off. I collared Hollenback and told him to start digging in the wedge of the tree that stands next to my bunk. He started that afternoon. I got a little spare time and went over to see how he was doing. He was down fairly deep, but a report came in that the bomb that had killed the most men had exploded hitting a tree—I gave up the tree idea. All day I inquired about, finding out from the more experienced the best kind of hole to dig for protection. During spare moments, I carried over logs for a roof. Shrapnel had come over as far as our camp. Pieces had gone over David Nelson's head in his hole. A piece had torn through Lt. Wenz's and Lt. Reinhardt's tents—only 15 yards away from mine. I'm glad I hit that foxhole in a hurry.

Worked hard cleaning up after supper, anxious to do a little work on the foxhole. Got back to find Hollenback had abandoned the tree hole on his own accord and completely disappeared. I quickly got to work, cursing H. Logs went over the top of the old hole Denison and I had dug two weeks before. Managed to scare up a few sandbags. Then Hollenback turned up. He'd been gaily talking to the marines, he said, with a foolish grin on his face that H. can get. I bawled him out roundly for five minutes. He redeemed himself somewhat by knowing where there were about seven full sandbags. We added these. What we had now was a partial covering, not altogether satisfactory. I then learned why H. had been lax. He was going out to the ships at 11:00 P.M. The raiders usually hit well after midnight, when the moon is high and bright. Now we plead for rain and clouds at night. Anyway, this taught me not to trust anyone to do a job for you, especially when it comes to protecting your life— that's your job. There are too many things I want to do yet to have my life end so quickly. We finished working by flashlight; I hit the bunk at about 10:30 absolutely dead-tired. Last night H., S. and K. were going to work, which left me alone in the tent to have to wake up for an alert. I was so tired I knew I would sleep heavily. I made it up with Fazekas in the next tent that one should yell to the other if either of us heard an alert. To bed.

At 1:45 A.M. I heard three horn blasts. I never heard the guns go off; they must have jarred me awake. This night I had clothes, shoes, glasses (which I had knocked across the tent the night before and nearly broken), and helmet handy. I was wide awake in a second, dressed in 20. Meanwhile furiously yelling, "Fazekas, Fazekas." No answer. I was now paying the price for not wanting to sleep with my own section. Luckily, I woke on my own anyway. I dashed into Fazek's tent, shook his bed, roused him out. "Condition is red," somebody hollered. Fazekas came tumbling out, with Peterson and Kowalczyk behind. The Captain was out of his tent, standing by his foxhole. My nerves were raw to every sound, because of the horror of the night before. I was quite alone in my foxhole.

Soon the ack-ack began; everyone was up and out tonight, no mistake, no lying in bed. The ack-ack winked on and off, on and off. I hit the hole and crouched in it as low as possible. Began to shiver, nerves tight. Earlier every truck had sounded like an approaching plane. I couldn't get the sound of a buzzing plane out of my ears. Every roaring wave sounded like a bomb. It was an awfully bright night—not good for us. Several times I hit the hole while the ack-ack fired away, about every 30 or 45 minutes. The moon shone white and eerie, glazing the sand. I felt the dull thud and explosion of bombs on the airstrip, six miles away. This was one of the few times in my life that I regretted being alone—but, not too much.

Bombs began to explode, but they were distant; they were after the airstrips tonight. We were putting up a lot of fire. Then a plane began to roar, getting louder and louder. Peterson yelled, along with others, "Here he comes." The buzzing sounded ominous, louder. I thought we would get it sure tonight. I was thoroughly scared, crouching, waiting for the Z-Z-Z and the thud of a 500-pounder, and oblivion. Pictures of home, family, Carolyn pounded through my mind, like raging water down a gulley. I crossed my fingers, and waited. What else was there to do? The Australian's words of two months ago rang in my ears, "Man wasn't made for bombs." The plane roared over, headed out to sea. No bomb fell.

Soon after, the all-clear sounded. Again I found myself tense, jumpy. I was out alive. Took off my clothes (was wearing two shirts to stem the damnable chill), laid them again where they would be handy, got into bed, every truck passing in the distance making me start. Ten minutes passed, still wide awake—then suddenly I heard a motor. What was that, truck or plane—sounded more like a plane. Seconds later off went the three quick shots for the alert. Like the night before, I was dressed and out—in 15 seconds this time—and in the hole.

Up went the ack-ack. A half-hour later, the all-clear sounded. This time I got into bed clothed except for shoes. It was 4:45—we had been up three hours, and I felt it after the day before. I soon fell asleep, woke at dawn to breathe a sigh of relief, and then grabbed another few hours sleep. It was 9:30 when I got up. The other fellows were still sleeping. They had been on the ships and on the shore during the raids. Needless to say, little work was accomplished. Got up, went over to examine the Captain's foxhole. He had 10 years in the army and was a graduate engineer, so I thought he ought to know something about construction.

I put what I had learned into action. Started work at 10:30. At about 2:00 I had a hole dug about three-and-a-half feet across, seven long and deep. I laid the logs over, leaving a hole only for concussion and for entrance. Then sandbags—had to look for more, found some, filled them. Worked furiously padding, excavating. H. slept on, oblivious to the world; but he was dead tired, scared to tiredness out on the ships last night.

Went for a swim at last to get dirt and sweat off. Meanwhile, continual dynamite blasts rip my nerves to shreds. Am tired, the last few days have been trying.

In a little while I go to work till midnight. Hope I can stay awake. It will probably be difficult unless we are attacked again. All day the fellows with free time have been digging, reinforcing. It's raining now, after a beautiful day, bordering on hot. The good weather reminds Kas and me of home. What a distant thought now. It gets more and more difficult to write home—especially to keep saying all is well. Hope it stays cloudy and rainy tonight.

Though the foxhole is pretty good, it needs another layer of sandbags. Told Hollenback about the new foxhole when he awoke—result—he's asleep, mouth gaping, hands again clutching his private parts. Must be enjoying some sexy dreams. Oddly enough, I had one too last night. Strange. Can this be a reaction to recent events? Also had the first premonition in my life the night of the damaging bombing. Dreamt only a few hours before the raid that we were heavily bombed, bodies lying about with shrapnel wounds gaping. I was there with crude scissors and knife and tourniquets, extracting shrapnel, cutting into flesh, seeing faces horribly twisted in pain, applying tourniquets. Odd it should all be true a few hours later—except for my medical aid.

Since the first landing, Cape Gloucester has experienced 140 alerts and bombings in about 45 days. We've had about 50 of them. Perhaps it's not too strange that I should be a little jumpy.

February 15

It was not 15 minutes after I made yesterday's entry, while Milligan was sitting next to me, that I heard a faint Z-Z-Z and then an explosion. Just a few seconds earlier I was explaining to Milligan how those truck motors were playing havoc with my nerves. It was broad daylight when a lone Jap Zero sneaked over the mountain. He dropped his bomb and left. This was so unexpected that we all sat stunned when the explosion occurred. At first I thought it was another dynamite blast, but doubted it because I am fast getting used to distinguishing between sounds. The bomb didn't do any damage, landing between the little island offshore and some LCMs. The apparent target was either the island or ships. About 10 or 15 minutes later we ate early because we were going on the 6:00 to 12:00 shift. We call the 12:00 to 6:00 shift the "dead man's" shift, because most of the bombings take place after midnight. There wasn't much kidding or talking or laughing in the mess hall. Some of us are beginning to get very jumpy or morose. I was surprised how worried Watts was because he is usually so cheerful.

We decided to work in three-hour shifts. I drew the second three, 9:00 to 12:00, so I ran up to the hospital to see Denison and Herbeck. Denison was in fine spirits, hard at his calculus book. He should come back today, and I'll be glad to see him. Herbeck is ill with malaria. Hadn't eaten in five days, couldn't even keep atabrine down. Doctor also told him he had something the matter with his liver. Herbeck was pretty disgusted with life in general. Denison exclaimed he had seen all the action he had wanted. That's O.K. with me. Denison told me he had watched one of the fellows have his leg amputated. Two marines lost legs in that bombing the other night. Everybody in the hospital area, in fact, all over the area, was digging in. Spent an hour with D. and H., talking, reading a few of Cecilia's letters. Funny, every time Denison gets a letter from Nancy, he thinks of Cecilia; when from Cecilia, of Nancy.

Back at work between the hours of 9:00 and 12:00 we had three alerts. After the first one, we ran into the jungle, laid alongside a log. Jack Harris remembered ———

AIR RAID!! Write later. (Ten minutes later. Raid still on. P-40s are in the air. A good sight. This is the first time we have had fighter protection overhead.)

Anyway, Harris remembered a foxhole dug into the side of a tree. We found it, a good big one, after groping around in the dark. After the all-clear, everyone was reluctant to get out—the Japs have a cute trick of coming over right after an all-clear and the lights go up. An officer's voice rang out, telling everyone to come out, the condition was all-clear, and that we had a job to do. We then got out.

When I got back to the crane, Stahl sent me over to relieve Sanchez. The gang then consisted of Milligan, Rouse, the worrying Watts, Morales, Nelson and Hudaick. But Milligan and I were the only ones there. The rest apparently weren't going to come out. We were loading empty oil drums on amphibs to take out to the ships. Milligan mentioned that the drums would make a hell of a blast because they were filled with gas fumes. Finally another alert was sounded, and M. and I headed across the road where he knew there were some shallow holes. We hit one of those and lay flat. Rouse, Watts, Nelson and Hudaick had remained in a well-fortified one. After a time the all-clear sounded. Then I urged the others out, and we all went back to finish loading the amphibs. Watts claimed he wouldn't work—but he did. Soon another alert—this one a long one. Milligan and I luckily found a big bunch of sandbags, full, and we started (all-clear just sounded) building some sort of protection. Soon we had Mike Hudaick and Nelson helping us. We were all tense then, and the signals seemed to be crossed. Some men yelled, "Turn the lights off, condition's red," and others yelled, "All clear." This time we stayed put. In a half-hour we had good protection built, but with four of us together we were rather crowded.

Finally all-clear again, and soon after the relief came out. I hit the cot and soon was asleep. About 3:30 A.M. we were up again, and this time I was in my foxhole. Now sleep all night with pants on. Half-hour later, all-clear. Got some sleep last night, although we've been getting most of it in the early morning. The raid this morning was our 42nd.

Four LCMs are in. That means mail tonight. Last night some fool had a fire going. One marine was going out after him with a .45. Can't blame him.

February 16

Norm came back from the hospital yesterday. I went to work in the afternoon loading empty drums on the ships. The LSTs were unloaded and took off. I knew there would be mail for me, and I knew there would be a letter from Carolyn. There was. News from home is good. Dick and Ginger write that the war is still far away for them. It's not far away from me though with these damnable bombings. I got a little angry last night, pacing up and down the tent, after reading in some letters about dances, gay weekends, college. If they could only experience one raid, even one alert, sitting next to your foxhole, half-asleep in the dark, nerves raw to every sound. I can distinguish noises now at a "glance" of the ear, as it were.

Might as well write this now. Norm and I were at lunch a little while ago. An explosion, another bombing! Didn't need to be told it was a bomb. Norm and I ran a few steps, hit the dirt. Then I yelled for him to get in the foxhole which was close to the kitchen. It was full. Then we saw the Zero wing off. Two of our P-47s were after him. They came back a little while ago. We thought the bomb had missed the ship again, but I noticed a haze around it. A few minutes later, the alert was sounded. Waited for the all-clear, and by the time I got to the supply dump, my detail had left. Kowalczyk just came in a few moments before I wrote this paragraph and said that the bomb had hit the ship; he was scratched up because he had dived. Six of our men are hurt, among them Jackman, Gligo and Digirolamo. Three or four Aussies were killed outright. They say D. got it bad. God!! When will this stop, this bitch of a war. Men getting killed, friends of mine now. I'm not tense much today, not half as much as I have been. Glad Norm and I finished our foxhole under the tree this morning. I don't know what to say, I'm sick at heart. I'm sick of war. They fired at the plane today, anyway. I can't write anymore. Two alerts last night. We've undergone 46 alerts and bombings now.

Later: We were paid this afternoon. Seems ironic to be paid here. Money worthless, men getting killed and killing, and we get paid for it. I asked Lt. Wenz about how the fellows were, and he said that our men were not too badly hit, that Jackman had a head wound that was not too serious. Report has it, so far, that there were six men killed, three marines, three Aussies, and our men hurt. I imagine Lt. Wenz is softening the blow, telling us that the men are not badly hurt. I hope it is so. Many of the fellows were badly shocked. Brothers seemed shell-shocked when I saw him in the mess hall, shaking badly, eyes as wide as saucers. He asked me for a cigarette which I did not have. That was a P-38 after the Jap bomber; it was not a Zero. The unofficial report has it that the Jap bomber was shot down. God, I hope so. When the Jap climbed, he was a perfect target against the sky, banking sharply. Could have got 10 rounds in the air with my 03 rifle which is powerful and accurate enough to hit him. From now on, I am going to keep it handier.

There was a Jap in camp last night; some of the fellows heard him during the night. He was starving and came looking for food. Probably cut off from the retreating Jap army. The guys in the outfit across the road shot him. Great stuff having Japs infiltrate. York was asleep on guard, a court martial offense demanding death. Sgt. Putt told York he would put him permanently asleep next time it happened.

There are a lot of drawn faces in camp. A few more bombings with casualties such as the one today, and we shall be badly under strength. My nerves are better today. Wonder why. Answered Carolyn's letter. Must write home, but it is difficult. The Aussie ship is listing somewhat and has been pulled close to shore. I can't quite understand why we get these pecking raids by one or two planes. If they came over in force, they could do considerable damage and kill many of us. Can it be that they have few planes; are they saving them for a reinvasion? A gigantic raid, such as we impose on them, would be horrible. Anyway, our air protection is getting better. Wonder if I'll ever see home. Have $85 in anticipation of a furlough. Ha! Will probably learn more when Norm gets in. Should be in in a few minutes. Fate plays strange tricks. Our section should have been out there this morning. We missed a shift last night, "dead man's shift," 12:00 to 6:00, and therefore missed the bombing. Any shift is dead man's shift now.

February 17

The bomb yesterday hit an LCT alongside, and they never even found a piece of her or the two men and one officer on her, all marines. [*Landing*

*craft tank: About 120 feet long, this was the smallest of the various land-
ing craft built during World War II for the purpose of transporting men
and equipment from ship to shore. The craft had a bow ramp which could
be lowered for the discharge of cargo.*] Our men weren't too badly hit
except for three. Gligo is O.K., just a bruised arm. Several have small
cuts, like Hartley who got it in the hand. None of these men I know well.
Digirolamo got a piece through the arm. Shaw got it badly, getting six
pieces of shrapnel in his right side. They say it will take three months to
get the pieces of metal out by single operations. Jackman is bad. He got
it in the head; I understand they operated on him last night. He also
has a case of amnesia. The rest are just shocked and I guess will be
O.K. except for jangled nerves. [*Actually, eight men of the 244th were
wounded: Jackman, Dininny, Morris, Shaw, Hartley, Digirolamo, Wagner, and Moore.*]

This morning we had an alert, the first one I did not hear. I was soon
aware of it when I saw the fellows in their foxholes. It was a welcome
sight to see about 25 P-40s zooming around in formations of two and
four. We felt fairly safe this morning. That's the first real protective air
strength we've had. This morning was our 49th alert.

The news is mixed. I understand part of the 2nd, 3rd, 4th Marine
Divisions have hit New Ireland, which is close to us, and are established
there. On the other side of this island, at Arawe, the 32nd Infantry Division has been pushed back to their original beachhead, which is bad
news. I imagine that Cape Gloucester, this base, is now the strongest
point on the island. The campaign in Italy is going badly, and that is even
worse news. Sometimes it seems we shall never win, but, of course, we
will in time. But how long? How many more graves or bodies blown to
smithereens?

February 18

Worked on the bombed Australian ship today. Work went slowly, as
usual. Got a kick out of the Australian first mate directing me down in
the hold and calling me "son." He was an old sea dog. Once in awhile
he would yell, "Good on you, good on you boy." They handed down a
platter of left-over fried chicken and brown potatoes in gravy. It's the
first time in many months that I tasted these things, and it was ecstasy.
The Aussies are anxious to get out. They are especially courteous to us,
because without us they are liable to sit out there for weeks instead of
days, and the Japs seem to want to get this ship. It rained like the devil
this morning, and this afternoon I got a five-gallon can of fresh rainwater
for washing and shaving or, should say, to keep my beard trimmed. Norm
and I have had interesting talks of late and have become practically insep-

arable in the past two months, though we have been fast friends ever since Pittsburg.

Had two alerts last night. That made numbers 44 and 45, including 14 or 15 bombings. My earlier figures were a bit wrong. Art Monroe has been keeping an accurate count. (This prickly heat has been raising hell with me for the past two months.)

The Captain left yesterday, quietly and without any adieu. Most of us didn't even know he had gone. He gave me a lift to camp about 20 minutes before he was to leave. I wish I had known it; I would have liked to have said goodbye to him. Our ride was in a strained silence.

Bud returned from hospital today, not looking well, but fairly recovered from malaria. His skin and eyeballs were quite yellow. The disease hits the liver hardest.

February 19

Today Norm and I went to the evacuated Jap bivouac area and hospital not far from here. We carried a machete, which we needed, and Norm's carbine and my heavier Springfield 03, just for emergencies. We walked through a dark green jungle filled with thick vines, squawking with parrots and infested with huge spiders, mosquitoes and myriad insects. When we reached the deserted Jap camp, swampy and hardly cleared, it seemed foreboding and mysterious.

There were many Jap foxholes, much larger than ours and difficult to enter. I was surprised at the length that they extended underground from the entrance. There were also numerous shacks made from bamboo, saplings, and vine. Apparently they had no tents. With helmets, mines, detonators, all kinds of shells, and rifle and machine gun ammunition scattered about, the gloomy camp suggested an army in hasty retreat.

We were quite careful what we moved and where we stepped because of booby traps. We didn't fool much with the ammunition. There were parts of rifles and machine guns about, abandoned rations (mostly salmon, rice and dehydrated foods in powder form), packs, leather covers, mosquito netting, shoes, etc. There were also many bottles and vials of various pills and powders, as well as bandages, first-aid kits and other abundant hospital supplies. We collected a few baskets woven from some sort of plant, a few cans with Japanese writing on them, a few rolls of pills and a few vials of yellow and white colored liquid. I haven't the slightest idea what they contain.

Gloomy. The battle here took place only a few weeks ago. It seemed I could hear a distant dirge. The horror, excitement and action of battle were still there in the scattered and mysterious evidence.

After wandering to our hearts' content, and, incidentally, finding contraceptives all over the place, which perhaps substantiates the story of the Jap nurses killed there, we left that silent, morose area. The sun filtered through the trees and the already deteriorating hospital buildings. Norm and I struck out along a swift stream, cutting through the jungle leading back to a walkable road. We were following a small trail when Norm stopped in front of me and said that the object in front of him looked like a bone. And so it was, a leg bone, lower leg from all appearances. Then we found two ribs. We each took one. (Norm later lost his when we were helping a fellow get his truck out of deep mud.) A few feet further down the trail we were following I spied a skull. I presume it to be Jap from the high position and prominence of the cheek bones. Part of the skull had been blown away. There were five teeth in the upper mouth, all molars; the lower jaw was missing. All of the flesh was gone from the muddy skull. I wrapped this eternally-grinning gargoyle in a cloth and took it with me. The skull was of great interest to me and still is. When we returned to camp, I took the skull down to the ocean and thoroughly washed it, losing one of its teeth in the process. Now it has two teeth on each side as it sits out in the sun drying and bleaching. There are sharp, jagged edges left where part of the skull was blown out. Am going to use it for a candle-holder. We have named him Charlie.

I keep thinking about this shattered skull I found lying in the muddy jungle. Here was a living man only a few days ago. Perhaps he was an unwilling Jap soldier; perhaps he was educated, wise, had a wife and children. He might have been a good man, or he might have been one of the rapists of China, or an invader of the Philippines; he might have ended many American lives. Now he was this bodiless thing whose ignominious destiny was my washing his skull in the sea, toying with this recently living-and-thinking head, running my hand around the inside of the smooth, hard shell where once there were brains and living matter, fingering his gaping eye sockets and nose, and pulling at the loose teeth. And years ago he was born on the other side of the world, and now we meet alongside a jungle stream, nothing remaining of him but his shattered skull and a few bones. I could not help a little ironical laugh when I plunked his rib in his skull and wrapped them up. I said to Norm, I bet he never thought he would have parts of his anatomy in so grotesquely-exchanged places. And now his broken skull is a candle-holder for me. When I look at it, I think about him, but I feel no pity. Have not our own men been blasted before my eyes, and might not my end be the same yet: some curious Jap plunking my rib in my shattered skull, and using me for a candle-holder? And we are human? Perhaps all our human feelings are farcical, and our lives nothing more than ridiculous flames briefly, comically, cynically burning in the candle-holder of our skulls.

February 21

Except for an accident yesterday at the marine camp next to us, life has been quiet. A marine burned his arms very badly; luckily there is a field hospital (dispensary is more accurate) stationed nearby where a doctor was available. I was not anxious to see burning flesh again, or smell it. The last time is still too vivid in my mind. There were enough men to help him, so I didn't rush over. However, passing the dispensary on the way to dinner a few minutes later, I saw him stretched out on a cot, writhing in pain, the skin burnt and hanging loosely from his arms. The ambulance came a few moments later.

The war news has improved. The Australians are advancing slowly up the coast of N.G. and are now threatening Madang although Bogadjim has still to be reckoned with. This part of N.B. is now quite consolidated, and our air protection good. The indomitable Russians continue to hammer away at the retreating Germans, and our forces in Italy have strengthened their lines south of Rome. But the most important and startling news to us here was not the air and naval bombardment of the Carolines (Wake being situated in that island group), but the Japanese claim that we landed troops there. This would be a bold move; Truk is one of the largest naval bases in the world. It is said that all the navies in the world could ride anchor in that lagoon. The landing seems highly improbable to me, but what a tremendous victory if we took Truk.

February 22

Received only two letters at mail call, one from home and a long, good one from Dale. I hope that I shall see Dale again someday. It would be pleasant to get a furlough and spend it in Sydney with her.

Yesterday, at Milligan's suggestion, Norm, M. and I took a trip to famous and bloody Hill 660. The afternoons have become unbearably hot lately. It was such an afternoon when we struck into the jungle. Jungles are nice to look at from a distance, but hellish to be in. The humid heat sucks your strength, you are host to myriad insects, the undergrowth hinders your movements, and half the land is swamp. Fighting on that terrain is nearly impossible to imagine. Yet all the evidence of recent battle was there.

The jungle is in continual struggle. Trees and vegetation rot in the swamps, and the smell is pungent and prevailing. Everything alive strains toward the sun and is in a fitful frenzy to grow and survive. The only pleasant parts of tropical islands, it seems, are the shore lines, where the cooling sea makes life bearable.

I developed a bad case of heartburn. It began to cause me unusual discomfort, along with the oppressive heat. Adding to my discomfort was the swamp water which had seeped into my shoes and soaked my pants. I decided to leave Milligan and Denison, who pushed on. I observed along the way abandoned ammunition and clothes, rude shelters where marines had spent long nights, live hand grenades, an unexploded bomb, and innumerable deep shell craters.

I followed the coast and found a solemn scene: a graveyard of Japanese barges, piled into all kinds of battered and grotesque shapes, shell holes blasted through their sides, and with huge portions of the ships torn away. Smashed barges littered the coast for 150 yards. No booming breakers here. It was quiet and mournful, the sea hushed. Shell-torn trees reached over the battered and half-sunk ships, water sluggishly swirled in and out of cabins, portholes and scuppers, and lethargically washed over the sides. A sight of utter desolation; a place for dead things.

Ducking under the large branch of a tree, I managed to clout myself sharply on the head. The fastener to the insignia of my sun helmet cut my scalp. Blood slowly leaked down my face and clotted in my eyebrow. I had to wade a few streams, the deepest waist-deep. After a slogging five-mile walk, I was soaked from the waist down. Meanwhile a burning sun beat down on my throbbing and bleeding head. Ill and dizzy, the return to camp seemed endless. This little adventure turned out to be a minor fiasco. When I finally reached camp, a swim greatly helped to revive my spirits. However the heartburn which began this chain of events did not leave me till this morning. It was just one of those bad days.

February 25

Today Lt. Wenz made the exceedingly unpopular announcement that the 3rd platoon will clear and level an area 100 yards down the shore to which we will then move. We are badly crowded at present, and one well-placed 500-pound bomb would about wipe out the 244th. But I don't think any safety is gained when Lt. Wenz also says that our tents will be lined up, that uniformity must be maintained. A strafer likes nothing better than a nice, exposed row of tents all neat and straight in his sights. Then, our astounding Lt. W. informs his belligerent platoon that it will have nothing in one tent that will not be in the others. And the crowning point—we will have to sleep with the men of our own section. For me this is nearly a major catastrophe because I find living with those men nearly impossible. It will break up the quiet bunch of fellows we have now—and peace will be gone. Norm and I have lived as close as brothers these past few months, but now we shall be separated. We shall still spend time together, but not as often or as easily.

In our rage, Norm and I built a place out of an abandoned gun emplacement. We spent most of the afternoon and early evening building it. We secured an old canvas with some difficulty, and used it as a roof over our commodious, partly underground room, which is now lined with sandbags. Plenty large for both of us, it serves our purpose well—a reading and writing room where we can be alone. We intend to put our desk in there, with some of our effects, mainly books and writing material. The room is located some distance from where we will camp. We should be able to find some sort of seclusion and quiet there. What a luxury that has become!

February 26

Norm and I finished our room today, and a marvelous job it is, too. Waterproof and windproof, comfortable and roomy. Once again we have our desk with our books, writing material, pipes, cigarettes, pictures, and our other little comforts of this life. If we can only keep it!! It is half-underground, well-lined with sandbags, only a few yards from the sea. And it is a place where one can be alone, sit and write, read and smoke without any disturbance. It's wonderful. It is highly soundproof too, except for the voice of the sea.

We could not get candles tonight. So I dug up our old rusty lantern, managed to get a limited and precious amount of oil from Brothers (thank goodness he's a good friend of mine), and we did get the old thing to work. Am writing by that very stingy light now, sickly yellow, its radius about 18 inches. On top of our desk our macabre skull gleams hideously in the dull light. A few Petty pictures [*so-called because painted by Petty for Esquire, these prints of scantily dressed women were popular as pin-ups during World War II*] give this hole-in-the-ground a little color and cheer. Except for Norm writing alongside me, I am alone; we both enjoy this clean and isolated place we have made.

February 27

One year in the army today. Here I am sitting and writing in a dugout on the island of New Britain. Exactly a year ago at this time I was getting into a bunk in a barracks at Fort Dix, a very tired, disgusted green soldier who had just stood four hours in the rain, after a gruelling seven-hour train ride. And was I hungry—and now I'm still hungry.

February 28

Spent this morning fixing up new area which is very nice. Built washstand, etc. Before I forget to correct myself, I was in error yesterday in writing about Fort Dix. It took place exactly one week later. February 27 I took my physical exam and was sworn in. Exactly one year ago tonight to the hour I was with Carolyn, with whom I spent nearly half the time of my last remaining week as a civilian.

[*I still remember the night of that physical exam. Stripped naked, we men of various ages waited in slow lines to have various parts of our bodies briefly examined. I was eager to be accepted because I felt the war was the most important event of our century, and I wanted to have a part in it. I hoped I would be sent against Germany. I quickly memorized as much of the eyechart as I could because without glasses I could only see a wavery large E at the top.*

The psychological exam consisted of one question: "Do you prefer to go out with men or women?" Only my surprise at the question kept me from laughing. When I said, "Women," my examination was over.

After the exam, a strange thing happened. Papers in hand and still naked, I stood in front of three officers seated on an elevated platform behind a long desk. In front of the colonel seated in the center were two large rubber stamps, a blue one for "Accepted" and a red one for "Rejected." After the three officers briefly examined my papers, the colonel nonchalantly picked up the red marker and stamped a large "Rejected" across the first page, and handed the packet down to me. Stunned, I stared at that red word stamped diagonally across the page. I turned back and said, "Sir, why am I rejected? I think you may have made a mistake." After glancing through the papers, he said, "You are right. I picked up the wrong stamp." And that is how I passed my physical and was inducted that day.]

As a result of the 47 bombings and alerts to-date, which now have ceased, our company suffered only light wounds, except for Jackman, whose head wound was serious enough to warrant a special brain surgeon to be brought up from New Guinea. It is said that he is progressing, but that he shall never return. Also Alexander has not rejoined us to-date, still in the hospital in N.G. Maddox has not returned, and I don't know where he is, but I've been told he has been evacuated.

This afternoon I got my first close look at Japanese soldiers. There were two prisoners, and a more miserable sight I've hardly seen, except for the pitiful old flower women of Philadelphia. They were small, as is typical of the Japanese. One looked on the verge of dying from starvation. He visibly trembled, his eyes sunk far into his head, his cheekbones a sharp outline against his pasty flesh. Both soldiers were so weak they immediately sank to the ground upon disembarking from the LCM. Three more days without food and medical care would have finished that one fellow. Both were dirty and barefoot; the weaker Jap had badly ripped pants. His legs were no thicker nor heavier than my arm. The other fellow seemed in better condition, though he had a wound in the foot which caused him to grimace now and then. He had a round, chubby face, very crafty and shifty eyes, and a small black beard. He wore a hat. Both were toothy, and a sad-looking sight they made.

I felt sorry for them, until I remembered the fellows they may have killed, and how easily it could have been me. The wounded fellow was the more active of the two; the other sat dumbly, holding his decrepit body. The one with the beard made signs of desiring water, and if someone had not given it to them, I would have. His hands shook terribly as he drank. Little did they know what good food and hospitalization awaited them in Australia even though our P.W.s are atrociously treated by the Japs. So these pitiful prisoners were the vaunted "Sons of Heaven," the supermen who were going to exterminate the white race. They didn't look very super then. One American soldier, to show his contempt, poured out a cup of coffee before their noses. I doubt whether they knew what was going on; they seemed in a fog. The marines report that the Japs are on the run in the north and that they were being starved out. These two prisoners were good examples.

February 29

I wrote a sonnet based upon the white crosses I saw recently. The ending was suggested to me by something Carolyn wrote in her letter about Mrs. Roosevelt. While in Africa Mrs. Roosevelt said, "I wonder how many dead there are here, and how many women's hearts have died with them?" Here is the sonnet I wrote:

> From black-green shade there peers in starchy white,
> Like upturned faces toward the candlelight,
> Rows of crosses. They mark eternal night,
> Mid sylvan scene that shows no cause for fright.
> And golden coins are strewn about the mounds

By yellow light that works its way through leaves,
And streaks black earth with strips of yellow ground,
While in confusion vines and trees do weave.

This is the final resting place of men
Who died in one great burst of rage and sound,
Or final decree in pain did mark their end;
But they are dead. Their crosses mark the ground.
That solemn scene, sad names of life bereft,
But sadder are the ones who still are left.

March 1

We really worked today, loading LCMs with supplies for advanced bases. We worked nearly all six hours in a pouring rain, and for the first time in a long time I was chilly. We have acquired many useful things for our hut. Today I got in some rations. Norm yesterday acquired letter paper, ink, band-aids, prophylactics (of all things), friction tape, writing paper, pencils and a pair of pliers.

Thomas is with me here tonight. He comes here frequently. A nice kid—from Texas. Norm and I are working different shifts now, so we haven't spent much time together here. Thomas, handy with tools, has made two oil lanterns which serve admirably.

March 2

This morning, at about 5:00, a terrific explosion blasted us out of bed. The burst was like a bomb, but I knew it wasn't by the sound. It was followed at intervals of two seconds by four more. At first I thought it was an air-raid signal, but never have they been that loud. Thomas nearly went through his mosquito netting to hit the floor. I then surmised it was either a big gun going off to signal some ships, or warn them, or a warning for gas attack, which wasn't a pleasant thought—especially that early in the morning. A little later we found out it was the marine outfit next door. They had set off dynamite charges to scare some of us, which it did. Cause: we wouldn't let them go through our chowline. We supposedly get fed better than they do, but we don't get stuffed ourselves.

Our company is considerably under strength. Men in the hospital all the time now. Hendel is in, and Fazekas with an ulcerated stomach. Egan got out with his. I can understand why they both have them. Sonnier has gone off his head. He is in the hospital under observation. He's harmless enough, but he says crazy things all the time about going home, too, of course—that seems always a part of the ravings when fellows go off. I can understand it; however, I don't feel on the verge of insanity, yet.

March 4

Robert Prince was caught stealing food from the kitchen, and he faces a courtmartial. Also Jack Harris, for arguing with Sgt. Putt. He refused 48-hours extra duty, which is company punishment. Sonnier is definitely out of his head, and I doubt whether he will ever rejoin us. Wayne has been evacuated because of a concussion as a result of the bombing on the ship. This may be legitimate, though some of the fellows think it's mostly faked. We are about 10% under strength. Jack Harris has been wanting to talk with me for some time; he's all mixed up in himself and thinks I can help straighten him out.

We have acquired T-5 Adams in our section and have lost Scarborough. We need new blood badly. Harris told me last night that he heard Lt. Wenz mention me for T-5. That's possible, but I refuse to get excited nor do I anticipate it. I expect nothing. I have been doing my share of any job that has come up. I want only that and to be left alone, which this hut permits. I spend nearly every free hour here. I hardly have to bother with anyone in the Co. I can read poetry, write and dream in more quiet and solitude than I have ever known in the army. I am satisfied to have this for the time being.

March 6

Had a few short alerts today. Our section worked on the dock this morning. We also work at 12:00 tonight. We are unloading the supplies and personal belongings of the marines, which have been well-rifled both by marines who worked in the hold and, now, our men. On the dock stuff was pitifully ravaged by all of us, and much personal property was destroyed, lost, stolen. Every man in the company has booty from this ship. What a sad sight all that largely spoiled equipment made, thousands of dollars worth. I got an old but usable cigarette case. I have no scruples about taking books. I acquired a very wet, but complete, book on the *History of Surgery*. Our hut is now well-stocked with almost everything.

Thomas is here so often that I suggested he build his own desk. There is enough room. I don't mind him about; he's a good fellow. He's somewhat of a carpenter, which I am not at all, and Norm is almost as bad. Thomas has added to the comfort of the place, and contributed food, tools, pencils, a whole ream of airmail paper and envelopes, fuel for the lanterns, and other incidentals. So far, it's a happy arrangement.

Watts, Milligan and Rice are on an adventurous detail, accompanying an Aussie ship to land supplies at an advance base in N.B. about 100 miles north. They are expected to be gone three weeks.

Talk about ratings is prevalent. They are supposed to come out the end of this month. Norvell will not make corporal but T-5, though he doesn't know it yet. Rouse will be corporal. Norvell was too happy-go-lucky with the men, which is fatal to a NCO—especially under Wenz. I have been informed from several sources, mainly Sanchez and Harris, that I am in line for a T-5. I've heard this one before—but never as strongly as now. Sanchez informed me at chow tonight that Rouse said I was "on the ball" and was not reading so many books during working hours. Ha! If I have not been reading, which I have continued to do, it is because of the lack of reading material. I wouldn't give up reading for anything. However, I have never let reading interfere with my work, and I've been doing a better job these last months. Sometimes there are hours of waiting between barges to load, and that permits good reading time. I stick a book in my pocket in order not to feel that those empty hours are wasted. I am notorious for my reading and because of it an oddity to the men.

Today there were more than a few readers. The personal mail, as well as the belongings, of soldiers and marines was strewn all over the docks and ships. I found Harris reading a letter aloud which interested me— and which has led to a series of coincidences. Harris gave me the letter he had been reading, and I found it to be an 11-page letter to an American marine (possibly an officer) from an Australian girl, very much in love with the marine. It was not an ordinary letter, involving ordinary people. The girl, a divorcée with a little girl, is well-educated and writes a decent hand. The letter, though quite a bit effaced by rain, revealed an intriguing, poignant story. Because of her ability to write, it was largely unfolded to me. I have the letters and intend to keep them; they make a beautiful story. In this letter she mentions sending him Palgrave's *Golden Treasury*, and throughout the letter there are frequent references to poetry, and not a few quotes. It is all intimate. But the unusually fateful thing about it is that this is undoubtedly the same *Golden Treasury* that Norm brought to me a few days ago and sits on my desk this moment! Its description fits it, and on the cover is the figure 4/6 which means four shillings six pence. Later still, as if I had been fated to learn all this, I found quite by chance a 13-page letter, written by the same girl, on the edge of the dock quite apart from where I was first sitting. I gathered all the soggy pages together and, when I got back, dried them out. Much to my chagrin, some of the pages were half-effaced, but the very dim outlines can be perceived; perhaps I can eventually bring them out. I read the pages with some effort, and in that 20-odd pages a thrilling and unusual story unfolded. It had real romance, tragedy, war, emotion revealed so powerfully in these pages that they stunned me and set my mind going. I wish I knew the woman, and the man, too. At this moment I can see the story unfolding—how I should and perhaps will write it! Yes, it's a good idea. Here I've been searching for ideas—and now I have it. Laid right in my lap—Gad! Now, for the ambition to write it up. If I let this pass, I shall call myself lazy—it has everything. I feel very close to her. At any rate, I have her book and her heart in my head.

March 9

Milligan, Watts and Rice have returned, not having experienced anything unusual. M. and Perez have gone north again today—that is, to Talasea. It was announced last night that Talasea and the airstrip there have been taken. Milligan told me in our brief passing that it is about 50 miles north.

Saw Langham save a marine from drowning this afternoon, a big fellow who got a cramp quite far out. Heard the yells, but one hears so many yells that it is sometimes hard to distinguish what each signifies. However, it didn't take long to identify it as a yell of fear; once heard it's always recognized. Still thinking about that story and am lazily working it into a theme.

A thing too ridiculous to mention a few days ago has persisted at all hours of day and night. I hear melodies of various songs being sung as if from afar by a harmony of three or four voices. Of course it is all imaginary, but it invades my letter writing and reading almost to distraction and, on several occasions, to the point of distraction. Can't understand it; it's rather disconcerting and like listening to a radio only more difficult to turn off. Where it was a curiosity before, it now begins to be annoying. I don't quite know what to make of it. Perhaps it's just my subconscious mind reacting to something, perhaps the lack of music, though this seems a little preposterous.

March 10

Nothing like a little excitement to break up the day. The sea has become decidedly treacherous, and today three fellows were swept out. Their screams brought us out of our tents. Some of our outfit set in immediately. There were enough to handle the situation, and all went well. This has happened several times, to our own men also, to Rybicki and Stewart the other day.

The most interesting part of this rescue was when I saw, not far off-shore, a large flat fish leap into the air. It was a most magnificent leap, fully 20 feet high and 30 feet or more long in a perfect arc. It was astounding and beautiful.

March 12

Some may think how foolish is the moth
That flirts with flame and seeks a Viking's end.
He heeds the beck'ning finger to come forth,
A puff of smoke—that flitting life now blends
Into eternity. He teased the flame
That waited and swayed in sensual calm,
Then suddenly in one swift move insane,
Exalted moment—then a broken charm.

Perhaps the end was brief and seemed for naught
That ardent love the gloriol to aid,
But think I that 'tis better to be caught
In brief igneous gain than live in shade.

In one great truth much rather would I flare
Than live a life in shadow and despair.

Composed the above last night, or rather finished it. Had to laugh at my struggles last night. Suddenly aware of them—unconscious for the most part. There I was struggling and groping for the right words or phrase or timing. At least I'm learning a little form, I think. Wish I had a few textbooks.

Norm just showed me a letter he received from Gloria, at the end of which was a great, wide lipstick print, meant for a kiss. We both decided it rather disgusting.

March 13

It's a beautiful afternoon, the day filled with warm yellow light, a wonderful breeze blowing in from the sea, making the mosquito nets in the tents look like scudding clouds. The sea itself is blue and sparkling, with hardly a breaker over a foot high. An unusual, fine day, one that makes you feel glad you're alive to enjoy it.

We worked hard last night. It's a long shift from 12:00 to 6:00. We handled ammo and gas. My hands are pretty tough, but I managed to raise a few painful blisters. We've been working the twelve off, six on shift, which is really more eleven and seven. After a few weeks of it, the fatigue catches up with you. I find the cargo hook much easier on the fingers, but it is a dangerous tool and needs to be used with caution.

March 15

A sad thing has happened. Bud Herbeck has been busted from buck sergeant to T-5. This will be a hard blow for Herbeck, and especially for his family and for Jane. "Old Blinky" was out to get him anyway, as Sanchez informed me some time ago when he told me that I would make T-5. Today he said it was positive. I've been working fairly hard toward that possibility, but it is against my nature to "buck" excessively. It's too servile.

Rouse will no doubt make buck corporal. He has been most affable and likeable of late. I had to laugh the other day when he was hanging from one ponderous arm and scratching his broad chest in imitation of a monkey. The similarity was remarkable, with his hairy chest, great shoulders, thick legs and arms, great round head, piggish features and protruding teeth. Gad, how I should hate to be the object of his affections!

But speaking of size, I have filled out considerably. I can tell by the stretching of my clothes. I had been little aware of growth until the last few days when several fellows made reference to it. I know I have gained considerable strength.

Norvell has made T-5, which was inevitable. My old 3rd section, and one of the best in my mind, will not be the same without Bud Herbeck. I think it's a dirty deal, and Lt. Wenz has exercised prejudice.

I have come to like many of the fellows in my section, which is natural after living with them for so long. Sgt. Stahl is a fairly intelligent fellow, Pennsylvania Dutch, and we have had several interesting talks since we have Philly in common. Nothing unkind about him, considerably fair, but lacking in fight for his men, for which Herbeck paid.

Rouse, whom I have described often enough, is a Florida native who had a year at Georgia on football scholarship, and studied the good old athletic scholarship course—physical education.

Norvell, from Florida, is a good-tempered, pleasant, sunny person from a good family who are farmers—but not hillbillies.

Watts, from Pennsylvania, was a gay, handsome dog in his day, but at 26 is beginning to fade. He is influenced too easily by the raucous Southerners—a mistake I shall never make again.

Good-natured, humorous, don't-give-a-damn Kelly Rice can do the work of two hard-working men—but lately hasn't. Kelly is from Florida and intends to bootleg with Jack Harris after the war.

Then there is Harris himself and a real character—likeable and glib, and sometimes mixed up. Harris is a great converter of workers to non-workers.

Old, salty, rusty Milligan is a man who has seen and done much, is wise with experience, and has an amazing fund of knowledge.

Fazekas, another character, divorced, heavy drinker, non-worker and coffee brewer par excellence. He is a big fellow who is a great pilferer, as we all are, but he is a champion. I recall the 15-pound ham taken off a ship under a fatigue shirt. Slick. Also likeable.

Then the "Big Spaniard" Sanchez and the "Little Spaniard" Morales, whom I like very much and have always gotten along with most affably. They are typically Latin, which I find most agreeable. From Florida.

Then little Singleton and usually hard-working Horn from Georgia. Singleton I like for his wit, his manner. Horn is O.K. Both my tentmates and likeable enough.

Thomas is a Texan who still has the flavor of the West in manner and speech. A good enough fellow but, like Redwine, apt to get into too many details in his stories. It helps him get rid of his homesickness.

Then Redwine himself, the fellow I loaned half-a-dollar to my first few weeks in the army, so he could go to a service-club dance. He has nearly talked me into lunacy with his detailed stories ever since. But since I told him sharply about that, he has decreased them a great deal and is a good fellow essentially. Had an interesting talk with the powerful Parker, who is a fisherman in civilian life, and I learned much. Never knew much about him before.

Finally, there is Adams from Texas—no longer a young fellow—and a farmer, or rambler, rather. A hard worker, Adams gives too many orders, most of which are unnecessary. I regret to say I have "blown my top" at him several times recently. Can't stand orders, much less when they are petty and needless. I long ago discovered that the more I am ordered and driven, the less I do. It is an inevitable reaction. If left alone, I always do more than my share or, at least, my share. I have that kind of conscience.

They are all all right, and friends, but not close. I am happy, content with my lot for the present.

March 18

This morning we had an alert (it is said a light bomber was shot down heading for the liberty), and the cook came running out, a short, fat fellow, looking terribly scared, and biting his fingernails. He certainly made a droll figure in his life jacket, from which dangled knife, jungle light and whistle. He wore a white apron, and his short, fat, bare legs stuck out like tenpins.

Six of us went aboard the lib as a skeleton crew because we had air corps men and colored EM crews doing the labor. It was fun directing the work, instead of doing it, especially in that the work was heavy and it was beastly hot. I had six colored men with husky builds, and a fine, strong crew they were. I was foreman, and we got along fine and did a good job of stowing. Being in charge I worked twice as hard. If I could only get a chance at regularly being in charge, I could get a lot out of men. It's all in the manner of treating them, encouraging, and doing as much as they do, if not more, instead of just giving orders. Wish I had that colored crew all the time; they had the physiques for the work and knew how to take orders, better than most whites, including myself. The theory about having to take orders for a long time in order to give them successfully is not wholly true, I find. I can give them satisfactorily; they are much harder to take. And yet it felt a bit odd giving them, my having been in the ranks so long. It's true that the ranks largely destroy initiative. Gets to be a habit, to let someone else do all the thinking.

We also loaded the two-hatch Aussie ship that Milligan, Watts and Perez are on. We did the whole thing in eight hours with about 15 men. Some fun. Didn't get to bed till 3:00 A.M., awoke at 11:00 to eat, went to work at 12:00. The night before we worked two hatches, three winches and a deck crew with *12* men. It will either kill you or make a man of you. I feel more the latter these days. So far, so good. Sometimes it seems illogical to see the big fellows we could use in this work in other organizations not requiring as much brawn, while we have a lot of men of 120 pounds and only five feet two and three inches tall. Yet we manage to get the work done. The organization is building a lot of bodies and tearing down a lot of minds. I've tried to build both, but in both cases there is a long road to go. At lunch Denison and I argued on how men should be led. I'd like the chance to try some of my own theories; I'm sure some would work well. Norm is getting a little swell-headed and arrogant, but I'm sure he'll get over it. He's a kid in a lot of ways, but a darn good fellow. Nevertheless, we don't agree on how to handle men.

Been working 6-on-12-off for many days now, but the last two shifts have been light. Go on at midnight tonight. Breakfast this morning: two pieces of French toast and coffee. On that, we were supposed to do six hours hard work. It's a great theory, but it doesn't work so well. Corned-beef and potatoes for both following meals. I shall never again eat good old "Australian chicken" [*rabbit*] when I leave the army. Desserts were good. We have quite a supply of food in the hut. Good thing, too. It helps supplement three rotten meals, which sadly enough is often the case.

Heffle was broken to a private. He doesn't seem to be taking it badly. Strange too, he and Wenz were such pals. Basil Jones is building a sailboat with the enthusiastic help of our C.O., Lt. Reinhardt. Nobody misses C.H. Drown at all, yet I shall remember the man for certain traits and ideas, not all of which I agreed with by far. Still, it is pleasanter without old "Moose."

Watts told me the story about the taking of Talasea. We lost less than 10 men in the invasion. However, one day soon after landing, a group of marines were standing on the beach. Suddenly mortar fire started, but the range was long and the shells were dropping in the sea. The range shortened, and the marines just continued to watch, stupidly. Suddenly and inevitably, one found the shore, landed amongst them and killed 50! It was the biggest loss of men in the campaign!

March 21

It has struck again! Suddenly, even without the preparation of a rumor, an announcement blandly states on the bulletin board this evening that we shall move in four days! I was liking it here too, especially this well-stocked and furnished hut. I think it is very sad, but the usual gay anticipation has permeated the organization that was beginning to stale with routine. What a grasshopper existence. Good old Blink, with his real estate schemes, now all worthless. Already the place is showing signs of departure. Where shall we go, I wonder? Talasea seems doubtful; New Guinea, Finschhafen probably. We will no doubt join the battalion, something I don't particularly relish. Shall we stay there, or move on? I wonder. China perhaps, or India—that would be fun. But travel in the army, especially here, is always so damnably uncomfortable. I hope we stay in a civilized part of N.G., long enough to get furloughs. They seem as difficult to procure as the golden fleece.

The Aussies are taking over this place; a whole shipload came in today. No doubt we shall return on one of the liberties. I knew we were getting too comfortable to be left alone. The work has been easy, but the weird hours sometimes tiring.

No mail, KP tomorrow, a rather horrible mixture. Perhaps our move will bring an end to our corned-beef hash and salmon diet. We have had it two out of three or four meals a day. Tonight it just wouldn't go down. After half-a-slice of bread and a gallant attempt at the food, I gave up. I knew the breaking point had to come sometime. My appetite died a peaceful and resigned death.

March 26

Our move has been indefinitely postponed because of trouble getting the organizational equipment shipped. We shall probably be here at least another few weeks, which is fine with me. The *Augustus Thomas* and *Jochow* have pulled in, and the *Henry Reiney* is being unloaded. Another new lib pulled in, but I've not been aboard her. We have been working six and twelve for weeks, and I've become used to it. I make up for the shorter length of sleep by sleeping 10 or 11 hours from midnight to noon, which I have just done. This way I have enough to hold me over. The work has been light for our outfit since we've had Australian gangs to work the holds.

Because we have free run of the ship we work on, I often talk to the ship's officers and learn many interesting things. I've been talking quite a bit to Australian officers, learning about their class differences and experiences. This outfit took a pounding at Darwin when the Japs inflicted four million pounds damage. The officer I spoke with was in those raids and told me about them. An American fighter-squadron there consisted of 15 antiquated Kitty Hawks. It was sheer suicide to try to stop Zeros with them even on equal terms, much less heavily out-numbered, and with 100 bombers attacking besides. The Americans went up gallantly; all were shot down, and all but two killed. They accounted for four bombers, three Zeros. One Zero came down and touched his wheels to the airport runway—probably the first Jap to touch Australia. At Rabaul the same thing took place, except only one came out alive out of 15. They sent a message to Australia from Rabaul: "We who are about to die salute you." And they did.

Another white-moustached, aristocratic Aussie officer told me about the time some Kitties forced down a Jap Zero. When this officer was called to take charge of the pilot, the Jap addressed him in perfect English. He was a captain and educated at Oxford. He asked to be treated as an officer. He was then asked if there was anything he wished, to which the Jap replied, "Peaches and cream." He got the peaches. He was turned over to an Aussie non-com by the officer. A few days later the Aussie officer was placed under guard and taken to headquarters. He was charged with mistreating a prisoner of war. The Jap was beaten to ribbons and nearly dead. Of course it all was traced back to the non-com who decided to get even a little for the leg wound he had received in Malaya. There are many stories in this war.

Last night for the first time we heard Madam Tojo's propaganda program. The lib had a loudspeaker system on the ship. First she played a few popular pieces from San Francisco, but the reception was poor. Nevertheless, it was the first music heard in months and made us all feel good—especially when a female voice sang one of the songs. It was a funny sight to see the fellows dancing with each other on the deck of the ship, with big grins on their faces. I know what they were thinking; I was thinking the same thing. Madam Tojo, of course, accused us all of being butchers and murderers and twisted the recent facts. She said gangsters are prominent in the States and receive extravagant funerals, and that Elliot Roosevelt's wife sued him for divorce because of mental cruelty. He takes after his father, she added. Then, of course, she tried to split the Aussies and Americans. Meanwhile, to prove the futility of this, Aussies and Yanks were working and listening to the program together on the same ship and having a grand time. Furthermore, the American music helps us rather than makes us homesick. Poor Madam Tojo, with her sharp, clipped accent, is really quite unsuccessful in her attempts to demoralize us.

The other night I saw quite a sight. The gloriol of light around the hull of the liberty attracts innumerable fish. Some get playful and make huge jumps, causing great splashes. They shoot through the air in silver streaks, while flying fish go skimming about. They were particularly abundant, jumping all over the place when one huge silver fish took a tremendous leap and landed against the steering house of a tied-up LCM. I saw him hit with a flat bang, just missing the head of one of the fellows, and then twisting and richocheting back into the sea.

March 27

Announcement on board tonight states that we should be ready to break camp and move on 12-hours notice. I had better get my stuff ready. There was also a warning about pilferage, following a shakedown this afternoon. There is nothing in our tent, but in the hut we had considerable canned food. We've fed ourselves with the food, and I feel no guilt there. Six of our candles were confiscated. I would rather they had taken all the food than the candles. In the announcement Lt. Reinhardt appealed to the men instead of ordering them. I can respect this attitude, but I can see that most wouldn't. Many fellows are calling him spineless. That's the way of the common mind; it can't appreciate kindness and must be driven or ordered. Perhaps Drown was right when he said if you treat men decently, they will laugh behind your back. Perhaps I would never make a good officer if that is one of the doctrines officers adhere to. I guess I'd be too soft-hearted in disciplinary matters—like Reinhardt—with fatal results. He has already lost one C.O. job back at Wilmington. The gross ignorance of finer human relationships among men, after more than a year of observing it, still appalls me.

I don't believe this current warning has been caused by a few stolen cans of food, but rather the theft of gin, watches, brandy, etc. My section got gloriously stinko a few nights ago on a dozen bottles of gin. It is illegal to transport it so the Aussie soldiers, rather officers, can't complain too loudly. Our officers have a refrigerator in their tent and get the best of the food, facts that are beginning to pall on some of the men. If I were an officer, I think I would share more of my men's lot, and if I did have access to extra food, I would at least be less ostentatious about it. Anyway, all this disturbs me not at all. I have discovered I'm a quite hardy creature when it comes to survival.

March 30

We have received the news that opposition in the S.W.P. has ceased. Although the Japs still hold such places as Rabaul, Kavieng, Wewak and Madang, there is no Jap offensive and weak defensive action. That bears out here. However, these places still have to be taken. Recon shows no more than 50 enemy planes on N.B., and these grounded for lack of fuel. The whole S.W.P. should be ours soon. It signifies nothing more than a good start after a slow beginning. There is much yet to be accomplished. Soon we shall play another part in getting control of the S.W.P. It is logical to assume that we will be in another invasion of one of the important bases on the central coast of N.G., either Wewak or Madang. The Aussies are reported 20 miles from Madang. The going is slow. The Russians seem to be the only ones making notable progress, at last report only four miles from the Romanian border. In a few months all the Germans should be driven out of Russian territory. Where is that second front? It must come this spring.

April 2

These last two weeks have been pretty easy for all of us, with our outfit doing the directing and the Aussies and marines the heavy work. A few ratings came out today. York, Rouse, and Sanchez made Pfc. Especially glad Sanchez made it. Many of the fellows who had ratings before are getting them back, which pleases me. Thomas did not even make Pfc. That means the T-5 rating for checker is still wide open. Whichever way it comes out is all right with me.

April 4

We have been doing nothing but waiting to move these past two days. Our preparations have been mainly completed. We wait. I packed my jungle pack light this time. These two days off have rested me up. It is good to get off the schedule. Lots of rain too (it's going to rain any minute now), which I like. Nothing as pleasurable as lounging, listening to the rain, watching it, reading.

There was a formal notice on the board tonight concerning organizations of the 6th Army improperly registering complaints, and instructions to both officers and men in reference to treating complaints. Repercussions of our own little drama? At any rate, there seems to be quite a few such intra-organizational tiffs. Sorry to see it, though it's bound to occur now and again. Too dark to write further; no lighting available tonight.

April 6

Last night on the way to a movie I met a marine on the road who was also seeking transportation. We learned that there was no movie at the evacuation hospital and so fell into a mutually amiable conversation. We walked up and down the road for about an hour and then sat on the beach. It was pleasurable to trade ideas with someone out of the organization. He was Pvt. Leonard Perozzi, 2nd Battalion, E Company, from Mildred, Pennsylvania. We traded talk of home, experiences, opinions. It seems whenever American soldiers, marines, navy men discuss the war, there is never any thought but that of victory. Perozzi was one of those unenvied two-year men and was in Guadalcanal. Many of the stories I had heard before, but not the one about "Pistol Pete," his killed buddy, or about the close call he had when a naval shell landed two feet away and didn't explode, or about the wounded soldier he was carrying and felt he killed when he was forced to drop him, or the story of the face plastered in the coconut tree, or about the fellow who had smelled a Jap on the front-line and, thus, saved one of his buddies. Yes, there were many interesting tales about skirmishes, about the campaign here shortly before we arrived, and about how one feels. Then, he told me about the time he nearly died of malaria in Melbourne, and of his having 23 of 29 points necessary to go home. He was wearing his pants inside his socks because getting caught not wearing them thus, he would lose a point. An amiable fellow he was, dark complexion, black hair, and one missing front tooth, but that added to his homely pleasantness. We talked for at least four hours.

Report came through that the long-awaited naval battle between the

Jap force and ours is, at present, raging near the Philippines and that we lost 44 bombers. I hope the report of the naval battle is true. If their naval power is damaged, it will facilitate our advances. That reminds me of the story of the Aussie cruiser, *Canberra,* which knocked out three of our ships before the battleship *North Carolina* blasted her out of the water. A faulty searchlight caused that loss of four ships without their even meeting the Jap taskforce they were anticipating. [*Historical records report the* Canberra *was sunk by the Japanese in a naval battle off Savo Island, September 1942.*]

The Japs breaking through in India is not exactly good news, and it seems our forces are completely bogged down in Italy, though understandable, because of rain and terrain. The Russians continue to forge ahead, more slowly now. The end is a long way off.

April 8

We broke camp yesterday, and our platoon boarded the *Annui* [*British ship*] early in the evening. We were among the first troops aboard, because we finished loading her. I worked till midnight. The ship is fairly well-equipped for troops in the tropics. Ventilation good, hooks to set up hammocks, wash basins, and water. Also ice water to drink. I slept on deck last night because of the rather pungent smell of the latrine. Although I slept intermittently, I was not stiff or sore from sleeping on the hardwood deck, blanket for mattress, raincoat for pillow. Sanchez found a cot, as many of the fellows have. I am using his hammock, and it's fairly comfortable near open portholes; also, the smell has abated. There are four of us with hammocks slung alongside, Norm, Thomas, me and Milligan. Our quarters are roomy, which is unusual. This morning Pappy Milligan and I had our jungle-ration breakfast which took away a gnawing hunger since last night.

This morning, 6:00 a.m., was the sailing deadline. Some of our men got aboard only five minutes before. We could not get all our equipment aboard. Most of our barracks bags and tents remained behind with Blinky (Lt. Wenz) and a few men. Lt. R. flew down yesterday. Lt. T. is with us. Destination Finschhafen. It should be quite a mess when we get there if they have no tent area for us. Most of us, however, have enough gear in our packs and the bare essentials to make camp for a time.

And so the shores of New Britain are slipping into the sea, and on to new adventure. I wonder if I shall ever get home? On N.B. I learned a great deal more about war. I saw men die, I saw the enemy, we existed for more than two months on the most prosaic food. These were instructive experiences, and they have mentally and physically hardened me.

There were hardships, there was humor and tragedy. We experienced casualties, two men went out of their heads, our company lost some manpower. Nevertheless, I liked N.B., especially the lack of discipline there, the good tent area, the sea and the rainstorms, the sunrises and sunsets and flying fish and phosphorous lights in the water. I learned much from the many people I spoke with.

April 10

Events are and have been moving fast since we landed two days ago on the 8th. We arrived in the late afternoon and dropped anchor in a beautiful, large and good harbor. There were many ships there, at least 15 cargos and some flying boats. New Guinea looked typically tropical. We waited on board ship while a nearby navy vessel played recordings of "Begin the Beguine," "Night and Day," and other old favorites. It made me melancholy, recalling the good times associated with those songs and the many times I danced to them.

We disembarked by means of ducks and stood in them for a very uncomfortable half-hour, until we got a few miles inland. We had full equipment on, and it was quite dark. Then an unusual sight greeted our eyes: really fine roads, well-established organizations, well-lighted and picturesquely sprawling on the side of the hills, and large refrigerator plants. We all agreed it was like being in the suburbs of some big city, everything was so well-planned. This was, of course, Finschhafen—or rather a few miles just south of it.

We stopped in front of lighted barracks and the usual cracks about "short arm" [*inspection of genitals for venereal diseases*] and "area 1" [*fictional area for prostitutes*] split the night. We alighted in a foot of soupy mud, sloshed to an empty tent area, and willy-nilly tumbled into tents. Then we slipped and slid to a tent issuing cots, literally slipped back, and set them up. I threw my blanket on a cot, used my raincoat for a pillow, and was soon asleep. Home again! In the tent were Norm, Perkins, Parker, Havron, Wingfield and me.

The next morning we sloshed to breakfast and had really good pancakes, real butter, jam, drinkable coffee, and all such surprises. We remained in the tents for the morning, talking, kidding, and reading *The Reader's Digest*. There were a few wounded nearby from Arawe. We learned we were in a staging area! Then, the usual speculations. Then, lunch. The food since arriving has been nothing to rave about, but it is a great improvement. So this afternoon I read *C/O P.M.*, which I found typical of this organization's experiences and most, I imagine, that landed in Australia and stayed there a little while.

As soon as I finished *C/O P.M.*, we were alerted. We were packed in 10 minutes and onto trucks in a few moments. We drove a few curious miles and pulled into Co. B's area. It's a fine area, with raised tents and sides, mess hall, showers, ballfield, shop, etc., about all the comforts one can have in the S.W.P. when one is permanently stationed. I watched about 100 of our fellows walking in columns of twos across one of the spacious fields, like lawns, stretching down to the highway in front of this superlative area. It sure looked good to us. Meanwhile the old N.G. heat was rising; one really perspires here during the day. N.G. is truly a sudorific place. Well, we sat on one of these fields near the ballfield. The 100 men coming across, part of our outfit, in field equipment, but bedraggled after the tossing about we'd been taking, looked rugged. And it suddenly dawned on me that I look that way, too—that I do feel rugged, and that we are inured to much of the hardship of soldiers, that we were becoming veterans. It has been sneaking up on us for some time. Now it suddenly presented itself to me while watching my mates come across the field. Damn it all, we are soldiers!

We waited for about 1½ hours, and then in early evening we set to work putting tents up. It's an old story for us, and we had about 35 of them up in no time. It was well after dark when we finished. We had chow at about 10:00 p.m. They have a mess hall here, and we sat down and ate!! It was the first time we've had tables and seats with our meals in four months, an unusual sensation and quite enjoyable. It felt a little queer—too comfortable. I had a talk with Pappy [*Milligan*] who informed me that he will be 39 in a few days. If we stay in one place, he will put in for an over-age discharge. As long as we keep moving, old Pap will string along. He's quite an adventurer; I would not like to see him go. He is as hard as nails and a good friend of mine.

After some juggling, cursing, and carrying of equipment, we finally got assigned to a tent, and put the finishing touches on getting her in shape for the night. It's a good thing because it poured last night for several hours, but we were all dry except for a puddle under Adams' bed this morning. In the tent are Pappy, Sanchez, Adams, Redwine, Stahl and Eriksen. We took a cold shower last night, the first shower in months, and it was good. I slept well. One thing I forgot to mention was the PX that Norm and I visited at the staging area. We bought cookies, chocolate, fruit juice and gum, in rationed amounts, of course, but it was a real treat.

This morning after sloshing back from breakfast, good of course, but almost anything would be in comparison to the same food we'd eaten for months, I caught a detail with the Colonel of all people. Meanwhile, many reunions had taken place between friends in these two companies who have been separated for months. Their having been in Sydney seven weeks didn't make us feel too overjoyed. They were a bit respectful of our record and the Purple Hearts awarded to our casualties.

(Just informed Rouse that waking up men unnecessarily annoyed me. Sanchez is sleeping alongside of me, and Rouse just woke him saying, "There's a fly on your toe." Some fellows can't stand seeing other fellows sleep, and their waking them up has always seemed a damned stupid thing to do. I feel a lot better now having told him off.)

During this morning I worked with the Colonel and some of our section improving a fresh-water well. It was hot, but the old boy worked right along with us. He's well-liked for that. I believe him a good officer and apparently so do others in that he's a colonel. One feels more like doing a dirty job when there isn't an officer just standing and watching, but partaking. That's the kind of spirit I like and admire in leaders. That's the kind I'd like to be.

At dinner I was in for a pleasant surprise. I met an old NCO from the 496th! I haven't seen him in a year, but I recalled him instantly, a Texan and a swell, clean-cut fellow. He called to me. It was good seeing an old face, even though an army one. He was of the vintage of my early overnight passes to NY—the first ones. I asked him about Mathews, that unlikable fellow, whose repulsive manner is still strong in my mind, even though I left that outfit a year ago. He was still with them. He certainly gave me a bad start in the army. I have not forgotten it. Timmons, that self-inflated personality and quick-made blustering sergeant, was given a medical discharge in Seattle. I recall his great bellowing voice, supercilious manner, and how last year he used to give lectures about rifle marksmanship while we lay freezing on the ground. I can never forget those days of frozen face, fingers and feet—never being able to get warm, and then eventually a strep throat and 10 torturous days in the hospital. I have not been on sick call since. How ill and weak I was then, for weeks on end. I'm glad those days are over; they were difficult, but hardening. I watched Timmons make a score of about 65 on the range, and turn in a 145. That taught me at an early date about the morality of our NCOs. It was a bitter lesson then, but quite laughable now. Everything is always laughable afterwards. Although it's a year, there are still days I recall with a keen pain and grimace. I especially remembered infecting Carolyn with strep. God, that was horrible for both of us. I recalled the many complications between us that came from her illness.

It was shortly after lunch a few hours ago when the surprise fell. Lt. W. called a platoon meeting. In a short, rather dramatic 15 minutes our immediate future was mapped out. I suppose a lieutenant against a background of jungle, mountains and tropical sky, telling a bunch of soldiers seated under a tree about operations is good movie copy or novel material. This is the story: we are no longer attached to the marines, but will become part of a 6th Army taskforce for another invasion. This greeted in silence. Then the details. The 3rd platoon, with enough other men to make a total of 80 men, will be the first to leave aboard a liberty. We will go in D + 1, which means a day after the first troops hit the beach. We don't know where, of course. Havron's section will accompany the 3rd platoon along with a smattering of other men. The Lieutenant informed us that we may be in for a warm time and may have to work two or three days without sleep or rest. He stated that any man who did not feel physically fit to be up to that possible schedule should see him, and he would be left to come up later. Also, any man who did not want to subject himself to the danger would also be left to come up later, if he wished. I doubt whether there are many men who *that* openly would admit they were afraid. So far, I don't know of any men who will not go, though I heard Fazekas discussing the possibility which doesn't surprise me. It would be false to say the fellows are taking the thought lightly of "going in" the second day. Sure, we cracked jokes, and kidded, and I did my share of that. I said to DiPirro, "Going in on the first liberty will be like living on a bull's eye," which I later heard him repeating. Sanchez said, "Sure I'm scared, but I wouldn't miss it for anything." For the most part we are all in good spirits and condition, although Adams doesn't look happy. Our job will be to unload the lib we go in on and another following. I feel pretty good, although the initial announcement tied my stomach in knots, a feeling I always get when I know I'm in for something hazardous. But now I feel that I know more of what it's all about.

Our next interest was in "where." Most likely possiblities are Wewak or Madang, though it could also be N.B. again, close to Rabaul, or New Ireland or the Admiralties. The latter is very possible. It will be one of these places, I believe, though it might be some obscure place. The fact that a ship as big as a lib is going in on D + 1 day is an indication, I believe, of the lack of enemy air power. It is reported weak or nil throughout the S.W.P. If this is so, we should not be bothered with much, if any, air attack. I also wonder about the shore defenses. I suppose the theory is that the initial forces will neutralize them. Theories, especially in the army, don't always work. At any rate, I feel we are in for an experience. I hope I have written this with some degree of coherence; I've been interrupted about 10 different times.

It's chow time now. Am going to try to see a movie tonight. First one in months. Old C.H. Drown is here looking happy. I have found a nearby library. About 40 barracks bags came in and some of our equipment. The rest is sitting out in the bay aboard an Aussie tub that Jones and Williams brought in. Should get mine tomorrow. That's all for the present, and I believe it to be quite enough. I see that I have nearly completed the pages of this book. I suppose it might be called "The Book of New Britain." I shall have to start another.

April 13

We have added 32 replacements to our company, which brings us back up to full strength. Night before last we had two alerts, but nothing happened. During one of the blackouts there was an emergency call from aboard one of the libs. In the dark a man walked across a hatch where one hatch-cover was left off. He fell down to the lower hold, hitting a strong hook on the way down, which severed his head. He was brought up in a basket. The irony is that the Japs without even raiding got one man because of the alert and blackout. As Milligan, whose 39th birthday was yesterday, coldly observed, "Well you came over here to die." I don't quite agree with that philosophy, but he has a point.

We turned in our old gas masks and got back new ones of a different type. They are lighter and will be more comfortable. We are scheduled to move in about three days.

April 17

Long days and nights of rest, writing, reading, card playing, movies, and bull sessions. The 2nd platoon leaves this afternoon, presumably for Wewak. The 1st platoon leaves tomorrow—destination unknown. We have been moved from D + 1 to D + 8 days which considerably cuts down the hazard. Presumably our destination is Rabaul.

The mail I got was wonderful. Some letters from home reveal they realize I've seen action. I can well imagine what that is doing to them. A long-awaited letter from Carolyn came. There was a letter from Dale too, fascinating indeed. I believe if I had met her under more ideal conditions, it would have been a quite happy relationship. At any rate, our letters seem to be satisfying one another. I hope I see her again, too. What a furlough would mean! Companionship, civilization, a little kindness, tenderness, comfort. It's been a horribly long time, and the future indicates no leaving of this theater.

Besides the damnable ringworm, I am in good condition. Am living with Adams, Sanchez, Pap, Redwine, Stahl and Eriksen and this new fellow, Sigley, who flits in and out. We all get along well, and four are "old" men and have some sense. I got a kick out of the discussion of "love" among them, all unmarried and over 30. Eriksen showed us a picture of his illegitimate son, about two or three years old, whom he has never seen. The child resembles him and is good-looking. There are quite a number of illegitimate children in the world, I've discovered.

Had to laugh about Carolyn's question about my "status." Kahn the virgin, a veritable oddity.

Although I am isolated from my important relationships, I feel that it shall not be too difficult to weather the changes in myself and others. I hope I shall maintain all of these former relationships, even though my friends will all be grads or near grads and in a professional world. If most of my old friends will be alienated, as I feel they will, it should not be difficult for me to grow in a new world. I think much of Carolyn, but should we be separated by having years of education between us, I believe I could stand it, as could she. That is how I see it now. No matter what happens, I feel I shall manage.

I understand OCS applications are being considered. It annoyed me a bit yesterday to learn of it. However, in truth, I don't feel quite ready for it—I'm learning too much. Hope I'm not kidding myself, but I made my own bed through the mistake of the petition—now I shall proceed to lie in it. The mistake is a lesson I had to learn sooner or later. I have learned. Perhaps it is worth the sacrifice of OCS in the long run. Besides, so much has been happening so fast in our company that I would be a little reluctant to leave it at present, even if I did have the chance. Perhaps if the opportunity knocked, I would not be so reluctant. It is comfortable to remain in that everyone knows everyone so well.

Drew 60 more rounds of ammo yesterday. Am going to lug 100 rounds now. More fun.

April 19

The 1st and 2nd platoons have pulled out, and it was dramatic saying goodbye to some good friends, not knowing what they are getting into or when we shall see one another again. We have been loading their gear and drawing equipment.

Lt. R. told us we are going into a tough area where there are 145,000 Japs defending the terrain, airstrips, etc. Oddly enough, I am looking forward to it. I imagine that our platoons will land at various points on the New Guinea coast, largely wiping the Japs out of N.G. Our platoon may well hit Rabaul, while the rest hit N.G. These shall all be important blows. Saw some infantry boarding yesterday. We should be leaving soon.

April 21

A few days ago, and fully-equipped at last, we had a short talk by a rather young and pleasant lieutenant colonel in charge of the coming taskforce. He told us we are going into the stronghold of the Jap. This will be the biggest show in the South West Pacific so far. We are going to be well within the range of enemy aircraft, but we are well-equipped and have plenty to throw up at them. He didn't know how much action we saw at Gloucester, but we should prepare our minds for some nasty scenes. There will be plenty of dead men, plenty of horror. He ended on the note that we would receive the best hospitalization available. That last remark sounded facetious, following what went before, or perhaps it is my morbid sense of humor. At any rate, it was definite information, to the point. For the most part we liked the talk.

I don't feel any fear nor any particular bravery. It seems to be all part of the job. Besides, we have the added experience of Gloucester behind us which was, perhaps, an introduction to what will follow. I am not crazy about the future, and yet there is a certain magnetism in the hazard. Perhaps I have more of a yen for adventure than appears on the surface. Anyway, I must be careful of the feeling that because I have luckily come through the past unscathed that it shall be so in the future. I do like having, at least, the possibilities on my side.

Have read *The Red Badge of Courage* by Stephen Crane, well-written piece. The descriptive writing was superb, and his lavish use of color to describe emotion was extremely interesting. Of equal, if not greater, interest was the short account of his rather full life, even though he was under 30 when death claimed him. The more I read of writers, the more I realize that they are more or less ordinary people, but with a talent and a certain compulsion. Sometimes I feel this compulsion profoundly, but sometimes I am too lazy. Longhand is a tedious way to write, still many have done it. I think that I am afraid to put down my best effort only to find that it is poor in the end. Soon I am going to have to prick the bubble and find out if there is anything there. Damn it all, I know there is.

April 26

It's been raining, and everything is a quagmire again. I understand that the first landing was made a little above Wewak with about 20 casualties. They have taken the airstrip. It will not be many weeks before all of N.G. from Hollandia down will be in our hands. There should be some interesting developments. We are scheduled to move about May 1 or 2. We are D + 12. At that late date, the main danger is air attack. Their air force in this area is reportedly weak. Co. B is going to move to Saidor. Poor fellows, after building such a pleasant area. This will only be their third move since reaching N.G. We are preparing for our sixth, not to mention three or four small ones.

April 27

Ah, yes! The army is at work again. Company B, that was supposed to move out today, was postponed indefinitely. Landings have been effected at places a bit above Wewak and Hollandia. Good-oh! [*Australian expression picked up by our troops.*]

4

Hollandia, New Guinea

————— May 1–June 1, 1944 —————

May 1

On the 29th we went down to the LST landing, and we loaded into the LST the usual stuff: ammo, cats, gas, organizational equipment, etc. Going back to the tent, I listened to a radio report. Having learned that we are going to Hollandia, I was naturally interested in the news from there. The report stated that our troops were meeting disorganized resistance and that the Jap was being methodically wiped out. At that time 397 had been killed. Also, 20 of our men were recaptured after having been in Jap hands. Some American soldiers were so mistreated that they had to be carried into Hollandia. All the airstrips were taken.

The next morning we packed our bags and got our packs ready. We were all set, the tents taken down and camp broken, by about 10:00 A.M. It was an extremely hot Sunday. In the mess hall a handful of soldiers attended services. We lounged there through the remainder of the morning and all afternoon, the fellows amusing themselves playing cards, ball, trading rumors or reading. I read as usual. At 6:00 P.M. four trucks arrived, and we piled on; it was rather crowded. The truck trip was about 15 miles back to the LST landing. The dust was so thick that you could only make out the headlights of following and passing vehicles. It blew in our faces, lodged in our hair and equipment. In a few moments, rifle, men, everything had a layer of dust on it. It was fast growing dark.

After unloading, we boarded the LST by roster and were informed that we were to sleep on the top deck and to forage for ourselves. It was now pitch-dark. After climbing over numerous obstacles in the tank deck, with about 80 pounds of equipment on our backs, we made our tedious, panting, cursing way to the top deck. It was wondrously clogged with equipment (trucks, jeeps, etc.) and milling, sweating men. I was soaked with perspiration. Sanchez and I joined forces and picked our way aft. We found a clear space between some trucks and unloaded our equipment. However, we found the spot wet and muddy, as was the entire deck from the trucks which had passed over it, and the crusted mud from the fenders, guards, and carriages falling to the deck had become either mud or sand. So we circled the ship looking for another spot.

Men were sleeping everywhere imaginable, crammed into all impossible nooks and crannies. They were sleeping on the deck, in and on trucks and jeeps. They were sleeping sitting up with their equipment beside them. In our search we came across Monroe and Denison who invited us to join them. We did. All our equipment had to be lugged there, and with all the soldiers milling about, it was a major operation. Sanchez crawled under a truck with his stuff, and we three had an open spot on the elevator. After installing our equipment under various nearby vehicles, which hemmed us in, we considered the sleeping problem. After considerable difficulty, Denison got his hammock up; Monroe and I (a far cry from when we crossed the USA together in pullman berths) spread blankets and ponchos on the steel deck. Fortunately I spotted a broom, so we at least got the sand out of our beds.

After getting set, I wandered down to get water and found that a number of our fellows had made themselves at home in the crews' quarters and mess hall (where I am writing now), and they were playing cards, checkers, chess, shooting the bull, reading, and drinking coffee. We joined them in the evening. Knowing these LSTs from long experience, we made ourselves at home, and we have had this comfort, unlike the other troops aboard. Our men have had a great time lording it over the other men aboard, both army and navy, because they are relatively green troops. Our New Britain experience has seasoned us and also given us some prestige among these men, even though this is the second trip for the LST crew to Hollandia. They went in D + 1. We are D + 12. Harris, of course, has been especially shooting the bull. Before I forget, Hennel was transferred to HQ. He was too old to do the work anyway and for roughing it the way we do. Little by little the company is carved into a perfect cog.

I returned to deck to find Monroe and Norm asleep. Naturally the worst thing that could have happened, did. At about 2:00 A.M. most of us awoke to find rain in our faces. There was a general exodus from the deck to find places below. Monroe and I gathered up our blankets and ponchos and descended. Norm threw a cover over himself and hoped for the best, returning to sleep. Those fellows that did not go below put up makeshift shelters, stretching canvas from vehicle to vehicle. We were a sleepy, tired lot, too sleepy to curse. The rain got heavier, and it was very dark. Art and I wandered about the ship, seeking a place to sleep. Many found their way into the tank deck, but it was so dirty that I decided I would sooner stand in the rain all night. Art and I separated; he preferred the tank deck. I returned to the top deck and climbed on top of a truck. The rain had nearly abated, but not till I had made a regular pilgrimage seeking a bed. I was damp, tired, sleepy, and thoroughly disgusted because there was no place to stretch the old bones. I sat there quite at a loss for a few moments. Everything was wet from the rain. In a few moments it started again, and heavily, so I retreated down to the darkened corridors where bunks lined the sides, three high. Some fortunate crew and soldiers had cots. It was dirty and warmish in the darkness of the passageways, lit only by red lights. Men were sleeping on the floor. I was fast losing all hope when, by miraculous fortune, I came across an unoccupied lower bed. I thought surely it was taken, just temporarily vacated. It was a crew's compartment as I could tell by the mattresses on the other cots. Nevertheless, I tossed my blanket down, poncho for pillow, removed shoes and was soon asleep. I woke in the morning and inquired about the bunk, which I found all mine. I was extremely lucky. There are a few others with bunks: Pappy, Parker, Sig, Rouse.

We shall land probably on Thursday morning. Whether it will be a new landing or a reinforcement of the original is still unknown. It will be a jump of more than 600 miles up the New Guinea coast, and it will be in Dutch New Guinea.

Dinner and supper were excellent, though I had to wait two hours to get my mess kit cleaned. I am at the moment thoroughly bathed in perspiration and tired. Now for a breath of air on deck, and bed. This is a large convoy. There are 75 ships in all, the LSTs towing LCTs, PTs, destroyers, cruisers, cargos, corvettes. Stretched across the sea, within sight of shore, it makes an impressive sight. One can feel the power there.

May 3

We are scheduled to land somewhere around Hollandia tomorrow morning. No doubt we shall have to unload this scow in six hours which will make a hard job harder. We are all out of condition, not having done much during the last month. I have learned that this ship is going to return to Pearl Harbor with the 1st Marine Division, to which we were attached during the New Britain campaign. That Division has been overseas for more than two years with considerable losses in that it did the main fighting for some time. I am glad to see those marines relieved. [*Perhaps some 1st Marine Division troops were relieved, having fought in both the Guadacanal and Cape Gloucester campaigns. However, the*

Division itself, and with some veterans of those battles, went on to fight at Peleliu in the Palau Islands and at Okinawa in the Ryukyu Islands, sustaining over 14,000 killed, missing and wounded in these two following campaigns. See Sledge, With the Old Breed, for history of the 1st Marine Division.]

That friendly sailor who shared a midnight feast of fruit cocktail (that he secured) with Sigley and me is now in the brig. He was caught stealing some gear. Most of the men aboard have court martials against them.

Last night I could not sleep for hours. I didn't know why, and for the first time in months I was bothered sexually. I felt heavy, full, with a need for relief. This I did, as I have only had need to do once or twice in my life. Usually these feelings take care of themselves, but once in a great while I have need of relieving myself. I recall often reading that masturbation left one feeling ashamed of oneself, of detesting oneself. I examined how I felt and found myself impassive, with neither remorse nor pleasure, just necessity. Only after that was I able to sleep, which I needed and knew I would. It was an act like a reflex when one has need of coughing when the throat is irritated. I cannot possibly feel disgusted, ashamed or remorseful because of physical necessity. However, this was almost a unique experience. I suppose it is a result of my rapid physical development during these last six months. I feel a new strength, I feel myself growing, and sometimes I must flex and stretch myself because of a feeling of tightness. Many have remarked on my physical change during the past two months. I feel bigger, and the mirror proves I am. I must be over 180 pounds now. I'm glad of one thing. I don't like arguments or fighting, and my size saves me many. I am rarely belligerent.

May 6

On May 4th we pulled into the bay early in the morning. Through binoculars we saw attractive, white-sand beaches with no breakers. There were several picturesque rock-bound islands. As we got closer, we saw much devastation. The whole beach was lined with the burned remains of ammo, gas drums, vehicles, both American and Japanese.

We landed and unloaded the LST by hand. More than half the convoy had gone elsewhere during the night. About 12 ships reached here. We carried the supplies out, box by box. About 500 men streamed in and out of the ship, like ants carrying eggs out of a hill. It was beastly hot (we are only a few degrees south of the equator). As the afternoon wore on, we unloaded the cats and ammo. Then we had to roll out the drums, two men to a 450-pound drum. Carrying and rolling them in soft sand is no joke. Every man was streaming sweat. There was great confusion, with men and officers bawling directions, cursing, vehicles bogging down in the soft sand, and bulldozers not always successfully keeping a passageway of sand between the ship and land. Sometimes we waded in knee-deep water with 100 to 150 pounds on our backs. During all this confusion and activity, it was inevitable that some would get hurt. The first one was Colby who had a nail torn off and passed out. More serious was Herbeck who was run over by a trailer. His leg was fractured above the ankle. He was taken to the field hospital.

During the unloading, I looked around and gained some information. Considerable material was destroyed on the beachhead. A solid black line of gutted army supplies lined the beach for a half-mile. The jungle near this stuff was scorched. Tires were burned right off the trucks, shovel handles right out of the shovels. The heat had been intense enough to melt metals. An American shoe was found, partially burned, with a foot still in it. The fire was caused by a Jap plane that scored a lucky hit on the high octane gas. The drums, seen all over the bay, were bloated like balloons where the exploding gas blew huge rents in them.

There was, naturally, some loss of life. The cost of all this destroyed material is terrific, not to mention the strategic loss. I have never seen such a sight of utter devastation. There was another raid (the only two so far) that killed six or seven men the night before we got here. However, the first was as effective as 20.

We couldn't get all the drums out by dusk. It was nearly dark when we shouldered our equipment and started for a camp area. In our tired condition this turned out to be a difficult two-mile hike.

Walking along the beachfront on a crude road we saw captured Jap material. This had been a big QM base, and there were great mountains of rice, canned beef, dried fish, bottled oil, oats, vehicles, and many crated plane motors and wing sections. The Japs here were taken by complete surprise by our 600-mile advance. In fact, food was left cooking in the pots when the Japs hurriedly retreated into the hills. Hollandia is one of their last big supply dumps in the South West Pacific.

It was dark when we cut inland. At this point an alert sounded. About two-thirds of the company scattered into the jungle and fields alongside the road. About 20 of us wanted to keep going in spite of the alert. Then, to add to the confusion, we found ourselves leaderless. No Lt. W. and no 1st Sgt. Tipple. We didn't know if we were headed in the right direction. This got the better of me, and I said some things about not having leadership when it was needed. Pappy, Norm and I leaned against a nearby small dirt hill and waited. In about five minutes the rest of the fellows came plodding along, and we found, having pushed on, that we had become the vanguard. Had to laugh at Shorty yelling, "Let's go, we've been through a thousand of these things." We did elect to keep going. Electing under these conditions still strikes me as amusing.

We plodded along in the dark, passing bivouac areas, truck concentrations, gun emplacements, and a radar emplacement atop a hill overlooking the quiet sea and the scarred beachline. We continued inland and came to a sharply sloping hill, and down we went, finding ourselves in a huge basin where vehicles were concentrated. After we worked our way over wire entanglements (Clark tripping and rolling down a bit—nobody laughed), we then climbed up the red clay sides and reached the few trucks that were parked there. There Leo, who irritated everyone by hurrying us, gave each two men a can of meat. We hadn't eaten since noon, and we were all hungry, hot and tired. We sank down on the side of the hill and removed our equipment. That 10-minute rest did wonders for me.

Pappy and I had teamed up and decided to wait to eat until we settled somewhere for the night. By this time, the all-clear had been sounded by word of mouth. While we were sitting and talking and resting, the majority of the men pushed on without our knowledge. As a result Pap and I pushed on alone, getting directions from stray soldiers. We were about five minutes behind the main crowd. We trudged over the hill and down the other side which sloped to the beach—where we knew it would be cooler—by means of a small trail cut through the jungle. It was cooler. There was a light sea breeze in pleasant contrast to the stifling basin and jungle.

We reached the beach and followed the shoreline, sloshing through water half the time. The palms along the beach were burnt black. I thought what an adventurous sight we made, just the two of us marching with full equipment, Pap first and me following on the white sandy shores under a bright white moon. It was very quiet except for a somnolent, lapping sea.

Along the beach we found a hollow in the sand between two logs that was big enough for the two of us to lie down in for the night. Our men were scattered along the shore, most of them about 75 yards up further. We dumped our equipment, took off our clothes, and went into the sea. It was wonderful, and just what was needed, to relax our taut bodies and nerves. The water was warm and the bottom sandy. Twenty minutes later we got out, feeling much better. Because of the mosquitoes, we had to get back into our sweaty clothes. Then we ate our dinner, the single can of meat. Luckily I had enough foresight to pack a large can of roast beef and a small one of pork. We ate the pork too, but decided to save the roast beef. All the drinking water available was what we carried. We had been husbanding that. By the time we decided to save some, we had drunk ¾ of a canteen, which is almost a pint. I had two packs of soggy gum which I shared. We topped it off with a cigarette. With food under our belts we took a new lease on life.

We made our bed for the night by throwing down a shelter-half, blanket on top, poncho for cover. The hollow afforded some protection against shrapnel. We didn't worry about the close ones because we'd never know it. We laid down, remarking what a beautiful night it was for bombing. The moon was extremely bright, making everything visible. All those new supplies on the beach made a perfect target.

It was not 15 minutes later that we heard an alert. I was willing to give 2:1 that the Japs would be over. We waited for a half-hour, and finally a green light shining from across the bay indicated an all-clear. This method was used to foil the Jap trick of watching for the all-clear flare, while distantly gliding, and then dashing in for a quick surprise attack, which had been effective on New Britain. It was about 10:00 P.M. when we got to sleep. Twice more during the night there were alerts. The warning gun was only ½ mile away, so it practically blew us out of bed. During that night I spent the most miserable four hours ever.

The spatter of rain in my face woke me. Soon it was torrential and seeped into bed. When I was finally soaked and lying in a half-inch of water, I got up, threw my poncho over me, and leaned against the bank. It rained like the devil. Pappy was alongside me a half-hour later, having stayed dry a little longer. He miraculously managed to light a cigarette, and we sat in the rain, improvising jokes. After an hour of this, I was chilled to the bone, so I wrapped the wet, woollen blanket around me, which helped.

All night bedraggled soldiers straggled by. I was just dropping off when a stray soldier, whom we could not see because now it was so dark, plunked himself down next to me. He started to talk. I didn't even turn around, feigning sleep. He got muffled answers from Pappy. No doubt he needed some human comfort; misery seeks company. He asked all kinds of questions: "What do you think about the situation, the place?" etc. After a half-hour he talked himself out and disappeared into the rain and night as mysteriously as he came. Later it struck me as amusing. After another hour I dropped off in spite of the rain, though the tide was coming in and lapping and wetting my already-soaked feet. Not being able to get wetter or feel colder or more miserable, I let it lap. I awoke to the rhythm of Milligan's poking. Daylight was breaking, and I greeted it, stiff, wet, and with cynical humor.

Shouldering our soaked equipment and getting a kick out of watching the water run out the barrel of my rifle, we marched into camp. Everyone was stirring, and we got the horse-laugh for our sodden appearance, though everybody was as wet. We were just the vanguard of our fellows straggling into camp during the next hour. Some had slept on the hill where we first stopped and were covered from helmet to leggings with thick, red clay. What a sight. We were dry by comparison.

We did not have a bad camping spot, a sandy, clean stretch of shore. Behind us, at the edge of the jungle, there lay the exploded drums of Jap gasoline. Beyond them, a swamp.

Pappy and I finished the can of beef and the remainder of our water. That was breakfast. Soon the day was scorching hot, and just what we needed to dry everything out. Lt. W. was there, along with Sgts. Stahl, Eriksen and Tipple, as dirty and wet as we, and owning the only foxhole in the area. Hammocks were stretched among the burnt palm trees. Some men had laid their hammocks on the ground, as we had done. Pap and I put up a pup tent with our shelter-halves, swam in the quiet, clear sea, got our things out to dry, and put on dry clothing. The sun was murderously hot, and thoroughly wet clothes dried in an hour. We managed to refill our canteens after a muddy quarter-mile walk. Pappy miraculously produced a box of cereal, canned milk and chocolate. We made a rich mixture, and it was lunch—and good. Everything dried nicely, and life looked livable again.

(Sgt. Stahl wants me to remember—he's sitting alongside me—that a 178-pound box of ammo grazed his back the day of the unloading, and he narrowly missed serious injury and possibly death. Fate was with him. All he has is a slightly lame back.)

Denison and I spread a blanket over his hammock and talked awhile, and I cleaned my rifle. Then Lt. Wenz called a meeting and took stock of our situation. No food, no water, plenty of humor and direct orders. One party, under Norm, was sent to forage for water, and another for food. We set up a single tent to serve as orderly room, officers' sleeping quarters, supply. Norm's crew returned with about 40 gallons. With the 15 we had, that gave everybody a drink. It's funny how much thirstier you get when water is scarce. I got half-a-cup during the afternoon, spilling some in the process. Lt. Wenz jumped on me and I couldn't blame him. He has done a wonderful job keeping everyone happy and fed, and he has been very relaxed with us. All in all, we are 69 men at present. There is a great advantage in being a small unit because it is easier to supply.

That night we had the first hot food in over 30 hours: two slices of Spam and a half-cup of coffee. After dark we sat about talking in the warm, bright night, waiting for raids. During the day we got everything dried, cleaned and stowed away in the few pup tents that had sprung up—or under tarps. More hammocks were slung. Pap and I dug 2½-

foot-deep slit trenches on the beach shortly before an alert. I am sitting on the edge of the trench now. After the only alert last night, we slept in the pup tent, which wasn't bad. (Five alerts since we've been here.) Pap complained this morning, not liking the ground for his 39-year-old bones.

We spent today hauling rations over the hill on our shoulders. I went to see Herbeck in the hospital. He was in good humor in spite of the fractured and swollen leg and ankle. The hospital was packed with men who had the usual jungle diseases, wounds and accidents. No water was available for them in the stifling hospital tents. Herbeck had nothing with him. I got a carton of cigarettes from the weapons-carrier, telling him not to smoke himself to death, and that he would do anything to get out of work. Later in the day Miranda made the long walk to carry toilet articles and reading material to him.

During the morning a strength report was turned in to HQ. In a day or two we will probably move closer to the frontlines which are at the moment six miles away. I understand that they are having trouble getting supplied.

The front here extends 150 miles, and we have three divisions (100,000 men) engaged. It's one of the largest concentrations of men in the South West Pacific. We are less than 1,000 miles south of the Philippines, the next big objective. With the successful termination of this campaign, along with the isolation of Rabaul, and with Kavieng airfield on New Ireland largely knocked out by bombing now, we will have complete control of the South West Pacific. We have paid for it, but these are important steps that break the outer-ring defenses of the Japs.

We have done no work except for ourselves, clearing the area and keeping fed and getting water. Water was hard to get until this afternoon when fresh water springs were discovered about a half-mile up the beach. I spent last night in thirst. These springs are out of reach during high tide. During low tide the natural springlets come out of the rocks and jungle, cool and clear. We use water-purifying pills in this water to make sure it's safe. I lugged a five-gallon can, and Pap took our canteens. It is a beautiful spot there, yellow sand, green jungle, with white blossoms and broad, smooth leaves among the rougher stuff. There were various small paths, Japanese. (Before I forget, the day of the landing some prisoners were seen, among them a Jap nurse!) So, during the afternoon, and by the tedious process of filling up the cans, cup by cup, we got over a full Lister bag of water [*a canvas bag suspended from a tripod*].

The spot is a naturalist's paradise. There was a small, clear, deep, perfectly round pool caused by a bomb hit. Starfish and tropical fish and clams remain in the little puddles of the ebbing tide. The starfish are so plentiful that you can't take a step without crushing one. All kind of crabs, too. Pap and I spent a half-hour searching among the rocks and found myriad varieties of seashells with little crabs inside. He collected black shells with yellow stripes. There were many pretty ones of odd shape. The rock formations were extremely interesting. We discovered a peculiar animal, about as big as a fingernail when bloated with water. Upon contact it squirts out a stream and dissolves into nearly nothing. Many other oddities. The fellows are drying starfish of many colors, and some are now cleaning them to send home. Wait till they start to smell! I remember my old starfish-dissecting days. Now I can't even remember the names of the parts.

I would like to write more, but it is nearly dark. Alerts soon, no doubt. All the fellows are in good spirits, enjoying this area immensely. We are eating well, because we've foraged a lot for food. Everyone's well-equipped from looting the dump, as everyone here seems to do. The place is still pretty rugged. Finally got some stuff for that ringworm. Half of us have it. Otherwise we are in good condition and in good spirits. We keep too busy for anything else. The swimming is absolutely superb. Nearly dark now—must get some clothes on, take double dose of atabrine and a salt tablet.

May 12

Last six days have passed without any unusual occurrence. The reason I can't write more often is that we have been returning to camp near dark. There has been no Jap activity. We had three alerts during the last few days, but no attack. From reports, advances are going well everywhere, and apparently three more successful landings were made further up the New Guinea coast. We have received no official word.

Generally, the nights have been beautiful. The moon, bright and round, lights the dark clouds with silver and makes a silver streak through the water. During one of these nights while Pap and I were lying in the pup tent, looking at the beautiful night, and both sleepless because of our sinuses, he got unusually talkative about his personal life and told me a great deal. I have the honor to be the only confidant of this taciturn old sea dog. We talked, rather he did, and I listened for quite a few hours. He told me of his romance with a German girl prior to coming into the army. This ties into the letter he showed me on New Britain and the assumptions I drew from it. He has had many experiences. I have come to know the man and his philosophy and reactions well. We are good friends.

Today we helped unload an LST, mostly handling dynamite and ammo. We unload the dynamite by letting the truck dump it. The boxes go tumbling off, and one of these days one will fall too hard and set off about 500 pounds or more of explosives, and then they can send this diary home along with a few of my belongings. The stuff is heavy handling, and the sun beastly hot. To the horror of newcomers, we facilitate matters by dumping boxes of dynamite and ammo and then stacking them. It is necessary in order to get the LSTs out in time. Nobody feels comfortable watching the stuff slide off, cases breaking, and half-pound tins of explosives getting smashed in between crates. Meanwhile the shells and grenades (left by the Japs) have had the disconcerting habit of going off as the bulldozers maul the beach. Some fellows have been burned. One went off fairly close yesterday.

Herbeck has been evacuated by an Aussie boat, probably down the coast somewhere for adequate care. Before I forget, Milligan, Sigley, Wingfield, Demers and Walsh are in this tent with me.

I wish I could take an hour to describe what I saw today, but it is getting dark fast, and there is a blackout at night. So briefly in the remaining light: while we were unloading the ships about *200* Jap prisoners were brought in to be taken back to an internment camp. They were, for the most part, a pathetic-looking lot, ill-clothed, ill-fed, emaciated and very weak. They were so thin that the worst ones looked like walking skeletons. Some were carrying others. There was one Mutt and Jeff pair, with a tall, thin Jap with black-rimmed glasses helping another, who was exactly half his size, stagger along. They are naturally small. Compared to us, we are well-fed and generally taller. The Japs seemed of all ages, and some looked like mere boys. Many had bushy beards. There were several old men with scraggly white beards.

One prisoner spoke English, saying he learned it at the YMCA in Tokyo. When asked who would win the war, he replied, "Very difficult," and when he was informed that we intended to blast Tokyo and Tojo, he pointed to his head and said, "Bad headache." A bit later I saw a truckload of prisoners with some women mixed in, a strange sight. The women were either Jap, Chinese or Javanese, though they looked like Japs to me. They were very plain, with straight black hair, gaunt faces and bodies. There were two *babies* with them.

We returned to camp late this afternoon to find Capt. Drown, now wearing an Engineer's insignia, and a new officer who got here by mistake and the Chaplain. We heard that either the 1st or 2nd platoon was torpedoed while working a ship in the harbor. Our organization experienced some casualties (the number varies from three to eight), and four men were killed from another outfit. Check this.

May 14

We had a little excitement last night. The first alert was around 1:00 A.M.; I heard a Jap motor overhead. I can easily identify it. I hollered, "Everyone down on the beach, Jap plane overhead!" As in New Britain, we scattered down the beach.

We spotted the plane high up, and saw a light blinking on and off. We thought it must be friendly because of the light. The incident was soon over, but a few hours later we were out again. We didn't see anything, but from time to time one could hear the high whine of a Jap plane. We slept fitfully all night, jumping up now and again. Finally things quieted, but just before daybreak an alert was sounded, and soon afterwards we heard the chatter of machine guns. I dashed out of the tent but kept close to the ground. Red tracers of machine guns tore the sky into blue stripes. Even in New Britain I never saw such a concentration of machine-gun fire. A gun opened up across the bay. No bombs were dropped. In a little while the sun was up, and the hot day began.

We learned today that the planes overhead were recon planes, and that the blinking we saw was a camera taking aerial photos. We hear that a captain will be court-martialed for not turning searchlights on the planes.

We expect a heavy raid either tonight or soon. All along the beach men are digging in. In our area some of the fellows started to dig, but they all quit because the digging is too tough. The only ones digging now are Smith and Sam, the replacements. Perhaps they are the wisest. Everybody is a little jumpy tonight. Smith and Sam just quit digging. Church service just called. W. Harris said today, "Bombs and religion go well together."

May 17

During the past days I read *Dynamite Cargo*, a short adventure story, nonfiction, concerning a convoy to Russia, as well as *Sanctuary* by William Faulkner, a horrific tale of rape and murder by odd characters. It is unusually told. It skips, and in the skipping one learns what happened in the gaps of the previous parts. Sometimes confusing, but interesting. I also read *The Valor of Ignorance* by General Homer Lea, a philosophical study demonstrating that there is a cycle of rise and fall in the history of nations. He also points out that now, as 20 centuries ago, the races looked upon as wretched, barbarous, and inferior by so-called civilized countries eventually became their conquerers. Civilized countries, says Gen. Lea, become soft, indolent, vain, lose their military might and become an easy prey of a militant nation. He predicted the present war with Japan, gives its underlying reasons, and he discusses some of the technical matters of war unknown to civilians. He lays out in amazingly accurate detail the Jap campaign. He even went as far as predicting the capitulation of the States of Washington, Oregon and California. The one thing he overlooked, or rather didn't foresee, was the tremendous industrial superiority the U.S. has over the rest of the world, and this has been the factor that has saved our whole way of civilization, and the hides of our allies. It is amazing that he foresaw it all in 1909.

During the last three nights we had eight alerts which have cut large gaps out of our sleep. However, no bombing here, though we heard the airport 25 miles away gets periodically plastered. Three nights ago we planned to go up the beach a couple of hundred yards. I got tired of this, and the night before last I dug a slit trench for Pap and me. We got up for the first alert; the trench was intact. The second sounded some hours later, but when we went to the trench, we found only a smooth stretch of sand. The tide had come in. That was that. Last night I spent two of the four alerts in bed. I did get into a pair of pants and shoes each time. I have a distaste for being bombed without pants on. The official report stated that on the morning we had all the machine-gun fire, one plane was knocked down, back in the hills.

Today I saw 16 more Jap prisoners who had been captured two miles from here. Some were quite old. One was 50, a soldier for 17 years. They were in better condition than the others. The fellows got quite friendly with them and soon had some of the younger and, consequently, less stoic and more friendly Japs conversing and making signs as best they could. After being plied with cigarettes, a few started writing good-naturedly enough on papers and on Aussie, Jap and American money. One especially friendly fellow told Sanchez that he was 33, has an 80-year-old mother and no father. He showed a picture of his girl to Sanchez, who said she was quite pretty. When Sanchez asked him if he shot any American soldiers, the Jap, with emphatic gestures and noises, said no. That's very understandable with 200 American soldiers standing around.

We've been working rather hard these past few days under the QM. I got some pants today, but I own only one fatigue shirt which is rotting. No time to write letters, and have not received any in nearly three weeks. Getting dark. Oh yes, 28 planes were reported heading this way the other night. Sarmi, about 100 miles north, has been reported taken with little opposition. [*Totally false. It cost over 1,000 American casualties. Actually fighting in the area never ceased until the end of the war. See Ronald Spector's* Eagle against the Sun.] The taskforce that is supposed to hit

Wakde Island, some distance up the coast, pulled out tonight after lying in the bay for three days. It consists of a fleet of LSTs, destroyers, and perhaps light cruisers.

May 19

Yesterday I witnessed one of the most horribly magnificent sights, one of the most stupendous, gigantic fires, seldom equaled. On the beach millions of dollars of material now lies in black, smoking ruins. It all started yesterday afternoon at about 2:00. I was writing a letter home, during a lull in issuing rations, when an explosion cracked out. I knew it was a bomb and automatically hit the ground. I looked for the attacking plane, but there was none. The bomb, we learned, had gone off on account of a small trash fire built near one of the numerous Jap bombs lying around loose and half-buried. I had been expecting such an accident all along. I could see the smoke of the explosion because I was only 200 yards away.

In a few minutes Sgt. Stahl and York, who were returning from lunch, came up and told us that they had missed the explosion by 100 yards. Watts went to the site and came back with the report that he saw three casualties. One fellow had his abdomen blown open, another a series of shrapnel holes punched through his side, and another lay in a stretcher. After the initial excitement I went back to writing the letter.

About 20 minutes later a smaller explosion, probably a shell, went off. Then, in the next half-hour, there were a series of explosions. I counted 13. They were of various intensities, but none as strong as the first. Nevertheless, it was necessary to dive to the ground and pick myself up seven or eight times. Then, suddenly, many men came running by me with a look of panic, a look I have seen before. I glanced up for a second and saw a most horrifying spectacle. This was only the beginning.

A huge sheet of flame rose about 150 feet, yellow and wicked-looking and terrifying. For that instant it seemed to be heading right toward us, and I thought this was the end. As I automatically dived between two piles of rations, the loudest, most terrifying noise I'd ever heard seemed to tear and rend the very air. My sun helmet was blown off, and I could feel the concussion against my body. A few seconds later the shrapnel came raining down, and I could see and hear it landing against the boxes all around me. There was a large fire burning now, partially shielded by a palm tree grove and piles of equipment. After the shrapnel had stopped falling, I took to my feet (forgot all about the sun helmet which are so rare) and started travelling at a good clip, not running but stretching the old legs. Many men were running on all sides of me. I went about 300 yards further up the beach and there found Thomas reading *Topper Takes a Trip*. Most of us stopped there for about 10 minutes, discussing what had happened. It had been a rather close call for me.

Then, suddenly we looked up at a tower of black smoke several hundred feet high. We again hit the sand and then came the second big explosion, rocking us as had the first. The explosions were terrible, past description. It seemed as if the whole beach was going to be blown from the face of the earth. We retreated another 200 yards down the beach. I lost contact with the fellows in my outfit during the excitement and in the milling masses. I am glad to say that, after the first explosion, I didn't lose my head at all. I recall asking fellows I was walking with, "How far to Wewak?" which got a laugh. Now the explosions were coming steadily; several terrific ones shot flames and smoke hundreds of feet in the air. We were hitting the ground like clockwork. I continued along the beach and ran into King, Hellman, and Johnson.

The lower beach was a blazing inferno, flames shooting many feet in the air. The gasoline and ammunition dumps were going up like tinder boxes, rocking the island for miles around. Flames leaped out of the inferno like Roman candles, and flaming debris was blown a couple of hundred feet in the air, leaving white tails falling into the sea or starting new fires. Some explosions were so big that trucks and the sea itself jumped from the concussion. We felt it mainly in the ribs and stomach. High-ranking officers, colonels and generals, were dashing about in jeeps. Meanwhile, for miles down the beach a dark line of men streamed down to the other end of the beach-landing (a good two to three miles) and even into the hills. It reminded me of pictures of civilians retreating from bombed-out towns in Europe; the feeling, appearance and atmosphere were the same. Sullen files of men walked, sadly it seemed, away. We were about three-quarters of a mile from the inferno then.

Bigger and bigger explosions, if it can be believed, forced us back. We were close to a mile away now, and we could still feel the force of these blasts, when a file of men about a quarter-mile long came marching by us, armed with shovels of all sizes and shapes, and some men even with sticks, for the purpose of constructing a fire wall. Bulldozers worked closest to the inferno, about a quarter-mile away. They always seem to carry the brunt of work, and those drivers and machines deserve more credit back home than they get. They were ploughing back and forth across the beach, trying to build a firebreak. At each big explosion the drivers would jump off their machines and hit the sand behind them.

Gasoline went up by the hundreds of barrels. The flames got closer to about 3,000 pounds of dynamite. Great greasy balls of flame, 100 feet in circumference, shot into the air and blossomed out in wide flames.

The balls first looked like huge brains on fire and then like hideous blossoms, bursting for a few seconds' fiery bloom, then dissipating in black smoke.

Lt. Wenz came galloping along, headed toward the inferno "to help construct the fire wall." King, Hellman, Johnson and I followed. Then another series of huge explosions caused Johnson and me to use discretion as the better part of valor, and we stood our ground. There were hundreds of men with shovels up there now. We could see a wall of sand going up in the distance. We ran into Sanchez then who informed us that Sgt. Eriksen had boarded a LCT which took him and about 10 men, along with hundreds of others from other organizations, out into the bay away from the fire. This was the first evacuation. Sanchez also told us that some of the fellows were back about a quarter-mile in the weapons-carrier. We started toward that.

Violent explosions continued at our back. On the big ones we hit the dirt. Never have I seen such explosions—thousands of pounds of explosives going up at once, whole gas dumps, making horrible sights and terrifying noises. We ran into about 15 of our men, mostly of the 2nd section and some of the 3rd. I looked for Norm but he was not there. Morales was driving.

Millions of dollars of equipment were burning now, trucks and a radar unit which some lieutenant had tried to save, but no one would stop to help lift the tongue to hook it up to a truck. The ration dumps were ablaze where I had been working. The four tents there went up like matches. That was where my sun helmet was, and I'm sure glad I wasn't in it. Everything in the lower end was a hideous red. Black and white smoke streamed from the red mass. Palms were blown down, whole dumps went up, tearing the earth, smashing everything to atoms for yards around it. The ground shuddered under our feet.

We found the fellows near the QM dump at the other end of the beach. We waited there. Norm with five men had taken to the hills, as had Sgt. Stahl, Pappy, Langham, Thomas and a few others. The men building the fire wall were forced to retreat because of these recent explosions. All luck was against us. We were utterly cut off on the beach—but with plenty of room to retreat.

The wind fanned the fire toward us at a ferocious rate. This was our first windy night, and it had to be this night. The fire licked eagerly ahead; it seemed to pant to go forward, like a greyhound. Dumps continued to go up, flares shot hundreds of feet in every direction, incendiaries burned with white-hot flames. Even the green jungle was ablaze like a forest fire.

Sweaty and grimy, Fazekas was the first to come back from the wall. A few minutes later Hellman, King and Lt. Wenz came along, all looking the same. Hellman had a slight shrapnel wound in the knee. Nobody else from our gang had been hurt.

Gathered in the QM dump, we began stocking up on cans of food. Thousands and thousands of rations were burning. We also took some clothes and helmets. We didn't know how long we would be cut off from the company and to where we would have to retreat. Rainclouds were trying to form in the distance, but the stiff wind kept them at bay. We cursed that wind. It kept threatening to rain, but it never did. I got a new poncho, a fatigue shirt (at last), a compass and a helmet liner. I didn't take any food. We finished off a five-gallon can of water, and that was that.

It was dark now, and the night made the inferno even more hideous. It was moving up the beach uncomfortably fast. I learned from Hellman there were three fire walls constructed, each about eight feet high. The wind would not abate. The fire seemed to be gaining momentum as it destroyed everything before it in great explosions and tremendous heat and smoke.

Suddenly a stupendous tower of smoke shot up into the air, black and greasy. Debris was flying everywhere down the beach. At this moment I was sitting on the weapons-carrier. I jumped and hit the ground flat in the same motion. A second later the hugest blast yet went off. The sound is past description. It was a hundred times greater than the loudest sound I had ever heard. The concussion played havoc with our insides. After that, we finished loading up food and helmets, and we retreated down the beach. There we met Stahl's gang, Pappy, Thomas, Langham and a few others.

The whole working party was together now except for Eriksen's crew in the LCT, and Denison's who were somewhere up in the hills. Stahl's crew had been up the coast several miles. We were now under the direct orders of Lt. Wenz, and for a change we were getting some sort of leadership. After milling about for about an hour, we stuck together, trying to find out what was to be done. We finally settled down on the beach quite exhausted about one-and-a-quarter miles from the still-raging fire. Explosions went off continually during all these hours, some so large I still can't believe I actually saw them. I felt very tired. It was dark, and the display was fearful, yet in its terrible raging, magnificent too. It was fire with control over man. Flares regularly went off. Sometimes a whole section of beach would burst with a huge fountain of flame and sparks, like a giant fire-works display.

It was about 8:00 P.M. when the first alert came. At the time Pap and I were lying on the spread-out poncho. He had several cans of food. Near us were Lt. Wenz, Stahl and Langham. The alert was what we had feared.

The whole beach and sky were lit for miles around. All of Hollandia was a beautiful target, and the cut-off beach was chock-full of men, perfect strafing targets. I felt a little sickish for a moment. Because so much had happened, because death had been so close and was now so imminent, one reaches a point where one doesn't give a damn. I felt very tired. Lt. Wenz called all of us together (about 25 or 30 at most), told us to spread out but not to take off. Pap and I lay down, discussed the situation and watched the fire destroy dump after dump, blazing wickedly and triumphantly, fanned by that damnable wind.

At about 9:00 we saw the fire jump the first wall. At least half-a-mile of beach was now blazing red. Incessant explosions and stupendous, colorful and horrible displays blended together. Watching all that material gutted by the fire made me ill and sad enough so that one wanted to cry. I felt that way. I think nearly everyone felt it who lay on that beach last night with the weird light playing on their faces.

Because of the alert, men scattered all over the beach and into the jungle itself. Some men were digging holes with their hands. A lot of the night is a little hazy and mixed up in my memory. We spent much of the time cursing for rain, cursing the wind, and watching the destruction with horrible fascination. It was a great relief when the all-clear sounded a half-hour after the alert. The danger was bad enough without Japs added too. The fire jumped the second wall too, and it looked like the whole damn beach was going to be eventually reduced to one huge, glowing ember. Further back, where the fire had burned early in the afternoon, the blackened beach smoked with small spots of red here and there.

The fire continued to advance. We had been through at least 500 large explosions. There was talk of evacuating the beach. Out in the harbor, there was much blinking of signal lights. We continued to wait and watch. I turned my back to the fire, slumped to the ground, and hung on the verge of fitful sleep; explosions kept me from slipping over the brink. It got bad, and I remember Langham saying in a funny voice, "I hope the good Lord has some mercy for us." Nobody said anything. Jim is one of the strongest, bravest and clean-cut fellows in the outfit. Lt. Wenz kept trying to find out about transportation.

At about 10:00 a LCT landed, and several hundred troops boarded her, and she pulled off. I think I felt then during that slow evacuation a little like the men at Dunkirk must have felt. I remembered Carolyn once saying that the most impressive sight she ever saw were the faces of the soldiers who had been evacuated from Dunkirk. I don't think they had anything on us. The human face in silence is capable of mighty with the weird light playing on their faces felt it. Men were still scattering all over the beach and into the jungle itself on account of the alert, some men were digging holes with their hands. A lot of thought in a little happy and mixed upon my memory. We spent much of the time cursing for rain, cursing the wind and watching the destruction with horrible fascination. About a half hour later after the alert the all clear was sounded, and this was a great relief. The danger was bad enough without Japs added too. The fire seemed to have jumped the second wall too and it looked like the whole damn beach was going to be eventually reduced to one huge glowing ember. Further back where the fire had already passed early in the afternoon, it was smoking blackly with small spots afred here and there. As the fire continued to advance, and by then time we had been through at least 500 large explosions, there was talk of evacuating the beach. There was much blinking of signal lights out in the harbor. We continued to await and I turned my back to the fire, shrugged to the ground and hung on the verge of fitful sleep with the explosions keeping me from slipping over the brink. It was getting quite bad and I remember Langham saying in a funny voice "I hope the good Lord has some mercy for us." Nobody said anything. Jim is one of the strongest, bravest and clean cut fellows in the outfit. H.W. kept trying to find out about transportation at about ten o'ct landed and several hundred troops boarded her and she pulled off. I think I felt then during that slow evacuation a little like the men at Dunkirque must have felt like. I remember Cawly once saying that the most impressive thing she ever saw was the faces of the soldiers who had been evacuated from Dunkirque. I knew then they had anything on us. The human face in

Diary page, May 19, 1944, Hollandia, New Guinea.

expression. There weren't many men here whose bombarded nerves weren't drawn tight.

Then a bit of luck: the wind shifted against the fire, not strong, but against it. I think this, along with the third fire wall, saved the rest of the beach. The fire was still burning fiercely, but the explosions, though fierce and continuous, became less-and-less violent. The wind and third wall seemed to be holding. We avidly and hopefully watched the battle. We felt the heat and force of the big explosions over a mile away. It was still a holocaust. But the fire was held and even died down a little.

It was 10:30 when a huge LCM pulled into the beach and evacuated us. We waded to it and boarded in the dark. The discipline was good, no panic, everyone kept his head and followed orders. I was having a difficult time seeing what I was doing, because dust kept clouding my glasses up. I stumbled onto the ship, and we backed out into the bay and started off, taking a course around the fire and fairly far off. Luckily there was no large explosion during the 20-minute trip. As we passed the fire and looked straight into it, we could see the devastation even in the dark. It was horrible. The huge, 25 feet high Jap rice piles were glowing hills. Though the fire still burned fiercely in spots, it seemed stopped and was abating. All the equipment contained in a mile of beach, millions of dollars worth, was a black mess.

We landed a mile above where it had all started and walked another mile into camp. We literally straggled in, carrying boxes in that dark and through mud, up and down hills, and through jungle. Pap and I carried one together. I couldn't see, so I just followed in Pap's footsteps. (He later said I was pushing him ahead because he couldn't see either!) We finally reached camp and were well-received. The fellows in camp had been concerned about us. I fell into bed and just laid there. We had all been out of cigarettes (I had one left after having given most of them away while on the beach waiting to be evacuated). There was some chow left, beans and coffee. We all had a plate of beans, a swig of water, and a cigarette which helped to revive us.

So far nobody was hurt from our gang, though not all had returned. Some arrived earlier (Eriksen's gang), having been evacuated to Pim, several miles across the bay. Then they took the long ride to camp. I went back to the tent, lay down and could see the glow on the other side of Pancake Hill. It all seemed fantastic, as if it really hadn't happened. As we lay there, we could see the flashes, and then, a few seconds later, the explosions. There was a terrific one still left for us, a sort of final grumble of the dissipating fire. That was the last big one. Wingfield, Sanchez and Vierschilling in the next tent had rolled off their beds and hit the ground. There were more explosions, but they were minor.

In a few minutes an alert sounded. The alert used to sound like a loud explosion, but in comparison to what we had heard in the past 10 hours, it was as the striking of a match. Even a couple of 500-pound bombs would have been nothing. For hours thousands upon thousands of pounds of high explosives had been belting us, as if some giant were forging a huge horseshoe with heaven-shaking blows. There were five alerts last night. I didn't get up for any of them, though I woke and dressed for each one. It was a hard night. It was a nightmare. It was one of the most devastating, horrific, horrendous spectacles that I ever hope to see.

The morning dawned bright and hot. I didn't wake until about 8:30, and breakfast was at 10:00. The strain was mainly gone. Over the hill hung a white smoky haze. The fire is still smoldering this evening. Infrequently there is a small explosion. The worst is over. I doubt whether there is anything but black earth in that area. We had a company meeting with rollcall. Everyone OK. Norm and his crew had come back by way of Pim. Sweeney and Reynolds were the only ones who had disobeyed orders in the company. Lt. Wenz gave a good speech, praising our action, noting our faults, and he dressed down Sweeney and Reynolds who without orders had boarded a boat and returned by way of Pim.

Pap and I spent the rest of the day up the coast, swimming in the crystal-clear water, lying on the beach, discussing philosophy and books. We sunned ourselves on the white, hot sand, and then sat in the shade of fantastic rocks and palms. The water was actually hot, and the starfish and other odd sea-life studded the sea bottom. Pap found a magnificent shell. I built a sand castle (had the urge), while Pap read in the sun. I watched the weak waves slowly dissipate to nothingness, unlike the wild, raging sea of the previous night. We returned to camp late in the afternoon. It was damned good to be alive.

May 21

Night before last there were three alerts. Last night there were two unusual events. First, there were no alerts; nevertheless I slept fitfully from habit. Second, I received the first letters in three weeks, which were from Mom and Babs. This mail was six weeks old.

Yesterday afternoon we went down to the beach where the fire had been. We were supposed to work on LSTs. Everybody was jumpy because the fire still smoldered in many places, and every once in awhile there was a small, muffled explosion. The beach was marked by huge craters, larger than I've ever seen before. Ravished by fire, the area seemed melancholy. Among the gutted materials there was a lot of unexploded stuff around. We went down twice and both times were sent back, which didn't annoy us very much. Curiously, not all the rations had burned, though most have. We should be feeling the pinch soon. We sat in a large crater near the shore, in order to be below the surface of any blast. It would have been a dangerous job clearing the beach. Many ugly and ominous black Jap bombs were still around.

Last evening a company meeting was called. We learned that the rumors of a few days ago are indeed true. We have been attached to the 41st Division, and we are going on another blitz with them. Twenty-seven men will go in on D-day, the rest of the platoon to follow on D + 6. At present our strength is 68 men (Morales is a bag of bones in the hospital, and Herbeck evacuated). Men from two sections out of the three would be chosen. It was decided that the three section leaders, Stewart, Langham and Stahl, cut cards. Stahl lost, so our complete section goes D + 6. The winning section leaders chose 12 men each out of their sections to be led by platoon Sgt. Eriksen and 2nd Lt. Murphy, our new officer. All in all, a force of 27 men and an officer will help make the initial invasion.

I never saw Pappy so mad about anything as his not going. He was still complaining when he woke up. Very unlike him. Many of the fellows going are my good friends. The majority selected are from upper New York State, though not all. The two section leaders are Southern, leading a great majority of Northern boys, while Stahl is a Pennsylvania man leading mostly Southern fellows. Colby, Heffle, Flynn, Miranda, Denison, Monroe and DiPirro are going. I would like to be with the men from my home state, especially Norm. Perhaps fate has decided wisely, perhaps the cutting of those cards may decide lives. No joke, making an invasion. I am not impassioned one way or the other. If I had to go, of course I would have. Anyway, it's only a matter of six days.

Lt. Wenz, who heads the remainder of the platoon, gave those men leaving some words of caution in reference to firing rifles and emphasized especially the conservation of water. Even with two canteens, a man has only about a quart-and-a-half of water. He warned them not to be reckless and not to sleep in the hammocks but on the ground. He didn't want any throats cut. Anyone who would sleep elsewhere would be out of his head, in my opinion. Those hammocks are virtual traps. We now await further orders.

News last night reported that Wakde Island has been taken for all practical purposes, and the heavy bombing of southern Java. I would like to see Java. Though Java is a long jump from here, it is a strong possibility because the strategy seems to be to keep the present campaign rolling, and not to give the Japs time to consolidate their forces to make a stand anywhere. Hit them here, there, and everywhere—and fast.

May 24

The first 27 men are getting ready to pull out sometime today. We were briefed the other night by Blinky and learned that the landing will be made on an island far up the New Guinea coast and that we shall be the frontline troops in this theatre of war. Also, some new operations will be executed because it is possible that there is not enough water to bring the LSTs into shore. The rations will be lowered over the side by hand into alligators. That should be fun.

We've only had a few alerts lately, and I suppose that the Japs are trying to hit Wakde, now in our hands, as Wakde was their base of operations. We took it at the cost of 16 dead and 72 wounded. The Japs lost 34 men to our one. Two nights ago we had two alerts, night before only one, and last night none for the second time.

Learned yesterday that Lew Ayres is at the evacuation hospital as assistant to the chaplain, comforting the sick and wounded. Recall when Mom, Babs and I used to see his movies, usually week nights—and play bingo in the theatre and never win. Odd finding him here, half-way around the world. Morales got out of the hospital looking considerably thinner. A good little fellow.

While I was on KP yesterday, a very battered, old native appeared. In pidgin English he informed us that his hand had been blown off by a Jap bomb. One eye was awry too. We gave him a box full of candy and cigarettes. He was a very sad individual. Am on camp detail today. Probably rip down tents.

May 26

The 27 left on the 24th. I got a chance to say a hurried goodbye to Norm. They might have hit this morning, though I'm not sure yet. The fellows worked 36 straight hours loading the ship and then embarked. I talked to a fellow from the 36th Evacuation Hospital who informed me that the casualties on Wakde Island were much heavier than reported. That is possible. I believe little of what I hear and base opinion on what I can see.

These past few days I've been haunted with thoughts of death. I am not, I can honestly write, afraid of it. I get this odd feeling every once in awhile, and it has been particularly strong of late. The few times that I thought it was imminent I have just gritted my teeth and waited for

THE LORD'S PRAYER   THE TEN COMMANDMENTS

(Translated from the English into the tongue
 of the natives of New Guinea, Pidgin English)

PRAYER BILONG BIG MASTER

Fader ubilong mipella
Ustopalong Heaven,
All hearem talk about U.
Kingdom bilong U I kum
Along ground allsame along Heaven.
Give mipella Kai Kri alongday
Forgive wrong bilong mipella
Allsame mi forgive wrong alone nothapella.
Take along us not to wrongdo
Mipella folla U away from wrong
Upella bilong Kingdom cum
Same power. Same Glory
Allsame now. Allsame Time.   Amen.

COMMANDMENTS MIPELLA DO

1. Man I got onepella God, Ino got notha pella God
2. Man Ino try make nothapella God
3. Man Ino swear
4. Man I keep No. 1 day, No. 1 day bilong Big Master
5. Man I good along. Fader, good along mumma
6. Man Ino kill.
7. Man Ino take Mary bilong nothaman
8. Man Ino steal
9. Man Ino lie along nothapella. I talk tru all time
10. Man I see good something bilong notha man, Ino
      wantim alltime.

* *

Presented at Services, Sunday, 20 February 1944, by
Chaplain Walter D Owen, 495th Port Battalion.

* *

Examples of Pidgin English, distributed Feb. 20, 1944.

oblivion. I cannot help thinking of it sometimes, and of the effect my death would have on other people. For Mother and Gram it would be horrible. I think it would be a miracle if they recovered from the shock. It would be better if they were not so wrapped up in me. My death is not a remote possibility. Dad and Babs would weather it better. My possible death is the reason I estranged myself from Carolyn before I left. Those were biting words when she said one afternoon shortly before I left, "You are less a gentleman than ever before," during one of our tiffs. It hurt, but that was what I wanted. I've only received four letters from her in six months, and though they have been all I could hope for, the paucity of our correspondence annoys me. I have thought of her constantly.

Damn, there is so much I want to do yet, and I am just learning how to live. Tonight I told Thomas to see that my diaries got home, just in case. At least I want them to get home so that they can have that.

Mother, Dad, if you ever read this, feel not grief. It is my foremost wish that you be happy. Words are inadequate to express what I want to say, but I am only a single distinct life. It would grieve me to think that my death would haunt you for the rest of your lives. Bear the grief and forget. Life is too wonderful, too full, to be bound forever by a memory. This may sound cold, but you know I love you above anyone. Still it must be so. One life is an instant in the eternity of time.

Sometimes it seems to me a tragedy that we are animals capable of sentimentality. Nevertheless, the living must go on living, and the dead remain a soft memory, not a life-long grief. So it must be. I pray that should I die, which I shall do my best to prevent, you will remain firm. It is the way I wish it, and I ask it of you as a favor to me. It will be said that I died for my country, honorable in the eyes of the world. I do not always know if this war is necessary, or where the blame lies, but I believe in the principles for which men are being killed all around me. Perhaps my greatest satisfaction will be that the older people and youngsters at home will be spared the horror and terror of war on our own soil. I regret that my position does not draw upon my whole capacity.

May 29

The all-clear to a short alert just sounded. It was the third in the last four nights. The night before last, one plane came over, very high. We could see the 20 millimeters bursting in air, but they were so far away that we could not even hear the reports. Two searchlights poked the sky but appeared dim from where we were. Tonight at the company meeting Lt. Wenz informed us that we shall probably not go in D + 6. This news was not very welcome to Pap and Stahl. As for me, I am indifferent about when we get there. The news last night reported a landing at Biak in the Shouten Islands, establishing a two-mile beachhead. Tonight we heard of a five-mile advance, to one mile from the first of three airstrips. If those strips have not been neutralized by air and naval bombing and shelling, the fellows up there are probably catching hell.

Our advance in Italy is beginning to move. At the last report our troops were 20 miles south of Rome. We have been waiting anxiously day after day for news of the invasion, which must come off very soon. The Russians have not moved for 11 days. They are probably content to hold their present position, having driven the Germans out of Russia and penetrated into Poland and Romania. They are sitting back, and it is hard to blame them, waiting for the Allies to take over the brunt of the heavy fighting. Probably there is an agreement to strike again when the Allies attempt the invasion. By June 15th there should be some definite news.

June 1

Night before last I was sick. I was feeling bad, but not seriously, for several days. Appetite was falling off. All that night I had an attack of chills, and later the malady developed into the GIs. I am all right now, but I spent a miserable night. At first I thought it might be the start of a malaria attack, atabrine keeping it in check, or a reaction to the five atabrine tablets we take at one time now, twice a week. [*I was correct in the assumption of malaria, a malady I had for the remaining time overseas, and for some years later as a civilian.*]

We are most interested in the news about Biak in the Shoutens, because that is our destination. The campaign has gone as follows. The first day, we established a two-mile beachhead. Next day we captured another five miles, but none of the three airstrips though the troops came within a mile of one. The third day's fighting was very stiff, and there has been little advance. As of tonight no airstrips are as yet taken. The Japs are strongly entrenched on Biak. There is no retreat off the small island; they are forced to fight until annihilated. The Japs also have tanks there, the first ones they've used in the South West Pacific. Eight have been destroyed and three damaged. Later we got the private information that our troops took up defensive positions. To substantiate that, we are pushed back from D + 6 to D + 9. This delay necessitated our move here because the seabees were promised the other area by D + 6 when we expected to move. Tonight the report was that strong Jap counterattacks had been repulsed, and in one sector Jap resistance has collapsed.

Tonight our bulk-loaded equipment went aboard the LST, and we shall spend all tomorrow, day and night, loading the LST and sleeping on the beach when we can. There are dogs stationed down on the beach. Pap and I passed them as we went for a swim tonight. Big breeds, mostly police or half-police. I've heard and read a lot about their training. They have been extremely effective on sentry duty and in routing out Japs. (These mosquitoes have been hell these past few days.)

I have a month-old beard now.

5

Biak Island

———————— June 7–Dec. 17, 1944 ————————

June 7

So much has happened in the past six days that it will be difficult to get it all down. Chronological order will be best I guess: June 2nd, 3rd and 4th we spent travelling aboard the LST. We spent the night sleeping on the beach the day before we boarded. Once aboard we again had to bed down topside. I found a pretty good place under a truck and spent most of the trip looking into its clay-encrusted bowels. The clay kept drying and falling down, getting in my hair and making me extremely dirty. Sanchez was alongside me, and Pap and Stahl had hammocks slung nearby.

As we neared Biak Island, we heard the sound of heavy guns, and soon we saw the guns themselves. We pulled into the jetties the Japs had built here. They jutted from the coast of the island like spread fingers. The rest of the day we worked hard discharging the cargo. I rolled oil and gas drums over coral and sand, not an easy job. While I worked I saw several hundred natives evacuated by small landing craft: women bare to the waist, children carried high up on the back and held there by a band across the women's foreheads, and young men carrying the old, sick, and wounded. All who could carried loads of equipment, even the smallest children carrying incredible loads for their size. About 20 young-ish Javanese also were evacuated, most of them with bandaged hands and feet, and in jungle-green uniforms with high and wide-brimmed hats. We later learned from one of them that they had been tortured by the Japs. We had a few alerts through the afternoon. They have been con-tinual, day and night, since our arrival. The LSTs pulled out at the 5:00 P.M. deadline, some with a small portion of the cargo unloaded, including our organization's gear.

We marched into "camp" and found the most unreceptive terrain imaginable. Nothing but coral, and that as sharp as knives. I was anxious to see all my friends. The first one I saw was Ron with a hand bandaged, cut by coral. Quite a few fellows were cut. They were living in make-shift huts and in a few tents. Everyone was dug in, and tough going it is to dig through pure rock. Norm's tent floor is about three feet below the surface. Eriksen is living in a cave; there are many about. Nobody was seriously hurt. Howe got a scratch on the hand by a piece of flak.

Then we got the news of how things are going. The fighting has been very difficult. The Japs are dug in; they have had two years to do so. I had testimony to these facts by the casualties on stretchers I helped carry aboard for evacuation. These were strong young fellows, mostly from the infantry, and with horrible wounds. Each one had a tight grimace on his face.

The fellows have been subject to innumerable raids and bombings. And they have been under the constant noise of our own batteries, as we have been for the past days since our landing. They said that the gunners have knocked down about 25 planes so far, and even though the anti-aircraft company is a new outfit, it has accounted well for itself. They have fine equipment here. The night before we landed the fellows said they saw ships going between this island and the one directly across. Having been warned of the Jap navy in the vicinity, they were scared. A naval shelling is much more effective than bombing. They discovered during the night that all troops had evacuated the beach and had retreated back to a ridge at our rear. The next morning our men found themselves the only troops on the beach. Fortunately, nothing happened. The report later came through that our navy had encountered theirs, and we accounted for 18 ships, including several destroyers.

[*Unknown to us at the time, the Japanese made two attempts during late May and early June to reinforce Biak with additional troops. On both occasions their troopships and accompanying warships were spotted by our planes, and the Japanese were turned back with losses. The loss of Biak posed a serious threat to the Japanese, located as it was on the flank of the Japanese troops and navy in the Central Pacific. Consequently, they made a third attempt, as Spector tells us in* Eagle against the Sun, *and "assembled an overwhelming force, including the giant battleships* Musashi *and* Yamato," *but fortunately for us this powerful armada was halted when the Japanese learned of the American advance on the Mariana Islands north of us in the Central Pacific.*

Had this third Japanese attempt to reinforce Biak succeeded, Spector observes, "It would have probably inflicted a serious defeat on the inferior Allied naval forces, delivered a destructive bombardment of American positions on Biak, and gotten their much-needed reinforcements ashore. Such a Japanese success might have set back the whole American time- table for the Pacific War" (p. 293). On a smaller scale, the attack would have obliterated a substantial portion of the 244th Port Battalion, given our vulnerable position on the shore.]

One of the tragedies that happened here involved one of our own bombers (B-25). It came over and dropped some maps and photos. They said the insignia was as plain as day, but some fool down the beach apparently mistook the plane for a Jap aircraft and opened up. This trig- gered the other guns, and he was shot down. All seven of the crew per- ished! Also, an Aussie destroyer that shelled the Japs on D-day fell short in its range, killing 21 of our troops.

The problem facing Pap and me was to find some sort of shelter for the night. After looking around a bit, we went down a small hill in the vicinity of the general camp area and found a foxhole about two feet deep, which is a considerable depth in this coral. It was supported and boxed by heavy logs. Luckily, we found that we could sling our hammocks right in the hole. We also erected a shelter out of shelter-halves and ponchos. During the early part of the evening we had several more alerts. I cut my right knee when I slipped on a piece of coral going after my helmet in great haste. We finished our work just after dark, and we were fairly comfortable.

About this shelling: we are located among quite a few batteries of heavy artillery, and intermittently for three days and nights they have been laying down terrific barrages. They are right in our backyard, and one can feel the concussion of the salvos. The shells roar overhead. They sound like fast-passing freight trains. Then 20 to 40 seconds later, depending upon the range, one can hear the report of their landing. The frontlines are only six or seven miles from here. The range of these monsters is about eight miles. And so, day and night we have been under this fire, but we are grateful that we are not on the receiving end. These guns play hell with the nerves, especially with the high-strung fellows. For the most part we have become accustomed to the artillery fire, but sometimes, after a silence, when you've nearly forgotten about the guns, the sudden roar makes you jump. This morning, while Pap and I lay in bed cracking jokes, the barrage was terrific.

This beachhead bristles with all kinds of guns. Ninety millimeters, 30- and 50-caliber machine guns. One only has to walk a short distance along the beach road to see guns set up and dug in everywhere. We didn't get much sleep the night of the 5th. We were subject to about 10 alerts, and we could hear formations of enemy planes whining overhead during the night. They bombed, though not in the immediate vicinity. When they did come within range of the guns here, all hell broke loose. This happened quite a few times, and Pap and I spent most of the night bobbing up and down in our foxhole. Alongside the 90 millimeter, the 50-cals sound like whispers. The earth trembles when those 90s start to pound, and they make a terrific yellow flash. They give me a peculiar feeling, especially when they go off down the island, and you see them before you hear them because of the distance. The sudden yellow flares, the fiery streaks, look like silent shrieks, as if the color yellow were writhing in pain.

At about 1:30 A.M. the Japs went home, and we got some sleep during the remainder of the night. I can't get comfortable in a hammock and always awake with a crick in the back. The next morning we decided to renovate our home and make it more livable. We spent the morning rebuilding, Pap doing most of the engineering because I am poor at such things. We got it arranged so that I have a cot elevated above the hole and Pap has his hammock (he prefers the damn thing) slung right in the hole. It gives him more protection in case of a surprise bombing. We cleaned the coral rock bottom out, laid plywood and a Jap mat on the bottom, and constructed a good roof. It has been raining all day today, and we have been dry as a bone. It is so arranged that everything is within easy reach and *neat.* We are both passionate about neatness, and that is one of the reasons we choose to be together so often, besides the good company. We can use my bed for an excellent desk, with a supporting beam for a seat. The hill at our rear gives us good protection from that quarter. We are located in a hollow overlooking the rubble and shell holes of a war-torn hill. We also have a tidewater spring, and when the tide is in we have adequate water for washing. Pretty good so far.

In the afternoon we took a short walk. There is a lot of Jap stuff around (I've found the Jap officers' cigarettes pretty good). We found a burned and bullet-pierced sedan that the Jap officers probably used. The Japs are passionate about knives, bayonets, sabers and duelling equipment and do a lot of practicing of hand-to-hand combat. We came across wooden guns cut to the length of a gun and bayonet. The bayonets had rubber points for bayonet practice.

We now have access to a fresh water pump, so we all got good and refreshing baths. It was good to get that red clay off and dirt out of my hair, and get into fresh suntans. It was the first time I took my clothes off since we landed; we've been wearing them all night, too. While we bathed the report came through by means of an ack-ack telephone that THE ALLIES HAVE INVADED FRANCE!!! At long last, the second front has opened. So far, from the report, it has been successful; they are now 10 miles in along a 17-mile front. Our paratroops are playing hell behind their lines. Meanwhile, Rome is taken, and the Italian campaign is turning into a rout for the Germans! Our morale is up about 500%.

Last night was hell again, although we are all getting used to being under fire and take it pretty serenely. The alerts and raids continued all night. Early this morning a plane came in and dropped three bombs. I knew they were bombs immediately in spite of the racket. They landed about 300 yards away and injured six men. The Japs are undoubtedly endeavoring to knock out the big, stubby, powerful artillery guns which are firing as I write.

At this very moment, not far from here, we are launching a big-scale offensive on Biak Island. This morning tanks were loaded here and taken up the island by LST. The artillery has been laying down a barrage all day. Half-an-hour ago I saw eight of our bombers head toward the Jap lines, and we heard the "crump crump" of heavy bombs landing. (Boy, that was a huge blast. For a moment we thought it was return fire. Must have been three of ours at once. Gad, what a barrage. The earth is trembling.) For the past half-hour we have heard small arms and machine-gun fire, and the "crump, crump, crump" of bombs and shells. A big offensive is on, trying to take the airport. The fighting is heavy and all hell is loose. From all appearances, this looks like it's going to be a lengthy and costly campaign. The Japs are so well-established that they even have a railway on the other side of the island. "Boom, Boom"—terrific pounding now with 105s and 155s blasting away. At this moment Biak Island is a roaring hell!

June 9

In the past few days we have been subject to about 10 raids and alerts. The night before last we went through nearly the complete night without an alert. Toward morning I was jarred out of a half-sleep by the unmistakable explosion of a bomb. A single plane had sneaked in and aimed for one of the LCTs out in the bay. No damage. Last night no bombs were dropped in this vicinity, but there were planes overhead. We heard and saw them dive a few times, but our heavily concentrated fire-power drove them off. I fell asleep toward early morning and slept to about 9:00 A.M. We have only camp details today. Yesterday afternoon we worked hard loading ammo on trucks that were taking it right up to the frontline. Sleep has been at a minimum. Only the tension and excitement keep us from feeling the lack of it. I haven't had my clothes completely off for more than 10 minutes at a time in the past week.

The fighting here is extremely difficult. Though our ground troops have taken one airstrip, it cannot be used because of the heavy fighting for civilities I had about a dozen letters awaiting me in camp. I read from home, Dick, Shirley, Charlotte, Dale, Edith. Perhaps some more today. Couldn't get them finished before dark & so was forced to wait till the moon came up to read Dick's and Edith's. The moon is bright at nights, bright enough to read by. Also got this blister rash attended to by "Dr. Eaton" and the gash of my knee.

Last night was hell again though we are all getting used to being under fire and take it pretty serenely. The alerts & raids continued all night. Early this morning a plane came in and dropped three bombs. Knew they were bombs immediately & quite the racket. They landed fairly close. This morning we found they had landed about 300 yds away and injured six men. They are undoubtedly endeavoring to knock out the big, stubby, powerful artillery guns which are firing as I write this.

At this very moment a big scale offensive is being launched on Biak Island not far from here. This morning tanks were taken from this shore & taken up the island by L.S.T. The artillery has been laying down a barrage all day. Half an hour ago 8 of our bombers headed toward the jap lines & we could hear the "crump crump" of heavy bombs landing. (Boy, that was a huge blast. For a moment we thought it was return fire. Must have been 3 of our own. Sounded like a barrage. The earth is trembling.) For the half hour past we can hear machine gun fire, small arms, & the "crump, crump, crump" of bombs & shells. A big offensive is on trying to take the airport. The fighting is extremely heavy and all hell is loose over there. From all appearances this campaign looks like its going to be lengthy & costly. The japs are so well established they even have a railway on the other side of the island. Boom, Boom – Gunfire sounding now with 105's & 155's blasting away. Biak Island at this moment is a roaring hell.

June 9, 1944.

In the past few days we have been subject to about 10 raids and alerts. The night before last we went thru nearly the complete night without alert. Toward

Diary page, June 7, 1944, Biak Island.

concentrated around it. We have heavy casualties. The Japs have an underground network of caves from which they hold off an attack. They also can pop up behind our troops and cut them off, which they have succeeded in doing a few times. In recent advances we have used everything to batter the Japs. It is unusually quiet today so far, but the past few days we've mounted a constant artillery barrage, as well as bombings by Liberators and by the first Fortresses I've seen in action. On the way back from their bombing run, they dropped crates of shoes to us. Tanks, too, have been thrown into the fray.

There is a need for blood donors. Norm, Pap and I volunteered. This morning while we were chopping a huge tree into sections, a plane circled overhead. Flynn kept saying it didn't look right to him, and I didn't recognize it as one of ours. After the plane leisurely circled overhead a few times, the beach guns suddenly opened up. I hit the foxhole. The plane was in plain sight and a perfect target, but these gunners didn't live up to their reputation. They clean missed him. One could see the shells bursting around him.

There was a fighter plane expected over here to drop maps, and it may possibly have been him. They ought to get their signals straightened out before we start shooting down some more of our own planes. The B-25 that I saw mistakenly shot down over the ridge the other day had its crew saved. I am now quite cool and have no feeling of apprehension when enemy planes are overhead. I realize now how much training and hardening it takes to turn out true soldiers. I don't profess to be one, but troops must experience the actual apprehensions, surprises and vicissitudes of action before they can be counted upon to stand firm under actual fire.

June 11

These Jap cigarettes, one of which I am smoking, I find much to my taste. Not too strong and a different flavor.

On the late afternoon of June 9, Sgt. Stahl informed Pap and me to be ready to leave in three minutes with canteen, helmet, rifle, ammunition. We drew the conclusion that the Japs were making a counterattack, and more men were needed to hold a sector. Sans supper, we piled into the truck and were transported down to the end of the beach. There we learned that we were to help move an artillery outfit from one front to another, where the fighting is heavier. There was a convoy of about 15 trucks. Pap, Stahl (who seemed anxious for us to be with him), and I boarded the last truck with some others, and we set off. We rode for over two hours, and it was positively one of the roughest rides I've ever experienced. An extremely rutty road of sharp dips and climbs twisted through rough jungle nearly all the way. We were jarred until our bodies ached. One couldn't sit, one couldn't stand—one just bounced. Along the way abandoned Jap material littered the road: trucks, drums, food, etc. One could follow the infantry's advances by the slit-trenches and foxholes where they bivouacked.

We drove about 20 miles, which brought us within half-a-mile of the frontline and to the artillery outfit we were to evacuate. Our truck was driven into the brush and among trees for camouflage. It was nearly dark. We were split into four or five men to a truck. Pap, Norm, Heffle, Langham and I were together. I found sleeping on the truck floor difficult and uncomfortable. I lightly dozed for several hours. When awake I listened to the night noises of the jungle. There was plenty of artillery and small-arms fire during the night. At least, I thought, for one night we would not be subject to air raids. It didn't occur to me to be jumpy even though we were so close to the frontlines.

At 11:30 I suddenly awoke, and without a second's thought I instinctively dove under the truck. I was not fully awake and do not remember the movement. Nevertheless, Heffle and Denison were beside me, and overhead we heard a plane. All the guns in the vicinity were fired. A few seconds after we had hit the ground, we heard nearby three not-loud-nor-big explosions. The plane had dropped some antipersonnel bombs (fragmentation bombs) and they landed quite close to some of the other fellows. Flak was heavy too, but no one was hurt except Stahl who cut his hand seeking a foxhole. It was all over in a few minutes, and then Jim Langham told us what happened. He had been awake and watched the plane fly overhead and the gun bursts. Then he saw Heffle, Denison and me suddenly rise and jump from the truck. Jim said it was one of the oddest things he ever saw, the way the three of us simultaneously rose from sleep and hit the ground. Seeing this, he too hit the ground. Then Pap woke up, and finding the truck empty, he too followed. It was ironic that we had to go 20 miles into the jungle to get bombed.

We settled back down, sleeping in our helmets. They were slightly more comfortable than the floor of the truck. The rest of the night I was miserable. I could not sleep nor lie in any position more than a few minutes. Everyone slept fitfully except Pap. It turned cold, adding to our discomfort. I buttoned my shirt over my hands and head, and that helped a little. The floor of the truck, especially its metal parts, was like ice. I shivered and the night dragged on; it seemed interminable. I've seldom lived through a longer night. At about 3:00 A.M. it started to rain. Everyone got up and smoked a cigarette, though we weren't supposed to. We talked and cracked jokes for a half-hour, and then the light rain stopped. I had heard yelling in front of us during the night, but I didn't give it much thought. We had been instructed to keep our rifles unloaded. After we finished smoking and laughing, we lay down again. The other fellows seemed to drop off, but I couldn't. At about 5:00 A.M., when there was a very faint light in the east, I fell asleep on my back, unprecedented for me, and slept for two hours from sheer exhaustion. At about 7:30 after a breakfast of half-a-can of cheese, eight lumps of sugar, three pieces of candy, a few biscuits and a couple of swallows of water, we set to work. I was chilled and glad when the air began to warm.

We loaded the truck with 25-mm shells in bundles of three, 150 bundles (450 rounds) in about a half-hour. At about 8:30 we started in convoy to move out with the artillery troops and all their equipment aboard. The ride back was tedious, uncomfortable and hot. We were perched on top of the ammo; the trucks could not make more than four or five miles an hour.

We got back to camp about 3:00 P.M. I hadn't eaten much in the past 24 hours and was starved. There wasn't much to eat, just cold canned tomatoes, bread and peanut butter, and water. However, supper was good, and I ate hearty then. Spent the afternoon getting washed and cleaning my rifle. I was dead tired by evening and fervently hoped that Tojo would let up for one night so that I could sleep. Haven't had three hours straight sleep in over a week. At the company meeting Wenz informed us that all dogs were to be destroyed on sight, because it was suspected that the Japs were using them to find our installations. I look forward to the meetings as the only humor of the day. Lt. W. sometimes goes on and on about nothing. He repeats a single fact about four different times and ways, and in the end says little. Lt. Murphy is well-liked and has a great sense of humor. He bunks with Jim [*Langham*] and Stewart, does his share of the work, and acts like a kid and like one of the men. I don't believe the two lieutenants agree with each other's methods. Murph conducts a gossip hour every night, cracking jokes about the fellows, both dirty and clean. It's a bright spot in the day, and a few laughs quiet jangled and tense nerves.

The 105-mm's have moved forward as our forces have advanced. The Japs tried to reinforce their troops by means of six destroyers and lost four in the attempt. That yelling I heard the night before at the front proved to be infiltration by nine Japs and an officer. The nine were killed, but the officer managed to carve up a few of our men with his saber before one of our fellows choked him to death. The Jap was clever though, a good example of fast thinking. While the soldier was choking him, a friend rushed up and, in the dark, couldn't distinguish friend from foe. He yelled to his buddy, asking if he was on top or bottom. The soldier answered, "I'm on top," and the Jap, thinking fast, yelled, "I'm on the bottom." It was a chance, but he lost his life anyway.

Although I was dead tired, sleep was difficult during the early part of the evening. Two 105-mm firing close by kept me awake for a few hours. They go off with a tremendous roar and flash and concussion. Not a tonic for sleep. The shells land so far away that most of the time you can't hear the report of the shell exploding. A few times I was almost asleep when the guns fired, and I jumped six inches. Had Pap laughing at me. They soon let up, and I dropped off. Although I awoke several times during the night, I had the best sleep in days. And the Japs didn't come over last night; there wasn't even an alert for the first night since we arrived here.

June 13

For the past few nights we've experienced heavy raids and heavy casualties. Squadrons of bombers have plastered this area, but so far our outfit is fortunate. Bombs have fallen on each side of our camp. There have been six alerts and three raids. A number of men were killed because they failed to get in their foxholes at the alert, taking a chance that the planes would not come over. Result: death. The bakery and an air corps outfit received direct hits. Last night some medics got it.

There was plenty of action on the 12th when the LSTs arrived. Four planes came in during the morning, bombing the little offshore island and trying to bomb a PT boat. The PT zig-zagged like a water bug, with bursts all around. The warning sounded, and I headed for the beach from where I could see the burning wrecks of two Jap planes shot down by our fighters, the first that we've seen up here. Another was shot down by ground fire. However, we paid heavily. The Japs hit one of our destroyers, and to its bad fortune the explosion set off the torpedos, resulting in 53 casualties. The destroyer had to be scuttled.

We have been working hard of late. Today was one of the hottest days that I've experienced. The sun felt like it was burning holes through my body while we loaded LCMs with supplies. Heavy and difficult fighting continues here. I've helped carry the wounded onto an LST. There were at least 150 casualties on this ship alone, casualties from bombing, snipers and mortar fire. They were very glad to be leaving. Because of the frequent Jap strafing along with the bombing, Pap and I (mostly Pap since he doesn't trust me in construction jobs—"Might cave the sides in") are deepening our foxhole.

The atabrine is beginning to back up on me. I find that taking 10 a week is difficult. All I could manage to get down were three this evening. Even these made me slightly ill. Wish that mail would come in.

June 17

Company meeting going on now, but I'm avoiding it because I wanted to write this evening. Quite a lot has happened. We've had about six more alerts and one raid. Lately, alerts and raids have been light because of the rain and because the moon is in its last quarter.

Yesterday the fellows went up to the front with ammo trucks into an area taken the day before. Unfortunately I was on KP. It was an easy KP because we did not need to prepare lunch. The fellows carried rations. But, that didn't make KP one whit less distasteful. The fellows came back with all kinds of souvenirs. Pap found a wristwatch in a pack, Dutch invasion money and yen. He's been waiting for months for a watch from his mother, and then last night he finally received it. Two in one day. He also brought back a good stack of Jap records which we listened to with Lt. Wenz last night. We sat around under the stars, smoking, listening to *music,* and playing the records we liked. At that moment I liked the comradeship of the army. It felt good. The Jap music was extremely interesting, sounding like marches or light opera. I enjoyed the choruses and the solo singing. There was one soprano with a voice reminding one of a small bird, very sweet. Funny how your enemies' music will make you dislike them a little less. Some of the records were typically Japanese and thus not to our taste, especially those off-key string instruments.

While at the front the fellows saw some dead Japs. There was one, Pap told me, that had been squashed flat as a pancake by trucks running over him. There is also a huge store of Jap mortar ammo which we are using jointly. The Japs come down at night and get it, and we take from it during the day. The shells fit one of our mortar guns. Strange things occur in war.

We spent the day clearing out our new area. It was pure jungle, but we got it cleared off pretty well. It overlooks the cemetery, and while we worked we could see burial details bring in American soldiers, some from the hospital and others straight from the lines. It's a sad sight, seeing the bodies wrapped in blankets placed in sandy pits. A grave is marked by a simple white cross or Star of David with a dog tag nailed on. It would do selfish and uncaring people good to see that sight. Our casualties have been fairly heavy here. There aren't even enough crosses, and some graves are marked by just a piece of wood. A hell of a place to die, Biak Island.

The bugs in the new area are hellish. Millions of ants. While we worked with axes and machetes we were covered with them. Ron and I had fun picking them off each other, the red variety that like to bite. The terrain is coral and stubble, not very inviting. The only good feature is that the camp is on a hill overlooking the sea. Looks like we're going to have a colored outfit next door, the 296th Port Company. The fellows don't go for that too well.

The going on Biak has been slow and difficult. I believe an infantry regiment (34th?) is coming up tomorrow on the LSTs. More mail I hope, too. The war progresses so well on both sides of the world that we are swept by a wave of optimism. Nevertheless, I have a five-pound bet with Norm that we will not be home this time next year. I hope I lose, though I don't think I will. We are generally optimistic because: 1. The offensive in Europe, 2. We landed in the Marianas, 3. Japan has been bombed by the new B-29. There is no doubt of the eventual outcome. Wonder whether we shall all be here when the wars end. What a day for the world!! How many more shallow graves and broken hearts, though!

June 20

Today two cargo ships came in and are docked nearly alongside the shore. Should be easy to build docks here with deep water close to shore. We are going to work them starting tomorrow. We work from 7:00 A.M. to 1:00 P.M. The only other port outfits here are the colored 296th and the 503rd. We are going to try and work our watches with 48 men. If they run full blast, we shall have our hands full.

No raids during the last few nights, and only two alerts. Beginning to get more sleep. However, the fighting on Biak continues to be tough, and our cemetery grows.

Today we had our first casualty in this platoon from enemy rifle fire. It came about this way. Having the day off, most of the fellows (including Pap) went toward the front in search of souvenirs. They ran into plenty of trouble. Catching a ride on a truck convoy, they started through Jap-held territory. Harris, Rice and Wingfield were two trucks behind the one that received a direct mortar shell. It blew up, killing four men. Harris said it was horrible. One man was sent hurtling through the air.

Rouse, Norvell, Herndon and one other man were snooping about in Jap territory. Suddenly a Jap pillbox opened up, and Rouse said his cap was blown off. Inspection revealed a scalp wound. The men scattered and hit the ground. Rouse was behind a small rock, bullets spattering all around him. Herndon was also shot at. A Jap threw a grenade which landed six feet behind Norvell. At this, they all turned to run from it, and the Japs sent a bullet through Rouse. Norvell jumped head first off a cliff and gashed his skull. Herndon grabbed a tree and slid down, and the other fellow got down somehow. Rouse continued on despite his wounds and reached an infantry group. He told them three men were pinned down by the Japs. The infantry met our boys while going up to get them out of the mess.

Repercussions came tonight at the company meeting when Lt. Wenz in his emphatic manner declared all souvenir hunting out. I do not claim to be psychic, but today I felt that someone was going to get hurt snooping at the front. I feel you either go there for a purpose or you don't go. To ask for trouble is foolish, if you want to get back. They all narrowly escaped with their lives, especially Rouse. He will be saved penalty. Seems the reason he gave for being there was that he went to look for a wallet that he thought he lost there the other day on the ammo detail. I doubt whether any charges will be pressed, and he will probably end up with the Purple Heart. It was a lesson that the men had to learn, sooner or later.

June 22

Our rapid advances in both wars have caused optimistic conjecture about a near-future victory. In France we are doing well. Cherbourg is close to falling, and many Germans are trapped. In Italy our forces race northward in pursuit of the German army, and Russia is applying pressure from the East. I don't see Germany holding out longer than the end of this year. In our own war, things are progressing satisfactorily. In the Marianas we are advancing, and in a recent sea/air battle 300 Nip planes were destroyed, a good slice out of their air force. At present a great sea battle is being waged, the outcome of which will decide many future issues. [*This was the Battle of the Philippine Sea, on June 19 and 20, during which a number of Japanese ships were damaged or destroyed, but the Japanese fleet escaped when Admiral Spruance decided that his Task Force 58 should turn back toward recently invaded Saipan rather than sailing west. However, the battle destroyed just about the last of Japan's carrier-based planes and pilots. Indeed the Japanese lost hundreds of planes, and Admiral Ozawa's fleet lost several carriers.*]

On Biak, in a sudden push, all three airstrips were taken, and the Japs suffered heavy casualties. Our tanks are very effective. There has not been even an alert in our sector since my last entry. We have many fighters here now; silver P-38s whistle overhead and look awfully good to us. Today we saw 10 cargo planes come in, a sure sign of our air superiority. The batteries of cannon close by thunder now and again, the shells roaring menacingly overhead. Probably we are trying to destroy Jap pillboxes. Big guns seem impersonal because they are so far behind the lines.

July 1

During the past week and a half, we've had about 15 more alerts and three actual raids. On one raid we were caught out on the *Tamarakan*, a rather uncomfortable place to be. We finished the ship day before yesterday, after working our hearts out and earning a good reputation here. For 50 men we did more than our share. I've also been caught out in raids a few times at the movies that they have here now. I saw a movie at the hospital where Rouse is. He looked well, and he showed me his bullet wounds. The wound where the bullet entered his back is nearly healed. It entered to the left of the backbone under the scapula and left his body below the armpit. That wound was still gaping and ugly. His head wound was slight, just breaking the skin on top of the skull. He is to be evacuated. Not all of our men have been well. Stewart and Redwine are hospitalized with high fevers, and now Torre and DiPirro. There are also plenty of rashes and infections among us. The other day we went for tetanus shots. No after-effects.

July 6

Been working fairly hard on the ship. One alert last night. The moon was blazing white, the stars like diamonds. Lt. Wenz continues to make himself ridiculous by his dwelling on small points and going into long harangues, using a vocabulary that ¾ths of the men don't understand, and tripping himself with it. On several occasions he has made himself a distinct liar. Now he sends men to work who are marked "quarters" by the hospital and gives them extra details. He doesn't know what a smashed foot, a bruised arm, or any other injury feels like. Many of the fellows are ill or injured, including about half our section. We have about 12 men out of 21 actually in working condition. York was clipped by pontoon hooks and has a bad leg; Harris got his foot mangled by a pontoon girder, weighing a mere 700 pounds. Fazek has a bad foot, Shorty works with hands sore from jungle rot, Smitty has a cut knee, Mike is half-sick all the time with his sinus, Rouse is wounded and out, Redwine is banged up after tangling with a wild cable. That's only in our section. I had a narrow escape with the pontoon hooks when I signalled Charley to slack off and he tightened. The hooks let go and flew past, missing my legs by inches. Could have easily fractured them. No serious injuries in the company, but lots of little ones cropping up. We are doing good work for the small number of men. I've acquired a couple of cans of bouillon cubes, and they make a good drink while I am writing or reading at night. Been using Jap canned heat, but we're low on it.

The merchant marine seems to be a sinecure in the S.W.P. Even the lowest-paid hand gets four times the amount of money a private gets, takes less risk, lives on the best of food, has clean quarters, gets back home in much less than a year, gets 30-day furloughs, and gets paid extra for getting bombed. It's a soft life. I truthfully don't envy their having steak, chicken, iced tea, turkey, ham and eggs, etc. It's just the inequality of the services. The crew has been rather decent, getting us things to eat, clothes, books, cigarettes, etc. However, there was one fellow who sold sandwiches to us for a florin a piece, squeezing money out of the fellows who bear more and get paid so much less. Well, I guess one can't understand our life unless one has lived it, which they haven't. They are the healthiest bunch of fellows I've ever seen, the merchant marine. I guess anybody would be, living as they do.

July 8

Life has settled into a nice routine and pace, and it's pleasant for a change. We have a fairly comfortable camp. Night before last we had four alerts and a barrage went up twice. Last night we had one, rather this morning, just before breakfast. We've been working hard on the ship. Yesterday we put out 134 tons in six hours. Feel a little sick last day or so. Can't seem to take atabrine like I used to.

Just had a company meeting in which our own Lt. Wenz, playing sly, told us that we were stealing government property. The usual pilfering in the hold has been rampant. He was happy enough when one of the sections got two cases of boned turkey ashore, which we've had for supper these past two nights. Perkins was caught trading with a native, which is taboo. He traded an American bayonet with his name on it. Tomorrow he will dig graves as punishment. In my opinion digging graves here should be an honor. I don't believe the man laid in a grave would want it dug as punishment, but with honor and respect. One can be easily cynical and say that it makes no difference, but I can't feel that way. The Lieutenant threatened that he could assign men to dig graves at any time. Why, I don't know. I hate to be threatened like that. Perhaps he thinks we're imbeciles or children.

July 10

Had an alert night before last, none last night. Yesterday afternoon I saw an interesting air attack. Not far from here is the last pocket of Jap resistance within a radius of about 20 miles. They have been catching hell from our heavy artillery barrages during the last few days and nights. Before daylight this morning, I could see the flash of exploding shells.

Anyway, yesterday I watched an aerial attack by Australian Boomerangs. They flew in a large circle, then dove at a certain point, swooping down nearly vertically, strafed the target at low range, and then swept back into the air. The sound of the strafing reached us after the plane leveled off from its sharp climb. This attack continued for 45 minutes, the planes strafing in two or three short bursts. Then they dropped bombs. The Japs have an intricate and tough defense in that particular group of caves. It is in the vicinity where Rouse was shot. The Japs are taking a terrible pounding, but that area is tough to crack. Hundreds of shells have been fired into it.

I've been working hard on the ship, as we all have. We are turning out close to 300 tons a day, which is pretty good for 50 men. Today I signalled, worked in the hold, and checked. Handling ammo is rugged work, but I feel stronger as time goes on. We are wringing wet most of the time, those of us in the hold. It is pure, unadulterated hard work.

There were Japs close to camp the other night, and a Spanish infantryman who was visiting Sanchez was forced to remain the night. He told us of the action he saw here during 17 days at the front. He related that the 41st, living up to its reputation as the "bloody butchers," came upon a Jap hospital and killed everyone in it.

July 13

Just had an outlandish, senseless argument with DiPirro. Now I know where the word "balderdash" came from; someone listened to DiPirro.

Had two alerts last night, a couple more previously, none the night before because it rained all night. That night we waited in a pouring rain to see *Woman of the Year*. Katherine Hepburn is one of the few actresses for whom I would wait in the rain an hour to see. I can listen to her voice for hours. She reminds me of Carolyn a great deal, and some of her expressions were so similar that it was painful.

Some ratings came out. Thomas, Smith and York made Pfc. Hindmon made T-5. Keep trying, Kahn.

July 14

The pocket of Japs still holds out in the hills, and they have even infiltrated our lines. They got to the bakery, several miles above us, and killed some men. Fazekas is so jumpy he stays up all night, keeps his rifle handy, goes on sick call in the morning with a bad foot, and sleeps all day. They have moved a battery of 105s and a 155 about 150 yards away. For the past four days they have been intermittently shelling the Japs, both day and night, the shells whistling or screeching, according to atmospheric conditions. It is usually the roar of a big gun that fully awakens me. At night the concussion makes the candle flame jump. Even though they roar in our ears, I sleep well at night, right through the shelling. We work hard and sleep hard.

I had a very realistic dream the other night. I was going home, still in uniform, and was standing on a corner looking at Fort Tryon Park and the Cloisters. The hills were very green, and I was explaining to some middle-aged woman that this was the first sight of home I had seen in two years. It's actually over 13 months at present. When I awoke I couldn't remember where I was for about a minute, until the roar of a gun brought me back to reality.

Have just finished reading *Burma Surgeon*, the latter half written in diary form, covering the retreat out of Burma. I was struck by the similarity between Seagrave's diary and mine. I can easily imagine his difficulties in writing and, of course, know only too well the truth of his descriptions. So natural has this life become that I sometimes forget that what the people at home consider adventurous, we now think of as prosaic.

Our days now have a steady routine. Up at 5:30, work till 1:00, afternoon off to bathe from the barrel, read and play checkers with Pap. He beats me more often that I do him. We have a pretty quiet tent, but lately Mike has become quite garrulous, and a bit "jungle happy." He goes on for hours, and he's in poor physical condition. We have about half-a-dozen men in the hospital.

Speaking of physical condition, Sanchez just commented on how broad and big I am now, especially in comparison to my early days in the army. I feel in perfect shape. Sanchez claims I'm getting to be one of the biggest men in the company. This rugged life and work have benefited most of us, especially me. I have a beard, but it curls up and appears less than it is. It's a good one though.

Heard on the *H. White*'s radio today that the Russians are but 68 miles from the German border. I would not be surprised should the war in Europe end this year. I mentioned this to Pap, but he countered with, "A small infiltration on Biak Island concerns me more than the battles of Europe." Nevertheless, our eventual fate depends heavily on the duration of the European war, and the good news keeps us in good spirits.

July 16

Bud Herbeck arrived tonight in camp. It's the first time we've seen him since Hollandia. It was good to see him again. He flew up from Hollandia in one-and-three-quarter hours. He also informed us that our barracks bags are at Hollandia with Singleton and Devaney. Scarborough is also there and is coming to rejoin us. Scar and Singleton were hurt in Hollandia by a booby trap. They were wounded in the legs, and Scar just missed having his testicles punctured by shrapnel. Rouse came over to camp yesterday, looking quite well but claiming his wound is not fully healed. Geyer and Morales are in the hospital over on the island and are pretty sick. While I was writing a letter to Carolyn, using my last airmail envelope, Rouse came in to talk. Nobody was here except me; everyone went to the movies. He told me of the numerous mental patients over there, and he found himself a bit nervous, which is unusual for him. I told him that such a close call as he had would have its psychological effects. Then he told me a bit about his past life, and how he missed playing in the Rose Bowl game because he broke his leg. We discussed the schooling that the government is offering to veterans and that he might go back, taking Phys Ed courses. We are all seeking a postwar plan. We fellows of 18 to 24 are more or less in the same boat.

From the article Miss Sophian cut from *The Times* and sent me, my college education is assured. I wish I could be more definite on what I want to do. According to the article, a minimum of one year's education will be paid, and upon satisfactory completion of that, three more years. And we will be allowed $50 per month for expenses. It's like a dream, all one could possibly hope for. All I have to do is get back! This plan will assure my future, and I shall not be forced to lean upon Dad or to work for funds while I am in school. It's wonderful. Norm and I are jubilant. If only it will not be too much longer.

July 17

Mike has gone a bit "jungle happy." He babbles incessantly and says stupid things over and over. He complains of missing sex and liquor. I have come to like Wingfield. I like living with him because he is quiet, but when he does say something, it is remarkably clever or intelligent. I should learn the lesson that it takes a long time to find the true worth of a person.

The book *Coronet* is entrancing. The writing is wonderful. What experience and depth of character Kornroff must have. And what an eye for the dramatic, the symbolic and the esthetic. I shall write like that some day. I am capable of it. But I am lazy or afraid to start.

July 18

This morning the 2nd section went to work on one of the ships near Mokmer. While working they succeeded in dropping a 22-ton bulldozer overboard. A bulldozer is costly, and I am sorry I missed so expensive a splash. Hiller was going to ride it down but fortunately didn't. Luckily, the LST had swung away from the ship at that moment permitting the massive machine to drop between the two ships. Discussion of the incident has filled the rest of the day. We are like smalltown people, pouncing on every incident, embellishing it in repetition.

We have not had an alert for a long time, but the big guns roar often enough to remind us that there are still Japs on the island. The war progresses nicely; the Russians are only 45 miles from the Prussian border, and pressing. The Germans are pressed on all sides. In the Burma-India theater we advance against the Japs; in China fighting is heavy, and in the Central Pacific the Japs are catching hell. Another year perhaps.

[*From time to time we got a printed* News Bulletin, *published daily by the 41st Division Special Service Section. In the July 18, 1944, issue, typically giving war news from all theatres, there was a reprint of an entry from a recently captured diary written by a Japanese soldier. The entry was dated "25 June 44" and was found in nearby Mokmer Cave. I am including it here as a comparison to my own diary:*

> *Under existing conditions we are helpless. 'Let us be guardian Spirits of the Empire,' said one sergeant from the 35th division before he killed himself. There were about 30 wounded soldiers left in the cave; those who could move assisted the others. They all shouted 'Long live our Emperor' before leaving this world. My friend Nagaska stabbed his throat with a knife but did not succeed in killing himself. I finally decided to assist him so that he could rest in peace. I stabbed my own brother in arms. Who could understand my horrible predicament? I still have two grenades; one to destroy myself and one for the enemy. I don't know whether or not my rations will last until we are rescued. I am determined to kill myself before I lose the power to pull the grenade pin. I want to*

restore my health so that I can die on the battlefield and follow Nagaska. Long live the Emperor! Father and Mother, please forgive me for dying before you do. I hope that you will be able to live the rest of your lives in peace. I wish you good health. I have done my duty to my country. My dearest parents, I am committing suicide with a hand grenade. My ashes will not reach you.]

July 22

This kerosene lantern that I stole from the *Melgram* today burns wonderfully. It's the best light I've had. Just finished talking an hour-and-a-half with Bud, sobered by his long absence from the company. He's a good kid. I informed him about the opportunities for education after the war; he was interested. (Norm just came in for a 20 minute session; he wanted to know what ½ of the sine of a sine was. Ye Gods!) Well, Bud and I talked also about life in general. During his convalesence he met a nurse and a doctor who inspired him to want to study medicine. He wants to feel that he is giving of himself and not only pushing himself ahead. In short he has discovered that there is a lot more to life than self-glorification, and has reached that wall all young fellows of our age reach sooner or later. It is that wall of indecision, of not knowing what should be our route in life. We must hurdle that wall to find what is on the other side, or we will forever bash our heads against it because we lack the will to climb it. We talked of the problems facing youth today and, of course, of the war from which we have benefited in many ways. Perhaps it is not medicine that he wants; no doubt that is only another name for purpose. I need that myself, a purpose, a sureness, a determination. Just as Carolyn has. In this world of turmoil, living under high tensions, we must attain simplicity in the complexity of our modern lives. I believe we have reached an age where success depends not on making the simple complex, but the complex simple. We live in complexity but we will only find satisfaction in the simple. We are like new-caged mice seeking an entrance to liberty. Bud and I, and many others, face that quest.

Norm spoke about the insecurity of his stripes, and that Wenz has been dissatisfied with him and Monroe as corporals. Wenz wants non-coms to be editions of himself, in other words, bossy and weighty and profound about the trivial. These younger fellows are placed in the position of pleasing Wenz and straining their relationships with the men they command, the men with whom they have to live. Herbeck has already lost his rank because of Wenz's determination to install his type of person—or else. Bud has taken it manfully.

We finished the *White,* and began working the *Melgram.* The lack of barges made it an extremely light work day. We were witness to an interesting but terrifying sight. The new ship is about three miles up the bay, and about a mile above the Jap pocket of resistance which has been shelled for so long. They started heavily shelling that area for about an hour, and this time, instead of hearing the shells go overhead, we saw them land. Located behind the action, we could clearly see the flash of the bursting shells, the flying debris. It seemed odd to stand at the gunwales of a liberty and watch with complete detachment men blasted to death.

Not long after this heavy shelling, the first wave of Liberators came over. I was jarred from my reading, *Orchestral Music and Its Times,* by a series of terrific explosions, about 15 in staccato rhythm, which had the unmistakable crack of bombs. These fell about 1½ miles away, slightly inland behind the ridge which parallels the coast of the island. I didn't see much of this bombing, but I plainly heard it. A few moments later three more liberators came over, as leisurely as if they were on a pleasure trip. We could see the bombs fall from the planes, looking like dots, and then gaining momentum and plummeting to earth with blinding speed. The great explosions of 1,000-pound bombs again cracked the air, and great towers of smoke rose hundreds of feet. The third group of planes followed soon after, and their bombs hit much closer to us, on top of the ridge where we could observe them. Bluish concussion rings pulsated up from where the bombs hit. The very air lurched away from the impact. What these blasts do to a man's insides is hideous. There we stood, fascinated by this close-up action against the enemy. They have taken this continual brutal pounding for days. Then the area was enveloped in a thick haze, but we spotted one tank going up a road, and later heard that they were "softening up the area" for the infantry who were going to try and crack that defense again.

We learned that Guam was invaded this morning.

When we got back to camp this afternoon, Stahl gave me two rolls of film for my camera, and I had a few shots taken of myself, and the rest were of the fellows in the section and platoon. I put the films in a prophylactic to prevent them from getting damp. Hope they come out, because some of them were awfully good shots. Funny how ultra self-conscious most people become when they have their pictures taken. It was lots of fun though.

Other night we were blacked out in an submarine alert. Alerts have mainly ceased, much to our joy.

Had an odd dream last night. I woke up intermittently, but every time I fell asleep, I dreamt about Carolyn. Except for the first dream, the others were pleasant enough, because I always awoke smiling and feeling good. The first part was symbolic. I dreamt that Carolyn somehow had been converted into a knife, and that this knife was cutting a piece of paper exactly in half; on both sides of the cut were written the names of my family, first names, too. As the paper was cut, the edges of the cut became black and smoked as if on fire. Then they spread in opposite directions enveloping both halves of the paper. That is one of my queerest dreams yet.

I shall close on the cheery announcement that recently came through: "No furloughs are contemplated from this area to Australia in the near future." At least there is solace in our advances.

July 24

We learned this morning that we will soon move again, and that rotten feeling again takes hold of me as I think about the process of building a new camp. From what I hear of the site, we shall have to carve ourselves a camp out of the jungle. Our barracks bags arrived several days ago, and I found mine in wonderful shape considering the time that has passed and the difficulties of transport. I spent this afternoon and this evening once again packing my bags. I have quite a lot of stuff, and with my large collection of books, I have more weight to handle than the average soldier. The fellows handling the bags a few days ago remarked that mine was by far the heaviest. I have lightened it as much as possible, but it still remains remarkably heavy.

Except for the blasting the Japs took the other day, we have not heard any artillery fire. Before that barrage we had weeks of artillery fire. The scouting party that went up to the much-assailed area apparently found 200 to 300 dead Japs, which was about the size of the resisting force. There seems to be no other major resistance on the island. The spot to where we are moving is along the beach about a mile beyond that Jap pocket.

We are slowly returning to full strength, with the return of Butler, Scarborough, Herbeck and Devaney. Fazekas and Morales have been evacuated. Rouse is back, too. We are not so hard-pressed for men now. Stahl said the invasion of Halmahera is anticipated within the next 60 days.

I have come to be a sort of information bureau for the fellows. From all tents comes the fairly frequent cry, "Hey Sy," (or Kahn) "how do you spell ——— ?" That's the usual question, but they ask me everything. It keeps me on my toes, and I don't particularly mind. From sergeants down I have spelled words and answered questions. Most of the time the questions are easy to answer. Gosh, I dread tomorrow.

July 26

Moving proved to be the ordeal I anticipated. We broke camp early yesterday morning, loaded trucks, and travelled about 10 miles up the road past the first airstrip. Then we cut inland about ¼ mile along a road that was still being blasted between the thick green walls of the jungle. It started to rain, as it generally does when we've moved, and the rain continued for the rest of the afternoon. We unloaded our gear and set to work hacking at the jungle with axes. We worked steadily, slashing, sweating, swearing, and shivering for six solid hours until we cleared enough space for our tents and kitchen. The terrain is horrible; it is all stumps and lumpy coral. One cannot take a step without going up or down. The bugs are awful, especially these little stinging ants. During the last few minutes I have killed at least a dozen. We were soaked and disgusted.

At the company meeting we were handed another piece of disagreeable news to top off a most horrible day. We now work from 7:00 A.M. to 3:30 P.M., a very long day. We were also told to keep our rifles handy, and clips in them, because no one knows how secure this part of the island is. It's wild enough. I kept my rifle handy, but the clip close by rather than in the chamber. After that I got into bed, keeping my clothes on, and began to read Shakespeare's *Romeo and Juliet* by the light of the kerosene lamp. After I read a few pages, we were called out by excited voices yelling, "Come see." I went out, and there I saw two trees covered with thousands of fireflies, blinking on and off simultaneously. They looked like Christmas trees, and the light that blinked on and off, like a beacon, lit up the surrounding jungle for 20 feet. When the trees lit up at alternate seconds, one could see these pin-points of light moving rapidly in small circles. A most unusual sight.

About ½ hour later, we had the first alert in many days. We all felt pretty secure under this heavy cover of virgin jungle, with no important installations nearby. Soon we heard a plane circling overhead. The 90s fired at him intermittently, but it was as nothing compared to earlier barrages. Not far away a bulldozer was working with lights on, the driver not having heard the alert. The plane dropped seven bombs aiming for the "dozer" but hitting only the jungle.

July 30

At this moment I am sitting in the kitchen on guard duty, having drawn the 12:00 to 6:00 A.M. shift. The jungle is full of suspicious sounds at night. Anyway, I just finished two thick slices of fresh bread with real butter. It was like cake. Close by are my rifle and a clip of four shells and writing material. Perhaps I shall be able to get off a letter or two. It is a dark night. This is the shift on which so many fall asleep. Rouse did the other night and got a terrific laying out. Falling asleep on guard is a serious offense of which I want no part.

This afternoon, during our lunch hour, we heard a small explosion and, a moment later, an anguished cry for help. We all stood silent and still for a moment, as groups of men will at the first sound of calamity. Butler was the first one who started running toward the screaming man. Others followed; I held my place. I don't know exactly why I did not go too; I know a little about first-aid. But the sound of a man screaming is to me a most fearful sound. The accident itself, no matter how bad, does not affect me to $\frac{1}{10}$th the degree as does a screaming man. It sends a cold sensation all through me and causes a momentary paralysis. At any rate, I soon learned from the returning fellows that it was Warrant Officer Rountrey who was hurt. (What weird noises are about tonight.) It seemed while tramping through the jungle just outside our area on the other side of the latrine, Rountrey set off either a booby trap or a grenade. He saw a small bundle of brown paper and poked it. It began to hiss, and he had the presence of mind (more likely the instinct) to hit the ground. A moment later it went off, and several pieces of shrapnel pierced his foot. From the sight of the bloody shoe they cut off him, which I saw a few moments later, the wound bled profusely. He was fortunate that his injury was not worse. Some fellows got the truck. They passed me, bouncing and jouncing, with grimacing Rountrey. One must be careful all the time. It is when everything seems innocent and safe that one should be most alert.

Shorty brought back heartening news tonight. Manchuria was bombed in a daylight raid, and the Russians are 20 miles from Warsaw as they continue to sweep through Poland. It looks more and more as if the end is approaching for the Germans. The Yap invasion seems to have been just rumor. The continued good news keeps us happy and makes our difficulties less. Gosh, to see home again.

Last night I got the urge to write. I composed a poem called "Burial" which I shall include here. It was based on an experience of several weeks ago.

BURIAL

We stood and watched them digging in the sand,
Uniform holes with smoothed and straightened sides.
It is done with care, for frivolous land
Is sand, it must be coaxed. It plays with tides,
Flexing easily under the fingers
Of the sea that clutch at the naked shore.
In the small black caverns coolness lingers,
A black wound on the hot surface they tore.

A brown blanket is coffin for a man.
With painful care it's lowered out of sight,
The slowly shoveled sand eternal ban
To living eyes and to the burning light.
The black wound is healed, the simple deed done.
Rest peacefully soldier, the battle's won.

July 31

Last night we had a raid-alert. A considerable barrage went up. We heard the motors and the sound of bombs falling in the distance. It lasted about two hours. This morning we learned that six men are dead, 15 wounded. We got one of the three attacking planes, and one probable. One never knows when he awakes in the morning what fate lurks in store for him before another 24 hours is out. It sometimes seems that there is little one can do to alter what will be.

We are working the *Clayton Sage*. How bored I have become on these ships, checking or working in the hold. If it were not for the book I stick in my pocket every morning, the days would be intolerable. We are all tired of our existence. I still can find pleasure in my observation of people, but the mind hungers for other things, the body for some of the comforts of old, the palate for both hearty and delicate tastes. Thank goodness the war goes well, for that keeps us going. I wish there were some impetus for advancement, and sometimes there is, but it is not steady enough. I lose my ambition because the cultivation of favor to reach that goal is so repugnant to me. I am more or less satisfied as it is, doing the work emptily most of the time, and reading whenever and, sometimes, whatever I can. I have recently become more aware of the days, more so this last month than ever before.

Last night while emptying contents of my barracks bag into a box, I was stung by a small scorpion. The pain was sharp for a few minutes and caused my hand to swell. Glad he was a small one, as I understand a large scorpion can make one quite ill. Funny thing was that a few minutes later Pap was stung on the thumb by the same one. He spotted and killed it. We spent some minutes examining it, especially the effective stinger on the end of the tail.

August 4

We have had about five more alerts. We've been slowly building our area and working moderately hard on the ships.

Been getting letters now and then from home. I also received four packages including a new watch, canned food, cigars, etc. One package contained the ruined remnants of a cake, squashed and moldy. All the fellows have received a flock of packages.

A new landing was effected in north New Guinea between Manako-waii and Sorong. These, I believe, are the last strongholds the Japs have on New Guinea, and in a few more months we should have control of the island after more than two years. There are reports that a new secret weapon was used on Guam, described as "devastating."

This past week the men have been noticeably homesick and dispirited. How often have I heard: "I wish I could be home now," or "I don't give a damn what happens." Probably at the bottom of this depression is the drudgery of our particular work and our disgust with this particular camp site.

August 8

Yesterday afternoon and last night we put our tent up over the finished platform and moved our stuff in. This is the most comfortable we've all been in many months. After heavy lifting in the hold all day, I took a much-needed wash by flashlight, with water in my helmet, and then fell into bed and an exhausted sleep. Today was a similar day. Now I have the first few moments to myself in several days. We've got the tent pretty comfortable, and it is nothing short of a luxury to walk on a smooth floor of wood again. Last night I had a wonderful night's rest. By tomorrow night we should be comfortably settled, and I may add that we have worked hard at it. The insects are singing, the night is dark, I have a new cot which I took from one of the ships, I am in good health, and I received mail tonight. The world is indeed considerably brighter. If only this desk wouldn't wobble so. I do believe I am the world's poorest carpenter.

We've had several alerts lately, and one raid in which three ineffectual bombs were dropped not far from here. They landed on shore although they were intended for a ship. The natives have been rounding up scattered Japs. Some bring in the Japs, and some bring in their ears on a piece of string. Those of us possessing Springfield 03s have turned them in and will receive carbines instead. We will need to learn how to break them down. I liked the 03; one gets sentimental about a piece of equipment carried so long. Still the carbine, only half as heavy and half as long, will be to our advantage, especially if we move as frequently as we have in the past. Biak, however, appears to be our home for awhile.

The war news continues to be heartening.

August 10

I read tonight that Hengyang has at last fallen to the Japs after nearly all the Chinese defenders had been killed. A very great victory for the Japs, but I believe it shall be their last one.

Several fellows, getting quite fed up with Lt. Wenz and the organization, have again applied for transfers to the infantry: namely Rice, Scarborough and Herndon. The Lieutenant tonight made some ungracious remarks because, no doubt, men are not too enthusiastic about staying with him. He used the word "intrepid" in sarcasm. Any man who voluntarily joins the infantry, knowing the hell it is, deserves the adjective "intrepid" in its truest sense. Wenz is not a person I can respect. The men have my respect for wanting to transfer. Herndon is a funny fellow; Rice and Scarborough the "devil-take-it" kind of fellows. Rice is the most good-tempered fellow in the platoon, always raucous and jovial.

Adams found his lamp in the possession of Doran, who probably stole it. Adams is not pressing the point. I hate a thief. Sanchez has been in the hospital for several days now and, thus, there is a noticeable decrease of smutty sex talk. Have a carbine now, cleaned it today, and learned how to take it apart, and put it together.

August 12

Much has happened during the past few days. For one thing, the night before last one of the colored fellows across the road shot himself. They had obtained some gin, gosh knows where, probably from the incoming ships. I slept through the whole thing.

One of the most beautiful sights I have ever seen took place yesterday morning. We were on the floating dock waiting for a new ship, the *Nancy Hanks* to dock. The sun had not quite cleared the horizon when it began to rain lightly and, then, in earnest. Flynn, Johnson, Bud and I took refuge in one of the small boats tied to the pier. We watched the rain come sweeping across the sea, obliterating in murky gray the cargo ships lying in the harbor off shore.

For awhile it was a typically gray, heavily raining day (the kind which I enjoy), when suddenly the sun burst over the horizon with a sudden leap and made the air seem like spun gold, the most beautiful color I've ever seen. As the sun rose higher, a rainbow to the west slowly emerged in magnificent brilliance.

Everything around me became transformed, enchanted. The fantastic light glowed in greater splendor each moment. The whole world seemed in a hushed silence. The rainbow became stronger and stronger; the colors seemed on fire. One end rose out of the sea, arched majestically and perfectly across the sky and gently curved right before our eyes to the shoreline. If there is a heaven, the angels must surely live in this kind of golden air. The arch of the rainbow encompassed a delicate blue esplanade. It seemed as if some great hand had painted the precious colors in perfect symmetry. The rainbow reached a brilliance that I've never seen before, brighter and brighter like leaping fire. Then an ordinary, slate-gray cargo ship gently came toward shore. But it, too, was enchanted. The gray hulk was transformed into an ethereal blue, and as it cleaved the water, the bow wave was a foamy white feather, and the masts a golden pattern of light. It was dream-like. As the ship approached, it passed under the rainbow, catching its band of color, and then, lo!—at that moment a second rainbow directly behind the first, though of less brilliance, materialized out of nothingness. The yellow raindrops had become like a gossamer gauze settling gently to earth.

There it was, one of the most perfect moments I have ever known; the ship, the double rainbows, the golden air and yellow drops all immersed in a faint gray mist, the world hushed by the spectacle.

Then, as the second band of color began to rival the first, the sun seemed to lift itself from its lethargy, and the spell broke. Like shy deer, the colors fled at the sudden leap of the sun. The air turned blue and clear and fresh, the ship was again just a ship, the rain ceased. The second rainbow vanished into the sky, and only the first remained, reminiscent, like the aroma of flowers, of the beauty from which it springs. I watched the rainbow disintegrate from the middle downwards until the last faint colors at the base had dissipated, like smoke, back to the unknown from which it sprang. The day was then sunny and bright, and I was convinced that whatever ill fate might taint the rest of the day, it could not possibly spoil those moments, then or ever. It was a haunting sight, painful and delicately beautiful. That evening the sun went down among banks of magnificent fiery red clouds, but to compare the sunset with the morning is to compare the pretty with the divine, with the dignity of beauty itself.

Last night I received a V-mail from home (July 28) informing me that one of my poems was accepted for publication by the magazine *Drift-wind.* They chose "Nature's Gossipers" from among those Mother submitted. I am thrilled and gratified. It is a light, fanciful poem, and I don't believe it is my best. I have dreamed of having my poems appreciated, and now I shall see one in actual print. It gives a certain impetus to further my efforts. I have never heard of the magazine; it sounds like a poetical publication, though. I am anxious to learn more details which Mother said were forthcoming.

About 3:00 A.M. we had an alert. Not long after, I heard the sounds of motors. We all tumbled out of bed. I headed for the nearby shell hole, Mike following. The rest took to the base of the huge fallen tree that borders one side of our tent.

About 20 minutes after the end of the first alert, the second came, and the whine of approaching aircraft grew. Grabbed my helmet and rushed for the hole, Mike alongside. Adams joined us, pants-less. Shorty stood close by. The whine of the plane was close. Suddenly the "woosh" of a falling bomb jerked us into instantaneous action. Mike, Adams and I hit the large hole without consideration of the sharp coral sides and sharp coral bottom. But strangely the explosions never came. The object just crashed into the jungle, the same distinctive sound as the first bomb I ever heard in New Britain. We concluded that it was either a dud, a 90-mm shell that had not exploded and came back to earth, or a bomb that had hit some branches without contact on the nose and landed on its side. It seemed to have landed within a couple hundred yards. Planes continued to attack until near dawn, and there was no sleep for the remainder of the night. There were several more alerts, and in between these foxhole dashes we could hear the staccato of gunfire, the whine of planes, and a long burst of explosions as a pattern of bombs hit. Shortly after that an all-clear sounded, and I went to sleep clothed—for it was chilly.

August 15

Yesterday I received two shots, one in each arm. One for typhus and one for cholera. They were easy to take, but about four hours later we all began to feel the effects. Our arms and shoulders swelled painfully, and everybody got a poor night's sleep. Every time I moved, I woke up. The stiffness was bad and remained most of the day, but tonight it seems to be abating. Quite a few of the fellows were ill, and I wasn't feeling too well early this afternoon.

We've had one more alert, but it was short with no action. The raid a few nights ago was by a Jap force of two bombers and three fighters. A dog fight took place. Apparently our planes took off from the island off-shore. We lost a P-40, and they lost two planes. Also we had some casualties from the bombing.

August 17

Now situated in the new tent in our permanent position. Pretty comfortable. Finally stopped this tent from shaking by nailing it to the floor! I got quite a thrill when I found in one of Mother's letters the poem that was published with my name under it. Not quite my name. They spelt it "Kalin" instead of "Kahn," but Mother wrote that they were correcting the error. Spoiled it a little, but still there is satisfaction that the piece was published on its merit. Also they printed "tend" instead of "bend." No doubt Mom wrote them in longhand, and her writing being as bad as mine, the words were mistaken. In spite of all this, rather pleasant.

NATURE'S GOSSIPERS

The wind has made gossipers of the trees.
It must have brought the news of some fine plot,
For they stand in huddled whispers, tossing the breeze
In little violent gestures on the spot.

And as the wind rises to tell them more,
They bend to hear what he has said aright,
Then flail each other causing leafy gore,
It must have ended in a joke or plight.

In commemoration of my approaching 20th birthday, Mom wrote a most wonderful and sentimental letter, going through the years of my life recalling little events. It was very touching, bringing back vividly days that seem centuries back. It gave me a lump in the throat and made my eyes feel sort of wet when I finished. She does mean so much to me, as I know I do to her. These long months must be difficult times for her, I know. I love her very much, what else can I add.

August 20

How the days fly by! Last night I was on guard, so today I had the day to myself. Finished reading Sandburg's *Storm Over the Land*, a history of the Civil War, its generals and Lincoln. I have read of this period often, ever since I was a grade-school student, and never tire of it.

This afternoon I borrowed Plato's *Dialogues* from Eriksen and found new vistas. I have long wanted to read the old philosophers, and now I am intrigued by the truths and new concepts. From this well of time I have taken buckets of knowledge to water the seeds of new ideas. The *Dialogues* is an impressive piece of literature.

One sentence particularly hit home. Socrates said, "Poets are aware of wisdom and truth only through a certain genius and inspiration." These words ring true and are exemplified by the private lives of many of our great poets who did not live as they wrote. They had a certain gift. I believe it to be a sensitivity to beauty, whether abstract or objective, rather than clarity in the philosophy of pure logic and reason. Another of Socrates' observations particularly impressed me: "Why waste time arguing over things that all wise men disagreed about in search for a knowledge that would do no one any good. What men need to know is how to make the best out of living."

I recently came across a line of Oscar Wilde's which fits my feelings about my misprinted poem better than I could put it. "A poet can stand anything but a misprint."

August 21

Last night at about 11:00 we were awakened by a loud crack. Because I found it blowing pretty hard when I awoke, and just beginning to rain, I thought it to be a crack of lightning. However, flashlights cut the dark, and I heard someone yell that a tree had been blown over. To the call of "Anyone hurt?" there came a "No," so I rolled over and went back to sleep.

This morning I saw the tree, large and about 35 feet long. It was the same tree I had suggested we cut down when we first moved into the area and were clearing it. I noticed that the tree had been torn on one side by gun fire. That, along with the rapid decomposition of vegetation here, meant that it did not take too powerful a wind to topple it. The tree was situated a few feet from Kasprzyk's and Fitch's tent and just missed its corner. The top of the tree caught the corner of Thomas' tent, somewhat damaging it. In that tent Redwine was hit in the back by equipment knocked from his shelf. This evening he turned up with a taped back and a fractured rib. Thomas was shaken up but unhurt. It is lucky someone wasn't seriously injured or killed. It fell at a very lucky angle. Thomas and I had cut cards for the choice of tents, and I was going to take the tent struck by the tree if I won. Thomas drew the ace of spades. Pap would have been the one in Redwine's place. Strange how these things work out.

Sgt. Stahl just informed me that I am going to be a Technician 5th Grade starting September 1st. I did not expect it. All good things come to him who waits—and I have waited. I just told Bud, because I had to tell somebody. I got a warm congratulation. Damn, I feel good. It's about time Kahn—damn you!

August 23

I've been working harder than my regular pace, spurred by the impending T-5. York nearly smashed my ankle with a 450-pound drum, very close, but a miss is as good as a mile. Tonight we had a company meeting in which Blink gave us an elementary arithmetic lesson about conversion of American and Dutch money. When he gets started nothing can stop him. Add to that his habit of repeating phrases and his "short" meeting usually lasts an hour. One very sore spot with me was touched tonight. The C.O., Reinhardt, asked Blink to send him the names of those eligible for the good conduct medal—excepting those who signed the petition. Again, at hearing that, I got that accursed sunk feeling I always get with any reference to the petition. Will I never be rid of it in the army? It seems it will be a curse on me for my own misadventure—but much, much worse, it affects some 60-odd other men. It is difficult to live with. Technically I am eligible, not having signed the petition, but I hope Wenz will have discretion enough not to turn my name in for the medal. If he does, I think I shall request that he not do so—yes, that is what I shall do. Seems fated that this should come just when he gave the nod to my prospective T-5. Don't bank on anything Kahn; you've come close before.

Singleton is back after his lay-up because of the booby trap. Bud and I have been very close for some time now—comes over and talks with me about his private life. I enjoy having his confidence. His latest ambition is to go into medicine, inspired by the doctor and pretty Jewish nurse at Finsch. His father wrote Bud about it, and subtly discouraged his marriage to Jane. We have our civilian troubles.

I am enjoying having Dale's picture in front of me, her clear cut features and so much that is "woman" about her. Now for a letter to Carolyn; wanted to wait till I could put "Cpl." in the return address—but what the devil.

August 25

Had a shot day before yesterday, but only a slight local effect. Yesterday, as today, we were handling 260-pound bombs. Rouse came down into the hold and attempted to lift one by himself. That started something.

We all tried, Charlie, Smitty, Sig, me, and we could just about get one off the ground. Adams managed a foot. The lift puts a great strain on the body. Then suddenly we heard Mike say, "You mean like this?" and he bends down, stands straight up with it waist-high, no sign of strain on his face, and then puts it down easy as you please.

The word of Mike's power spread quickly, and soon we had a bomb on deck with everyone taking a crack at lifting it. Amazingly, Mike weighs about 135 pounds and doesn't look as if he could lift his own weight. Seven years a coalminer though. Nobody else could lift the bomb. Then, stocky, well-built Fitch tried. I knew he would get it fairly high off the ground. He did manage with all his strength to get it waist-high. You can only lift it once, then you feel like you've done a day's work. Jim, after several attempts, got it knee-high. Ted and DiPirro raised it thigh high. I don't believe anyone who was not used to hard, physical labor could have lifted it. Shows how hardened and strengthened we have become. I tried once or twice more, but just as I was exerting enough pull to lift it clean, I felt a bad strain on my left side and back. So I thought better of it. With a rope around it, I was able to lift it knee-high without much trouble, though any man in good condition could, I imagine. Oh yes, Hollenback lifted it waist-high. He is built like Fitch, but not as perfectly. Then came Parker, easily one of the strongest men I have ever seen. He's built squarish, heavy and thick, with a large, round head on top of a short, thick neck. Massive back and shoulders. I've rarely seen thicker, much less as thick, forearms and wrists. He lifted it *chest-high* without much strain, and he nearly succeeded in putting it on his shoulder! Amazing strength has this fisherman. Wally, Harris and Red could probably lift it, though they didn't try. I believe Pap could, too, though he didn't think it worth the strain. It probably would have ruptured many of us a year ago.

Lifting that bomb on the deck of a ship with all the men gathered around reminded me of the past. I mean the past when men gathered with men and demonstrated physical strength. The days of pirates, woodsmen, frontiersmen, rugged farmers, etc. Those sorts of men, proud and revelling in their strength. In civilization such occurrences do not happen. Perhaps physical strength has become too elemental and primitive in this day of students, scholars and those that live by the keenness of mind. I am glad that I am acquiring more and more physical strength, along with cultivating my mind in the past, and, I hope, in the future.

Blistering hot today. We worked the same cargo. We had to leave six good men back in camp; we had only three-men gangs in the hold. Very rugged work. I am tired tonight. I had Shorty, a good man, and Sanchez, who works well when the spirit moves, which is rarely. Adams and Mike were out. We were informed on the ship that we were to quit at 2:00 P.M. so that the men could see the Bob Hope show. A couple of trucks were arranged to take us down, which was pretty decent, and the show was only a mile or so down the road. That happily cut our day short in that we were so short-handed. We cajoled Eriksen down into the hold with us for the last hour, and we worked just a little harder ourselves to see him work. He's a pretty good fellow, this blond, white-skinned Norwegian, and I like him. He often asks me for interpretations of poetry, mostly on *The Rubaiyat*, while I still get the usual questions about "Who was he?" or "When did that happen?" or "What does this mean?"

Had a good time reviewing in my own mind and then explaining the gestation of the mammal embryo. It started when I mentioned the fact learned from Carolyn's last letter that a human egg cell has been fertilized in a test tube. Reproduction and heredity have always interested me a great deal. Before I knew it I was diagramming, from memory but not badly, the maturation of sex cells, and explaining Mendelian principles, and answering various questions that came up. Much fun. I have done this several times for groups of fellows, widening their scientific sexual knowledge. They are always hugely interested, because they don't know much about it, and I enjoy amazing them with the facts and curiosities intrinsic to the subject. Most men, I find, know only the essential physical facts of sexual intercourse.

After a two-hour wait under a merciless sun, Bob Hope and company and the 41st Division Band entertained us. I got a "seat" close to the front. We were all unbearably uncomfortable. We sat so close to one another it was impossible to move more than a few inches, and it wasn't long before men were grimacing with cramped muscles. It was not fun to be so closely crowded together in that heat. The hillside was absolutely covered with men, thousands of them, straining to see, cramped, and freely perspiring. The show was excellent as far as entertainment goes. Hope, of course, was his usual uproarious self. He looks much older and flabbier than in his pictures. His hair is sparse. He is very funny and got off some pretty raw stuff, which went over big. Jerry Colonna was there, also a good comedian himself. Gray hair streaked his black hair. There was also a guitarist and singer, and petite and painted Frances Langford, who sang two songs until dust in her throat stopped her. The sex appeal was supplied by scantily-clad Patricia Thomas, a dancer. She was medium-sized, heavily made up, smooth features, voluptuous body—and as little clothed as possible. All in all, a very entertaining show. Sitting so close I could see that they all looked fagged and tired. They do two shows a day, flying to the numerous bases in the South West Pacific. Not an easy job by any means. They have a week to go—and then home. First women I've seen in many months. Their kind of beauty has no appeal for me, however.

Paris has fallen.

August 29

We received the first beer issue tonight, three bottles or cans for two guilders. We have enough for two weeks, three bottles every three days. That long-sought beer has finally come. I'm not much of a beer drinker, but it goes well for a change. Some of the men are ecstatic.

Got a book called *Outline of Psychiatry*, which is interesting reading. Read the first chapter, found it simple and quick reading. Still feel listless. I don't know what's becoming of the days; they just seem to melt away. Got ahold of Red's harmonica and fooled with that; can play quite a few songs. Damn, if I don't believe I'm homesick!!

I feel certain that Germany will fall within the next few months. Our armored forces in France are only 188 miles from the German border. Bulgaria and Hungary will join Romania in making peace. Hitler's Europe is beginning to collapse around his head. One short alert last night.

August 30

"Effective this date . . ." Kahn, you are at long last a T-5. Long time no T! No work for us today except chores in the area. Too restless to read much. Rainy, gray days, the kind I like. Slept away most of the afternoon. I was glad to see Wingfield made Pfc and Watts T-5, DiPirro T-4, R. Miller and Fitch T-5. All of the petition-signers got their ratings back, which makes me feel better. Morales came back today. Good to see him.

September 1

Last night we got our second beer issue. Pap, Mike and I sprawled out on the floor of the tent and had an old-fashioned beer party with plenty of cigarettes. We swapped stories about women for a couple of hours, which was fun. Pap, of course, has the widest experience. Then Pap and I talked about what the next war would be like, its vast devastation with whole continents becoming battlefields, and whole peoples becoming soldiers, of races annihilated, and of the terrible machines of destruction the future would hold. Also, since most events are cyclical, civilizations not excluded, we speculated that we may be reaching a peak, and that the next giant conflict would throw us back to another dark period of history. Anyway, it is interesting to speculate.

We built a volley-ball court and played some games last night. Lot of fun. Time was set back an hour last night. As a result everyone was up around 6:00 this morning—except Sancho!

September 2

Last night we had a raid, the 126th on Biak. We heard the planes roar over us a couple of times or, rather, whine. Searchlights were ineffective, anti-aircraft light. It is reported that the 7th Service Group was hit and had casualties. Some of the fellows thought they heard bombs last night, but I didn't. Pap and I have been expecting bombings because of the moonlit nights we have now. Tonight looks ripe for another raid.

Every morning our planes take off and roar over our heads, waking us at about 5:00. They are hitting Halmahera [*an island northwest of Biak in the Dutch East Indies*] and the southern Philippines. Redwine was in today from the hospital, and he said they brought in four fellows who had been shot up. The pilots claimed they were intercepted by 100 Zeros, and flak was heavy over the targets. That rather conflicts with the newspaper reports of little opposition on these missions.

Got word today that the rest of the company was getting furloughs. That makes us the only platoon out of our whole battalion that has not received any yet. Damn, but I'd like to get one real bad. I do feel I need one.

ON SHAKESPEARE'S SONNETS

Thy truth and wisdom shines through dusty time
As the eternal sun through the ages.
The scattered gems of wisdom some pens mined
Compare seldom; thy constant line blazes
As a facet in a many-sided gem.
To withered curios have old ideas
Shrunken. Time-weathered facts prove them
Reflections of a moment, idle fears.

No thing more constant, nor can stay suppressed,
Than a truth, for it stands strong in time's trial;
Nor wealth, nor love, nor health, though it be pressed
In the book of time and hidden awhile.
Thy ink, the blood of truth, shall flow when
This day is dead, from the heart of all pens.

September 6

I've been working steadily. Got the pictures back we took when Frank Harris got out of the hospital. They came out well. Now I have some with my beard, which is over three months old, nearly four. I find it quite comfortable.

We had another alert about two nights ago, but nothing since. Fleets of bombers continue to go out day and night, hitting the southern Philippines, Palau Islands and Halmahera. We follow our progress in the European theater. The end is surely in sight with our forces in Belgium, Holland, and at the German border in France. Russia today declared war on Bulgaria, and, at long last, it looks as if Finland may pull out of the war. It can't go on much longer over there.

We have three men down with yellow jaundice, Hiller, Johnson and Meacham. Fazekas has been transferred to another outfit. Men who go to the hospital now are transferred out of the outfit, baggage and service records included.

Been reading the psychiatry book slowly. There is much of interest, although much goes over my head. Haven't been able to get at Plato for some time. Life is getting civilized here. During the past few days we've had fresh eggs, butter, meat, and real potatoes once in awhile, and even jello. We obtained a crude kind of ice cream (not too good but cold) in exchange for a load of dunnage, to which we have easy access. Last of the beer issue tonight. We spend our evenings lately playing a game of naval engagements. All that is needed is pencil and paper. Pap and I have been having a great time playing these last few nights.

Had a nightmare toward morning today. Dreamt I threw two men off a cliff and killed them. Woke up just as I was caught—glad I woke up!

September 8

Last night I woke out of a deep sleep in time to hear the second shot of the alert. A few moments later I was in a shell hole with about 25 others. The sound of planes was quite clear. At first they were down at Bosnek section, giving the little island a blasting, and then worked their way out here. They circled and made their bombing runs right over our heads toward the airstrips all around us. There was some anti-aircraft fire, and the searchlights poked the sky with long, white fingers. For a moment one of the beams picked up an enemy plane approaching us. That's not good for us, because any plane approaching may let go its bombs when caught in the lights. A plane overhead or going away is nothing to worry about. Anyway, this Tojo let go with something, for we heard it as it whizzed over us. It landed some distance ahead, causing a red glow but no explosion. We later surmised it was an incendiary.

The planes buzzed around for awhile amidst intermittent but light fire, and then another plane came toward us. We heard the distant whirring of bombs falling. I lay flat against the plane side of the hole. Monroe dove in head first, hit Adams, and lay uncomfortably with his head considerably lower than his feet. The bombs seemed an awful long time coming down; perhaps it was 10 seconds. Some prayed, though not audibly. I lay flat, head low under my helmet, not even feeling the sharp coral. I mentally cursed and hoped, with a sort of "lightning never strikes twice" confidence, that the damn bombs wouldn't land in the shell hole. Then we heard two sharp cracks somewhere up ahead, much to our relief. Tojo by now was overhead, and both 90s and 50s were firing. He buzzed around for awhile, and then we heard other bomb bursts in the vicinity of the ship. They didn't sound like particularly large bombs, a couple of hundred pounds. About five minutes after this action, the searchlights picked up an enemy plane. One especially bright beam caught him square. The plane was a silver dot in the sky, very high and quite far inland, heading away. He was way out of range of the 90s' bursts. They had him flush in the light for at least three or four minutes. It was irritating seeing him move along up there. Where the devil were our night fighters? The fellows have been asking that for a long time. Some say they meet incoming enemy planes out at sea and don't follow them in. That's all right if we had effective anti-aircraft.

At this point, fat Sam Owen came dashing into the hole. Lt. Wenz, who is always at the bottom of it, remarked that it must be a bad raid to get Owen out of bed. Sam, who has a ready and caustic tongue, remarked, "*You're* way down in that hole, aren't you Lieutenant?" I got a kick out of that and laughed out loud. At any rate, that plane finally got out of searchlight range, ending the raid. Today we could not learn of any damage done in the immediate vicinity. The bursts we heard landed in the bay, near the ships. The bay is so chock-full of ships I don't see how they missed them all. Now that the Japs know of the concentration of ships here, I imagine there will be more raids. Our fleets of planes go out every day to blast hell out of them, anyway. I still would like to see a dogfight.

Monroe was broken and then made T-5, no longer buck corporal of the 3rd section. We worked heavy lifts today, the heaviest stuff we've handled yet, some of it running 35 ton. We moved 168 ton in four hours. This afternoon the heat was oppressive and everybody's temper short. I'm very tired this evening; I've been too many days out of the hold, I guess.

September 11

Everyone has been a little jumpy these past few days. Last night two false alerts. Rumors going around concerning prospective large-scale Jap raids. Fantastic, like the 300-bomber raid expected tomorrow night. The Japs supposedly have dropped pamphlets. I'll believe it when I see it. Nevertheless, such rumors do throw scares into some of the fellows.

Still mopping up on this island and smaller, surrounding ones in this group. To date over 5,000 Japs have been killed on Biak. Herb passed out day before yesterday and is back in the hospital. The war in Europe goes well, with our troops fighting close to the border of Germany at several points, other troops have landed in Yugoslavia, Bulgaria out of the war, and the Russians moving. Not too much longer, but there is still heavy fighting to weather. Here we're pasting the Japs with air attacks, and occasionally in Japan and Manchuria. In China the Japs have taken Lingling, an American airstrip. They can't seem to be held in China. Their successes there will lengthen the war.

Have been working in the hold whenever possible; have broken Redwine in as checker. Hate the simple job; I would rather sweat in the hold.

September 12

Went aboard the *Henry Gantt* this morning to find two old merchant marines fighting. It lasted about 10 minutes, and then they decided to shake hands.

Saw a most wonderful sight today. I saw men boarding a transport to go home. They were mostly out of the 41st Division and overseas 30 months. We rode down to the dock this morning to find 1,200 men lining the road and waiting on the dock to board. The transport was tied alongside the *Gantt*, and they had to cross it to go up the gangway of the *Evangeline*. At 8:00 they proceeded to board. The band was there and enthusiastically played various marches while the bomber fleets roared overhead in an unintended but appropriate salute. Salute to these "30 month wonders," to the men who have sweated it out and started the drive at the Owen-Stanleys, that gains momentum every day. At the gangway the men were checked off as they boarded, dressed in assorted fatigues, suntans and camouflage uniforms. They carried half-full barracks bags, no rifle or gas mask or cartridge belt or helmet. A few carried prized souvenirs such as Jap swords. It is nearly impossible to describe the feelings they must have at the start of the long voyage home. We felt good to see them go. Some of them smiled, others were expressionless; none was boisterous. They were too well-seasoned for that. Officers and men shook hands, a two-star general was there. It was a happy and well-ordered moment. Colored troops were among those going back too.

On board the *Evangeline* the men settled into the routines familiar to travelling soldiers: card games on deck, men smoking and reading, and some just standing at the gunwales looking out at sea. Need it be written that the word "home" filled their minds and brought scenes to their eyes. It was quiet aboard that transport, but not sad; peaceful was what it was. Though the long line kept well closed up, there were unseen gaps there for men left behind, for men who shall never walk in the line that leads to home.

These men go back with memories of war and its horrors, its oppressiveness to the human spirit, and the memories of friends who lie in the sand. They accepted the good-natured cries of "Dry run," or "Don't let them fool you, you're going to make the beachhead at Halmahera." They smiled and did not answer with the customary sharp replies one expects from troops. And while they boarded, we worked unloading rations. I felt good watching them go back and glad to see that the old-timers are being replaced. By this time next year I believe we shall be close to going home. From home, too, I hear of the 2-to-2½-year overseas soldiers coming back for furloughs, and they have probably seen the last of the active war. Good luck to you men, you deserve it.

Tonight we played a ball game, the first one in many months. Going into the 5th, we were winning 4-3. Then a new team was put in for our side. I pitched. The whole thing fell apart, and they hit my pitching all over left field for clean hits. That, coupled with poor support, ended the game with the score—ouch—19-4. Rouse was pitching a good game. I pitched a rotten one; 16 runs in one inning is really some sort of record.

September 14

Heard something interesting today from Sgt. Stahl. He was talking with a small body of Aussie soldiers this afternoon at the dock. First I've seen up here. They are a specialized group of men versed in enemy message interception and decoding. As one said, "The blasted fools use Morse code." They have an outpost in the hills. Their job sounds interesting. The large raid we had the other night, officially announced as 12 planes with two destroyed, was foretold by them from intercepted messages. They informed the radar operators to set their direction even before the planes came within a 200-mile radius. They also picked up the 52-ship convoy, which, I learned today, was headed to retake Biak. Gulp!! This fleet was largely scattered and sunk. They also claim that the Japs considered using gas on Biak. The bastards might do that. If they do they are signing their death warrant, but our troops will suffer the first casualties, and not only our troops, but us, according to these reports. I can't conceive that the Japs will be that foolish. Still, it would be horrible to be caught down at the ships in a gas attack without a mask.

September 17

Two days ago I celebrated my 20th birthday by cutting off my 4½ month old beard. The day was also marked with good and long-awaited news. Morotai, a small island in the Moluccas, was successfully invaded. Little opposition was encountered, and already the engineers are clearing the way for an airstrip. The forces on Halmahera are still strong. I imagine it is a pretty hot place because of our air attacks. Also, Peleliu was hit simultaneously, where heavy resistance is encountered. Both marines and army were used to establish the beachhead which is at present only 1½ miles long. Probably another Biak. [*Peleliu proved to be one of the toughest battles in the Pacific, fought on terrain similar to Biak's. Attacked by the 1st Marine Division and the army's 81st Division, Peleliu cost these American forces almost 10,000 casualties, almost 1,800 of whom were killed.*] Here, small remnants of the Jap army are systematically wiped out or taken prisoner. A Jap admiral, whom the forces have been after for so long, is still hiding somewhere on Biak with 50 personal guards and 20 men handling his personal equipment.

The place is getting GI. It can't be recognized any longer as the island we first saw. We have been here longer than anywhere else since we were activated way back in Indiantown Gap, Pa. The checker now really earns his money by working tediously and steadily for eight solid hours. The heat here is constant and oppressive; consequently I would rather work hard in the hold for four hours than sit and check for eight. So I have maneuvered Thomas, who is my assistant, into the job and maneuvered Redwine as his understudy, while I willingly sweat in the hold of ships. Checking suits both of them better than it does me, though it is as tiring and more boring than the other jobs on the ship. Both Thomas and Redwine are rather scrawny and weak in comparison to the heavier-built fellows. Because I am now bigger and heavier than I was at 18, I need to work hard to expend the energy that, if bottled up, would leave me continually restless.

This work, however, begins to wear on my nerves. Our food is better than ever before. Last night we had all the rabbit we could eat. First time I ever ate it, though it was familiar to the Southern boys. It was fried and tasted like fried chicken, though it had a faintly repulsive odor. Today we had fresh meat twice.

I want to remember the story about Sanchez's wife and the fellow he met overseas, who had intercourse with her. He told Sanchez all about it, and then Sancho informed him that the woman was his wife and had given birth to a baby. I should like to have seen the expression on the poor fellow's face. This all came out when they met quite by accident in a latrine while at Hollandia. However, Sancho has his divorce and wasn't mad at all; rather, he congratulated him.

Helped Eriksen study his English grammar last night until 11:30. I admire him for it. Now to get a can of that pineapple juice we took off the ship today.

Yesterday evening I received a telegram. It gave me a start for a moment, and then I remembered my birthday only a few days before. To my delight, it was from Carolyn and read, "Birthday greetings, best wishes from all of us. Love Carolyn." Rather swell of her to send it.

We were issued beer tonight, a carton of cigarettes, and we ate ice cream and meat twice. Pretty soft.

Three letters from Mom tonight. In one she mentioned that on September 5th there was a report of Germany's capitulation, later proved false. Perhaps that was the rumor that just got here! Included in one of her letters was one from Sylvan Jacobs, of all people [*a boyhood friend*]. And from all places, France! He is in the 320th Infantry and has seen action. He vividly described the taking of a town where the people greeted them "screaming and waving like mad" and offering food and wine. They wanted good old American cigarettes, of course. Also the French underground men marched, armed with light weapons, and with Cross of Lorraine arm-bands. It is a more interesting war there. When you take a place, it's a town and civilized. Time must pass quickly for them.

September 22

Troops moved in all night next to our camp. Our area is built up now with camps and outfits everywhere. Wandered over about 5:30 A.M. and talked with a few of the men. I learned that these men were part of one platoon of the 604th Port Company. They were going to be attached to us! This was news to me.

To add to our woes, our Battalion HQ has arrived. Saw Honnel and Colonel Whitener, who had been "right behind" us, though this is the first time he's caught up. Good old bird, though. Also saw the various officers and clerks of HQ. Wenz is in his glory, of course. Funny that they should be here along with only one platoon out of the whole battalion. Romero here, too. I asked about Bartholomew and learned that he was with the show "Stars and Stripes." They heard him play at Finsch, and requested and got him. Good break for Ray, travelling around the South West Pacific, entertaining.

I knew our set-up was too good to last. Just the 70 of us were getting along fine with only Blink to contend with. Now we have a whole slew to complicate the chain of command. It's odd being part of a larger unit again after our small platoon has been alone for so long. The Colonel is an ambitious old cuss, and he does get a lot done. He had a bulldozer clearing land all afternoon. We did it with our backs. That's one advantage of having a colonel instead of a lieutenant in authority. He'll have his piped water and indoor theater going in no time, I bet. We'll probably get civilized as hell and soft; I'd prefer that we get no more civilized than we have. There's not one man enthusiastic about the turn of events. However, anything that gets to be good in the army doesn't last. Looks like we might remain here for a long while. HQ brought along a refrigerator plant and electric units. Damn, if I don't prefer candles and all that goes with it or, at most, kerosene lamps rather than electric lights and all that goes with *that*. Time will tell what this new set-up will be. Having an officers' mess again in the mess hall bothered everybody tonight. We were jammed up today because of the crowd. Fellows saying, "When's the next D-day? Let's go." I half agree with them.

September 26

Yesterday marked one year overseas. Since that day a year ago, we have progressed steadily in both wars. Yesterday's news disclosed that we bombed Manila and that we breached the Gothic line in Italy. Here, nearly all of New Guinea is in our hands. Fresh troops from the States are arriving. There is a huge transport down at Dock 1 now.

One of these rookies asked Redwine where the nearest town was; another wanted to know about the women and liquor situation. I do feel sorry for these fellows brought directly to this heat hole, and who will be in the S.W.P. for some time to come. The rotation plan is working, and a thin trickle of men is going back. At the 542nd there are some men ready to return home, on the list that is, and have only 19 months overseas. If men can be on their way at 20 months, there would be no complaint. Still, there are many 30-month men still here.

At Aitape it seems the rest of the company experienced a fire much as we did at Hollandia, and at about the same time. They were less fortunate because they lost nearly all their company and personal equipment. Last night, while working in the hold, we learned the sad news that Brock, a Southerner in his 30s, had been killed in an ammo dump explosion.

September 29

Have received mail from Carolyn, Enid, Edith. Carolyn says she is subject to the dumps, but of course blames herself for it, and says she is not giving enough of herself to the life and people around her. I wish I were there; she could give some to me, and we both would feel better. Her letters have been sweet and as much as I could expect or want under the conditions.

We are going back to the army routine and GI life. For one thing, our steady KPs are quitting in another day, and that means back to the roster and KP once a month. I absolutely detest those days.

Also, starting the 1st, we shall go on a 6-on, 12-off schedule. It is a killing routine. It slowly wears one down. Twelve hours in 24 is a lot of hours doing something you don't like. It's difficult to sleep well during the day. I feel one of those long-absent feelings of disgust and lassitude coming over me. God, we're so helpless to do anything. Never have I so intensely felt the lack of freedom. I hate the army.

October 1

I'm back in better humor. Pain in my jaw gone.

This morning at about 10:00 I heard the unmistakable roar of a bomb explosion. I thought instantly it was a sneak attack. A high column of smoke rose from the airstrip inland. We learned later that a P-38 had caught fire and blown up. It was quite a blast scattering parts of the plane all over the field. Don't know if anyone was hurt. It's said the pilot got out in time. A rumor sprung up this morning that we lost 15 Libbies over Borneo to a new Jap interceptor, some sort of secret weapon. This has since been classified as a false story. The lights were on last night, throwing up a huge cross in the sky. This was supposedly to guide in any limping planes whose instruments had been destroyed. It sounds too fishy to be true. If it is, we're in a tough spot. Fifteen Libbies lost in the S.W.P. is no joke. There are always stories cropping up about secret weapons. Tip got the report on Brock, killed by shrapnel in the head by an explosion in an ammo dump.

Denison got photo-developing equipment, and he has rigged up a good darkroom in his tent. Watched him develop some snaps last night, a simple process. Think I'll develop my own when I get home. Took a roll of film today, will develop it tonight. Bud and Monroe drew first KP. Funny, former sergeant and corporal of the 3rd section. Now we are all T-5s.

October 3

The unusual windy weather kept us from working for over two days. It was a welcome respite that was broken last night at twelve. We worked in the stream on a freighter, loading it with heavy lift equipment from a powerless cement barge. The wind, that had caused some of the docks to give way because of the choppy sea, again rose intermittently during the night, causing the big, heavy cargo-hook to swing dangerously. When we stopped working during these times, I read Hilton's *Story of Dr. Wassell,* a true story dealing with the evacuation of Java. It was simply and well-told. I always liked Hilton's definition of writing. Tell a story.

The moon was bright all night, very round, and silvered the choppy sea. The warm wind, a bit wild, the clear air, the bright sky and low, dark, scudding clouds were all beautiful. I felt great peace and satisfaction. I also felt impersonal, as if I were an object absorbing the natural good of the scene and, in turn, imparting a sense of well-being. I felt at peace. Thank goodness for these moments in which the mind can escape into a beautiful void.

A few days ago Bud and I, who hold long discussions on anything from sex to politics, went to the 41st Division's hospital to see about the wisdom tooth that was bothering me. While waiting all morning to see the dentist, we watched the cargo planes land nearly sidewise because of the crosswind. We saw some nurses, the first white women in a long time. This is the same wisdom tooth that has troubled me periodically for the past two years. The dentist claimed that the upper tooth was cutting the gum of the lower because the wisdom tooth hasn't broken through yet. "Come back Monday," he said, "and I may pull it since it's not as good a one as the other." I have no desire to have even my less-standard teeth pulled, and besides the pain completely abated a few hours after he dressed it. I haven't gone back.

On the way back to camp I had a brilliant conversation with a nurse. We were thumbing a ride when she passed in a jeep, looking attractive and nonchalant in slacks, sun glasses and wind-blown hair. One leg was adolescently propped up. She smiled and said, "Sorry." I yelled, "Me too." That was that.

October 6

Good old 6-on, 12-off—a weary schedule.

There has been much talk of possible furloughs. It is more substantial than a rumor because we are all eligible. The sergeants took the names of those who want them. Most everyone did, of course. A furlough list has been compiled. Sgt. Stahl is number 1. Pap is 7th. I believe I am around 25th or 30th. There goes my hope to spend spring in Australia. With extreme luck I might get there in summer, though I doubt it. It depends how soon furloughs are issued, available transportation, and how many go at a time. I should imagine about five or six at one time, tops. It would be good to see Dale again if I ever do get back.

Dale has been a steady and interesting correspondent. In her last letter a few days ago, she recounted an interesting tale. It was a grand hoax pulled by two soldiers on some poetry critics and proved them pseudo-intelligentsia. Having little respect for the muddled impressionism of modern poetry, the two soldiers composed a so-called modern poem by combining jumbled and lifted sentences from an American article on drainage systems. The piece was hailed by the critics as an excellent example of modern Australian poetry and included in a book of poems, the preface of which was written by a friend of Dale's. When the hoax was made known, the critics who had praised this hodge-podge piece were, one might say, rather embarrassed.

Letters from Ginger and Enid yesterday. Enid still after me about the colorless way I end my letters. I object to using "love" at the end of my letters, because using it promiscuously destroys the value of the word. I have respect for words and the shades of meaning they imply, and I like to preserve them.

About a week ago 60 of our planes attacked Borneo in one of the biggest raids in the S.W.P. It is a long distance to Borneo, and the planes barely made it back on their gas supply. The planes only carried 75 tons of bombs among them. The raid concentrated on the oil dumps there and is said to be effective, though heavy fighter opposition was encountered. The report claims we destroyed seven out of thirty attacking Zeros while we lost three Liberators. It is stated that our men who parachuted from destroyed planes were machine-gunned in the air and in the water by the Japanese. The Japs continue to advance discouragingly fast in China while we slowly hack away in Burma. The Palau group is all in our hands now. [*This report is an example of the sometimes over-enthusiastic battle statements we received. Stubborn Japanese resistance continued in these islands, particularly Peleliu, for weeks later.*] There have been no raids here for some time in spite of the clear, bright nights. I guess we have seen the last of them. Old places like Rabaul and Wewak are still being bombed; they are occupied by isolated and non-attacking Jap troops.

The war in Europe goes steadily but slowly now. That defeat of our airborne troops in Holland was a bad blow. Only 1,800 out of 8,000 escaped the trap. We were forced to abandon 1,200 wounded. The rest were killed. Twelve thousand Germans were said to be killed. This I somehow doubt; I think we just must have taken a beating there.

October 9

The other evening Sig, because of an irresistible desire to have some fun, stole a weapons-carrier and had a jolly time tearing around. He took it at Bosnek, 10 miles away, and as fate would have it, the vehicle belonged to the 542nd just down the road. Sanchez was lucky. He got out of it before Rouse and Sig were picked up while gadding about. The major of the 542nd forced Wenz into preferring charges, and both face court martials. Watts is acting corporal in place of Rouse, who will probably lose his stripes.

October 13

Been loading ships heavily with ammo these past few days, including the new 240-mm shell. The invasion of the Philippines is rumored to take place before the month is out. These ships are supposed to be going there from Hollandia, where a huge convoy of some 400 ships is assembling. I truly hope so. It looks like we will be here for a number of months yet.

Morales stole a beautiful victrola from a recreation center down the line, and a whole new package of V-Discs. We have the old victrola in our tent now. It's pleasant having music right in the tent with us. If only I can get some classical music.

Yesterday I received a package from home containing four civilian shirts and socks. They made a familiar sight, and they smelled so wonderfully fresh and clean, and they smell of cedar from lying in my bureau for so long. It was the most beautiful perfume I ever hope to smell, it was the smell of home. The shirts are wonderful to wear around the tent to relax in.

Sig and Rouse drew 30-days extra duty, ⅔ of a month's pay lost, and Ray lost his corporal's stripes.

At the show the other night, which was pretty horrible, they showed films of Biak Island. At the end of the film there was a shot of the American flag fluttering in the breeze, and there was not a sound from the audience. It was a strange, dramatic kind of silence. For some reason it would have seemed ridiculous to cheer.

October 17

At the moment we hear the rumors that the Philippines have been invaded and that there is a great sea battle going on off Formosa. I would not be surprised. Both these actions seemed in the making and imminent. Not official, however.

I've scored something of a triumph in finally getting myself to run a winch. I ran the jumbo yesterday, and I fooled with one of the two handles of a one-man winch, which is by far more difficult. Haven't reached any advanced stage, of course. It made me feel good to run them because these machines, as do most machines, perplex me. Besides, it is easy to hurt someone with them. Still, it was a thrill for me to move that five-ton tractor. It is valuable to know in a pinch. I hope to become more proficient. Been working with Watts' gang as hold foreman, whenever possible, giving the checking job to Redwine. Been thinking about transferring permanently to it and letting Red take over the job. I am happier when working hard, and especially when I am in charge. Still I would hate to get out of Pap's and Adams' gang, who are the best holdmen in the platoon. What fellows to keep up with!

Been getting along wonderfully with everyone. I don't know whether this is a reflection of my own amiability, my being able to make the fellows laugh, or quite what it is. For some reason I am more at peace with the whole world and, for the most part, happy. I do miss female companionship lately, my home and family, of course, and sometimes I lament the time slipping by without further gain in education. Still, it is not bad—and we are winning the war.

Sig, Watts and I stole five gallons of coke syrup and we have been having cokes. No conscience about it, it's air corps stuff, and they get the cream of everything. Morales stole a beautiful radio set which now adorns Norm's tent. Norm, Bud and I have become especially fast friends. Bud will make T-4 as soon as someone slips up and gives him an opening.

Bud and I went out to see Flynn this afternoon. After chasing about the island, because he was evacuated from the 41st Hospital to the 9th General, we found him. The 9th is a beautiful hospital with really fine wards. In fact, we were amazed at the medical equipment and personnel. There are many hospitals being built all over the island—in anticipation, perhaps. Biak is now a tremendous base. Anyway, we found Flynn with a good case of yellow jaundice and visibly ill. We saw some rather ugly-looking skin disease patients. It was strange to see white sheets and pillow cases, pillows, springs and mattresses. There were numerous nurses about, some rather pretty, and more women than I've seen at one time in nearly a year. We killed an hour or more cheering Flynn up and told him about the 35-ton crane that was dropped and which ripped a hole in a LCT. This morning a barge crane was lifting it, a cable snapped, and 35 tons and about $50,000 worth of equipment went for an eternal dive. Jim's gang was supervising but not responsible for the accident. A colored winch operator was nearly killed.

Coming back we cut through the airstrips and made the return trip in less than half the time. It was interesting because we saw all the various planes at close range, something I've been wanting to see. The planes look much less impressive on the ground at close range than in the air. Some of the fighters had two or three Jap flags on them. We saw a Fortress, P-40, 47, 38, 61. Also C-47, Catalinas, A-20, B-25. The P-61 was by far the most impressive and imposing. It's a night fighter called the "Black Widow," and it looks lethal. It's a huge plane for a fighter, carrying a three-man crew and painted black.

Read Ernie Pyle's book, *Here Is Your War*. Excellent. He writes from the heart and is frank and truthful; he captures the real mood of the soldier better than any other newspaper writer. He writes human interest but good reports; I'm glad somebody is handling this angle for the people at home to read—and realize.

October 22

The war goes well on all fronts. Advances in Holland reported. Aachen has fallen after a week of street fighting, and other minor gains in France. In Italy continued small gains toward Bologna. Russians are fighting in Belgrade. Greece is close to completely liberated. The Russians are beginning to pierce Prussia and advancing south from Riga. The net tightens, it will strangle Germany soon.

Our landing in the Philippines [*on Leyte*] met little initial opposition and proceeds well. Here, we continue to load ships destined for there. MacArthur has "returned," and it is 6th Army troops that are in the show. The 41st will occupy, I imagine, when they finish taking it.

As MacArthur said, from Milne Bay, the start of the push against Japan, we have come 2,500 miles in 16 months. Another year, 1½ on the outside, to finish these Japs. More troops landed on D-day in the Philippines than in France on their D-day. Seven divisions it's said. This landing in Leyte right smack in the middle of the Philippines is of great strategical importance because it splits the defending forces on the islands in two and neutralizes, to a great extent, the Jap bases to the south in Borneo, Java, Celebes, Ceram, etc. There are ½-million Japs behind our lines. A funny thing, modern war. Only in China does the situation

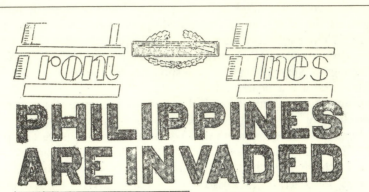

PHILIPPINES ARE INVADED

LUZON

Bataan MANILA
Corregidor

Mindoro

SIMAR

Palawan LEYTE

NEGROS Bohol

The Point
of
Invasion

MINDANAO
Davao

Talaud

Morotai

HALMAHERA

FRIDAY, 20 October, 10 AM
--Three years after the fall
of 'Corregedor the greatest
amphibious task force in the
Southwest Pacific landed once
again on Philippine soil. The
forces were reported as having
driven 750 yards inland in the
face of mortar opposition. It
was reported that all beaches
have been secured and that the
third and fourth waves have
gone ashore. The landing was
made on Leyte, 340 miles from
Manila. The land operation
was supported by bombers and
naval warships.

An eye-witness account to
the New York Times by war correspondent Frank Gluckhorn stated that the American flag was
once again on Philippine soil
as wave after wave of experienced Southwest Pacific jungle
fighters made their landing on
Leyte, which is above Mindanoa
and above Luzon.

A convoy of more than 1500
vessels of every description
left Dutch New Guinea Friday,
October 13. They hovered in
the vicinity of the central
Philippines for three days
during which time carrier-
based planes pounded targets
in the Philippines. The troops
landed without opposition.

They advanced inland toward the airdrome in 15 minutes. The troops
progressed under heavy mortar bombardment. It was reported that by
nightfall more troops will have landed on Leyte Island than on D-
Day in Europe. The Philippines have been under heavy bombardment for
14 days while the great task force waited in the vicinty of the central Philippines for a favorable in the weather, A task force carried
the 'cream of American troops ashore.

GENERAL MacARTHUR WITH TASK FORCE

General MacArthur came personally with the task force aboard the
cruiser Nashville. He was accompanied by Sergio Osmena, president
of the Philippines. General MacArthur said, "American forces are
on Philippine soil once again." He told the Filipinos that the
force came dedicated to the task of destroying enemy control "over
your lives". "At my side," he said, "is Sergio Osmena." He called
upon a supreme effort by the Filipinos to let the enemy know than m
enraged populace faced them from within as well as a force from
without.

Newsletter describing the invasion of the Philippines, dated Oct. 20, 1944.

look bad. China has already lost much ground and four airbases. The Japs still push forward, and the Chinese are unable to hold. The Jap advance there is more or less a countermove to our advances in the S.W.P. How effective it will be, time will tell. The Jap navy, time and again, has avoided a showdown fight. They will be smashed when they do stand and fight.

At work I have been handling Negro gangs. They are really funny sometimes, and I like to work with them, and sometimes prefer it. The other day one fellow said to me after a hard first hour, "I don't mind working with you, but you moves too fast"—and later—"When I carry this hook, I needs two men to hold me up." They have a great sense of humor and are most always bright-spirited. They are combat troops out of the 93rd who have been converted to service troops. They have colored officers, one of whom I saw today. Norm told me about him, a grad of a Midwestern school, studying for a M.A. in music when called into the army. He drives the men under him hard.

Today "stringing them up" on the dock, I told one colored fellow to be careful that a cable caught right in lifting an eight-ton truck, while he stood between truck and ship. "If she comes your way," I said, "jump into the water."

"But," he said, serious and wide-eyed, "I can't swim!"

October 25

Yesterday morning at breakfast Stahl informed me that I am now a buck corporal. Though I have expected the promotion, I didn't figure it to come so quickly, and so it was a surprise. Langham and Bud were at the table with me, and Bud offered sincere congratulations. The only other person I cared to tell was Norm, who was very pleased. Although I have long thought this was the spot for me, it throws upon me quite a responsibility because I will be in charge of a hatch by myself. Also, I have some difficult men to deal with, and I am the youngest man in the section. Nevertheless, I welcome it. For one thing, no more KP and guard duty. Technically I am over Pap, which is really a laugh. But this is what I need to build up confidence, poise, and to get used to giving orders instead of continually carrying them out. It does feel a little odd, but so did T-5 when I first got it. The only other rated men in my gang are Watts and Hern, who will make T-5.

Couple of nights ago, just before making corporal, I had charge of a gang and ran the winch with Watts for three hours. I have to learn to run winches alone and more about rigging. Bud gave me a lesson the other night. I had a close call when claws tore lose the top of a box holding an airplane motor. Happily the box fell on deck, and we eventually got it off, but it was uncomfortably close. I'll have to watch for Eriksen; he is notorious for picking on new non-coms and testing their mettle with his harangues. Colored fellow pulled a knife on Eriksen the other night, and Eriksen did the wise thing and backed away and out of the argument. Nothing came of it. With Stahl going on furlough soon, that will leave me acting sergeant and in charge of the whole section. That will be a test. Use your head, Sy.

Evening—later.

Just got in from ship. It's after supper. Put in quite a day. Three hours in hold, 2½ on the electric winches. I'm dead tired, absolutely too fatigued to write a letter. Being corporal means nearly steady work, no more three on, three off. New system now. They send out five gangs of 10 each, which means the gang off will have to supply the deficit. This will probably take half the men or more in the gang off. Talked to Ray Rouse this afternoon and he was quite decent. He can be when he wants to be. He told me that I was letting myself in for a headache, which I knew; and I strained my good judgment and told him in a general way the reasons that I took the job. He told me that some of the fellows didn't like the way I bossed them the first night I had charge. I didn't particularly want to, but my being new and a bit nervous in addition to their under-average work were, I believe, the causes of my bossiness. Ray gave me a good tip: "Let the men make the decisions whenever possible and on unimportant things." This is good advice. The one thing I have been and intend to be is absolutely fair and unbiased, and to give the men under me every break I can. In a few days my new role should wear a little more comfortably. It is quite a metamorphosis.

Teddy handed in his corporal's stripes; he wasn't the kind of fellow to be a non-com in the first place. Harris and Hiller both returned yesterday, though Harris has a pending transfer to the 119th Medics. Harris still the same and full of talk about the various rackets at Finsch. This may all be true; I have heard it from other sources. Williams (now a private) and Fazekas, who was at New Britain and headed for Sudest for reclassification, have written letters with company news. Lake is reclassified as a 1st looie and has a nurse at Finsch. Finschhafen is full of women. Morris is back in the States, NYC in fact; Basil Jones transferred to amphibs, and three others transferred out. Reinhardt (Bobby) is strictly GI now and so is Aitape. Hope it doesn't get that way here.

Last night worked out in the stream on floating crane unloading LCIs [*landing craft infantry, a shallow draft assault craft smaller and faster than the bargelike LCT*]. Gave Mike the shift off. Today Sancho and Singleton were ill, so these three will be the first to fill gaps in other sections where they are needed. I plied Sancho with atabrine this morning; he's better now. A touch of malaria, perhaps.

Fellows stole case of Milky Ways, chocolate mints, and a case of grapefruit juice. We divided it up tonight; it was chocolate all day. First real candy I've had in many months, and with the first piece I found that I've completely lost my taste for sweets. Damn, but I'm tired.

October 28

Been working steadily and have found the job of corporal no cinch. Also, I have been short-handed, so work has been no picnic. Last night I did four hours on the electric winches and learned something about rigging. Today did another three hours. Was so tired last night that I slept from 12:30 straight through to 11:00 this morning. Now I know the difficulties of being a non-com, but as Ray said, "Your troubles are just beginning." He was right. Not only am I responsible for the hatch I work, but I must contend with various officers on the dock and ship, and with non-coms of other units, all making different demands, and I must try to appease all of them. Besides this, I try to give my own men the breaks, something I believe in doing as often as possible. I'm up to my neck—and love it. No more time for reading on the ships, though. I have become proficient on the electric winches, but have yet to master steam winches by myself. My gang has been running pretty smoothly. I hope Eriksen gets this new system working so that the fellows get at least one out of six shifts off. Hern will make T-5, Perkins and Redwine Pfc. Glad to see that. Haven't had two T-4s in the section since Cape Sudest when Jim got transferred. Anyway, I am beginning to feel the strain of the job. In a few weeks, the rough edges of my status will wear smooth. Watts and Rouse have been especially helpful.

Norm and I had the tiff that has been brewing between us for several days. His arrogant manner was slowly getting my goat, adding to the pressure on me these past few days. Consequently when he accused me of "bitching under my breath" about his not getting the films developed, which was absolutely untrue, I was peeved. I don't believe he exactly meant that, but simply expressed himself poorly. At any rate, it was enough to make me lose my temper. I wrote a letter for Bud to the University of Buffalo, requesting information on their pre-med program.

A very funny hoax was pulled on Charley Norvell yesterday when he received in the mail his Captain Marvel pin [*comic book character popular in the* 1940s] and membership card, personal letter from Captain

Marvel telling him to help the war effort by saving scrap paper. That was a tremendous laugh. Herndon is the one responsible. Poor Charley will never live it down. Fellows go about yelling "Shazam" at him, and "Here comes Captain Marvel!" Everybody has been hilarious about it.

Now to get some sleep; I need to be up at 5:00 A.M. The report (nothing very clear yet) has us victorious in that big sea battle off the Philippines. If so, this is a big victory and a giant step toward the end.

November 1

Night before last (little after midnight now) worked the ship, a liberty with steam winches. It was my first crack alone at them, and I worked them two hours. After the first hour I handled them fairly well. My first five minutes I had the fellows in the hold jumping. That inboard winch was stiff as blazes. My hands were cramped after an hour of shoving those handles. They are much more difficult to handle than the electric winches, and twice as dangerous. It is very easy to hurt a man, or get hurt in our work. Our luck has been excellent, but bad accidents have been happening among the colored infantry working the dock. A load from the electric winches the other day broke one man's neck when it landed on his head. Today, a man was caught behind the ear by a flying chain, and it killed him. I'll have to keep my eyes open for the safety of all of us.

Officially today I was made buck corporal; the announcement was on the bulletin board. Gang was off today, and tomorrow too with only two remaining hatches. General cargo, slow to handle.

This morning we had a terrific rainstorm for an hour, and just as I write this it's beginning again, drumming on the tent, with gusts of wind. Really pouring again now. Ron got back from the hospital today.

Have been thinking of Carolyn comparatively little this past week. My mind has been occupied with running the gang and learning more about winches and gear. Of course, I still do think of Carolyn, but not so intensely, and I have developed almost as patient an attitude toward waiting for her letters as for anybody else's. For some time and for some reason, I'm increasingly feeling independent of everything and everybody more than ever before.

November 2

Last night we had the midnight shift and I had my first tiff with the sergeants, Stewart in particular. Harris, a notorious goldbrick, was sick, and therefore Stew didn't give me the man I was entitled to draw from

Harlan Thomas, signalman to the winch operator, unloading a liberty ship "in the stream" off Biak Island, 1944.

Ray Rouse, shortly before he was wounded by rifle fire, Biak Island, 1944.

Charles "Bud" Herbeck, Biak Island,
1944.

Leland Watts, Biak Island, 1944.
Note coral terrain.

the off-gang. I went to see him on the ship. We were working the jumbo boom on number four, and I knew we needed every man available. Stewart got sore, but I was in the right. I can't possibly call a man with a fever out to work, notorious goldbrick or not. He sent W. Harris over. When we opened number four and found organizational equipment instead of heavy lifts, I returned Harris, for I didn't absolutely need him. However, I was right in principle in requesting another man. We supply men to other gangs when they are short. We took off two ton on the jumbo, and then finding what we did in the hold, we changed to the regular booms. This entailed a full job of rigging, about which I was somewhat ignorant, up to last night. Learning rigging never appealed to me; now it is imperative that I learn it. Our men could probably have done it, and better, the way it turned out, but I wanted the merchant marine on it. The mate, boatswain and a few men did the main work while I helped, watched and learned in the process. I picked up a lot of facts and learned the principles. Rigging doesn't worry me so much anymore.

It was an extremely foul night, chilly, with a steady, cold drizzle. The lighting was poor. We had the jumbo up, the booms down and spotted, and nothing more to do but to tighten the midship. The boatswain fouled that by tightening with the runners instead of hooking on the combing and pulling down. I learned plenty, but I was cold, dirty, tired and wet by 4:00 A.M. I sent most of my section back at 4:30 A.M. The fouling entailed bringing the inboard boom all the way down, and at 6:00 when we left, they were still trying to loosen the fouled runner from the block. We didn't get any more cargo off, but the time spent was worth the lessons to me. A couple of weeks and I'll have learned what I need to know.

Had to inspect the fellows' rifles today because I'm acting sergeant since Stahl left [*recently on leave to Australia*]. Eriksen has been particularly easy on me, and even helpful. Maybe he's taking it easy because I'm in charge of my squad with such limited experience. It's quite an effective way to learn to be a good corporal—by being acting sergeant!

Sent $100 home for Christmas presents for Dad, Babs, Carolyn, Enid and Edith: smoking jacket for Dad, Beethoven's 9th and notebook holder for Babs, "Duchess of York" perfume for Carolyn, "Indian Suite" for Enid, letter paper and box for Edith. Flowers to all. Hope Edith gets something nice for Mom with the money I sent her. She wrote jade bracelets cost $100. Mom writes I have $706 in bank to date. Hope to have $1,500 by the time I get back. That, with government tuition, ought to get me through four years anyway. I must not lose sight of that road to education. I must return. Not sure what to study—but I must get back. If only the damned war won't take too many more years. Can't complain, there are fellows in a lot worse spots.

November 5

Everything was going wonderfully well. My gang was running smoothly and I was and am learning by leaps and bounds—and acquiring the confidence which I originally sought. I gave the fellows every break I could, and I know they are used to my position. We did have a close call yesterday when Ray hooked the strongbacks in the 'tween decks and pulled three of them into the hold. Nobody hurt, however; that is most important, that no one get hurt.

Yesterday afternoon the six gang leaders were called to the platoon sergeant's tent and informed that one gang would be dissolved into the others, making five full-strength gangs and most likely eliminating our days off. The plan wasn't enthusiastically greeted. Anyway, it was decided that high card break his gang, delivering two men to each. I knew I would lose before the cards were offered—I felt it as a sure and foreboding fate. That ace of spades came to my hand as if it had a handle. I called the fellows together to give each his choice where he wanted to work. Having the choice, I naturally chose Pap Milligan's gang where my rank makes me automatic gang leader. I shall be glad to have Pap's experience at hand. Singleton drew the other spot in the gang. The fellows, of course, didn't like to be broken up, and I felt pretty rotten about it because it was my first gang and everything ran so smoothly. It had me down but I'm over it.

Last night I went to the boxing matches across the way, which weren't bad at all. Reminded me of the old days, when Dad and I used to go to the matches at Dyckman Oval.

The rest of the 604th is up here now. The camps look permanent. In fact, at this moment a machine is drilling a well near the officers' tent. Bulldozers cleared the coral that has been around our tents for months. It doesn't look like we shall be moving for awhile. The kitchen personnel had an argument with the 604th fellows, and now the cooks are out on the line. We got Owen, and he put in a good night's work last night. Good thing we had him, short as we were. Most of the fellows are resentful of the 604th moving in and taking everything over, and volatile tempers break out now and then. It's rather foolish, because the men haven't much to say where they camp or to whom they are attached. The 604th brought improvements, the best of which is the refrigerator. We have a good shower now, too, and even electric lights in the tent. If it weren't that I lost my gang, it would be pleasant. However, the new system isn't in effect yet, and perhaps it will not happen. Other plans have vanished. If we remain on the same schedule, my gang will be off tonight.

November 6

This morning I had a little episode which may possibly cost me my corporal's stripes. Informed that there was mail, I went to the orderly tent. There was a pile of mail on Dowdle's desk. He had his feet propped up on it and was reading his. I inquired when ours would be handed out, and he said that because the men were sleeping, he would not call it now. I pointed out that phonographs were blaring, card games were on, and that no one was asleep. It was already 10:30, and we had to have chow at 11:00. I decided to wait until he finished reading his letter, but my temper was rapidly rising. Dowdle has gotten under my skin for a long time with his lackadaisical attitude toward delivering the mail. Mail is one of our chief pleasures, and the fact that he makes us await his pleasure has long infuriated me, along with his supercilious attitude. When he finished the letter, I saw him proceed to open another, and so again I asked when we got ours. He replied when he was good and ready. I cursed him out. In between oaths I told him that because we worked steadily we'd like to get our mail in time to read and answer it. He came back with how he was going to mess me up, so I took a light swing at him and grazed the top of his head. To my utter amazement over he went, hitting the floor, the chair tipping over. I know I just barely touched him. He began to come at me, and I stood there ready for him. Tipple and Sanchez stepped between us, and that was that. However, I told him to get the mail out or else he and I were going to have a set-to. Five minutes later we had mail call, and I got a letter from home and from Enid.

The news spread in no time, of course, and at lunch I could hear the story told and our names spoken. I received many thanks from the fellows for my action. There has been talk that Dowdle turned me in to Wenz, which as Pap says would be typical of Dowdle. If he does and I get broken, I'll take it out of his hide as a private. In the heat of my anger I forgot my position as a non-com. Anyway, I have my side of the story to tell, and though ethically I am right, I am actually in the wrong. For one who rarely uses physical violence, I certainly picked the spot. I must admit I will regret if I do lose my stripes because I was and am so happy having the position. However, he had it coming to him for a long time. We shall see.

November 9

Dowdle apparently decided not to turn me in. He wouldn't have stood a good chance, though it might possibly have gone hard with me. Anyway, mail delivery has been better, it seems. Got a couple of packages today, mostly food. One from Dad is a large, sealed can with no markings. Probably something to eat; hope it isn't Spam. That would be the last straw.

November 12

This non-com job has been keeping me very busy. Trying to appease the fellows and the various officers is a tough job, and I'm a tired lad at the end of a shift.

Last night I had chills and fever. I haven't been feeling right the last few days. Stuck it out for the shift though I hurt all over. Got 10 hours sleep, and when I woke this morning I felt better. Dosed up on plenty of atabrine, which probably helped. Haven't been taking as much as I should. Fever's been fairly common; Demers in the hospital with it, and Shorty has not been right for a few days. I sent him back early today, and when I got back to camp, I found he was taken to the hospital, too. Might be that malaria is breaking out and my good condition prevented it from getting a hold. Atabrine keeps it down.

Read and enjoyed a collection of short stories by Ring Lardner. Don't get time to read much anymore. Find it takes more discipline to lead than to be led.

November 17

Played basketball against colored engineers the other night under lights on a good gravel court. I was very tired after the game, having played all but three minutes when I was out with a bloody nose. It's been a long time since I've played any basketball, but it was fun in spite of Harris' grating voice. He's not a bad player. Score was 24–13. We lost.

Last night I went to an entertaining stage show put on by the 41st Division. On the way back to camp, Smitty tripped and laid his arm open, requiring stitches.

Colby flew out of here a few days ago. He was third man on the furlough list; Miranda turned his down. Right after he left all furloughs from Biak were cancelled. Anyway, two men went, which puts me 16th on the list. I doubt whether I will receive one before I get back to the

U.S. It would be fun to see Dale again after a year now, and to browse around a big city.

November 20

I've been sick these past few days. Chills and fever hit me as suddenly as last time, after I worked two shifts in the hold. We were short-handed with Hendricks in the hospital, now back, and men on camp detail. I missed the last three shifts, first two in part, and last night I didn't go out at all. Fortunately there wasn't too much work these past few shifts, though Pap can easily handle everything.

Last night was especially bad. Bud took my temperature, and it was 102. I figured I was good for a week in the hospital had I gone to the dispensary. However, these past few days of no food, heavy doses of atabrine and some aspirin, along with two days and nights in bed, getting fitful sleep, have brought me around. I decided to go to the hospital this morning, but my temperature was nearly normal, and it is normal this afternoon. The pain in my back is nearly gone, and some amount of strength has returned. That's one advantage in being a non-com; when you're sick you have only yourself to ask if you stay in or not. I have that control over the fellows in my gang, though if a man tells me he's sick, I immediately send him in.

The fellows have been getting liquor from the merchant marine who sell it at about $40 a pint, and several men have been drunk. Sanchez was pretty sick for a couple days. Scarborough got caught drunk in the hold and got 24-hours extra duty, which is no fun to make up in off-time during our steady 6-on, 12-off. Mike had a pint this morning. I took a small drink, and I believe it helped me. The warming effect felt good after these chills.

Furloughs to Australia are definitely frozen. Cobo flew out just in time. Rumors of a new system, though nothing clear yet. We, with 14 months overseas, need not be concerned, I suppose. Almost one year in the tropics. I hope to be out of the tropics before it becomes two years.

November 21

Yesterday the fellows stole two cases of whiskey. Last night the heavy drinking began; tonight it's still going strong. We've been lucky in that none of the sections has been drawing hard work. In fact, we haven't pulled a full shift in the last six. Last night the party was centered in Norm's tent. I went to bed, but York came over and woke me up. I had a half-cup of bourbon. It was powerful stuff and hit the fellows hard.

When I went to bed at about 2:00 A.M., my head throbbed just a bit. The fellows were still going strong, and most everyone was high, and some were thoroughly stinko by the time I left. Norm acted like a typical drunk and was awfully funny. Bud was high, Langham, Eriksen, everybody. This morning the fellows recuperated pretty well; we didn't have to go on till noon. There were an awful lot of big heads. Sigley was a mess. He had a mean cut on his forehead, and one side of his face was battered pretty badly. York hit him with a bottle. Of course nobody remembers anything. Kasprzyk was still out this morning, and several were still pretty drunk. The first thing I saw when I awoke this morning was Devaney staggering about, very drunk. Stewart and Eriksen were especially sick, throwing up, as did a number of others throughout the night.

Taking small shots during the day, the men started drinking heavily again tonight. I was sure that every drop had been consumed last night. Hindmon was stewed silly when I left with Bud for the movies tonight. I guess it must be all gone now since Rouse and Watts were just in here, pretty high but not quite drunk, looking for more.

Last night the merchant marine got hold of some of the bourbon (they attempted to hijack some trucks too), and they were pretty well stewed at the docks. It resulted in some free-for-alls. It's been a fast-moving three days.

This afternoon, after finding out our stream ship was finished, our section returned to camp, that is, those who had not gone "for a drink of water." Capt. Smith wanted six "volunteers," so we were detached to him. Our detail took us down to the Red Cross area in order to dig a small ditch for a water pipe. Now I know where all the women come from that I've seen running about in jeeps. Their deluxe tents were in a stockade-like area, MP at gate. Our work took us right into the camp. It was strange to see women's silk underthings fluttering on the line! It was warm pick-and-shovel work under the afternoon sun. We got the job done in a couple of hours, in spite of the constant parade all afternoon of females in scanty attire coming out of the nearby shower house. It was more women than we've seen in over a year. Air corps officers were much in evidence, which got under the fellows' skin, and mine also because of the principle of the thing!

I can say this truthfully. Seeing all these women suddenly I had the strongest reaction of aversion. My reaction was not only toward these women but all the girls I used to know: Enid, Carolyn, Shirley, all of them. These women here with their mincing steps, small bodies, long hair, and especially those whining, typically American female voices irritated me as if they were sandpaper rubbing on my brain. Odd. I was glad when we got out of the area. I don't like seeing women over here, and for the life of me I can't see any good in it. They cause more trouble than they are worth. Of course they are good for the officers' morale!

The afternoon was not without humor. We broke a pick during the digging operation, and so I sent Redwine back to camp for a new one. During that short time he managed to get half-crocked and to bring back half-a-bottle. He even offered Capt. Smith a drink. The fellows had a few shots. I mixed mine with some cold pineapple juice, and it made a refreshing drink. The newly-finished Red Cross building nearby was the source of the juice. Anyway, we finished the job, and I sent Frank back for transportation. He made a most ludicrous sight standing on the side of the road, his hat cocked over one eye, his thumb up, and wavering on his feet. Meanwhile a brigadier general came to the women's area, and he and another officer picked up two of the women and drove off, going past Frank. And there was poor Frank wavering on his feet trying to bum a ride from the general! Frank finally got a truck to stop for him, and when he started to run after it, his head preceded his legs by about three feet so that he ran slantwise. He stumbled along in this peculiar form of locomotion, with all laws of equilibrium apparently repealed. He made it without falling and killing himself, but it was a minor miracle. It has indeed been a busy two days!

Two of the women stopped to talk with me about the work; the conversation lasted about a minute. I mention this because it is the most extended conversation I have had with a female since leaving Dale.

Shook off the fever all right.

November 23

Thanksgiving dinner this afternoon consisted of turkey, dressing, tomatoes, potatoes, peas, pumpkin pie, tea, and oranges. I took exactly one bite of everything and nearly threw up. Excluding the egg sandwich this morning, I haven't touched any food in three days. I've been pretty sick with chills, fever and sheer exhaustion. Of course you need a fever to prove you're sick here. Went to the dispensary across the road and got a couple of aspirin and some small, bitter, white pills. Today, a little while ago, Bud drove me over to the Port dispensary where a pretty good captain talked to me. I told him all that I've been experiencing these two past weeks, including the cough. He asked about my work and how long I've been over. He said that I was probably run down from being overseas so long, or that I had a touch of malaria. Next time I get a chill I'm to report to have a smear taken. I guess this is the saddest Thanksgiving I've experienced. I hope I shall not spend another in the tropics. I'm getting weary.

The fellows have been working steadily, thanks to Lt. Wenz. Any time we have an opportunity for a break, he calls up to find us a ship in the stream, or a barge, or anything. I guess he's scared of leaving here now. Many of the fellows are sick. Monroe is in the hospital, and Howe also, with jungle rot which he's had for months. The only thing that's been keeping me going on this 6-on, 12-off schedule is the fact that in the 11 hours off, I've been on my back 10½ of them, sleeping intermittently with frequent nightmares. Damn, I just need some rest.

Perkins stayed in last night; he, coupled with the two men off on detail, left us plenty short-handed because we needed men to work the guys on the single boom. We were left with two two-man hold gangs. Good thing the work wasn't very heavy.

November 25

Fourteen months overseas today, a long time.

Been pretty sick these past days. Can't eat, sleep only intermittently. Ate a little supper last night and threw it up in the middle of the night. My back has been bothering me considerably, feel very weak, still have that persistent cough. Urine has changed to an orange color.

Went to the dispensary this morning, and the doctor examined me and asked some questions. He sent me to the Base Hospital for a blood and urine check. He also marked me "duty." I don't know how the doctor figures I can do any work, or hitchhike eight or nine miles to Base H. and back again in the heat and dust, feeling as I do. I'm really sick, and yet at midnight out I'll go to the ship for six brutal hours at the end of which I'll be so exhausted I can hardly stand, just as it has been for the past week. I'm trying to arrange with Nix for transportation to the hospital this afternoon. Absolutely out of the question to attempt 16 miles of hitchhiking. You positively need a fever to prove you are ill here. Sanchez just came in off the ship with a fever, went to the dispensary, and was just carted away to the hospital. It wouldn't surprise me if more are to follow.

Fellows got hold of a lot of beer last night on one of the ships, and the usual gang was drunk. We have again the tentative plan to form six gangs to work the dock and ships in the stream. Personally, I'm too sick to give much of a damn right now about anything.

November 27

Here I am in the 105th General Hospital. Yesterday after several visits to the dispensary with the reports of my tests, I was sent here with acute caudural jaundice. My back and liver had become acutely sensitive, and the uncomfortable jeep ride up here yesterday jarred them painfully. Today I feel about the same: weak with discomfort in the back and abdomen, low fever, no appetite, and my eyes turning yellow.

It is comfortable, clean and fairly cool here. It is good to lie in a bed with springs and clean cool sheets. The doctor in charge of this ward is decent, and the nurses seem all right. One is oldish with a gentle voice and manner. The other is a brunette, of about 26–27. Naturally the main conversation in the ward concerns this nurse or when the men will get home. I'm considered a bed patient. I guess I am, though I can move around to a degree without difficulty. As a bed patient I have all meals in bed. My status also resulted in my having a rather embarrassing experience this morning: a bed bath given to me by the younger nurse. I didn't mind the head, back, torso and shoulders so much, but when she said, "Take off your pants," I got worried. However, she moved away while I undressed, and I lay with nothing but a sheet between me and humiliation. She then bathed my legs, and I felt very foolish—and then I was informed to finish the rest of me. I told the fellow next to me that I was glad that was as far as she went. In fact, very glad. Tomorrow I'm getting up early and taking a shower no matter how bad I feel so that I won't have to go through that again. I am enjoying this rest, but will enjoy it more when I can get hold of some decent reading material. There doesn't seem to be much here.

The other day when I was up for the blood and urine tests, the fellow giving them got to talking with me, and he told me he was in need of an assistant. He said he was serious and he would accept me as one and teach me what I needed to know about the work. He had a beautiful microscope and swell lab to work in. That's the kind of job I would have loved getting into at the beginning. However, even if I could change now I wouldn't because I've been with the same group of fellows and outfit for so long. Besides, my position as non-com wouldn't very well permit it. It was good to use the scope for a few moments anyway.

Received letters from home, from Dale and from Ginger. Dale's letters continue to be swell. I'd give a lot for a furlough to Sydney. Ginger's officially announced her engagement to Dick, which comes as no great surprise.

Good-oh! Here comes some cold coke!

December 1

Feel somewhat better with some return of appetite. There are many jaundice cases coming in, and the major who examined the fellow next to me said that it was taking on epidemic proportions. This fellow next to me just came in yesterday, a big Italian fellow and friendly. We talked some last night in the most extended conversation I've had here so far. He flew down from Moratai where they are still being bombed, though not heavily. The Japs said they were going to counter-invade the island within 10 days. I guess there must be a number of them on Halmahera.

The worst part about this place is the lack of reading material. If I had some good books I'd be perfectly happy. Tried some poetry but couldn't go it yesterday. Tipple and Dewey came over last night with four cans of beer, three cigars and a month's pay. I must have about $500 in hand. I guess I'm good here for another week; I still have jaundice.

December 4

Yesterday Bud and Norm visited. They inform me that work is easy these days and that I've lost weight. My appetite has returned, though I still have jaundice. Bud, Herndon, Rice and Harris hopped a ride to Noemfoor for the hell of it. It's only a half-hour run. They claim there isn't much doing there, though they had a chance to go on a bombing mission to Leyte. They also brought me a package containing sardines, canned chicken and melba toast from Mrs. Kastor [*Enid's mother*]. That melba toast is especially good. The hospital food is nothing to rave about, not much variety, mostly beets and potatoes for dinner and supper.

Last night I went to the movies and saw *Summer Storm* with George Sanders whom I like very much. A good picture, kind I like. About 11:30 I was partially awakened by a man yelling while running by the ward. This morning I found out more about it; it was a soldier hysterically yelling that Japs were coming. I was so tired last night that he never did fully wake me.

I am reading a book of plays and *Flight to Arras* by St. Exupéry. [*I had discovered the Red Cross Library in the hospital.*] No other change. I'm just taking it easy in the hospital which fills with more casualties every day, mostly from Leyte. A Negro quartet sang a few spirituals in every ward. They weren't bad.

December 7

The Japs attacked us three years ago today; I was 17. I remember the day clearly. I first heard about it coming out of the 181st Street Coliseum [*movie theatre*]. The next day all the students and teachers gathered in the George Washington High School auditorium to hear President

Roosevelt's declaration of war. And now, three years later, I'm in the hospital on Biak Island with a case of jaundice.

Anyway I'm feeling a lot better, and even played some ping-pong last night at the Red Cross, and then ate the sardines Mrs. Kastor sent. Still have traces of jaundice in my eyes though, so I guess I'm here for awhile yet. Yesterday I read Hugh Walpole's *The Killer and the Slain,* an interesting story. Sort of a Jekyll and Hyde theme, but unusual story. Browsed through the library last night but could find nothing of interest.

The European front is ablaze, and some commentators claim that the final battles of that war are now shaping up. It is maddening to read of the bickering and small-scale revolutions that are taking place in countries that have been cleansed of Germans. I do not say "liberated" because, in truth, I don't know if they are truly liberated or not. In Greece, Belgium, France, Italy and Yugoslavia, various factions are trying to control the government and people. Some monarchs are trying to get back their thrones, but the day of the monarch is over. How many years is it going to take for all these countries to settle into peace? And how big a part must the U.S. play in rehabilitating the world after the Germans are defeated? Probably the U.S. will have to unravel the political knots and keep the peace with U.S. soldiers. Democratic and communistic factions will try to secure a hold on the governments, not even to mention minor factions.

In China the situation is gloomy. The Japs are preparing to make a drive on Chungking, and it would not surprise me if it is successful. Their advance will set the day of final victory back months and months. If Chungking falls, the backbone of Chinese resistance will be broken. The recent, frequent raids on Japan are heartening. The Philippine campaign seems stalemated at present, torrential rains slowing it up. The strategy is hard to understand. We draw closer to Japan on one side while she continues to advance in China. I hope that the European war can be ended within the next few months so that we can bring more of our forces to bear on Japan. There is a long road to travel, I'm afraid. As for home, that's at least another year away.

December 9

Finished *So Little Time.* I enjoyed it so much because it deals with settings, time and people I know so well. The setting is mostly New York or the part of Connecticut I know. The time is the past few years, and the people are familiar. It's good writing in that Marquand has captured the tempo of the times, and his characterizations are vivid. I paused often, because there was so much in the novel that was familiar, and sent me off on my own memories.

There was a piece in the paper yesterday about a paratrooper who had been hung at Oro Bay for a murder in Brisbane. The trial was held there because there is no capital punishment in Queensland. Odd place to be hung, Oro Bay, New Guinea.

Doctor was around this morning. He said I would be here for another 10 days. I don't care, it's like a vacation. Getting plenty of good sleep. Been thinking of writing, but then I always manage to find something to do to avoid it. I believe I'm both afraid and a little lazy. My appetite is back, and I'm hungry half the time.

December 13

Saw a picture I much enjoyed last night, *Devotion,* with one of my favorites, Ida Lupino. The story dealt with the Brontë family and the writing of *Jane Eyre* and *Wuthering Heights.* The part I liked best was that distant shot of Wuthering Heights on the wild moors, with dismal clouds scudding low in the sky. Her monologue there is stirring.

To add to my infirmities I have contracted a rather severe case of either jungle rot or athlete's foot, which is now being treated. Only several toes are affected so far, and I hope it doesn't spread or get worse. It's messy stuff and painful. I still have traces of jaundice and may, indeed, spend Christmas here. This makes 18 days that I have been here now, and I've enjoyed it, despite the heat in the new ward. It's been a welcome rest in a bed with springs, sheets and mattress. I feel quite well now, and my hospitalization serves as a furlough, in a way.

I have written a short story called "Murphy Burns at Eleven." It is a good short story, though not remarkable. The theme is a little unusual; I could not ever write anything that didn't have at least one point out of the ordinary! I feel sometimes I have the capacity to write something great, and as always my head is filled with ideas, snatches of dialogue and characterization and description. So many things rush into my head when I start to write about writing that I always end up feeling a little distraught and foolish—as now. Yet I can, I know I can, and one day I shall.

Am half way through *Anthony Adverse.* For one who wants to read so much, and loves it so much, my reading speed is pitiable. I absorb novels as if they were textbooks. Much as I sometimes try to speed my reading, I am too steeped in the habit of careful reading that I can't break it. Although I have been here for about three weeks, being lazy and doing nothing physical, the thought of returning to camp is not comfortable. It has been so good to get away from everyone.

The Leyte campaign seems to be drawing to a close. Ormoc has fallen. In Europe, Budapest is surrounded and expected to fall soon. That has been a long campaign. The Russians are 20 miles from Austria, while continued pressure is applied on other German fronts. How long can they last now? A few months perhaps. Japan is bombed quite regularly. Also, it seems as if Chiang Kai-shek has made some agreement with the communists in China. This will add 500,000 troops, reportedly good troops, to his forces. He had to acquiesce because of the latest Jap drive, which now is halted and even thrown back a little. That's a serious situation there.

December 17

Events move swiftly. This morning Lt. Wenz and Tipple came to see me and to give me the surprising news that we pull out tomorrow! Lt. Wenz wants to get me out. Happily the doctor was nearby, and we conferred with him. He consented to let me go tomorrow on the promise that Lt. Wenz would allow me to rest in camp for about a week. At this the Lieutenant waved his hand deprecatingly and said he would give me a month if necessary. Luckily my urine specimen went in yesterday, and the doctor is overlooking the blood test.

I got a pass in order to get back to camp and get my things together. Lt. Wenz drove us back in his brand new jeep. Camp showed the signs of breaking up, stripped of all the luxuries we accrued during these past months. Driving down, Lt. Wenz informed me that we are to pull out tomorrow, head for Sansapor, and there join the rest of the company. He intimated another quick move after that, which I gather will be the Philippines. Mindora was invaded yesterday, 150 miles from Manila. They must be catching hell.

Our tent was stripped, my desk out, and all my stuff packed. Pap explained that the original move orders at midnight gave four hours to pack. Of course these orders were rescinded in usual army style, and the men have been waiting for three days. They had the tents down and had to put them back up. Sanchez did my packing, the sloppiest man in the outfit, and his job made me sore at heart. This stuff is all I own in the world. However, I couldn't blame Sancho because he had such short notice. Lots of stuff had to be thrown out because of lack of space, and the fellows had to decide what to discard in my absence. I couldn't agree with all their choices. All my food supply was devoured. That was all right. But in repacking my two bags I found much valuable equipment and some personal effects gone which I shall sorely miss. The equipment can eventually be replaced, but the pipe that Dad gave me, the Peterson, is missing, and the old cheap ones still there. I'd give $50 to have that pipe back. I didn't care about anything else that was gone, though I would not like to be rushed into a campaign without the missing equipment.

Pap gave me a hand and was surprisingly sympathetic at my losses. For these I cursed Sancho, I'm afraid. All my stationery was gone, but Pap made sure my journals and all my books were saved. Those would have been a terrific loss. These journals are irreplaceable. Happily they were in good order. Packing, I separated the stuff into two bags. One I have at the hospital containing things I will need for the voyage, a few books, and, of course, the journals and pictures and other papers of value to me, along with some letters, all of Carolyn's—the last dated October 2.

Had lunch in camp, wrote a quick letter to Mom, and then Tipple drove me back to the hospital with the half-full bag containing essentials to life and spirit. Here I got things in order, replaced my dirty towels with clean hospital ones. Not ethical, but necessary at this point. Everything I own is ready to move in three minutes' notice.

Among other things missing are my maps, lantern, etc.—well, why think about them, they are irretrievably gone. I shall miss the presence of that pipe surely. Slowly all the old things are gone. My rifle was packed away and will not be available until we land. I hope we do land at Sansapor so that I can get my things back in order. I imagine we will be there for awhile in order to get re-outfitted. I need that badly, at the moment. All our Dutch money was handed in. Pap handed 250 guilders in (for he had my wallet) under his name, and I gave Tip 130 more this afternoon. The rumor is that we are to get American money which doesn't quite tie in with a Philippines move. Time will tell. Fellows in camp seem well. Was glad to see Bud and Pap, and a lot of the fellows were cordial indeed. I must have made a strange sight in my hospital pajamas. The men have had lots of access to liquor. Mike was drunk for nine days running, causing trouble by menacing people with his rifle. He was sober but drinking when I saw him.

I still face some difficulties getting out of here in time. The plan is to pick me up between 8:00 and 9:00 A.M. tomorrow. My service record and gas mask have yet to be obtained. The former, I learned tonight, has to go through "regular channels" and may be delayed till noon. I may have to swim to make that ship. Tomorrow I will do what I can in order to get out early, although I wish I could talk to the Captain. Am waiting now, in case he comes in. If I don't get that service record, I'm stuck. Stahl and Colby [*on furlough to Australia*] ought to have fun catching up with us. Pap told me orders came through stating all Yanks out of Australia by January 1. So long Dale!

I feel pretty well, but even the exertions of packing this afternoon stiffened me up. My foot is not healed yet, and that shall probably get worse when I hit my feet again. Tonight shall probably be my last in a comfortable bed for some time to come. Rainy season now; plenty of mud in Guinea, I bet. Plenty of rain here.

That Philippines deal is pretty rough. I've been talking to many of the fellows here. One last night told me of a 20-year-old with a leg off. He was hit by a sniper. Lying in the open, he tried to knock himself out with his helmet so any investigating Jap would leave him for dead. Another soldier had half his face torn away by our own machine guns. I've seen plenty of wounded here. The air attacks are heavy in the Philippines with 30 to 40 plane squadrons, heavy for the Japs—and they do hit the shipping. Well, I'll face that when I get to it. Take things as they come. I'm better at that than ever before. I'm glad of that.

I was able to finish *Anthony Adverse* this evening. The end was excellent. It's a moving and often profound book. I discarded some of my lesser books this afternoon.

Well, that's the present situation. I hope I don't run into difficulties tomorrow. It's a good feeling to be moving again; we were growing stale here. I'm looking forward to seeing some of the fellows in the other platoons, especially Blanco and Seth. I probably shall not write again until we are at Sansapor. The world is still wide and the path long.

6

Luzon

December 27

We are aboard the navy transport *LaSalle,* lying off Sansapor. We've been kept continuously on the move this past week, so that there has been no time to write. I'll start chronologically and try to include all that has occurred.

After remaining in camp and waiting until the 21st, we loaded equipment and personnel, boarded a LCT, and proceeded on an hour hunt around the bay looking for our ship. We boarded the *John Marshall* via the nets, which continue to be a lot of fun to climb with full equipment!! The Colonel, Lts. Wenz and Murphy were with us. The platoon loaded its own equipment. That afternoon the fellows went fishing and caught 27 good-sized fish, using corned-beef hunks and egg for an effective bait. We had delicious fresh fish that night. In fact, throughout the trip aboard the *Marshall* the food was way past complaint, and we lived most comfortably. We had full run of the ship because we were the only troops aboard her.

The night of the 21st a colored outfit was unloading a barge full of mail at a snail's pace. It would have taken another full day if we waited for them to finish. Our gang took over the work, and we had all cargo aboard and the hatch battened down in two hours. The ship was full of cases of beer, and for our speedy work the Colonel got each man four extra bottles of beer besides our regular issue of three cans. Naturally we would have gotten that beer whether it was issued or not. All that night, actually for the duration of the trip, everybody had as much beer as they could hold, with the result that most of the platoon were in various states of drunkenness, especially for the following few nights. It was a simple matter for the men to steal case after case of beer and consume it.

Pap and I bunked together as usual. We set up our ponchos in tent form. He has been carrying a thin mattress ever since leaving Biak, and it has been most useful for him. Eriksen, Pap and I spent the early part of that wet evening drinking, later joined by Bud and Flynn. We drank quite a bit. I didn't by their standards, though I did by mine—about seven or eight cans. They made me very sleepy and seemed to soften the deck a bit. Pap was slightly drunk but knew it. We turned in about midnight. Fellows were sprawled everywhere in half-drunken stupor. I slept intermittently. It rained hard during the night, but we stayed fairly, though far from completely, dry. Wingfield drunkenly rolled into our tent alongside me and remained there for some time. He didn't know where he was, though he remembered rolling in the next morning. It was not the most comfortable of nights, especially in contrast to my recent hospital bed. The following morning Mike continued his drinking spree and remained quite drunk, consuming huge quantities of beer for the next few days.

The morning of the 22nd the engines throbbed in the gray hull and the ship moved through a gray, wet dawn. During the day I lolled and read *Not Peace But a Sword* by Patrick Gibbs, a story concerning the torpedo branch of the RAF, and though all in narrative form, it is well-written and holds one's interest till the end. The night of the 22nd proved clear and dry, but sleeping on a hard deck is never restful. During the day and the following morning (the 23rd), we sailed up the New Guinea coast; it was in sight nearly the whole way. There was one submarine alert, but nothing came of it. The coast was very mountainous all the way, with low-flying clouds seemingly resting in the valleys before they continue their fast-flying trips overhead. It was hot and my hospital-sheltered skin got a good burning which caused some discomfort for several days. Lt. Murphy, still "one of the boys," Stewart, Smitty and I played a morning's worth of pinochle in which Smitty and I were consistently beaten. Oh, yes—about Rouse. Ray complained several times to me before we pulled out of his feeling ill. At 4:00 A.M., an hour before leaving Geelvink Bay, he had an appendicitis attack and was taken ashore in a launch.

Although New Guinea scenery has long been familiar, I still enjoyed watching its huge, mysterious, haze-bathed coast slip by. It still has all the mystery of a little-known land.

We dropped anchor off Sansapor at about 1:00 P.M. on the 23rd. Thus, we have travelled just about from one end of New Guinea to the other in the past 13 months. We didn't go ashore that afternoon as expected, and just as I broke open my pack to get bedding out for the night, orders came through to board an LCT. My section drew the job of loading our equipment into the LCT. We started work at about 7:00 and finished loading everything by about 11:30 P.M. Naturally a whole mess of beer came over the side, and the crew and our section quickly broke into that. It was a hot night, and the beer was welcome. By the time we were completely loaded, so was ¾ths of the section, including Adams and Pap. Half-drunk, Pap got sore at Wenz. Whenever he gets mad, which is seldom, Pap stomps off leaving the whole job to me, as he did this time. We also unloaded some mail, and in every draft under the bags were four to six cases of beer which the fellows stored with our rations. When we later unloaded on shore, we found that we had stolen a whole truck-load of beer.

Speaking of mail, some of the colored fellows who worked the barge at Biak were seen stealing packages; in fact, I saw several stuffing packages under their shirts. This got us all pretty angry. Breaking into mail is a serious and low act. John H. told Murph who told the MPs, but nothing was done, and they got away with what they stole. I would have no compunction about turning a man in who would break into the mail.

It was too rough to land at Sansapor, so we anchored offshore until 1:00 A.M., during which time everyone got drunker. Mike was just about out; I didn't call on him for any work throughout the night. On shore we loaded our stuff on trucks and drove to camp, arriving there in pitch-black night at about 3:30 A.M. Soon after, the other platoons were woken up and old friends rejoined. After eight months' separation, a peaceful camp became a party of night revellers. Lights were lit and cases of the stolen beer broken out and flowed like water.

I got all my equipment into the mess hall which had the old stand-up tables. After getting everything in there, I took a quick look around camp, and ran into Monroe talking to Anderson and Meyer. Though I knew them both well, I could not recall their names until someone else spoke them. I found this true for many of the fellows I knew well eight months ago. All night and next day I got innumerable handshakes and many congratulations for making corporal. Surprising how many knew of it so quickly. We talked about close to an hour, and from them I learned the general news about the rest of the company, about how Brock was scalped and killed instantly by a piece of shrapnel from an exploding ammo dump, and the close call they had on the torpedoing. Billy Dixon got a Purple Heart on that action for burns received. He was sleeping in the hold. Awfully lucky no one was killed then. I learned more about our coming invasion of Luzon, and other news. Over beer that I supplied, we talked until Capt. Reinhardt came bellowing in our direction, hollering for quiet. We then broke up. I stretched out on the three spaced boards that make up a mess-hall table, and though I was quite uncomfortable, I got about two hours sleep.

The morning of the 24th broke with reveille. The first two platoons fell out in suntans and leggings. We grinned, but not long after it was they who grinned at us when, after breakfast, the 3rd platoon fell in for the first time in many months. The platoon made a ludicrous sight, everyone still half-soused. It took me some time before I could finally get Mike and Redwine out of bed and into formation while the Captain impatiently waited. Finally our wavering platoon was there in its entirety.

Mike was completely shot and maudlin and uncaring. While the Captain was telling us of uniforms to be worn, preparations for the trip, etc., Mike kept yelling out that he didn't have this or that piece of equipment, that he wanted to get out of the outfit and into the infantry. At this point tears were streaming from his eyes, and he looked a mess, much like the men I use to see lying in the gutter of NYC on a Sunday morning. He put the final touch to all his remarks by yelling out to Lt. Murphy that he wished Murphy was company commander instead of Capt. Reinhardt. Naturally the whole company was laughing hard. Later that day Mike went to the Colonel and asked for a transfer to the infantry but, of course, it was rejected. In the long run there was no punishment meted out to him, and I didn't call on him for details, and so as time went on, and the beer evaporated, he finally sobered up. We spent the remainder of that day setting up tents, cots and getting settled. Spent all day packing and repacking to fulfill the orders issued on what is to be taken on the next invasion.

Although I had my cot up, I had not the chance to lie down on it till that night. Christmas Eve proved the only good night's sleep I had in five. Even after chow Capt. R. and Sgt. Eriksen had me jumping on various little details, besides my having to check on the fellows getting equipment in shape and taking care of the ones still drunk. Gas masks had to be waterproofed in case we have to wade ashore, and a green ribbon patch sewn on to identify us as beach personnel, equipment to be drawn such as halazone tablets, gas capes, soap, etc. One fatigue uniform, socks and blanket needed to be impregnated against insects. It was a busy day. After sewing Shorty's and my own patch on, I fell into a deep sleep, the first in four days. During the night I thought I heard two shots, and then felt somebody fall down next to my cot. Then I saw Sam Owen sprawled on the ground next to me—and I remembered nothing more. The next morning I found out that Mike, in his drunkenness, had fired two shots, gunning for the Captain, and the fellows along the line had scattered when he started indiscriminately firing. Owen had stumbled on our tent ropes and crawled in alongside my cot. So tired and deep in sleep had I been, I thought it all a dream.

Christmas was marked by an unusual dinner, turkey with stuffing, pumpkin pie, etc. Norm got pretty high, but he's happy when he's drunk. During the day I saw a lot of the old fellows: Blanco, Hillsberg, Henehan, Pietrangelo, etc. There were quite a lot of new fellows around who are replacements, and one 32-month man who was transferred from the 32nd. I noticed that the first two platoons as a whole were not looking well; most of the fellows had lost weight. Seth was down to a shadow. Many of the fellows are lamenting the loss of their girls and wives. Basil Jones, who transferred out, used to talk of nothing else but his girl, and now he is no longer engaged. Butler's wife divorced him, etc. There haven't been many changes in ratings, and some of the fellows were broken without prejudice to comply with the new T.O. Seth lost his Pfc. Beal is in the orderly room, Russell is now 1st Sgt. and Sgt. Putt on his way home after 30 years of service. William P. Jones is out, as he should have been long ago. Much as I hate to say it, his skeleton body serving out the food did not abet the meal. Sonnier is in a California hospital, Maddox discharged and drawing $60 a month on a medical discharge. Poor Jackman's mind is gone as a result of his head wound, and he is partially paralyzed.

The afternoon of Christmas Day we were ordered to take down tents and get equipment together. We spent the rest of the afternoon breaking camp and getting set, though we kept our cots. That night we lay out in the open on our cots waiting for orders to move. Some of the fellows were singing Christmas carols, and with the moon coming through the trees and the night warm, it was a very peaceful few hours. I got intermittent sleep, waking up colder each time. At 2:00 A.M. we were waked and had coffee and doughnuts. We then finished folding cots and donning equipment in the dark. The packs were and are very heavy because of the amount of equipment we were required to carry, besides that of our own choosing. My gas mask is packed full with odds and ends. A fire was burning at one end of the campgrounds, and we made weird-looking figures filing past, the firelight and shadows licking faces and bodies and equipment. At 3:00 A.M. we loaded into trucks which took us to the beach, and there we waited until dawn. Blanco and I filled most of this time trading talk.

During the few days at camp under the new, strict leadership of Capt. Reinhardt, I learned the general plan of the invasion. Lt. Wenz has turned out to be an especially "right guy" and has been treating the fellows fairly. He's inquired about my health several times. He gave a good talk to the platoon about sticking together, about operating as a platoon, and reminding us that you never feel the bomb or bullet that hits you: "You just go down." Anyway it was the kind of talk that hit all of us right. I don't believe there is any love lost between Lt. W. and Capt. R., and events of the past few days seem to substantiate that. We also have a new 2nd Lt., one Lt. Pranke, I think, but have had no contact with him.

Smith went to the hospital with a fever Christmas morning and so has missed the boat, along with Stahl and Rouse. Owen is back in the kitchen, and so we're back to 17 men of the 21 that comprise a squad. The new T.O. calls for two platoons with five sections each. Eriksen will be busted to a section leader instead of platoon sergeant if this comes about. A checkers' section is planned as part of headquarters, and these men will be meted out to the other sections.

At about 6:00 A.M. we boarded a LSM and were taken out to the navy transport *LaSalle* which we boarded by nets after the usual tedious wait. The harbor is full of all kinds of ships that will make up part of the huge invasion convoys. The transports are big affairs with jagged designs of dull colors on their hulls. We found the quarters aboard the *LaSalle* much like those aboard the *West Point,* tiers of four bunks. The sleeping quarters are crowded, dusty and extremely hot, as usual. I finally settled in a bottom bunk and made it serviceable. There is a stand-up mess hall. So far the food is good, and the meal schedule not too bad. The ship provides trays which save the bother of mess kits. The latrine and washing facilities are the best we've had aboard a ship. There is also a PX. Last night there was a movie aboard, and there will be others as long as we lay in port.

After the show I went to my bunk in the hot hold of the ship. With a towel under me and a handkerchief wound about my head to absorb the sweat, I fell into the bunk and was soon asleep. Today, while waiting to pull out, I've been writing, though the wind and dust make it difficult.

This invasion of Luzon is supposed to be one of the biggest, and the blow that will destroy Japanese power in the Philippines. There are to be several (three, I believe) landings made on Luzon, involving thousands of men, including Ranger outfits and Australian troops. Our particular ship is carrying 900 men; she carried 1,500, including 500 marines, to Leyte. We are rumored to land near the San Fernando Valley, about 130 miles north of Manila. We are the 15th wave which means we may land anytime within the first few hours of the invasion up to several days. Time will tell. Our specific job is to unload the supplies on the landing crafts, and, if needed, we are available for combat. We are to provide guards for the supply dump. Life for the first weeks ought to be very rugged, though we are inured to that. Still, this is a big show, and there should be plenty of opposition. The convoy is said to be 500 ships, includ-

FIELD ORDERS)

NUMBER   1)

244th Port Company
APO 159
23 December 1944

MISSION:

(a. This unit is attached to the 543d EB &3R for operations in the objective area. The mission of this unit is to furnish labor and supervisory personnel for unloading of LCT's, LCM's, LSM's, and self-propelled barges.

DEFENSE PLAN:

a. The 244th Port Company under the 543d EB & 3R is responsible for beach and dump defense and will furnish necessary air sentinels to assure timely warning of imminent air attack.

b. All personnel will dig foxholes with overhead cover at the first opportunity and will sleep therein until instructions are issued to the contrary. The construction of such foxholes will not interfere with the jobs to be done.

c. Work will not cease at the sounding of RED ALERT, but will continue until the beach is actually attacked. Work on the ships will never cease except to seek individual protection against direct attack.

d. Work will cease to defend against ground attack only on the order of the Shore Party CO, except that in an emergency, the CO of this unit will take the necessary action for defence

e. All personnel will have their individual weapons readily available at all times.

f. A shell will not be kept in the chamber of any piece unless hostile action is unquestionably imminent. There will be no firing or throwing of grenades except against a positively identified enemy. BE SURE BEFORE YOU FIRE AT NIGHT ESPECIALLY. STAY IN YOUR FOXHOLE AT NIGHT, FOR YOU MIGHT BE TAKEN FOR A JAP.

g. On order of the Shore Commander, necessary men for line combat will be drawn from the company.

ALERTS:

    a. **Navy:**
        Flash Red: Air attack imminent. (Corresponds to Army Red Alert)
        Flash Blue: Air attack probable. (Corresponds to Army Yellow)alert)
        Flash White: All Clear. (Corresponds to Army All Clear)

    b. **Army:**
        Normal: No enemy or unidentified targets.
        Yellow: Unidentified aircraft twenty (20) minutes from defended area.
        Red: Enemy or unidentified aircraft ten (10) minutes from defended area.

WARNINGS:

    Yellow Alert: No alert will be sounded.
    Red Alert : Selected Bofors guns will alert adjacent units by firing three (3) rounds at one second intervals. This warning will be spread by three (3) short blasts of sirens or Klaxons. NO MAN IN THIS UNIT WILL USE A FIRE-ARM TO SOUND THIS ALARM.

- 1 -

Field orders for the invasion of Luzon, distributed Dec. 25, 1944.

CARGO CONTROL SECTION
SHORE PARTY
543d ENGINEER BOAT & SHORE REGIMENT

C O N F I D E N T I A L

22 December 1944
A. P. O.   159

SUBJECT : Labor Detail Plan (FAR SHORE)

TO   : Commanding Officers 294 Port Co., 244th Port Co., APO 159

1. The plan for organization of labor details, and the manner in which they report, of far shore S Pay is outlined below:

Off in charge	NCO	Slot	Detail	Orgn
Capt Jackson	Cpl Hambley	W	1 Off: 1 NCO: 50 EM	294th Port
Capt Long	Sgt Herbert	O	1 Off: 1 NCO: 50 EM	294th Port
Capt Knight	Sgt Fisck	S	1 Off: 1 NCO: 45 EM	244th Port
Lt Arden	Sgt Stacey	P	1 Off: 1 NCO: 45 EM	244th Port
Lt Huntoon	Sgt Mawyer	K	1 Off: 1 NCO: 50 EM	294th Port
Lt Usoskin	Cpl Patrick	C	1 Off: 1 NCO: 45 EM	244th Port
Lt Trentacoste	S/Sgt Kearnes	L	1 Off: 1 NCO: 45 EM	244th Port
Lt Martin	M/Sgt Stewart	CP	1 NCO: 15 EM	294th Port

2. Details will be organized as shown above. All details will be organized and assigned before departure from near shore, and every individual will be unquestionably familiar with projected location and relative position , Officer and NCO in charge, of the slot at which his detail is to work.

3. When organizations reach the beach at the far shore, they will proceed under company direction to their assigned bivouac area. There they will drop all equipment immediately and proceed under direction of Officers in charge of details to Cargo Control CP, where they will report either to Capt. Rodgers, Lt Martin, or M.Sgt Stewart. From here details will be dispatched to their slots. If for any reason, either of the three of these individuals cannot be located, report direct to their assigned slot, and inform Officer in charge that they are reporting <u>direct.</u>

4. a. When details report to slots they will be furnished with
      * rations and water arms details will not return to bivouac area, nor be released for any purpose except by O in C.
      b. Do not quit work for air raids unless told to do so by O in C or O in C detail.

DISTR: 1 Ea Indiv 294th, 244th Port Co.
         2 Ea Orgn concerned
         1 Ea S/T Off.

PAUL R. RODGERS, Jr.
Captain, CE

Shore party orders for landing at Luzon, distributed Dec. 22, 1944.

ing 40 aircraft carriers and many warships of all classes. What we can see of it ought to make an inspiring sight when we get to sea. I believe we shall land on or about January 7. Little did I realize when reading of the Jap invasion of the Philippines while a junior in high school that I would be a part of the liberating forces in the greatest invasion of the Philippines' most important island. Luzon is one of the most civilized islands of the Pacific. It will be good to see some kind of civilization again.

The outfit has high hopes for eventual stationing in Manila. The Colonel has mentioned it more than once, and he will probably try to get the battalion together so that we can take over the port. That would be a break. Lt. Wenz thinks this is our last campaign—but one can never tell. The time ought to go quickly in the midst of all this activity and danger, and our 18 months should be behind us before we know it. I hope we survivors don't experience any serious casualties after being together so long. The news today claimed Leyte completely ours. Germans are still raising plenty of hell in their recent drive in France and Belgium. Enough for today.

December 30

The days move but we don't. We are still anchored in the same spot as when we boarded four days ago. Since then we've become acclimated to life aboard this transport. Our time is mainly spent in lines for chow, reading, and carrying out the orders of Capt. R. Wenz continues to be a good fellow to all the men in the platoon, and we pass pleasant words every time we meet.

We are now operating under the new T.O. of two platoons. My squad is the 10th and remains intact with me as squad leader. Demerle has been assigned as our checker. Capt. R. has been exacting in his orders that we mark our clothes, read the rules, and that squad leaders see that these orders are carried out. I don't mind, though he insists upon using the old Drown method of threatening his NCOs: "If you men want to keep your stripes, use them." The fellows have been cooperative with me, so far. Anyway all this checking on them, reading rules to them, as I had to this morning, and my responsibility for their dress, equipment and well-being serve to fill up the time. Reinhardt doesn't seem to like Eriksen at all and rides him at every opportunity. Eriksen is platoon sergeant of the 2nd platoon.

Though we do nothing strenuous during the day, I am thoroughly tired at night. I sleep soundly from the moment I lie down till reveille. It is hot in the hold during the day, but it cools off sufficiently for sleep at night. Read *The Axis on the Air* by Ettlinger, story of Axis propaganda and how it works; most of it I've heard of or read in other books and magazines. During the early part of the evening there is a movie aboard ship, which serves to break up the long night because there is no place to read. This routine will last only as long as we are in port. To break up the latter part of the evening, there are air attacks.

Night before last during the middle of the show an alert was sounded, then "general quarters" on ship. About five minutes later the long fingers of the searchlights were stabbing the dark, and they found a Jap plane fairly high and going away. Undoubtedly he came over to secure information on the convoy forming here, and probably got some pictures. He didn't attack the ships, and our ack-ack was ineffective. We learned yesterday morning that he attacked the airstrip and hit a B-24. Apparently there were several Japs in the area, but I only saw the one.

Early this morning, about 2:00 A.M., I was waked by the "general quarters" alarm and by the blaring PA, "All men man your battle stations." I dressed and took my life preserver and headed for the deck. In the 'tween deck I heard the pounding of ack-ack and the chatter of machine guns. Upon reaching the deck, I saw that all fire was directed immediately over our heads. It was a very bright night, full moon, and the luminous plane was easily spotted quite high up. With red lines of bullets chasing him and ominous black puffs of exploding 90s all around, he flew very fast, headed away from us toward open sea and a thinnish cloud bank. Just before getting to the bank, two 90s shells burst close on each side of him. A moment later he was in the thin clouds which weren't adequate cover. The ship's machine guns continued to rattle, but the range was too great for anything but ack-ack. Just as I thought he was about to get away, he began to dive out of the cloud he had sought for cover. A moment later a huge streak of flame burst from the falling plane, now out of control. The Jap fell a long way, burning brightly and viciously all the way down. I could hear the whine of the motor as he fell earthward in ever-increasing speed. The pilot didn't have a chance; he burned like tinder. It was the clearest sight I've had of a hit Jap plane. While he fell, all the men aboard were silent and fascinated by the orange streak that marked the end of a life and enemy. No guns fired. As soon as he hit the water, a tremendous yell split the air, and we continued cheering, me included. He fell in the sea some distance away and continued to burn brightly for some 10 minutes after crashing. Soon there was just a tiny, diminishing flame—the fiery and brief marker of one less enemy.

Undoubtedly the Japs have wind of this convoy which is forming all up and down the New Guinea coast. I hope we have all the aircraft carriers rumored. It is said there are 200,000 Japs defending Luzon. Leyte is taken and mopping-up operations remain. Our report states that we lost about 2,700 men in that campaign to the Japs' 113,000!! It is difficult to believe these figures. If these odds are anywhere near accurate, it is a decisive victory. [*Actual postwar figures: Japanese casualties numbered 67,000; American casualties were 3,504 killed and 11,991 wounded.*] There is continued air attack on Luzon, on Clark and Nichols Fields, and other less famous ones, with 214 Jap planes on Luzon reported destroyed so far, that many less we'll have to face. The Japs shelled Mindora (ineffectively, it's stated) while we sank three destroyers and scored hits on a cruiser and battleship!

The battle in Europe continues to sway from side to side, and we all hope that this will prove the last German offensive, the last spurt of flame before the candle goes out.

Living aboard the navy ship has accustomed me to the terms the navy uses, some of which sound odd. Each announcement over the PA system is heralded with "Now hear this" or once in awhile with "Listen." When it's an announcement for troops, it starts with "Attention all army personnel," or "All army troops." "Turn to" is the equivalent of our "Fall out." For sweeping the deck the loudspeaker voice blares, "Sweepers, man your brooms! Clean sweepdown fore and aft, all decks and ladders," instead of the army's "Sweep de goddam floors." In spite of a slightly sore throat, I am feeling fine and in good spirits. Took Willie Harris to sick bay with fever the other night, where Clark already was with a boil.

Some of the fellows drew "gun watch," seven from my section. Norm and Bud were on it too. Don't know exactly what that means, except it's 4-on, 8-off. I wouldn't have minded drawing it, but then I'm a section leader. Sometimes I forget that I'm not eligible for regular details anymore.

December 31

Just after I finished writing yesterday we started to move and have continued to do so, but at a very slow pace. Today the convoy has grown. All around there are long lines of ships of all classes, LSTs, tankers, and many large navy transports, each carrying at least 1,000 men. There is a screen of destroyers and other protective vessels. I don't imagine we shall run into trouble for another three or four days yet, and meanwhile the convoy itself will get larger. For the past 45 minutes all the ships have been practice-firing at flares. Each ship is capable of a fearful barrage; with all of them firing together, the noise is indescribable. Black bursts of ack-ack pock-mark the sky, and the three-incher firing from the fantail is loud and jarring. They've stopped now. All this should be adequate fire power against air attacks, I hope. It looks and sounds menacing enough. It is now required that we have life jackets and full canteens at all times. Abandon ship drill now—write later!

Tonight is New Year's Eve. It's rather an odd place to spend it, aboard ship headed for an invasion in the Philippines. This move signifies to me the end of a phase in my army career and the end of our campaigning in the S.W.P. Some time last night or this morning, we crossed the equator and even that makes me feel a great deal closer to home. Tonight is a period at the end of a sentence in the paragraph of my life. On the great swinging circle of our travels, the landing in the Philippines marks a bit more than half-way home, and at least a half-way mark in the winning of the war against Japan.

There is nothing funny about the campaign facing us, and I hope fate continues to be kind so that I may one day return home well and in good spirits. It will be a great thing just to live peacefully again. Though this invasion will be the toughest and most hazardous, I feel less fear than at any other time. I hope I am able to maintain myself; I shall do my best and act well under any future circumstances. I go into this with a certain amount of responsibility, and I am glad. It makes me feel more a part of the operation. Perhaps I shall be able to remember this New Year's in more comfortable circumstances and after our inevitable victory. The year 1944 is gone; it has been momentous for the world. Personally, I have learned a great deal. What better reward to ask of time than increased knowledge?

January 4, 1945

Am writing with difficulty in the mess hall of the *LaSalle* under dim lights. This evening we raised the Philippines. My first look at them was under a beautiful sunset. The sun sank behind a mountainous island, and the sky was splashed with vivid colors. There was that rare, delicate, blue-green color I don't believe I've seen since I described it to Carolyn while crossing the Texas plains. That was my last letter to her in the States, I recall. The islands from a distance look like others I've seen in the S.W.P. We seem to be at the southern end of the group and expect to be at Leyte soon, where we are rumored to remain for eight or nine hours. Pap and I watched the sunset from the fantail. It must seem strange to him to be in the Philippines again after so many years and under these circumstances. Wouldn't the family at home be amazed to know where I am at this moment!

We've had several alerts during the past few days. This morning a Jap patrol plane was spotted. I have seen several of our carriers, but at a distance. They lie way off tonight. During previous days of rainy, cloudy weather, they looked ghostly. The other morning I could make out the black dots of planes landing and taking off. We had our own patrols in the sky tonight before sundown. Our convoy (what I can see of it) does not seem increased in size. The fleet of about 40 LSTs continues to plough along off the starboard bow and aft, while several long lines of transports cut the water. We are flanked by cruisers and destroyers and numerous small craft, which range on the perimeter of the convoy like shepherd dogs guiding the flock of fat, slow-moving transports, LSTs, LSDs, etc. We've been moving at the slow pace of about five to eight knots an hour, from what I can judge.

The convoy must be much bigger than I can see for the task we are undertaking. The sailors say there is another convoy in front of us, and one aft.

Life aboard ship goes smoothly. Boat formation drills, alerts and meals break up the day. The food is good. I spend my spare time reading, playing pinochle with Seth and Muscles, or just thinking. I've talked at length with Lt. Wenz, who approached me one evening. He's a great one for talk. We discussed politics, world policy, government, intolerance, the coming campaign, the condition of the men, both mentally and physically, after two years. We hope, as do all the other officers and men, that this will be our last campaign. It's expected to be the toughest. Luzon will be well-garrisoned by Japs with a great quantity of their best equipment. Most likely we'll run into tanks and artillery as never before. Every mile of the way will be hard-fought. I do not doubt that Manila will fall to our hands only after a stubborn battle and with much of the city in ruins. Once again we will be the troops closest to Japan from the south. We have the distinction of engaging in what will probably be the bloodiest, the most hard-fought and important campaign waged against Japan to date. I expect life will be difficult for the next two or three months, possibly longer.

I am acting in the full capacity of section sergeant, and extremely glad to have certain reponsibilities. They will keep my mind off myself. I've attended several non-com meetings in which we've been briefed on the coming operation and the part that we will play. We land on I-day, part of the 15th wave, which is the last. Hdqtrs, the battalion personnel, miscellaneous men attached to HQ, and some of Havron's men will leave before the main body of men, and proceed to our bivouac area. Our area lies close to the beach directly behind slot one. There are eight slots planned for the beach. I am in charge of the 16 men that compose boat team #9. When the time comes we will go to the net assigned and go down nets into landing boats. When we land we are to be led to the assigned area. The men I have in charge for this operation are 10 men of my own section and six of Stewart's from the 3rd. Pap is on another boat team.

At the bivouac area we will dump packs and form a working gang. Our group, composed of my section, Stewart's section and half-a-section under Cpl. Scott, 45 men in all, will be under Eriksen and Wenz. I am glad that we have drawn our old platoon leaders to work under; I regard this as good fortune. From this area we will proceed to slot eight at the far end of the beach and unload cargo coming in from the transport *Calloway.* It is hoped there will be trucks to load, but it is not definite. We may have to lug supplies ashore as we did at the Hollandia landing, which will be difficult. That is the plan and our job for I-day. Lt. Wenz has warned me that no man is to break away from the gang in search of souvenirs or to examine dead Japs, if any. How many of the enemy we shall see after the beach is shelled is a question.

There should not be much enemy fire. Air attacks are to be expected for the next few months at any time. Pap and I expect to spend our nights together in a foxhole, as we have during past campaigns. The terrain appears to be relatively flat; whether the ground is sandy or muddy remains to be seen. In the vicinity of our area there are fish ponds, rice paddies and some small towns. Even these will be a treat and seem like civilization to our long jungle and native-filled eyes. Thank goodness New Guinea is behind us. The landing is rumored for January 9. Maps, aerial photos, and project-like sand map available to us in the "briefing room" (which is the 'tween deck of No. 5 hold) are intriguing. I hope our luck holds as well as it did in the S.W.P.

Ron Flynn is now acting assistant section leader of Stew's section. Glad to see Ron make it. I shall probably get one more opportunity to write before we land. I guess all the presents and flowers that I arranged for have been received at home. Wonder what Edith got for Mom. It will be weeks before I get any mail again, I guess.

January 8

We hit tomorrow. Action and plenty of it these past few days, climaxed this morning by a stunning spectacle. At present, we are steaming up the coast of Luzon, right in the teeth of Japanese territory. Attacks are to be expected—and they have not failed. During the past two days the convoy has been attacked from various quarters, subjected to bombing, submarines and suicide crash-dives. Most of this action prior to early this morning was centered on the convoys to our rear and in front of us. Several ships have sustained bomb hits, but none is reported sunk. The PA system gives us some information about the air attacks. Yesterday we passed southern Mindora where we could see a burning liberty, a hit having been scored in the vicinity of No. 3 hatch. A report came through that another had been sunk. That place has been catching hell. However, prior to this morning, all we've seen of air attacks has been distant ack-ack.

Last night I slept on deck till a GQ at 3:30 A.M. sent us below. I slept the rest of the night below decks until about 7:00. The alert was still on. During the night a Jap plane was shot down off our port side by a flanking destroyer. Also, some small Jap craft were blown up; the story on this is not clear. This morning the PA announced that a Jap plane attempting a suicide dive on a ship to our front was shot down and missed its objective. A little later another announcement told us of a suicide attempt on one of our carriers (officially we have 26 with us, 16 babies) and narrowly missed it. Pap saw this action.

When I went on deck, I found myself a few moments later in the midst of an air attack. I spotted two planes. One was quite low, attacking a transport off our starboard bow. It was the *Calloway,* the ship our work gang will handle. The Jap dive-bombed the ship, but the bombs fell short. While climbing away from his dive, he was caught in our fire and seemed to be hit, for I saw smoke trailing from him and the flicker of fire; however, this may have been his rear gunner firing, if he carried one. The Jap circled deliberately, ack-ack bursting around him, and then he started a long, steep dive for the rear of the ship. He dove as straight as an arrow. We all stood silent and transfixed as the Jap crash-dived his plane into the naval transport! He appeared to hit high in the after part of the superstructure. A second later a huge blossom of flame billowed out amidships enveloping the plane. We all stood still and silent a moment. Then a great coordinated groan of sympathy rose from us who viewed this nearly unbelievable scene from our transport right alongside the *Calloway.* A few moments later, I noticed another plane high overhead. Everyone remained strangely transfixed, but I broke this frozen scene by calling out that it would be safer below deck during these suicide attacks. This started a hurried exodus to go below, as the PA system directed shortly afterwards. The sight of the attack on the *Calloway* is burned in my memory forever. It shook me up viewing it. Miller completely lost his head and ran screaming and wild-eyed about the ship. During this action, we were unaware that our own ship was under attack. The other Jap plane had dropped a bomb astern of us. The explosion sent shrapnel into the fantail, causing several casualties among the navy gunners. Undoubtedly the *Calloway* has numerous casualties.

Out of four attacking planes, three were destroyed; the one over us was the one that got away. There has been no further action. Our naval taskforce, while under Jap air attack, is shelling Lingayen Gulf. A report came to us later that the Jap pilot who attacked the *Calloway* had managed to bail out just before hitting the ship and was picked up. This is surprising. The *Calloway* continues to steam on, apparently not extensively damaged. It is likely that we shall experience more attacks before we land some time tomorrow. All we can do is keep our fingers crossed. It will be some time before I can write again.

January 15

The last week has been such a jumble of activity and sleep-snatching that it is difficult to mark events as chronologically as I would like. We woke 3:30 A.M. on the 9th for early breakfast. In Lingayen Gulf all types of gunboats, including our huge battleships, were firing on the shore installations. We could see that parts of the coastline led directly into mountain ranges and other parts were flat for some distance. There were hundreds of ships dotting the gulf, steaming through the haze of smoke, especially heavy over the shore. On shore we could see the orange blaze of shell-bursts. Sometimes salvos from the battleships made billowing orange clouds belch from their sides.

At dawn four planes tried to attack, but they were driven off by a terrific barrage from the ships. There were so many tracers that the sky seemed filled with red rain. The boat teams pushed off all during the morning. It was after mid-day by the time my boat team was called to disembark. The others used LCUs but we drew a LCT which we loaded with vehicles. After that job, we boarded with several more teams and started for shore, passing numerous and various vessels. It was very hot. As we were half way to shore, the harbor was attacked by a single plane. He came in fast off our starboard bow, swerved out and made a crash-dive for a destroyer. I couldn't see if he hit the ship or not because he landed on the other side of the superstructure. The ack-ack started falling around us, and then several small shells exploded about 20 feet away.

We drew toward shore through rough surf and waded with full equipment through waist-deep water to get ashore. The beach was sandy and level. John A. [*Horn*], Charley [*Norvell*] and I were first off the ship. As soon as our group formed, I led them to where I thought the maps had marked our camp area. We went through a large pasture, the grass green and dry, the land rolling. After about ⅛th-of-a-mile walk, I found our area which lies in the first fringes of a coconut grove, near an abandoned hut built on stilts. It was one of the best campsites we've ever hit. The ground wasn't torn up a bit except for an occasional hole and a few pieces of shrapnel. The ground was dry and grassy. It was hot then, and some of the men, with all the equipment they were carrying, just about made camp.

As soon as I got my section together, we headed down the beach. Along the beach were all kinds of landing craft with supplies and ammo. That was our job, unloading ammo from landing craft. We carried ammo from ship to shore through waist-deep water all afternoon. Each box weighed from 100 to 170 pounds, so it wasn't easy work in the surf and sand. Nevertheless, I enjoyed the hard work. Though there were several alerts, we had no air raids or shore opposition. Some of the landing craft were swamped along the shore by the heavy sea, and the men still coming in had trouble getting ashore. Some nearly drowned. A number of trucks and other vehicles were swamped. We worked steadily till nightfall. We were all so tired by then that even Pap had to drop boxes and rest. Though I was tired and stiff and sore, I felt in good spirits and worked steadily till 2:00 A.M. when we quit. There were several planes over during the evening; at those times we scattered along the beach and inland. Capt. R. brought some 10-1 rations for supper [*a type of boxed and canned food*]. I had a piece of cheese, a couple of fruit bars, a half-cup of coffee. We walked the few miles back to our campsite and sprawled out on the ground, exhausted. At 5:00 A.M. we were up to go to work again. For the next few days we worked in the dumps along the shore or unloaded the landing craft. The days and nights were filled with air raids and work. We had little sleep but adequate food, considering the conditions. During the first three days I was not able to remove my clothes or wash. There were so many raids that I couldn't possibly keep track of them. I've heard so many bombs whistle down and explode that now I have hardly a trace of fear of them, nor have I once felt that old empty feeling in the pit of the stomach. (Hello, veteran Kahn!)

The morning after we landed, we had our first contact with Filipinos. While riding down the beach in a duck, after I spent half-an-hour trying to round up the fellows after an alert, we suddenly heard the whiz of a shell. Most of us hit the floor of the duck. It later proved to be a mortar shell that landed about 75 yards to our rear. It hit several men. During the day while we worked, groups of Filipinos came down to the beach, including a number of women. We spoke to many of them and found that the great majority could speak fairly good English. The older, educated generation were Spanish-speaking. I had a chance to use a little of my Spanish. They told us about the Jap occupation, atrocities, general conditions, and how glad they were to see us. During the day the army began to hire the men to work the beaches at a peso (50 cents) a day. I met and spoke to some intelligent and educated Filipinos who had attended college in Manila, men who had been guerrillas, men who had fought with the army on Bataan and Corregidor, and men who had been prisoners and released, having endured the hardships which are so well-known at the hands of the Jap. I learned much more of all this a few days later. Since landing and up to right now, I've had one full night's sleep, and that was on the ground. But I slept. I could get a full night's sleep tonight—if I'd go to sleep now.

(Am aboard a liberty but will get to that later. In fact I'll finish the whole story tomorrow. My eyes are beginning to burn, and I am very tired.)

January 18

Exactly one month since I wrote my last letter. I fear they must be worrying at home, but it is impossible to send one yet. Though I intended catching up a few days ago on events, there has been no rush because I've been aboard a liberty for the past four or five days, and there have only been alerts. The Jap air force is astonishingly absent and perhaps very weak. We were not without raids during the days ashore, though they were light and scattered. One morning while we were in the chow line, a bomb's whistle drove us into foxholes or to the ground. Some of the fellows had coffee and food in their hands, and it made quite a mess when we hurriedly dove for cover. Another close call came one night when we were walking double file along the beach, amidst a few scattered and necessary lights. Suddenly we heard the flat, splattering sound of a machine gun in a short burst. We hit the ground immediately. We heard and saw the orange burst of a bomb about 200 yards directly inland from us. Nobody heard the plane approach, and nobody got a shot at it. During this time Pap and I, crouching very low and moving fast through an ammo dump, found an open spot of sand. This was the first strafing attack I'd ever directly experienced. There were probably some fatalities because the bomb landed where troops are camped, and I did see one fellow who had caught two slugs in his shoulder. Strafing is exciting but not much fun. We passed a dead sailor who was washed up on the beach, lying face up with his hands folded on his chest.

We worked hard during these days, but having the Filipinos around spiced up the long, hot hours. The night work was trying because we used very limited lighting. The worst of all was unloading an LCM at night in rough weather under a few spotlights and with flashlights. Every so often a wave would make the boat lurch heavily against the shore. While throwing over 100 pounds, I was caught off balance and was pitched forward between the dock and ammo pile, a fall of about six to eight feet. I relaxed as best I could and remember thinking it was perfectly natural that someone should get hurt doing this. Fortunately I was wearing my helmet. On the way down one box caught me in the pit of the stomach, knocking the breath out of me. I escaped luckily with a few light bruises to my right arm. That was the night we pulled the 11-hour shift.

January 19

(I'll catch up on the days yet.) This whole operation seems to have gone quite efficiently. I guess the army has made so many beachheads that it's now down to a science. This observation was corroborated by a newscaster the other night. Also, there are new ideas and equipment developed during the past few years that help to make the war a little less costly and more comfortable. For example, a bulldozer digs a great trough, into which gasoline drums are rolled and piled up. This gets them below the surface of the ground. With added protection from the dirt piled at one end, there is less chance of the gas going up in a bombing or strafing. If it does, the trough contains the force of the explosion and reduces the possibility of fire spreading and of further explosions which occur so frequently with gas. That's using the old bean. There are other improvements such as in the taste of the water and in better emergency rations. Instead of the old D-rations' chocolate, there is very palatable caramel substituted in the K-rations. Add all these many improvements together, they count for a lot in the final score.

The first time off we had, Pap, Redwine and I went on a sightseeing tour. We headed for a Filipino community about a mile from camp, but we took a roundabout way in order to see some of the surrounding terrain. We walked through neat coconut groves, and then through numerous rice paddies cut into squares by dirt walks and rickety wooden bridges. We passed scattered farms and houses of palm fronds and local wood built on stilts, with a variety of farm animals running about. It was wonderful getting into open country, seeing civilians and regular clothes, farm animals and cultivation. The word is "exhilarating"; I got a tremendous lift out of it. By modern standards, these people are still primitive in their ways, but by ours it's a bustling civilization. Nearly all the younger generation can speak good English. The people are happy to see the American soldier and are more used to the American army than the people at home.

The Jap is generally disliked; atrocity stories are common in the Philippines. Food under the Japs was scarce; they took whatever they wanted, and they flooded the country with their special Philippine invasion currency. Everybody has hundreds of Jap pesos which are now worthless.

The first few days I obtained several hundred for a few cigarettes and a little food. Most clothes are ragged, though very clean. Nearly all the men wear straw fedoras and spotless white clothes when they can. The women wear colorful cloth dresses. Nearly everyone goes barefoot.

The hardest hit seems to be the old generation. I saw them, brown and wrinkled, emaciated and impassive, sitting at the windows of their huts and watching out of rheumy eyes their little part of the world go by. The huts are filled with children. We watched the younger Filipinos pound rice, spread and dry corn, and wash clothes. We examined the pottery and old carriages.

We were still curiosities to them, too, and everyone had a smile and a "good morning." I think I must have said "good morning" at least 300 times in those two days. It gets hotter inland. We rested in one place and watched American plane formations going over to bomb the Jap, and we heard our artillery barking like hounds on the hunt in the lush green valleys. The people ignored this. The community had been hit by shells during our landing and a number of their houses were demolished. All in all, it was an entertaining morning and a real treat after the months in the jungle.

The next morning Eriksen, Pap, Demerle, Baker and I slung our rifles and started for Daguapan, a community of about 30,000, and the largest in this area. We got a ride to the road that turns inland to Santa Barbara, which was captured the night before. We walked the remaining 3½ miles in the hot Philippine sun. We passed through communities similar to the one I described, and we also passed many people coming from the city to see American installations. "Good morning, good morning, good morning," every step of the way. The five of us were taking it in shifts to save our voices.

As we got closer to the city after passing over American pontoon bridges, we began to see things long unseen: beautiful houses, grounds and gardens, homes as high as three stories, glass in the windows, paint (though somewhat weatherbeaten), a good-looking school, long and spacious and fresh-looking against the bright green backdrop of the land. Then we saw a large hospital with marble floors, a grand driveway and civilian cars!! There were small, bare shops, and other features that resemble the main street of an American village.

We entered Daguapan itself to find some paved streets, a railroad station that is four hours from Manila when the trains are operating, shops, and an amusement dart-throwing concession that was closed down. Some of the shops were in ruins from the shelling, as was much of what we saw of the city. We walked around and saw old American signs and newer Japanese ones. A couple of Shell gas stations were in ruins, along with a Jap machine gunner's emplacement. The city appeared rundown. The Daguapan River cuts through the heart of the city, a good-sized one that flows to the bay. MPs blocked off the larger part of the city because MacArthur was making it his headquarters. Filipinos were ferrying many soldiers across the river in canoes, and we were debating whether to follow when Eriksen struck up a conversation with two passing girls. Dem and Baker had dropped out just previous to this, and we went our separate ways. All the way along the hike, we bought and traded for the nipa wine which the Filipinos sell. We kept emptying Pap's canteen and refilling it throughout the day. It's rather mild-tasting, but, as we were to find out, it has its effects.

Pap and I joined Eriksen in talking to the two girls, who were both carrying bundles. They were short and dark, as most of the women are, and one was far advanced in pregnancy, to which the other girl made tactless allusions. About one out of every five women is pregnant. It seems the Jap occupation didn't stop that. As we walked along we noticed many weathered shingles swinging in front of the weatherbeaten or partially ruined houses of lawyers, dentists and doctors. Pap offered to carry one of the girls' bundles, which he proceeded to do Filipino fashion on top of his head. Eriksen took the other. The two girls spoke pretty good English and looked very young. We were amazed to find that one was 20 with three children and the pregnant one was 18. These people go in for production! Pap gave me the bundle to carry awhile, and I was surprised to find it weighed about 50 pounds and that one girl had carried it on her head. This head-carrying probably accounts for some of the fine walking postures among the women, who are mostly short and dark, with a great quantity of black hair. Some are pretty, with thin but well-formed bodies, tending toward roundness. The men are slight. On several occasions I saw one very beautiful girl, dressed as a woman dresses in the U.S., including shoes and cosmetics and hair arrangement. She is light-skinned and striking, and always accompanied by two well-dressed men. They look like they are Spanish.

The non-pregnant girl invited us to her home and we accepted. It was one of those stilt-houses; their other home had been blown away. The stilt-house had two small rooms which served as bedrooms, dining room and kitchen. The structure looked fragile, but it is sturdy. There were several chairs. It was cool and comfortable in the hut. The girls and the family who were our hosts kept apologizing for the smallness and bareness of their abode. Many neighborhood children came in to view us. All the kids were well-behaved, watching us with round, wide, dark eyes. It was not long before we were all having a good time. First, there was the less-than-year-old baby who had a bad cut on the forehead. Out came my first-aid kit where I had several extra bandages, and Pap and I did a job on the child. Then we attended to a man who needed a leg bandaged. Next we were unloading all our extra rations and cigarettes for which they were thankful. Then we settled down to talk.

The girl's husband, exceptionally fond of one young son, talked with considerable fluency and an expressive face. A typical young Filipino, he was a corporal in the 21st Medical Battalion. He fought at Bataan and received a bad shrapnel wound in the small of the back. The scars looked nasty, and he walked with a limp. He suffered from malaria, and his wife had brought back about 40 atabrine tablets. We directed him to take two a day.

I learned firsthand about the conditions under the Japs, the beatings, whippings, torture, murder and rape wrought by them. I also heard about guerrilla operations in which he played a part for some months after the fall of Bataan, and about American officers who were captured and shot, and about life in the prisons. [*See Lt. Col. Harley F. Hiebs's* Heart of Iron *for his autobiographical account of survival and guerrilla warfare during the Japanese occupation of Luzon, from the fall of Bataan and Corregidor to the American invasion and recapture of Luzon.*] He directed most of his talk at me, and he took a good 1½ hours to explain in detail one guerrilla operation in which a Jap general and his interpreter were shot. His patriotism and loyalty to the U.S. ran deep, if I'm any judge. When he spoke about the women sexually taken by the Jap, one of the Filipinos showed us Jap contraceptives in front of the women. That embarrassed me at first, but it didn't seem to faze any of them. In fact, the 20-year-old girl proceeded to nurse the baby while talking to us. In a moment it all seemed quite natural to me, especially in that atmosphere and place. Eriksen meanwhile occupied himself with comb-ing the black hair of one young girl who was sick with influenza. Her combed hair was an improvement.

There was one rather pretty young girl of 14 who stood next to me the whole time. Impetuously, I put my arm about her waist as I might around my sister; in fact she somewhat reminded me of Babs. Well, that was all she needed. For the next two hours she held and stroked my hand and occasionally my hair. It felt strange getting all this feminine affection after a complete absence for nearly 1½ years. Eriksen meanwhile was picking up phrases of the local language from one of the young women and having a great time of it with much laughter. We were offered din-ner, but we declined because we didn't want to use up their food, not that we weren't hungry. However, when three heaping bowls of rice, hot and flavored, and a small bottle of wine were presented, we could not refuse. It was very good, but I was a little wary of the water. Though it was clear and cool, I only took a polite sip.

About 3:00, after exchanges of goodbyes and an examination of our carbines by the young former soldier, we took our leave with promises to return. We all agreed it was a most unusual and enjoyable afternoon. Later I recalled several remarks made by the young fellow that interested me. He said the old 03 rifle was too heavy for the light Filipinos to fire; they were battered and bruised by the 10-pound rifle during the campaign. Indeed I recall my own sore shoulder when I fired 100 rounds from it. He also told me that when the Japs landed, they had many Korean soldiers with them who could be easily identified by their long beards. They didn't lie flat when fighting, but advanced upright and made wonderful targets, he said.

On the way back through town we met several of our company. Together we found a small shop, operated by a rather pretty girl, selling liquor for a dollar a bottle. Several men there were already drunk. We replenished our wine supply there. The prostitutes were operating in town. Earlier in the day we passed several; a nearby Filipino informed us they were "taxi dancers." He got a resounding oath from one of the girls in English for this. On the way back through town, I spotted a large house with a veterinarian's shingle swinging out front—and a pretty girl in the second-story window. If I ever get back to Daguapan, I intend to stop there.

To top off the day, we saw General MacArthur wearing his new rank of five stars. He had two lines of staff with him, was immaculate, and seemed as curious and interested in gazing around the town as any other soldier. We tossed him a snappy salute which he returned with a "How do." We then started back to camp, catching several rides and making it in good time.

We returned to find that the whole 2nd platoon was to go aboard a liberty to live and work on it. Ordinarily we would have welcomed that, but we were a little reluctant to leave behind the first towns we had seen in so many months. Most of the fellows got back on time, all having experiences similar to ours. Some of the fellows had already visited the prostitutes—and without protection. They took quite a chance, and now they are a little worried and "sweating out" the time for something to develop.

I loaded about half my equipment into my pack, leaving the other half in camp. We piled into ducks and got thoroughly wet going over the breakers. Wet and chilled, we transferred to a LCT, and then proceeded to steam around awhile through the evening smoke screen, trying to find our liberty. This search was soon abandoned when it got too dark, and the fellows bedded down on the deck. I spent the night, up to 3:30 A.M., in the galley drinking coffee with Pap. Then I went out, lay on my pack, and slept for three refreshing hours from the sheer exhaustion of the previous day's activity.

The next morning we found the *Perkins* and the missing men from my section who had been delayed in town after dark. We started work immediately on a 6-on, 6-off schedule, which now more closely runs to 6-on and 18-off. My section is working No. 1 hold which is filled with rations and cigarettes. We have our own kitchen personnel and are eating hearty, keeping clean, and smoking unlimited cigarettes. We have a good deal on this job, especially as food conditions ashore aren't good. We are living pretty comfortably in the 'tween decks of No. 1 hold. Most of us have cots and are sleeping well; some fellows are in hammocks, here and on deck. The hatch is nearly empty as I write this; my gang goes on at noon in a few hours, and we should finish the job this afternoon. We've spent six days out here unloading in ducks, LCMs and LSTs. Willie Harris got his leg caught in the windlass ropes and bruised it. Otherwise, everything is going all right. Out in the harbor there are a number of battleships and other heavy and light naval units. There is a rumor that they are lying in reserve for an impending sea battle. Very likely.

Close by lies the *Carl Johnson,* a liberty which caught a torpedo in No. 2 hold. It killed over 100 men and just about wiped out an aviation engineer outfit. They were taking the bodies out in nets the other day. As Ron said, "We're all sick of the war and knowing what it's like, just hearing about this is painful," or words to that effect. I know what he means; I feel that way myself. We passed the ship coming out to the *Perkins.* She has a bad list. The campaign continues to go well. The radio tells us that our forward troops are 1/3rd of the way to Manila. The White Beach landing has met the most opposition so far and has advanced only several miles. The naval guns continue to pound that sector. It is rumored that our company will move to White Beach, but so far we are still at Blue, in our old area. Those of us here shall probably remain on board for several more days.

Last night I heard on the radio that the Russians have taken Warsaw and are only 15 miles from the German border in some sectors of southern Poland. We on Luzon naturally have our hopes pinned on taking Manila and occupying it as soon as possible. It's about the most civilized spot we could hope to find in this part of the world.

January 27

I am sitting on the beach on this hot afternoon looking at the many cargo ships clogging the bay. On the morning of the 24th we came ashore to find Blue Beach nearly completely evacuated. While disembarking via the nets from the *Perkins,* I had a close call. The duck taking us ashore was carried out by the swell, and I was left dangling by my hands from the lowest strand of the net for some 30 or 40 seconds. At one point I was sure I was going in the ocean (with the thought of that shark Redwine recently shot still vivid), but I managed to hang on until the duck got under me again. I only bruised my toe in the maneuver. Good thing I didn't have my pack on or I might still be going down.

Upon returning to our old area, we immediately set out for the new one about 15 miles up the beach, located between the shore and the railroad line. The area itself was formerly a rice paddy, but it is now dry and suitable. Little clearing had to be done. There are cultivated fields around us. We are restricted from sleeping on the cool beach because the officers are down that way. We are forced to sleep in the open, pasture-like fields, where it is extremely hot.

During the first night here we found that our area was outside the perimeter! Indeed, when we went 100 yards further up to a well to get washed that first night, we passed machine-gun emplacements. Over the ridge nearby is an observation post still subject to snipers' bullets. There are still isolated spots of resistance in this vicinity. As the nights go by, the artillery fire has diminished to an occasional roar, and there is a smattering of small-arms fire. We were all rather jumpy the first night as we were the first to establish a camp in that particular area. Some of the fellows dug foxholes. I did not. At the moment I am bunking with Demerle, a good worker, with a sort of liberal, small-town air. I like him, and he is a valuable addition to the section. Pap is alongside in his old reliable hammock—which collapsed this morning. We tried to keep from laughing, Dem and I, but it was impossible.

We are working a 6-on, 12-off schedule, in theory. Actually it's much more than 6-on because it takes so much time to get to and from the ships. We're working under a new system known as "key gangs." We supply a three-man gang for every hatch, consisting of a winchman, a signalman and a checker. Labor is supplied by various outfits on shore. My responsibility is great. I no longer have responsibility for just one hatch, but the whole ship. I control the working of all hatches, my own men, and the workgangs. I now have the authority of an officer, and indeed I did not avoid telling several of them off last night when they got too pestering. I am also responsible for all transporation; in short, my responsibility and job have increased tenfold. I am still learning plenty, especially about heavy lifts. I have no fear of the winches, and I can struggle along on most any kind, except on vehicles and with the jumbo, on which I have had limited experience. There are some reliable men in the section, mainly Pap, Watts, Norvell, Dem, Hern, Hindmon and Adams, who help relieve my burdens.

It's hectic out on those ships with inexperienced officers to contend with, inexperienced merchant marine, and sometimes inexperienced men in the hold. If more than three hatches are working, it's a damned mess—but the cargo does get off somehow. Most of the time only one or two hatches operate simultaneously, and I have to keep the key gangs shifted accordingly. As long there is work on the ship, I am busy, and when nothing is doing, I am busy trying to get something started. The job leaves me tired at the end of a shift, and I am so occupied that I have little time to think much about anything at all except work and army routines. I never thought I'd come to that. I feel myself a very different person, one I have not had time to introduce fully to myself. Glancing in a mirror last night aboard ship, I even found that my features had considerably changed, and I was surprised at the new set to them, a more mature set I judge. It's all curious.

The wars go well. The last report gives us control of Clark Field, with our ground forces 25 miles from Manila. The Russians, in their steamroller drive, are 125 miles from Berlin. The British are 40 miles from Mandalay, and the Burma road has been cleared of enemy troops to the Burma-Chinese border. The Japanese, however, continue to advance in central China, the last theater in which any enemy is successful.

January 31

It is on a sour note that I must end this particular notebook. We had our first mail call in over a month on the afternoon of the 29th. I received a long-awaited letter from Carolyn, and two V-mail from home which state they're anxiously waiting for word. Carolyn's letter was dated December 30. She received and liked my gift, which she stated in the first paragraph, but the second hit me a square, hard blow. The words have burned in my mind for the past two days. It read:

> Life has been hectic of late. Tomorrow Jim Heilbrun and I are officially announcing our engagement. It will probably be several years before we can be married—he's due to be sent out almost any time now—but we both decided we would be happier this way.

It goes on to tell about Jim getting his degree from Harvard via the V-12 program and that he will be an ensign, a communications officer on an LST.

I read the words several times and then just stood with hands over my eyes. Thank goodness nobody was with me when I read the letter. I was pretty numbed. After getting through the rest of the letter, I walked down to the beach, sat there awhile, and then took a long walk down it, walking the misery out of me as is my habit. I felt better and more composed after that. Although this turn of events is not wholly unexpected, it is difficult to get used to these new circumstances. Running the winch that night I would suddenly think of Carolyn and her present relationship, and the fact would irritate me and give me an awful, empty feeling. She has been so much in my thoughts for so long that it is difficult to accept her new, sudden and unheralded status. It's made me absent-minded, such as starting to shave with my comb a little while ago, but I have been able to laugh at myself. Except for the initial shock, I have controlled myself very well. I have no desire to play a dramatic role.

None of Carolyn's letters during the past year mentioned Jim, but I knew it would be he. He seemed a persistent fellow, and he is from the same background as Carolyn and the others, Enid, Ginger and Dick. I remember Jim, a rather clean-cut fellow who Carolyn once said was "a more normal person than you are." Her letter goes on to say how often they have thought of me, and how she wants to show me around Wellesley, and of the times she wishes I was there. But that is the kind of attitude I expect from Carolyn, nothing emotionally unstable. Somehow her letter seems too understated to be real, or is it that I have lost my perspective as to what is understated and what is not? To top things off, she writes of going to visit my family. She ends the two pages by saying that she takes it I am essentially the same. No Carolyn, I am no longer essentially the same. I am much changed.

On D + 18 Stahl and Parker arrived. Stahl spent 42 days in Sydney. I was glad to see him, even though it makes me second in command in the section. He leaves a great deal of the work and directions to me, and indeed his indecisiveness, his vacillating attitude have piqued me during the past few days. I have become used to my own definite action. I've been regularly working the winches on the ships, and the time, though not actually flying, moves along. We have had a little action. A plane came over a few nights ago; Company B next door talked half the rest of the night about it. I was asleep, as most of us were, less than minutes after the last shot went up. Air attack continues to be negligible.

The Russians are less than 100 miles from Berlin, our infantry 30 to 40 miles from Manila, with Clark Field taken. Two hot rumors have MacArthur relieved by Stilwell, and the Marines landing on Formosa.

That about winds things up at present, and indeed the next entry on a new pad will be a new start, in more than one sense.

February 7

I've not been able to write for a week and for good reason. So much has happened that I haven't had much time to think—and, perhaps, just as well. Steady work takes huge chunks out of the days and nights. We finished the *Singer* after several dragged-out weeks of work. Since then we've worked several other ships, and at present the *Blackburn,* which was at Biak—and in the European theater before that.

There has been some light action in our vicinity. We had two definite scares during the past week. One was a night air raid while we were on the *Singer.* The planes came over, and there was the usual ack-ack in the air. Soon we heard the close hum of a plane. The hum built to a crescendo as the plane went into a long dive. We took cover in the fantail. The scream of the diving plane got louder and more terrifying with every second. It seemed an eternity, though the dive must have lasted only about 20–30 seconds. Everybody was scared, faces drawn. I steeled myself for either the crush of a bomb or the crash of the plane. As the scream reached its highest pitch, the plane levelled off and flew right by the ship, very low and going fast. The guns opened up on him as soon as he was clear of the ship. Those who got a good look at him said they thought some shells went through his wings, but he did get away. For some time we remained frightened; everybody unreservedly admitted it. During the plane's dive, I was positive that we would be hit.

A few nights later, toward early morning, the whistle of a shell woke us. By the time the second one came over, we knew it to be an enemy gun. We could see the dull flash in the hills, and then about 10 seconds later the shell whistled overhead and landed on the beach. Only four rounds were fired, and one of those was a dud. There was not much we could do except sit in the dark and hope the Japs would not shorten the range. The shelling caused no damage, we later found, and we haven't heard from the gun again.

"It doesn't rain in Luzon in February" is now the standing joke. Three nights ago we had a terrific rainstorm, one of the heaviest I have ever been in despite its coming out of season. It started while we were on the way back to camp in early evening and rained in torrents for six hours. We were soaked and cold by the time we got to camp. The violent storm knocked down Dem's and my flimsy shelter, Pap's abode and the mess hall. The officers' tents were also down. (We were so dreadfully sorry that *that* happened!) The area having been a rice paddy and meant to hold water, did so. Water and mud were ankle-deep. I luckily salvaged a dry blanket and my raincoat, and then I sloshed my way to the orderly tent, the only one that remained up. Fortunately this was a huge hospital tent, and therefore the whole company was able to take shelter there. Everyone was shivering with cold and miserable. I made sure my diaries, pictures and wallet were dry; I didn't care much for anything else. Fellows worked in the nude in ankle-deep mud to put up a tent and to push water trailers by the light of a jeep. That tent was our improvised kitchen, and the cup of coffee and bun really helped everyone. Happily my crew ate aboard ship or we would have been hungry that night, as many were. The whole area was under water when the rain became a steady drizzle about midnight. Dem and I repaired to our "tent" and waterproofed ourselves as well as we could by the light of a candle which I was lucky enough to have. The shelter leaked, of course, but not heavily enough to soak through the dry blanket in which I wrapped myself and slept the sleep of exhaustion till early next morning. The sun was hot the next day, but the ground is still drying out.

That night the cots sank into the mud up to the cross pieces. While working on the poncho, which formed part of our shelter for the night, I stood on one of the dikes a little above the water. An army of small pisants also had taken refuge there, and in no time they were in my socks and shoes, stinging with the sharpness of needles. I was bitten at least 30 times on each foot and ankle before I could fling off my shoes and socks. My feet swelled. Now several days later, the bites and itching are still present from those tiny insects. Dem laughed that evening, but he got a similar dose next morning. Then we killed the whole nest with an insect bomb. That morning the camp was strung with wash lines, and everything from money to mattresses were hung up to dry.

Our equipment has arrived, and my barracks bag is in excellent shape. Now we have tents up, a mess hall, and a fair latrine. Everything is going GI, and because everything has to be so uniform, our details have absorbed the little free time we've had. In typical disorganized fashion, we have changed tents several times as well as their arrangement. Last night at midnight I went to sleep for the first time in 24 hours, and for a wonderful nine hours straight. Another good break was getting this afternoon off. Naturally when I got up this morning, we had to change the tent arrangement again. I am disgusted with the disorganization of and the pettiness among the officers for the past several days. One would think we are still a rookie outfit of six weeks.

This afternoon, at last, I have a chance to write. Since leaving Biak I've written one letter and one V-mail, both home. Though mail has been coming, I've received none at the last two mail calls and little during the past few months. I did get a letter from Dale, who remains interesting

in her letters, and always answers promptly. I have a lot to catch up on.
I still don't know what Edith got for Mother. I'm pretty well used to
Carolyn's engagement now, and mostly over it. It shall not be difficult
now to answer her last letter.

We get our clothes washed by the Filipinos who usually hang around
camp. A few of the girls are neat looking; all are clean with thick, black,
glossy hair. From some of them I have heard of brutal atrocities and
stories of the guerrillas.

The war news is good. Our troops now occupy Manila! We took it in
less than half the time expected. The Russians are only three miles from
Frankfurt and 25 miles from Berlin! How long can the Germans continue
to fight? By next spring ('46) the wars should be over. We are all anxious
to push on to Manila ourselves, though we are more comfortable today
than we have been for the past six weeks. There is also the long endemic
rumor of going to China. That wouldn't be bad, though I'd like to see
Manila. I'm not too keen on another campaign.

February 18

We pulled a double shift yesterday unloading heavy lifts so we got 24
hours off. Some of us are going to town in a little while. We are working
beer, and this morning cases of the stuff came in. I've developed a certain
taste for it myself while in the army.

Last night Sanchez, out on the *Mana Mitchell,* was solicited by a
homosexual. There seem to be a number of them on these ships. The
fellow himself is an effeminate Puerto Rican who had a year of journalism
at Columbia. Though he was extremely pleasant to all of us, securing
food, etc., it made me creep a little to have him near me, and yet I realize
more than most of the fellows the cause of such aberration. Sanchez told
me in minute detail about the homosexual's actions, his speech, and what
homosexuals wanted and the reactions they felt. Sancho is not perspi-
cacious; he simply repeated what the fellow told him. It was all extremely
interesting, as far as that goes.

Yesterday we unloaded ducks. Parker drove one into shore, with an
officer on board. While he drove, the motor got hot. When he opened
the hood the radiator cap flew off and hit him in the face. When we saw
him in camp he looked a mess. One eye was completely closed and the
other bloodshot.

Norm and I went to Daguapan a few days ago without passes. We had
hardly arrived there after 15 miles of hitchhiking, when we were picked
up by two MPs for not having passes, and taken to headquarters where
our rifles were confiscated. The captain of the MPs gave us a good break.

We were then escorted out of town by a sergeant who drove us in a jeep. Although orders of arrest were made out, we have heard nothing about it from the C.O. yet. I expected to be called on the carpet for it by now. It is ironic that we were arrested in the first town we have seen in a year-and-half, and that the next day we could have easily obtained legitimate passes.

February 20

Went to Daguapan day before yesterday with Sig and Frank. While there I met nearly everyone in the company. Now having passes, we weren't, of course, stopped by MPs. It was a nice day, and I felt especially good going to town for a much-needed change. While there we ate in several one-arm joints that served meagre meals of fish, chicken or eggs, with eggplant or tomatoes as a constant side-dish. No coffee available. It was fun eating in the dirty, shabby little shops with flies using the food as landing strips.

As we walked around town, we were invited to an apartment that was once luxurious but a bit worn now. The family had a little shop down-stairs. I sat in a room for the first time in months, a room with hardwood floors, civilian furniture, a nonworking radio, and a piano. It was all pleas-ant and congenial. We discussed (Eriksen did, that is) the Filipino custom of meeting girls' families before being allowed to go out with them. It is just like the old Spanish-courting system. The women, both married, were pleasant people and well-educated. Both had attended Manila Col-lege. One was a teacher, and the other majored in home economics. It was wonderful to be among educated, well-mannered people again. One of the women was quite pregnant. In the apartment there were children of all ages, kids with pleasant, chubby features and great, animated black eyes. I should like to go back and talk with them myself sometime. At another place, a wine shop, we found a girl who sang several songs for us in a beautiful soprano voice. It made an odd picture, the girl standing and singing in the corner of a squalid shop, the old toothless crone of a mother squatting on a stool, while we stood listening. Outside the dust rose from the dry, dirt road and glistened in the hot sun in golden, float-ing particles.

On the way back two soldiers in a weapons-carrier picked us up. The driver took off so fast that Demerle was thrown off the vehicle and luckily only slightly bruised. Later we realized the driver was half-drunk on nipa. A little more than half-way back, he ran off the soft shoulder of the road, and the vehicle slipped down the sharp incline, skidded along the top for about 20 yards, and then slid down at a dangerous angle. I thought I was in for an accident, but the car narrowly escaped turning over. It was a close call and shook us up. A bulldozer near where we ran off the road pulled us out. The driver's buddy, who was sober, drove the rest of the way.

At midnight as we came in from work and lined up for the midnight meal, we learned the astonishing news that Cory was dead. Eriksen had been picked up by MPs and when they noted his outfit, they informed him of Cory's death. A Filipino who was at the scene reported it as follows. There was a gunfight between Cory and a colored soldier. The latter was reported limping away down a road, probably hit in the leg or foot. Cory had twelve bullets in his body, eight in the chest, four in the abdomen. Demers, who saw Cory's body only a half-hour after it all happened, didn't know it was Cory until the next morning. He said Cory was sprawled out under a tree with blood all over his face, probably spewed up when he was hit in the chest. He was found near a house of prostitution situated out in the swamps near Daguapan. Several of the fellows saw him drunk earlier in the afternoon. The last time I saw him was that morning when he signed out on pass right in front of me. I remember, as my name went down, reading Pvt. William A. Cory—and, then, that night dead.

We were all grieved to hear of Cory's death. Because I know his pugnacious attitude, especially when drunk, and his deep-seated hatred of Negroes, it is not difficult for me to construct what probably happened. Most likely he resented the Negro having intercourse with the same girl he had, or perhaps his even being there. One word led to another and blam—blam—blam! Cory's rifle was found with an empty clip that holds 15 shells. We have no further word as to the capture of the killer. It is probable that Cory was shot in self-defense. In any case, he is now buried. A notice on the bulletin board advises that no one will mention anything in reference to this incident in letters. Most likely his mother will get a "Killed in the line of duty" notice. As Jack Harris said, "Some men who walk around with a chip on their shoulders are destined to die young." Cory was 21.

It seems a shame that a man has to go through all the hell of the army and campaigns only to be killed over some slut and because of a bottle of nipa. The occurrence is not unique; it happens frequently. It seems unreasonable that the army should require that troops in this area, which is now secure, carry their rifles and permit them to go to towns where there are liquor and available women. That combination of gun, liquor and women has already made for several deaths. Here frontier conditions exist; it is a place for a man to stay sober. This nipa, or tuber, is powerful stuff. A quarter bottle was enough to make me feel light-headed for several hours. Some merchant marines have been killed; Filipinos and MPs have killed men for rape or attempted rape. Carbines are fired all the time.

Yesterday Tunison, one of our 36-month men who was in the old 32nd Division, got his "walking papers." He expects to leave shortly. It's about time; we were all happy for him, even those of us who know him slightly. Joe Ward shall probably be next.

Received letters from Edith today. Her fiancé is overseas four weeks, and naturally she is worried and waiting to hear from him. She and the English professor at Queens were pleased with "The Veterans" [*an essay I wrote and sent*]. I wish you'd get a little more ambitious Kahn, and do more writing. All the old mail is beginning to catch up. Latest is Jan. 28th. Dad's guess of Manila is pretty close.

February 23

Cpl. Kahn came very near being a private again. These past three days Norm and I have been really sweating it out. The other day our delinquency reports came through just after we thought that they would not. Norm and I were called in separately—Norm first. He came out and told me he had drawn a week's extra duty. I didn't think that was bad, certainly not as bad as being broken. I went in, saluted, and told the truth about knowing we needed passes but going anyway. The C.O. said he would break me, and I said that I thought it was too stiff a punishment for a first offense, and a trivial one, though I didn't mention the latter. He had several delinquency reports in front of him. He blew his top saying that he had to make an example of someone. I figured, Kahn, you're an example and your goose is cooked! It seemed odd that I was going to be broken and Norm not to be.

About 10 minutes later, Norm was called back and told he would also be broken. The C.O. did not know he was a corporal!! It is strange that a C.O. doesn't know his own non-coms. Well, that was all day before yesterday. Just a few minutes ago, I was called in. The Sgt. said, "The C.O. has had a change of heart." It was short and very sweet. I remain in rank with nothing but an admonishment and a few days wondering. Norm and I, every time we saw one another upon changing shifts, would yell from the dock or Jacob's ladder, "Not yet!" Norm doesn't know the good news because he's working until this evening.

Pap also was on the carpet for his drinking binge with Eriksen. Pap was charged with firing his rifle in town and faced with a court martial. However, he came out pretty well also with only a week's extra duty and no loss in rank. Glad to see the old codger get out of it lightly, though he's been more than usually irascible and sarcastic these past weeks.

Tunison left a few days ago. The night before he was to leave we had a raid, and he really sweated that out. After three years overseas, it would be a supreme irony to get it the last night before starting the long journey home. We've had a number of alerts and several raids these past few nights; the moon is bright and full again. Bombs were dropped the other night on the beach in the QM dump, and strafing set a few cans of gas on fire. One bomb landed right in the middle of a tent—but was a dud. I'll bet the fellows in that tent are still thanking whatever gods look over them.

The war goes well, but the going gets tougher. The Japs hold a square, 100 by 500 yards, in Manila. Bataan is ours and Corregidor just about ours. Seven beachheads were established there in three minutes. The marines who landed on Iwo Jima have ⅓rd of its eight square miles, but they have sustained over 3,600 casualties in 48 hours. It's reported as the toughest battle in 150 years of marine history. The Japs are using plenty of artillery, mortars and rockets. This supports what we have always known: if the Jap used artillery, we would be slaughtered on the beaches. On Iwo Jima the gains are counted in yards. [*Fighting did not end until the end of March. The Marines sustained almost 27,000 casualties, 6,821 of whom were killed. Except for a few hundred prisoners, mostly wounded, the Japanese defenders died almost to a man. As noted by Ronald Spector in* Eagle against the Sun, *for the first time in the island campaign in the Pacific, "the Japanese had inflicted greater casualties on the invaders than they had suffered themselves."*]

March 1

I have read Sherwood Anderson's *Winesburg, Ohio,* a real piece of writing in an extremely simple form. He provides a picture of life, its meaning and meaninglessness, sharply depicted by the episodes in constricted lives. He seems to be able to grasp life firmly and attain the realism many writers unsuccessfully strive for. The lives of his characters, in their aberrations and complexities, beautifully shine with all that is human.

As for us, we continue our work and army routines. Occasionally I am assailed by nostalgic waves of the past beating against my mind. I have a great and growing need for affection, for people I knew, for the touch of women in my life. My mind has periods of this hunger during my waking hours and also at night when it runs through the crowded corridors of dreams, distorted and burning. I have a great emptiness in body and mind yearning to be satisfied. What makes me keep my balance—

and even to be cheerful, with periods of jubilation—is that I understand what these missing things are; and they are very human. And I miss them sorely.

Several men in the company have already picked up venereal diseases.

March 4

Happy birthday, Mom!

Last three nights we've had alerts and raids. Three nights ago was the worst. There seemed to be a number of Jap planes up. The lights picked them up frequently and, sometimes, for long periods. They seemed mostly centered around Magalden airfield, one of the largest around here. We were out on the *Hurd,* a four-hatcher full of ammo. One raid lasted two hours. A heavy bomber came over, caught in the lights about 25,000 feet up, I judge. The ships opened up with small stuff, but they didn't come anywhere near him. He was a sight, though: a pin-point of silver illuminated by tunnels of light from the searchlights and at the apex of a cone of fire shaped by the red tracers.

I was sitting on a bitt on the upper deck aft, and unwittingly under the three-inch gun. When it let go without warning, the concussion and surprise knocked me off the bitt and on my butt. The sudden roar, flash and pressure of air against my face, made me think that we had either received a hit or near miss. For some of the crew it was their first action, and one of the seamen caught me around the shoulders and clung tightly to me in fear. Two more terrific roars followed, and my ears rang for an hour afterwards. It's funny now, but at first I was sure we were hit.

A flock of ratings have come out, and under the overseas rule nearly everyone is at last a Pfc. Charley at last made T-4. Hendricks made Pfc. I thought Sigley deserved Pfc., but apparently Stahl didn't. The fellows have been dissatisfied with Stahl's keeping too many men for the easier jobs on deck and shorting the hold gang to three men each. I agree with them; there should be four. The other night I took the section out and used two four-man gangs without trouble. Company B is in Manila. I can't understand why we didn't rate the spot because we have ¾ths of the battalion's missions to our credit. I guess they are saving us for China.

March 8

An announcement on the company board states that of all the Port outfits in this area, we have attained the highest efficiency rating, 130.4%. The next closest was the 294th, the Port outfit that made the landing with us, with 101.6%. The 293rd was next to last. There is no doubt that we are a good outfit. Our high record here probably means we will stay at this base as long as possible, and then be included in another invasion.

Capt. Reinhardt read the Articles of War to us this afternoon. His pronunciation is poor. Wagner made a fool of him when the Captain made him read several of the articles. Wagner read slowly and asked how to pronounce three syllable words. At first he claimed he couldn't read, and Capt. R. had Sgt. Russell trot out Wagner's service record to prove his literacy. Finally Wagner told Reinhardt that it wasn't his job to read the Articles of War. Reinhardt seems to leave himself wide open for ridicule, and he is not quick enough with a comeback, nor does he correctly use his authority. Now he has the company restricted for a week because of the men who were picked up out of uniform or AWOL.

Lt. Pranke nearly got himself in a bad jam. When Cory was killed, Pranke remarked, "Some of these rebels are better off dead." Purley, who was Cory's close friend, warned Pranke that he would do him harm. It's a stupid thing for a man to say, especially an officer.

We had several more short alerts, but no raids. The 33rd north of us has started a push on Baguio. Planes were bombing this morning, and artillery started again.

We started a new ship last night, the *Bamburger* out of the States since mid-January. Their kitchen was *selling food* to soldiers. The merchant marine is getting to be a sore thorn in our sides.

March 11

Some alerts last night. Bombs might have been dropped on the airstrip.

Rear echelon came in with Smitty, Cobo and Rouse. They had a week in Manila, which they say is flattened, with people living in the streets, and, of course, it's all wide open. Smitty told me that the guerrillas are active in Manila, and that they are shooting all the Chinese in the city who collaborated with the Japs, after they dig their own graves. He saw some of them shot.

The final drives seem to be on in Europe and going well. Yanks have taken Cologne and Koblenz. The Russians are advancing on Stettin, Danzig and Berlin again. I guess everyone is anxious for it to be over this spring if possible. Hand-to-hand fighting on Iwo Jima continues. We now have over ⅔rds of the island. Luzon campaign in final stages. Getting good meals on the *Bamburger,* though we pay a peso a man for them. It's worth it to us.

March 16

The following is an excerpt from a letter of Enid's to Mom which she forwarded to me in one of hers.

> Feb. 20 '45. I don't know if Cacky [*Carolyn*] has been in touch with you or not, I do know she is planning to be married. She went to N.Y. this week to make arrangements and if possible was going to get married this week. Her husband will be stationed up here in Boston for close to two months, and I believe C. plans to commute to college.

It seems as if Carolyn's prediction of a marriage a few years hence has been radically changed. I don't know why I should have expected to hear the last of it. I suppose I shall always be hearing snatches of Carolyn's life.

The other night while I was working a ship, a duck carrying gasoline blew up on shore. It made quite a blaze. On the initial explosion something was thrown high up and burning, perhaps the driver. Rumor has it he was killed. Fire trucks got down there and used a fog spray. The duck continued to burn viciously, and then suddenly, like a candle flame in an enclosed bottle, the huge flame was snuffed out—just like that.

March 23

Last night was hellish. We experienced one of our heaviest raids. In the bright sunlight of this afternoon, last night seems like a horrible nightmare.

We were seated at the movie, Pap, Dem and I, drinking beer and enjoying *Sunday Dinner for a Soldier*. The moon was fairly bright; it's getting full again. Suddenly I heard in the distance the soft purr of a plane coming in low. Because there was no alert, no one suspected that it was other than ours. The "woosh" and "crump" of the first bomb found us stretched on the ground. The bomber had slipped in unnoticed and was laying down a pattern toward us.

I counted five bursts advancing toward us and assuredly waited for the next bomb to land square in the movie area, where we were still lighted up. The movie machine continued to run for a little while after the bomb bursts began. Then a minor miracle; the bomb pattern fell short of us. The second the bombs ceased falling, the alert went off, which struck us as funny, the lights went out, and several hundred men stampeded, knocking others down and trampling many. Fortunately, we were seated in the mess hall on the outer edge of the stampede. I only got my hand stepped on. We rose and quickly raced through the camp area to the railroad tracks and got away from an area that was a probable strafing target.

Out on the tracks, where most of the company converged, we could surmise by the faint, rosy glow not far away that hits were scored in the ammo and gas dump (recently unloaded) on the edge of the other side of the tracks. The ammo dump extends to within a few hundred yards of camp, and I can see it as I write. In 20 minutes there was a raging fire, along with the sounds and sights of exploding ammo. By the time the fire trucks went screaming up there, the blaze was out of control. A few minutes later the fire trucks came back, battered and damaged.

Meanwhile, we went for our helmets. I found mine gone and later on Hendricks' head, from where I retrieved it. The sounds of the explosions, though not yet comparable to the Hollandia fire, were assuming proportions reminiscent of it. Many men started to evacuate the area, making up small packs. Because the dump was so close, we stood an excellent chance to be burned out. I stuffed my diaries in my shirt, the only things I cared about saving.

Bud and I took off down the road about 50 yards. As the fire and explosions increased, we retreated another 100 yards and sat near a ditch alongside the tracks. Bud suggested moving away from the tracks and road, which shortly afterwards proved a fortunate suggestion. We headed beachward and hit the shore near a small Filipino community. At that time the planes returned to the attack. Ack-ack went up, and several times Bud and I stretched out until we finally found a shallow hole beneath a thorn bush about 40 yards from the water's edge. We could hear the planes' motors while ack-ack peppered the sky in almost unbelievable quantity. Hern, Bud and I found ourselves in the hole with Filipino women and children diving in alongside us. They were hugging babies and small children to their breasts. I never saw such looks of fear as the flickering fires revealed on the faces of those women. Some were whimpering with terror. "Where shall we go mister?" Where indeed? One little boy of two or three was fascinated by the noise and raging fire; he sat up and looked at it, unabashed by the danger. I grabbed him by the arm and pushed him down into the sand. Bud was saying, "Over here mother; get down mother," to the women. As soon as the ack-ack let up, they ran like frightened rabbits.

We spent about another hour with our noses in the dirt, getting as low down as possible in that shallow hole. Most of the time I wasn't frightened at all. The sky was a reflecting, flickering red; great billows of flame and smoke rose into the night. Silhouetted against the red night were the figures of retreating soldiers, civilians, loaded trucks, jeeps and weapons-carriers. Planes circled overhead. In fact, they were all over the bay last night. One bomber did frighten us when it flew over the fire, wheeled, and came up the tracks and road strafing. We didn't know it at the time, but that was where Pap, Dem, Thomas and most of the section were. They were all narrowly missed.

Everyone had close calls last night. I heard one plane diving toward us, laying down a pattern near the gas dump, fortunately hitting nothing there. Nevertheless, the dump became the hell that only a burning ammo and gas dump can. Birds wheeled and screeched on black wings against the red sky. Phrases and images ran through my head, good lines, as I tried to find language to capture the mood and scene. By this time our nerves were raw, alive and straining to every sound, our stomachs contracting sharply in fear now at whistling shrapnel. It was going to be one of those long, bad nights. We lay in the shallow hole, eaten by bugs and not much minding.

We were there about three hours. Bud fell asleep several times, lying in the sand. A fellow from the 243rd wandered along saying that they had asked for volunteers to fight the fire. I spoke to some Filipinos who were working right in the ammo dump. From them I learned that 42 Filipinos and three soldiers were killed in the initial blasts. The Filipinos were amused by Bud's snoring as he lay with his head back, his helmet on.

The huge billowing clouds of smoke and flame lit the sky and mountains; the flash of explosions lit the ships in the bay. After resting on my back for awhile, I looked about me and dimly saw the figure of a woman laying a small child on a nearby board. She rubbed the child's limbs, warming him. I lit a cigarette and handed it to her. I then bent down to see if the child was all right. She said nothing, apparently knowing no English. The woman was rather pretty, with her smooth features and gold earrings shining in the firelight. Everything seemed all right, and before Herbeck and I headed back to camp, I gave her a few more cigarettes.

Camp was unscathed. Only a few men were there. The officers had stayed. I met Stahl who had been in Daguapan at a church service. He told me that the planes had flown over there and that the benediction continued for 15 minutes after the alert. He and others drove back in the dark, passing an overturned truck. As we talked the all-clear sounded, and a cup of coffee went rather well at this time. It was only, to my amazement, 12:30 and so we organized a relief for the men out on the ship. Our section had only six men in camp, but by the time we got to the ship we had 13, and Curtin came aboard later. We unloaded kerosene drums during the night while the fire died down. We got a clear view of the fire from the ship because the dump was only a few miles away. Everybody related his experiences. Pap had to dive into a Filipino latrine during the strafing. The seat of his pants showed the unpleasant result. He had a close call.

At about 5:00 A.M. the dump began to burn and explode with new fury, surpassing anything we had seen or heard the previous night. Flames shot hundreds of feet into the air; explosions made one continual roar for over an hour. I sat watching it, fascinated by hundreds of anti-aircraft shells and small arms ammo exploding in giant fountains of light and flame, lighting the country for miles around. Large red gashes cut into the dark skin of the night.

At 7:30 A.M. half of us went to shore in a duck. There was no relief section. On the way to camp we picked up about 15 men straggling in from miles around. The renewed fury of the fire had caused the camp to evacuate. However, we found camp again unscathed. After arranging for a relief gang, I had breakfast. The relief went out shortly afterwards when enough men returned. By then the fire completely dissipated itself to a smoking ruin. Claud Young was in the hospital; the stampede at the movie had broken a couple of his ribs. He was the only man hurt among us last night, although the experience shocked all of us. Reports tell us that communication lines from the dump were cut last night. It may be that the raid last night was a pinpoint bombing—a pile of secret ammo was destroyed in the attack—certainly suggesting that Jap collaborators or sympathizers helped in identifying the target.

I slept about four hours this morning. We've received word that General Patrick was killed, the general who gave us the pep talk back in Australia. [*Patrick was killed by enemy fire, Mar. 15, 1945, in northern Luzon.*]

Rouse's old wound has been bothering him, and he is now on company details, leaving the section with 13 men and Curtin, who's been sick for a week. Eriksen was finally broken, and Peterson is platoon sergeant. Stahl thought he was in line for it, but Reinhardt claimed he did not get it because we were undisciplined up to the time of Finschhafen. If he got it, I would have been acting Sgt. again.

Rumor has us slated for San Fernando which the guerrillas liberated a few days ago. This fire may slow down the drive on Baguio and liaison with Filipinos in San Fernando. Understand it would be a good break to be up there; they have actual seasons of the year in Baguio [*the summer capital of the Philippine Islands up in the mountains*].

Pap and Dem are working on a slit trench. I might do same in a few minutes. The Japs will probably be back.

March 25

Eighteen months overseas today.

Received a letter from Enid yesterday informing me of Carolyn's marriage. The passage read:

> I imagine by now C. has written you. Gather yourself together, I wrote your Mother she was planning it. Cacky is married. The great independent career girl is married. Jim you see was going to be in Boston for two whole months before putting out to sea so you can understand why she did it. No, she hasn't quit college, she commutes. Marvelous, I know I could never get my work done, but I suppose it's all a matter of good organization.

Finis, and good luck Carolyn.

We've been cut to the bone on army equipment and have turned in all extra articles. Thus we forfeit a lot of little comforts, such as lanterns, extra clothes, my mattress—in other words, all that wasn't issued. Even our water pump was turned in, and now the showers don't work. That's the worst part.

I had a close call in the hold yesterday when barrel chimes swung at me from a sudden release of the winch. I ducked in time to protect my head, but my sunglasses got clipped and the frames broken. The lenses are still in one piece. I've had numerous close calls with my eyes.

There was a "Flippo" band and girl singer here last night. Not bad show. Tonight's movie is *To Have and Have Not.* Midnight shift off for me. Surprisingly, we've not had an alert these past two nights. I thought surely the Japs would try again after their recent success here. A false alert last night had everybody up and on edge.

Ten men leave for San Fernando tomorrow with Lt. Murphy to start getting a camp area in shape. We'll probably go up in a few weeks. Guerrillas just took the place several days ago, and it's liable to be pretty hot yet. As far as my rotation chances go, I'll save the ink.

March 29

We've got two new officers, which brings us up to full strength on officers for the first time. Both are 2nd Lts., named O'Loughlin and Walker, one from Buffalo, one from San Francisco. They're young, seem pretty good fellows, and both have been overseas three months. We talked about an hour when I went to keep Norm company on C.Q. I'll be pulling that in a day or so since they are going through corporals now. T-5s now pull KP—poor devils. We are operating with a 15-man gang, going to work

with 9 to 11 men. Not easy. The working gangs are too small. Lt. Cald-
well, one of our few good officers, is transferred.

Word has come through that Capt. Drown, who was in Leyte, is on
his way home, a psycho case after combat experiences [*never substan-
tiated*].

April 1

Pulled C.Q. night before last and yesterday, and then I slept for 12 hours
last night. Woke KPs an hour early yesterday morning by mistake and
felt rotten about it all day.

Got a most entertaining letter from Dale. In my last letter, I wrote
her the unexpurgated parts of my diary concerning our relationship way
back in October '43. She, in turn, wrote me some of hers. It is gratifying,
especially from one whom I admire so much, and it also proves that I
was right about what she thought. If I had my choice of going anywhere
excluding home, I should choose Sydney. It would be wonderful to see
her again, especially now. In her letter she wrote:

> November 1, 1943.
>
> Sy left on Thursday and I have only just realised how much I will
> miss him. O Dale you are a silly little fool, why do you always find
> out things like this when it's too late. I have the most horrible
> feeling today. Saying good-by to a person you like very much is an
> extremely painful operation at the best of times, but when you know
> there is little chance of ever seeing him again it is positively hellish.
> He is such a wonderful person too. He has practically the same
> tastes in most things as I have, can be lots of fun and is so easy and
> interesting to talk to. He is so intelligent he makes most of the boys
> I know seem rather gauche. When I come to count up his virtues
> I find he has almost all the ones I have always thought my ideal
> man would have. In fact I think he is the nearest I have ever met
> to that man. (Note: I've a list drawn up some years ago of all the
> characteristics of my idea of my ideal man) But of course it isn't
> the mere separate points that make me like him so much, it's just
> that he is, as a whole, a very very dear person. I have a feeling that
> if he had stayed here much longer I might have fallen in love with
> him and that would have been terrible as things stand. Then why
> O you idiot were you so (as he said) cold and unresponsive? I'm
> sure I don't know, maybe I didn't realise what I realise now. But if
> he were here tonight I'm sure he wouldn't have cause to say that.
> I love the way he looks at me sometimes with that little half smile

on his face. I love the way he is never dogmatic like so many men, and will always listen to your side of the question and give due consideration to your opinions instead of, like Gordon, give the impression that you are merely a silly little adolescent and your ideas are to be listened to with a tolerant smile. And particularly I like the way he says "student." Don't know what it is about his accent but when he says it it sounds so sweet and cute. For some obscure reason it makes me feel maternal and I feel I would like to take his head in my arms and stroke his forehead. O Dale, Dale stop going on like this, it's quite ridiculous and anyway he has gone and you will probably never see him again so please be sensible and try and put it out of your mind. Whether I do see him again or not I know I'll always admire him tremendously and regret having so little time to get to know him.

It's all very tender reading, and when I thought about her and what she wrote during the long early hours of morning, I felt a poignant, futile, tragic and yet beautiful and tender episode slip out of my life. I, too, believe I could have fallen in love with Dale. The whole thing seems fraught with potentialities, but in all probability never to be realized. I do not think my feelings have been distorted by my long absence from women. I have missed her always, a dull, aching sort of missing; perhaps the kind one feels when a baby dies—when a possibility dies. Her letters continue to be punctual, wonderfully lengthy, and among the most interesting I've ever received. Who knows whether our paths will ever cross— or whether I shall attempt to make them cross.

We had an alert during my night on C.Q. The growl of night fighters overhead jangled our nerves, Norm's and mine. He was there talking after coming in from work at midnight. He told me about the time Dale floored him with some remark. He said, "She was too much for me."

The camp area is getting ready at San Fernando. I understand that it is a good area, near the docks, but the water is rough. Rybicki has been transferred out into Base M. Special Service. Probably a good break.

April 6

I have been working hard this past week. John had a close call in the hold when a box fell from the net at the top of the hatch and missed him by a scant few feet. You can't be too careful in the hold of a ship, especially the way we work. Adams is back, and that gives us 14 good men. This is the best group of working men we've ever had in the section, with no goldbricks. We've got it arranged so that under favorable conditions we can go out with a 10-man gang leaving four men off every shift. Though we may sometimes work harder, it is well compensated in time off.

The ship we're unloading, the *Dona Matis,* has quite a history. She is Italian-built, Filipino-manned. She was the last ship out of Manila before the Japs took it, and one of the three surviving ships of a 12-ship convoy sent to relieve the beseiged Americans on Bataan. Since then she has had her share of adventures plying the Pacific.

These days the crew sells liquor for $20 a quart. All of us bought some. Frank and I went halves. I felt I wanted some, although $10 a pint is not hay. I've consumed about half of my half. It does go well after working hard, especially if it's been chilly.

The wars in both theaters progress. Our armies are 140 miles from Berlin; the Russians are six miles from Vienna. I can't see how the Germans can hold out until summer. Here, we landed on Okinawa in the Ryukyu Islands—only 250 miles from Japan itself. Landings were also effected on a few islands 30 miles from Burma. The Burma campaign continues to beat its way toward Rangoon after the fall of Mandalay, but in China the Japs still manage to have it their own way. They have established a land route through the heart of China. We now have an effective blockade in the South China Sea, if one judges from the daily reports of ships sunk.

Minesweepers have been operating around San Fernando. There is still hard fighting in central and northern Luzon. With the landing at Pagupsi, southern Luzon is effectively enveloped. We should move in about a week. I hope for once it will be an efficient move.

April 11

We should move in several days. I've heard so many conflicting stories about the place that I will not venture writing anything.

Mail has been coming through better these past few days. Received a long, entertaining and pleasant letter from Mrs. Kastor. I received letters simultaneously from Jerry Ryan and Mother, both telling me of his visit to my home. For a few minutes I couldn't quite place him, and then I remembered him as the mess boy from NYC aboard the *Perkins* that I asked to look up my family. The visit pleased and thrilled Mother. At least it somewhat assured her of my well-being.

We had a short alert last night, the first in a long time. The Filipino crew have brought some women aboard the *Matis* who are members of their families. Some of the crew haven't seen the islands in years, and some are finding their families decimated or even wiped out.

With all these showdowns [*a surprise inspection to see if each man has all his standard equipment*], I got hooked for 23 cents for a missing canteen cup! Rains now once in awhile, and it is very hot in the afternoons. Lt. Walker certainly likes to bat the breeze. Lt. W. told me last night that quiet Lt. C., overseas only six months, is on his way back to the States, a psycho case.

April 16

Three mornings ago the astounding news came to us that President Roosevelt is dead. He died unexpectedly from a cerebral hemorrhage at Warm Springs, Georgia at 15:35, April 12. The news shocked us all; undoubtedly the nation is more poignantly feeling the grief of his loss. He will go down as one of our greatest presidents, and one of the great men of all times. He has been President for over 12 years, ever since I was eight years old. We of the younger generation have never known any other man as the nation's leader. Truman is now President, and we don't know what kind of man he is. He got his start in Kansas City, backed by the Pendergast machine. He made a name for himself in the Senate. We can only hope that he can successfully handle the peace plans and post-war world.

In true army style our move to San Fernando has been called off. The harbor is not yet cleared of sunken ships. Lt. Wenz and Sgt. Tipple are on detached service to Hdqtrs of the 495th. Lt. Wenz is a well-liked officer, and almost all the men were sorry to see him leave.

I have been working especially hard these last few days on the *Ashley* which is filled with heavy engineer equipment. All day yesterday I was bothered with a severe headache, and my back and arms were sore. I thought I was in excellent condition, but those 200-pound boxes got the best of me.

One afternoon it must have been about 130 degrees in that hold. I had the midnight shift off last night, and that has refreshed me. A number of fellows are sick, some with malaria. Muscles is down with a typical case of yellow jaundice. Hellman fractured his ankle when he fell 20 feet from the gunwale of a liberty to the upper deck of an LCT. He was fortunate in escaping that lightly. Baker is leaving the company today with a bad case of jungle rot. A great many of the fellows have touches of it, especially around the hands and knuckles. The only thing I have are those small white "blisters," which nearly everyone has. Infection is almost impossible to stop in the smallest of cuts.

Our length of time overseas, the hard work, the nervous strain, and the sterile army life are beginning to manifest themselves in various ways.

H. W. told me last night that quiet Lt. Cald-
well, who has been overseas but six months
is on his way back to the States, a psycho case.
Everything else going along as usual.

April 16, 1945.

Three mornings ago the astounding news came to
us that President Roosevelt is dead. He died unexpectedly
from a cerebal hemorrhage at Warm Springs Ga. at
15:35 April 12. The news shocked us all; undoubtedly
the nation is feeling the grief of his loss more
poignantly. He will go down as one of our greatest
presidents, one of the great men of all times. He has
been president for over 12 years, even since I was 8
years old, and thus we of the younger generation
have never known any other man as the nation's
leader. Truman is now president and what kind
of man he is remains pretty much a question
mark. He got his start in Kansas City, backed by the
Pendergast machine. He made a name for himself
in the Senate. We can only hope that he can
handle the peace plans and post-war world successfully.

In true army style our move to San Fernando has
been called off indefinitely. The reason being that the
harbour is not yet cleared of sunken ships. Lt.
Wenze and Sgt Tipple are on detached service to Hdqts'
of the 495th. Lt Wenze is a well liked officer and
almost all the men were sorry to see him leave.

I have been working rather hard, especially these
last few days on the ashley which is filled with
heavy engineer equipment. All day yesterday I was
bothered with a severe headache, my back and arms
were sore. I thought I was in excellent condition
but those 200 lb. boxes got the best of me a little.

Diary page, Apr. 16, 1945, Luzon, Philippines.

Tempers are short. Occasionally my own escapes my better judgment. Some men are sexually starved; it seems Filipino women don't give much satisfaction. Cases of homosexuality are occurring, probably much more than I know about. The "fruit" are found amazingly often on board the various ships we work. Some of our men's experiences do not surprise me, but I was surprised to learn of J's having intercourse (if it can be called that) with a "morphidite" aboard the *Dona Matis*. His intimate, detailed description, though a little repelling, was interesting from a pathological and psychological standpoint. Another year of this life and there shall be even greater changes among the men. Lt. Walker, recently married and overseas about four months, frequently has discussed various aspects of sex with me. As for myself, my mind is ordered on that subject, though we are all in need of feminine company in a fundamental way.

I've been reading several novels, and sleeping lightly and uncomfortably. The 6-on, 12-off schedule (which is really 8-on, 10-off) is wearing. It always is after three months of it without a break. Alert at 4:00 A.M. this morning. I was awake at the first shot. I'm beginning to feel unaccountably old. I think I badly need a rest, a complete rest from army life.

April 20

Joe Ward leaves this morning. When you do go home, it comes all at once. He's the most eligible in the company, having been overseas three years. He flies to Leyte—and then ships home. The next eligible will probably be Berchin who has several more months than the rest of us. Then Pap, I imagine, because he was just 40. Anyway, it's a start. It's good to see someone going home. Joe was the head of the bastard 12th section. Skivvy drew the job to replace Joe.

Demerle is now out of the section and in the supply room, assistant to Gibson. He replaces Baker, who was evacuated for jungle rot; Baker replaced Grant, who was removed for inefficiency. It's a good break for Dem because the work is much easier, and he gets a full night's sleep every night.

As for us, we are cut down to 12 men, which substanially reduces our days off. Stahl, Power and I went over the men who are available as replacements, but we decided they would do harm to the morale of the section. Harris has an order from the doctor stating that he can do no hard work. What a farce! Many fellows are in the hospital, legitimately ill or hurt. Our platoon, having had few accidents, is getting its share of them now. Yesterday Herndon fell from the ship into a LCM when a rope he was handling gave way. He was rushed to the hospital, and no one knows how badly he is hurt.

During a surprise inspection yesterday, the Captain discovered I had five pair of shoes, one pair more than I was supposed to have. He took my best pair. When I awoke and was told about it, I took the Australian-made ones down and exchanged them. I really don't know why I was keeping them; they have nail cleats and are useless on the ships. I expected to hear more about this, but so far nothing has come of it.

There are tryouts for OCS again. I have thought it over and decided not to apply.

Yesterday we had a lecture on venereal diseases, by both a chaplain and a doctor, because there have been 25 cases since the beginning of this month.

On board the *Ashley*, I met a young 3rd mate who thought he remembered Bob from Kings Point. Received mail from Bob who is now in North Africa. Anyway, the 3rd mate had a victrola and some classical music, the first I've heard since leaving Australia. It was mostly Tchaikovsky: "The Romeo and Juliet Overture," the "Concerto No. 1," and "The Nutcracker Suite."

I dream almost every night, more, it seems, than I've ever done before—disconnected dreams. Almost always I am home.

Germany is reported cut in two. All organized resistance has ceased in the Ruhr. We control ¾ths of Okinawa. They are getting the heaviest air raids in the Pacific up there.

April 22

The 243rd has moved out; it at least lets some air through here. The Captain yesterday picked up my white blanket. When I went to reclaim it, stating it wasn't army issue, he blew up as he has on the other few occasions I have seen him. I retrieved it after he stated that I would have to take full responsibility in case of an IG [*inspection general, often called without warning*]. Lt. O'Loughlin vehemently backed me up, arguing right back. He told the Captain that he should confiscate his camera because he, the Lt., had bought it in Manila and had no sales slip. Last night when I thanked the Lt. for his help, he told me that he doesn't get along with the Captain and has had six or eight arguments with him. Lt. Walker also has had disputes. I don't know how much longer I shall hold my rating. I have two strikes on me already. The Captain is unreasonable. I've never been able to have a sensible talk with him; he goes into childish rages. The whole episode made me sick at heart. As for Lt. O'Loughlin standing up for me, I shall not easily forget it. If he wants a favor, all he has to do is ask. You could follow a man like that through Hell.

Dem informed me of a strange thing. When the Captain returned from seeing Joe Ward off, he was crying! He said that he was so happy for Joe that he could not help crying, and that if he had to send many more off, he didn't know how he would take it. He is extreme in his emotionalism, but I can understand that.

The report came through that Ernie Pyle was killed by a sniper's bullet on a little island, Ie Shima, off Okinawa. He was one of the few civilians that saw the war through the eyes of the common soldier, painted it in its true, mostly drab colors.

April 26

A crew member of one of the ships was killed by a shark. I have anticipated this, because so many men go swimming around the ships in deep water.

Forister hit Heffle in the jaw the other evening. He was wearing a pair of brass knuckles. Forister was drunk and stopped Heffle who was returning from a small dance down the road. He was talking with Heffle when, out of a clear sky, he smashed Herb's jaw. Herb was out for 20 minutes. His jaw is a mess, badly lacerated by splintered false teeth, and his lips are bruised. Forister is a bad actor from way back.

Out of curiosity I attended one of the small dances, walking down and back with Herb, who went in spite of his swollen jaw. The dance was in a cleared square, with a perimeter of rude chairs and benches, in the midst of a small community. Our orchestra consisted of two guitars and a mandolin, and some expert singing by Herb, Sanchez and me! There were a number of neat, clean, small Filipino girls about, and some Filipino soldiers. For light there were coconut oil lanterns. The girls danced a simple two-step to everything. I danced three times, and it certainly felt strange after so many months. Part of the "floor" was covered by an overhanging, palm-covered roof which was low enough so that my head brushed it whenever I was under it. The girls are much too short for us, for me especially, and there is no conversation. So I simply danced with small, brown, shy, silent girls under the light of the coconut oil lamps.

When some colored soldiers arrived, the Southern fellows especially started hooting. Soon a heavy, brooding atmosphere settled over the little square, accentuated by the weak, flickering lights and the general silence. Some of the Southern white soldiers carried revolvers under their shirts, looking for trouble. It would have taken very little to start a fracas. I have no sympathy and a rather deep disgust for fellows who continually seek trouble with the Negroes and who voice their stupid arrogance about how Negroes are subjugated in the South. The Southerners' prejudice effectively binds them together in what they feel is a common cause. If these fellows continue to carry weapons, their courage fortified by drink, hatred and each other, there is bound to be serious trouble. I often hear of the predicted trouble that will arise between whites and blacks after the war, and I am afraid that there will be.

There was an interesting incident at the dance when a Filipino accidentally fired a short burst with a machine gun. In a flash, rifles seemed to materialize in the hands of the Filipino men who held them at the ready. Actually, they were speedily handed out from the doorways of nipa huts.

April 28

During this past week we've only been working about every other shift—and not working much even then. The only shift when we really worked I had charge of the gang, and for the first time I completely directed the jumbo boom and windlass while discharging 25-ton LCMs. I felt pretty good at the end of that day, even if it cost me one of my favorite fatigue jackets, the camouflaged one. It's a good thing that the work has been light; Thomas has been out these past four days with a bad ankle.

Sometimes I am scarcely aware of the men who slip out of the company because of illness or injury, and who don't come back soon. House and Lewis have been out some time. Our hospital list grows all the time.

Read a book called *Larry, Thoughts of Youth*, the writings of a young boy at college who is killed in Arizona. He writes of the frosh and soph year at Lafayette College in letters, essays and poems. I enjoyed it, because he wasn't writing with an eye toward publication, and because he so simply reveals his high idealism. I am disgusted with myself because there has been time off and I have not done any of the writing I intended. Indeed, action has become stagnant from contemplating itself.

May 4

At the moment I am pulling C.Q. in our new area at San Fernando. We have been here since the 1st. Across the tent Capt. Reinhardt and Lt. Walker are discussing army regulations, as Lt. W. reads excerpts from the A.R.s, discovering with glee the various things officers can do. They are like a couple of kids, which in fact Lt. Walker is.

The move was one of our smoothest. We've had enough practice! We also had plenty of leisure to prepare for it. We covered the 40 miles via truck, and for the first time in many months we travelled on concrete roads. Only sections of the road were paved, but those were a novelty to us. The ride was interesting. We passed through numerous little towns, some of which were badly scarred by our rolling campaign. The town of Bauang was especially burned and battered. The countryside was green, with a great deal of the land under cultivation. There were many small farms and some substantial-looking homes. The railroad stations, churches and other large buildings were usually damaged. We passed over several pre-war built bridges of considerable size.

We arrived in camp to find the area right on the beach and still under construction. The mess hall, orderly and supply rooms were completed, along with a little less than half the men's tents. The tent frames and floors, built with bamboo, are being constructed by Filipinos.

Our mess hall is a super-deluxe job, not much different from Stateside halls. Our tent area, when it is completed, will be the best we've had overseas, and better than some we've had in the States. It looks as if we will be here a long time.

This is surely the hottest place we have ever been in. It gets hot earlier, stays hot later. Despite a good many trees in the area, it is hotter than when we were in open rice paddies. This area is all sand, a fortunate circumstance what with the coming rainy season.

San Fernando, now Base Hdqtrs, is a hot, extremely dusty, war-torn town. It already has the look of another Finschhafen. In the town are shell-ruined buildings and gas tanks that received direct hits and strafing. There is miscellaneous Jap equipment scattered about, as well as several shot-up and burned Jap planes. The shore, both in front of our own area and at S.F., is a graveyard of torn and battered Jap landing craft, looking like those we first saw on New Britain. The gaping holes and ripped sides testify to what happened to that Jap force. The harbor is small but deep; thus, the ships can anchor quite close to shore.

After arriving here, we set up tents for those of us whose tent platforms and frames have not yet been built. Under this new set-up, I'm with Stahl, Pap, Adams and Shorty. It's a good, quiet tent group that Stahl arranged, and one I'm glad to be in. The unusual thing about it is that the other men are all over 33 (Pap was recently 40!), which makes us four old men and me. At the rate the Flippos are building the tents, we'll be a long time in the one we're in now, which is pitched on the ground.

A half-mile from camp a Jap cargo vessel is beached, a four-hatcher of good size. Yesterday morning Pap and I ambled down there to investigate. We walked along the beach passing the many Jap landing craft until we stood opposite the freighter. I brought my camera along. The ship lay about 60 yards offshore at low tide. We decided to board her. From where we stood she seemed a battered hulk, badly burned. Her name was still visible on the bow, something like *Karashu*. We waded out to her, with our shoes slung around our necks, and the handle of my old box camera between my teeth. We boarded her by lifting ourselves by rope until we reached a Jacob's ladder and gangway, which hung straight down but proved secure. Pap went up first and let down a rope for the camera. The ship was stripped of all souvenirs, but she was interesting to us. She had burned with such intense heat that the metal decks were buckled and glass was fused together. She was a coal-burner, and in one of the hatches the stored coal was still smoking. It must have been burning for weeks. Booms were charred sticks, and gaping holes in the hull, gunwales and wheelhouse testified to the devastating aim of our guns or bombs. The binnacle had dropped to the lower deck; parts of the superstructure were burned through. Some of the rotting cargo, rice and rice bags, was still in the holds. The greatest surprise came when we went aft and looked down hatch four. There we saw a great gaping hole torn in the ship's bottom from a direct bomb hit, and through it we could see the coral bottom of the sea through cool, placid green water. The whole after-end of the ship was blown out of line.

We investigated storerooms, festooned with spider webs, each with a vicious-looking black or gray spider in it. Pap was interested in the engine room, so we descended into that rank and musty part of the ship. There amongst the rubble of gear and engines we found some Jap newspapers and a *Brooklyn Eagle* of 1940. It was odd reading the news and movie ads, and seeing photos of the actors and actresses at that time. I shot a roll of film out there. It was fun exploring the old wreck, just Pap and me. We got down without misadventure and not any too soon, for the tide was rolling in, and I would have had difficulty keeping the camera dry.

Walking back we came across a Filipino woman dressed in white and too heavily powdered, rouged and lipsticked. We stopped and spoke to her awhile. She spoke good English, and I wish I could have gotten the conversation verbatim. She had the unmistakably hard lines, hard features, and hard talk of a prostitute. This was confirmed when she told us of the "establishment" she had in a sort of barroom, and girls who "entertained." She hated the Japs and with good reason. They had taken her house in Manila, and when she protested, they "tied her up and threw her on the ground." She told them to take everything but to let her go. They did, and she fled to Daguapan. It was the familiar story of Jap cruelty, of slapping and beating people. She opened a little place in D. with several girl "entertainers," but the Japs took everything they wanted

Sylvester "Shorty" Hendricks (l.) and Victor Stahl working in a ship's hold, Luzon, Philippines, 1945.

Sy Kahn with bombed-out and beached Japanese cargo ship, San Fernando, Luzon, Philippines, 1945.

Sy Kahn and Andrew "Norm" Denison relaxing against a bullet-marked car, Luzon, Philippines, 1945.

Sy Kahn, winch operator, Luzon, Philippines, 1945.

and paid nothing. She had a friend, a Jap Captain, who had studied eight years in the U.S. He explained that the soldiers took everything because they got paid so little. She claimed that she didn't care if they danced with the girls, or even took a few drinks—but they "took all!!" She closed up on this account. As she told us all this, her language became more profane. First it was "goddam Japs" and then "goddam son-nama-bitch Japs." However, one got the impression that if the Japs had treated the population better, more people would have been content with them. The Japs largely defeated themselves in the Philippines. When we invaded Luzon, she told us she got drunk for two days and sick for two weeks. Got a big kick out of Pap discussing places in Manila and Legapsi with her. He then offered to get drunk with her on bassi on the beach. I half expected her to accept the invitation, but she was returning to D. that afternoon.

Bassi is a new liquor sold to us here. It comes in bamboo sections, cut to hold it, and is very cheap. The first I bought was good, best native stuff I've ever drunk, and tasted like a cheap wine. However, Rouse and Hudaick drank it all in my absence and got plastered. Subsequent bassi has been inferior, as it probably will be from now on, with the demand exhausting the old supply. It's made from sugar cane. The last batch I bought was so rank I gladly gave it away. Eriksen came in last night and told of a poisoned and unconscious soldier picked up on the road and foaming at the mouth. That's another good reason to shy away from the stuff.

The swimming here is wonderful. Pap and I have gone several times and had some good conversations. It is not often one has the time these days. He expects to go home soon, and I hope he does, though I shall sorely miss him, as will the section and the outfit. He is an excellent man, and I've yet to know him to lose his presence of mind or use faulty judgment.

Amazing news has reached us. The completion of the war in Europe seems only a matter of days. First, Mussolini was caught, tried and shot by partisans in northern Italy. He was caught in a little town called Como, then carried to Milan, where he was strung up and found by 5th Army troops arriving there. Along with him when captured was his mistress, and the secretary of the Fascist regime.

(Damn it's a hot, sultry night. Poor Sam Russell is wringing wet—and so am I.) Anyway, last night we got the news that all Axis troops in Italy had surrendered unconditionally to the Allies. In short, the long, heart-breaking campaign in Italy is finished, and the soldiers there sleep easy tonight. The capitulation involves a million enemy troops. Italy fell quickly after our troops were, at long last, able to break out of the mountains and into the open. They are now only a few miles from the Brenner Pass.

Germany is collapsing fast. First of all, there was the astounding news of Hitler's and Goebbels' suicides! Admiral Doenitz heads what's left of Germany. Von Rundstedt is captured and says it is hopeless to continue to fight. Berlin has fallen, and only isolated pockets of resistance prolong the war in Europe. It looks like the long-sought end is at hand. Meanwhile, the San Francisco Conference continues, preparing for peace and the post-war world. [*Attended by representatives of fifty-one nations, the San Francisco Conference, held during April–June 1945, drafted the United Nations Charter.*]

Over here the Aussies invaded the island of Trakan, off Borneo and near important oil deposits. Half the Jap merchant fleet has been sunk, our navy claims. The British are fast winding up the Burma campaign, long and heartbreaking, and Rangoon is surrounded at long last. The fighting on Okinawa is still hard. Our air force pounds the southern islands of Japan proper. We may invade there in a few months. In China the Japs continue to push deeper toward our air bases. Everyone has been excited by the turn of events during the past few days, and we, as the rest of the world, anxiously await the end of the war in Europe. (Just heard news that practically all resistance has collapsed in Germany.)

Our longstanding record for having no one seriously hurt on the ships has been smashed to smithereens in the last few weeks. I hope we are out of the streak of accidents. First Hellman, and then Herndon were hurt in falls. Devaney was hit by a gas drum, which broke his collar bone. Yesterday Egan, while taking in the midships' guy, got his leg tangled in the line when the boom suddenly swung out. He was pitched from the boom table and got his head severely cut. That makes four badly-hurt men in less than a month after more than two years.

Lt. O'Loughlin has been forced into applying for a transfer. The Captain caught him gambling with the men. He's a good fellow, but he should have known better. I really hope he stays on. Murphy went to the hospital today with yellow jaundice, along with several more boys with various ailments. Well, I have seven hours to go yet, and I'm plenty tired right now.

May 9

The war is over in Europe.

At last the anti-climactic finish is official, but the world is still shouting. Of course we are happy, but we still have a hard war of our own here. For several days the unofficial news had been circulating. I still don't know the official day of surrender, though I believe it to be May 6th. This morning I heard a description of the milling, screaming crowds in London, and martial and patriotic music. Churchill showed himself, and the ovation was terrific. It was very stirring. The news here has been accepted calmly.

Many Nazi officials are dead. Goebbels and family were found poisoned. Schacht is a prisoner, as is the traitor Ezra Pound. [*Hjalmar Schacht, German financial expert, was a nationalist, but not a Nazi. He took part in the 1944 plot against Hitler's life. Surviving the war, he was tried and acquitted at the Nuremberg war-crimes trial (1946). Ezra Pound was an important American expatriate poet who broadcast pro-Fascist propaganda from Italy during the war. Following his capture, he was declared legally insane and incarcerated in a mental hospital in Washington, D.C. Released in 1958, he returned to Italy where he died in 1972, at age eighty-seven.*] There is a rumor that Russia has given Japan an ultimatum, but there is no official word on it. These are great days that mark the end of a war nearly five years and eight months long, 3½ years for us, in Europe. We have great strength, along with our allies England and Russia. It must be used rightly this time, to enforce the making of a good world, with the principles of the Atlantic Charter as a foundation for all peoples. Yet I know there will be grave difficulties in the days of peace to come among countries and each nation's people. We must meet all problems wisely, as individuals, as nations. If there is a God let Him be just and give us strength and wisdom to avoid future killings.

Work is moderate. Baker got home, and Willie Harris is in the hospital paralyzed! Lots of fellows in the hospital, two more of Stewart's gang today, Johnson with jungle rot again—and Geyer.

Went to San Fernando recently with Vic Stahl. Drank bassi, talked to people. Got a big kick out of the old women smoking their tremendous cigars, and my making them laugh. Got a lump in my throat seeing the ragged little kids with their tremendous black eyes. S.F. is a ruin.

Jack Harris got an old beat-up violin I fiddled around with for a few hours. It has only three strings. I've forgotten how to read music. It frustrates me to realize I've forgotten so much.

May 16

At this moment I am comfortably living in a bamboo-frame hut. Yesterday we wove the door, built the frame and put up the tent. It is pleasant.

Gas is reported used on the frontlines in Luzon. We have been reissued our gas masks.

Dale's letter was good to get, and we have reached the stage of using endearments—something that is rare with me. Our letters get more and more intimate, and I look forward to them with increasing anticipation. She asks me all sorts of questions about myself, and we have a surprising number of interests in common: music, literature, travel, etc. I wish she were in the States to return to. My chances of ever seeing her again are hardly bright, yet I feel that it may happen sometime. I seriously hope it does.

Received letters from Dick, Enid, Rusty, Allan, and a *Cherry Tree* [*George Washington High School newspaper*] from Miss Sophian. The latter contains excerpts from a letter I sent her over a year ago in reference to the war. I was surprised to see it there. Seeing one's writing in print is a first-class thrill. It's a sensation that cuts deeply to see, nicely blocked and in neat lines, words that I have scratched out in my unlovely scrawl. Sometimes I am sure that I shall do some writing of merit.

Dick's letter contains comments on Carolyn and me. It pains me to read it, even though I have been quite over Carolyn's marriage for many weeks. Consequently, the hurt confused me a little. I have not stopped to figure it out. I don't want to be plagued with Carolyn, and this shall be the last entry concerning our former relationship:

> I know that no matter what I say will not change the way you feel or help matters any—I felt a long time ago that you and she could not make things work out, and it might almost be better this way than to find that out later. . . . Jim is one of the finest fellows I know, and they are extremely happy. Don't let this let you lose contact with her. . . . She's too swell a girl for that.

That was an awfully grim judgment on a relationship that was cut off when I was 18, and Carolyn less. But, in my heart I know that Carolyn and I could not have made things work out; our backgrounds were too dissimilar. As for keeping contact, that would aggrevate what little "situation" there is—or was, rather. Yet she is inextricably bound up with my life and with so many of my friends. But isn't everything that "was" becoming alienated?

We now have Filipino labor to help. They aren't very helpful though, padding around in bare feet in the hold. Some are boys and some old men; I hate to see them doing heavy work as hold men. They aren't very effective, but they are willing. They get paid a peso and 75 centavos a day (about $1.25).

Other day I bought a counterfeit five-dollar gold piece for two packs of cigarettes. It's a good-looking coin, but clearly fake. Work goes on at a fair pace. Frank's reported on his way home; Forister was broken for being drunk four days and refusing to go out to work.

May 23

There has been a lot of excitement these past few days. First, we were rated on the point system. I got a total of 62. There are a handful that have 85, making them eligible for discharge. I had 27 points for months in service, 20 for months overseas, and 15 for service stars (5 each). A man with a child gets 12 points. Those fellows who have seen this much service and who have children are the ones eligible for return to the States. Sixty-one or 62 is the average for young fellows in the outfit.

Some more excitement: we received a quota of one man to go home on TD [*temporary duty*]. Late last night a drawing was held from among the eligible men. These men must have 21 months overseas, which eliminates our replacements except one; they must never have been court martialed, which knocks out a few more; they must never have been reduced in rank except "without prejudice," or had an overseas furlough; and they must not have signed the petition against Capt. Drown.

I cannot describe what gloom the last requirement cast me into, not for myself, but for the men who lose their chance because of the petition. I still feel a great responsibility for that. The "instigators" are out of the outfit; some are home because they were ill, others are eliminated on other counts. But there remains a group of men whose only cause for elimination was signing the petition. The only consolation I have is that I asked no one to sign it, and I attempted, too late, to get it destroyed.

I was thinking of talking to Capt. R. about these men, but I'm sure that it would be to no avail and only stir the mess up again. Two of those requirements seem to me to be quite unfair because the men who made their mistakes have sufficiently paid for them in rank reductions and company duty. To make them pay the high price of not having an equal chance to go home seems to me like forever branding a criminal though he has paid for his crime. Besides, we were all very green and young soldiers then. It seems that this is the cross some of the men must bear, and one that I must especially bear for the rest of my army career in this organization. The responsibility for the misfortune of others is not easy to live with. Reinhardt's decision, which lengthens overseas service for some of us, is nothing less than a prison sentence.

At the suggestion of some of the men, Lt. O'Loughlin kept a list of those of us who pledged five pesos each to the winner of the furlough. This would give the first healthy man to leave from among the original men in the outfit about $500 to do everything we dream about ourselves.

The idea was accepted almost unanimously, even among the men who were not eligible.

Sgt. Gibson, supply sergeant, was the winner of the drawing. Gibson is an old woman. It was not a fair fate that gave the furlough to a man who has a soft job, and spent six months in Australia because of an accident, rather than to a man with a tough job who has put in long continuous service. The final irony was that Gibson, in true Gibson style, did *not* sign the five-peso pledge. Because of this, O'Loughlin tore the pledge list up, and Gibson lost the $500.

May 27

After a five-day vacation, because there were no ships in, we went back to work. We have 15 men in the section now, which is plenty. We all get one out of three or four shifts off, not bad at all.

Letters from home are full of the point system. I guess everything that happens in the service these days directly concerns civilians. Dad wrote about future plans, but everything is hanging fire until my return.

Got a most pleasant surprise in receiving another letter from Dale, a short one written on impulse because she had dreamt of me. I wrote back that I wish I could look forward to her being a part of my homecoming. I *really* mean that, too.

Notice came through a few days ago that men over 40 would be discharged within 90 days. Pap is most happy about this, and he should leave in a month or so.

Capt. R. stated, after considerable pressure was brought to bear by non-coms, that all the petition-signers would be eligible for the next quota. Thank heavens that's over, a thing that's hung fire and haunted me for 16 months. I should not have to make any further entry on that subject, and I think it will finally die the death it should. It taught me plenty, but most painfully.

He also stated that all those men who were broken or court martialed under his command would be eligible after three quotas. So the two conditions that I thought unfair have been eliminated.

A few days ago Sanchez and I went to Bauang to visit a school teacher he knew. It's about eight miles from here over partly concrete road. I found her a pleasant person, except for a high soprano nervous laugh, and one of the prettiest Filipino women I've encountered. Her name is Brasilisa Pachelo. The house was sparsely furnished, but what was there was good. In a glass case at one end of the main room was a richly adorned Christ. It was good to sit in chairs at a table, with a hardwood floor under us, and with pleasant country and people about. We had a kind of fruit that was like a grapefruit. I was much taken with a little eight-year-old named Opine, one of several small girls in the house. It was fun to have them sing for us, and then we reciprocated. I enjoy these Filipino children, girls especially, more than I do the older women. The children strike a very soft spot in my heart.

Sancho and I escorted Brasilisa to a dance in a two-story building on the outskirts of the town. The gathering was large, with a smattering of soldiers, mostly from 243rd. I danced a few times, but mostly I enjoyed watching. The proceeds of the peso entrance fee and a basket raffle went toward building a home economics school. We soldiers wanted to buy one of the baskets, especially Brasilisa's. None of us had much money, because it was the end of the month, so I suggested that we all chip in. We raised 25 pesos, but we were outbid twice for baskets that sold for 85 and 100 pesos to civilians! The high bidder was entitled to dance with the basket donor, but, as one soldier said, the girl ought to go with the basket for that price. The Filipino orchestra sounded like a record playing at half-speed. It was unbearably hot, but the musicians played a song for 20 minutes without a break. Dancing became a feat of endurance. The people in that vicinity seem well-to-do. The girls wore fine dresses and shoes. They surely were not the peasants we usually see. It was a change to be able to talk to intelligent people.

That wonder DDT, sprayed over the area by planes the other morning, completely eliminated flies for three days. However, they are annoyingly back in force this morning.

June 5

A few nights ago Norm, Sancho and I went to Bauang. We went to Brasilisa's house and met another teacher, Jane, a very pretty Filipino. We spent the evening dancing to a surprisingly good band and had a most pleasant time, Norm especially, who hasn't been out of camp for months. There is another dance next Saturday which I will try to get to.

Norm and I left about 10:00 P.M. and got a ride from a couple of MPs into Bauang. I caught a glimpse of their MP bands in the flash of passing headlights. When Norm and I had passed through the town earlier we were surprised at the number of "nite clubs" and shops open, little dark places lit by coconut oil lamps. Now the town was silent as a tomb and thick with MPs. We learned from the MPs who gave us the ride that several nights earlier a 32nd Division man had put seven shots into a Negro soldier in an argument over a slut, and that was the reason the town was so heavily patrolled and so dead. It also accounted for the pumping the MPs gave us when they picked us up and asked us about

Negro troops at San Fernando, and if we had experienced any trouble with them.

After getting out at Bauang, Norm and I walked out of the town a little ways, and there we ran into a very drunk 32nd man with a lugar in his hand. It was pitch-black except for a nearby street lamp, and this fellow came lurching up to us handling the gun very haphazardly. He was looking for some corporal, and was going to "kill the son-of-a-bitch." He was belligerent at first, wanting to know if we were MPs. Meanwhile a tall fellow came ambling up with his hand in his shirt, where there was a .45. The drunk didn't know this and became friendly. About that time while we watched him carefully, a MP came up and grabbed him. Then a jeep stopped and picked the three of us up. In the jeep the other fellow explained he had seen the situation and because we were "clean" (unarmed), he had kept the drunk covered. We were grateful, although we hadn't known it at the time in the heavy gloom of the night. Bauang is a rest camp for the 32nd Division, and it has become a tough little district. Men just back from the front, bad liquor, firearms, and women do not make a healthy combination. Despite our danger, there was something sad about the whole episode, like a scene out of an O'Neill play. I am afraid that our post-war world will see much violence—especially if times are bad.

Gibson left yesterday, the first man to return home via furlough. Pap signed his papers; he will probably leave any day now.

June 10

Out at the ship the other night, Sig showed up drunk and acted disrespectfully toward Lt. Walker. As a result, Walker had a talk with Stahl, who sent Sig to camp. Sig will forfeit his next two days off, a good action by Stahl. The same night a colored truck driver drove his truck off the end of the dock into 45 feet of water. The truck has been salvaged, but not the driver, who is still missing. He was either very sleepy or drunk. I suspect the latter. Despite the thick block at the edge of the dock, the truck had so much speed that even with its load it hurdled the barrier.

The rainy season has set in, and we have had nothing but cool, gray, wet weather these past three days. It is a relief from the heat of May, and I do like rainy weather.

We are winning the war here at a good pace. The Okinawa campaign is in its final stages. Japan continues to be pounded by bigger and bigger raids; the last was by 600 Superforts. The Chinese hold 105 miles of coast around Fuchow and continue to push the Japs. There is still fighting in northern Luzon.

June 23

Luzon, rain!

Today our four high-point men left: Sgts. Peterson and Walsh, T-5 Joslyn and Pvt. Mike Hudaick. Said goodbye to Mike last night and was especially glad to see him go. He's had nearly seven years in the army. Lots of rumors out concerning proposed changes in the point system (to our benefit), but nothing official yet.

Yesterday, the battle of Okinawa, after 82 bloody days, was declared closed. We lost 10,000 killed and suffered about 45,000 casualties—along with heavy losses in shipping. The Japs lost 90,000 killed and 4,000 planes, it is reported. There should be a new move soon. [*Spector wrote in* Eagle against the Sun *that by June 21, when organized resistance ended, "Fighting had claimed the lives of 7,000 U.S. soldiers and marines. . . . Close to 5,000 sailors died and 5,000 more were wounded" (p. 540). As for the Japanese, 70,000 died, along with 80,000 Okinawans, who were mainly civilians.*]

Coming in from work after midnight a few nights ago, we were directed to see a movie called *On to Tokyo,* a short film in which our generals answer questions on the war against Japan. It contains nothing much new. We all know that this war against Japan will not be short.

There have been several race riots lately, and during one a number of Negroes were killed. The situation does not get any better. Race riots are the antithesis of one of the main principles for which we fight. A Filipino told me not long ago that a colored soldier told him that after this war the blacks would rise against the whites. It will be a problem after this war for the less liberal, which constitutes most of humanity.

June 26

Pap got his orders on the evening of the 24th and left the morning of the 25th, the day that marked the completion of our 21st month overseas. He was, as he stated it, "Happy as a fucking bird!" I am truly happy to see him go, though I lose one of my best friends in the army, and from whom I have learned a great deal about life, independence, and how to take things as a man. This may sound a little trite, but nonetheless it is true.

Though he hated the thought of flying, he was scheduled to fly from Lingayen to Leyte, where he most likely is at this moment. He was, besides tops in other matters, a really good soldier. Before he left, Stahl, Adams, Horn, Redwine, Rouse and I got together 50 pesos for a going-away present. He promised to write, and he surely will. I hope I shall see him again after I get back. Though he's been gone less than two days, I greatly miss him.

Redwine moved into our tent in place of Pap. His leaving also opened up the issue of ratings because it leaves a T-4 and T-5 open. Henehan, without too much surprise to anyone, made staff, and Hancock is going to the buck. There was talk about shifting Pelham or Skivington into our section for Pap's T-4, but that would have been grossly unfair. As it worked out, Watts will get the T-4 and Smitty the T-5. Stahl told me this afternoon not to be disappointed in not getting the rating and that my "efforts were appreciated." Can't honestly be disappointed because Watts deserves the rating. He has performed a T-4's job for over a year. However, I was, and now am, next in line for promotion. Haven't been in the hold now for weeks, and it looks as if I'm going to become a full-time winchman. Sigley and Hindmon will be alternates, the way we stand at present. I've largely gotten over my antipathy for running winches now that I am well-practiced on them. As Stahl said, "Your promotion will come in due time." And I replied in turn what I have come long ago to believe in the army, that if you keep plugging you finally get what you want.

Got letters from Mom and Babs, telling me about her plans for the rest of this month which include a round of parties, a prom and graduation. She is definitely in that blissful adolescent stage. Indeed the world is bright and glittering for Babs, and how glad I am that it is.

June 30

Two or three days ago I received a letter from Carolyn. It felt a little strange to hold it and see the return address reading: Carolyn Gold Heilbrun. I can't really say whether I wanted to get one from her or not. I felt both ways about it. The letter was worded graciously and said all I expected this kind of letter would say. She mentioned dinner with my family and the date with Barbara, that she is very happy, and that Jim is in the Pacific. His LST is 1069. It would be strange if I should run into him. I remain, she writes, one of her favorite people, and she wants us to be friends. I don't know. I dreamt about her the night after I received the letter. Perhaps she meant even more than I was willing to admit. Anyway, I know I shall not answer the letter for some time. Our past is pretty much dead, though once in awhile it causes me pain. That's paradoxical because I know deep in my heart that we could never really have made things work out. Our relationship would have been sublime in some ways but disasterous in other ways. It is better this way. I am not sorry for myself, and honestly am very happy for Carolyn.

(There goes pay call.) A few nights ago saw a picture called *The Clock*, which takes place in NYC. God, it caused conflicting feelings; I felt depressed and elated all at once. The film showed many places that in themselves and in their associations have played a large part in my life. There was Penn Station, Times Square, the Palisades, my beloved Washington Bridge and Hudson River, Central Park West, Central Park itself and its zoo, and the lake where I told Carolyn I loved her for the first time—in fact, the first time I said that to any girl. I was 17. I suppose one always remembers that time.

It was a wonderful film for a New Yorker, recalling places not seen for over two years. There was Riverside Drive, at about the spot where Edith and I used to walk and talk, and where I told her I would send her my writings—and have. And there was the Astor lobby, and the subway stations I know so well, and the Art Museum, with numerous shots taken inside, and the buses that run along Fifth Avenue and Central Park West—it was all there, New York, my home for nearly all my life.

Sometimes the fellows talk about another campaign, but none of us especially wants it. I feel, as many of us do, that because our luck has been so good so far that it would be foolhardy to risk it again. Yet we cannot stay here forever. We have been on Luzon nearly six months, and soon there will be more invasions. Because we missed Iwo and Okinawa, we might be due. The campaign in Luzon is drawing to a close. Here and in Mindanao around Davao seem to be the main pockets of remaining resistance in the Philippines. We keep busy working, not too hard but steady. Reading *War and Peace* by Tolstoy.

July 8

Got a 13-page letter from Dale a few days ago. It was a good letter. She wrote she wished that she could kiss me. I wish she could, too. I wonder whether we shall ever meet again. It's been great writing to her.

Saw Ray Bartholomew today for the first time in 15 months. Seeing him again reminded me that way back during our basic training, because he had a wife, I gave him a three-day pass I had won. I'd never had a three-day pass before then—or since. He has been playing with the "Stars and Stripes" show which has been touring the Pacific for a year. He looks much the same. He noticed right away how much broader I've become. If I look so different to him after 15 months, I ought to be quite a sight to those who haven't seen me in over two years. Ray was at Biak during a sneak raid. He said it killed about 60 who were watching the show, and that a lieutenant in the show had his eyes blown out. He says Biak is a paradise *now.*

July 23

I've found it difficult to write these past 10 days. I've been playing some basketball. Our regular team is undefeated. Our section played Stewart's yesterday and beat them, 18–17, in a rough and tumble game on a wet floor. I scored three points, Vic scored 10. John H., Hindmon, Sigley, Sanchez—and even Shorty Hendricks—make up our section team. This afternoon we played Milewicz's gang and beat them in a rough game, 19–18. I scored two baskets, Vic scored five. It's been a great deal of fun, though we're all a bit stiff.

Japan is pounded daily in ever-increasing raids, and by 1,000 and more planes. Our navy has also been active. There is talk of an invasion of Japan, and although none of us is particularly keen on going, I, along with others, feel that we will surely be included. We will inevitably invade either China or Japan.

When I work the 6-on, 12-off schedule too steadily, I get tired and moody. Our days off are few and far between now; we pull six to eight shifts before getting one. That schedule wears us down. Curtin is again in the hospital, and we are down to 13 men. We are supposed to take 12 men out always, but have been taking 11—and tonight we shall take 10 on the midnight shift.

A new ruling says that a man must have 30 months in before he is eligible for TD. There goes even a slim chance for a furlough. Nothing new on points. Heard on the radio that 21,000 men sailed into NY harbor on transports. Certainly must look good, that New York skyline.

My eyes have been bothering me these past two weeks, first time in a long time. Have trouble seeing the signalman at night. Too much reading, I suppose, and eyestrain under the strong sun by day and under the poor lights at night. Been running the winches steadily, and now I am a good winchman, and the regular one in the section.

Five-day passes are under consideration, although the red tape is interminable. I asked Stahl early for one, because Norm and I want to go to Manila together. Section sergeants are supposed to turn in two names. Other sections drew for it, but Vic picked Hendricks and Harris. That really annoyed me, especially when he named Harris because he has 85 points. Harris went AWOL and has visited Manila. It's a bit raw. Truthfully, it is the principle that burns me, because I don't give much of a damn about myself. Every man who wants a pass should have a

start practicing despite the shortage of
players. We hope at least two more men
will welcome the opportunity to try out
their arms and legs. Sgt. Wallace McCor-
mack is the non-com in charge. We hope
the other companies will challenge us to
a game or two. Come out, c'mout, where-
ever youse are! Ed Kosnoski, secretary
of the horse-shoe tournament, reports the
contest is in full swing, and asks the
other companies to organize and bring out
their best for a Battalion tournament.
What say? First prize is 36 pesos, second
20 pesos, show is 8 pesos. ... The juke
box deal is still in progress. There are
still a few stubborn fellows who don't
care for music, but the box will be obtained. ... We welcome back Gil Deverdorf
from the hospital. How long do you think
you'll be able to stay put this time?
And that is not sarcasm either!

---

up last Tuesday's movie by putting diesel
oil in the generator instead of gasoline?
We hear "Gramps" Gilligan can tell or pre
dict an approaching storm by the way his
rheumatism acts up. Huh? .. "Glamour Boy"
Keys and "Rabbitt" Quick certainly have
set a couple of Filipino hearts aflutter
the past few weeks. .. How come we don't
see Hank Basso Profundo) Aldrich around
joining in on the evening bull sessions
anymore. Another attraction? ... "Tarlac"
Tarock seems to take a special delight in
giving the boys their shots. His perfect
aim and coordination has never yet let
him miss an arm he has thrown at. .. Why
was "Articles of War" Knox asking about
how one goes about signing up for a 30
year hit h in the army? He was quite concerned. Yes, the chow has been good of
late.

****
* *
* INTRODUCING *
* CHAPLAIN RINEHART, Capt. *
****

* * * * * * * * * * * * * * * * * *

Now it can be told! At last the censorship restrictions have been lifted
on what can be said about personal experiences 'South of the Equator'. Result:
The volumes of outgoing mail have reached
an all time high. .. Most of the boys can
write a novel on the rugged Cape Gloucester campaign. When and if they run ou
of New Britian palaver they can fall back
on 'Bloody Biak' or even Aitape. ... All
the reenforcements can talk about is the
voyage of the Sea Star(though I don't see
why). According to them that liquid safari was rougher than Gloucester or Biak
combined (true, how true). Our worthy cen
sor won't need scissors to go through
this new crop of mail, a shovel will be
more in order. .. Homeward bound are our
four "high point" men, Joss Joslyn, Mike
Hudaik, Pete Peterson, ans Leo Walch. Jos
had 97 points, while the others had 98
each. The point system is off to a good
start. .... Also heading for the States
is George Milligan. George is over the
40 year age limit now set for automatic
discharge. .. Don't worry if you don't go
home right away on the point system.After
you hit the 40 year mark the army can't
hold you for more than 90 days (O Yea)!
.. Spoked by Red Glasgow, the Birmingham
Bullet, the fast 244th basketball quintet
is now clicking smoothly in practice sessions. The boys are primed to top any and
all competition in Base M. .. Al Bow hin,
the Bronx pundit, is now on detached service in Manila. .... Ed Odom's section is
very quiet and peaceful these days. From
"Buffalo" Hudaik, just before he left us
last week, came this famous last word,
'REST! '

All the men of Protestant faith have
been waiting for a formal introduction
to the new Battalion Chaplain, Captain
Fred A. Rinehart. Chaplain Rinehart
hails from Cincinnati, Ohio, and is a
real native of the "Buckeye" State, he
having received his education in its
universities and seminaries. He was
ordained in 1930.
In October of 1942 he entered the service and his tours of duty have taken
him to such places as the Station Hos-.
pital at Fort Lewis and the Infantry Replacement Training Center at Camp Roberts
California. He was recently with the
80th General Hospital.
Now with the 373d the Chaplain says
he will be glad to offer assistance to
all personnel of the command in every
possible manner. The Chaplain says:
'My first responsibility is for the
spiritual life of my organization. I
urge you, therefore, to take advantage
of the religious services provided for
your particular faith.' His greatest
wish is that all men of the Battalion
attend the services of their faith.
The Chaplain needs your support and
friendship if he is to accomplish the
work assigned him. The Chapel is a part
of your organization and we urge you
to take pride and interest in its services. Feel free to counsel with the
Chaplain at any time. Your interests
are his interests too. Show your wel-
coming spirit by having a full strength
Protestant attendance at Church Sunday.

HEADQUARTERS DETACHMENT NEWS
* * * * * * * * * * * * * * * * * *

"Midge" Young wants to keep his stomach
in good shape until he gets back to the
States, so he is keeping it pickled in

****
* HE THAT HAS NO CROSS DESERVES NO *
* CROWN *
* Quarles--Esther *
****

Weekly bulletin, dated July 1, 1945, distributed in the Philippines.

chance. I've still to receive my first three-day pass in the army. Another year of this damnable life and I guess I wouldn't care what the devil happens. It gets bad at times now, and that midnight shift is rapidly taking the kick out of me.

July 29

An ultimatum to Japan for unconditional surrender has been issued jointly by the U.S., Great Britain and China. It is highly improbable that Japan will acquiesce to the terms. She is willing, according to reports, to let us occupy Formosa and Korea, but not the homeland. It looks as if ground invasion will be necessary to bring home the realization of defeat. Our air force is now so powerful that it has been telling the Japs which cities will be next bombed. This is not idle bravado but, I've no doubt, has strategic and psychological importance.

Spent free time reading Somerset Maugham's *The Razor's Edge*, a novel that I much enjoyed. I particularly liked the way it was put together, its mysticism, and its religious discussion and analysis. One passage particularly struck home: "A religious man who did not believe in God." The novel is the story of such a man.

August 7

This afternoon I heard over the radio about the "greatest war invention." It's called the atomic bomb. The information we know about it is as follows: When a test explosion was made in New Mexico, where the research took place, it *vaporized* a steel tower and left a huge crater. The pressure waves knocked men down at a distance of five miles; forest rangers 150 miles away thought there had been an earthquake, and it rattled windows 250 miles away. The bomb is equivalent to the bomb load of 2,000 Superforts or 10,000 tons of TNT. President Truman stated that this invention is capable of destroying civilization, wiping out everything that stands above ground. The first of these bombs was dropped on Hiroshima yesterday. Further facts are that the research involved two billion dollars and five years. The bombs are in production now at Oak Ridge, Tennessee and Seattle, Washington.

This must be an almost unbelievably powerful weapon. If it is as powerful as stated, then it should bring this war to a speedy close.

In the letter I received from Mom today, she included an article that stated that many Washington big-wigs thought that Japan might surrender as early as the end of this month, but at least by Christmas. Naturally I scoffed at this, for even the latter date seemed improbable, and I was annoyed to read these optimistic predictions handed to the people at home. However, this new weapon may bring a much quicker end than we anticipated.

It has long been known that atomic energy is extremely powerful, if it could be harnessed. Such a weapon as has been developed forecasts what is in store in future wars. Although these words may sound fantastic now, they may prefigure the destruction of future civilization or, at least, destruction beyond the realm of imagination. The U.S. has stated that the secret of the weapon will be carefully guarded while a defense against it is developed. Once again we have the vicious circle of powerful, new, destructive weapons and more intricate defenses against them, until this frenzy of diabolical invention shall backfire into the faces of all humanity. As other eras have had their rise, peak and decline, perhaps we are reaching the peak of our machine age and beyond lie the black pits of decline.

Meanwhile, we are harassed with endless and petty army regulations, and Vic gets more annoying by the day. Our shifts off are now negligible. After much ballyhoo about lowering the point system, it remains status quo until at least the beginning of next year. Seven million men will be used to finish the war with Japan. By June '46, two million will be released, one-and-one-half of them via points. Demers got his papers to leave, but they were revoked because he lost two points for guard-house time in California. However, he will be eligible on the next quota with Dininny, who are our two highest point men with 91. It nearly broke Jack Harris' heart when he was told he would lose two points also, but he got a most fortuitous break in that they weren't taken from him. Jack doesn't know why, and he considers himself too lucky to inquire about it. He has turned into a surprisingly cooperative, pleasant, and mature person these past few months. His point status and basketball success have probably helped to mellow him. The regular team has won 19 straight games and has built a considerable reputation. Some games have been real thrillers.

Pamphlets about China have been distributed to the company, a logical indication that operations will begin there shortly, and that we may be included. There are rumors of a strike next month.

Geyer is in the hospital. He was attacked by four Flips, so the story goes, on account of some woman. He suffered knife cuts on the head and a severe cut on the arm, which severed some muscles. The towns of Luzon are still pretty rough places. There are continual stories of race riots, marauding gangs and killings.

Had a close call on the winches recently. I was taking long pipe out of the hold, and I nearly got mashed against a running winch. Fortunately, the draft just grazed my arm.

August 11

Breathtaking, whirlwind events these last few days. Last night at 10:00 Colby told me the stunning news that the Japanese had offered to surrender. We were just returning from a movie, and so we rushed down and piled into the orderly room. It was true. We all just stood there smiling and laughing, not really able to feel the full impact that the end was near. However, we kept in check our full exuberance until we got the official word from Washington. Going to work on the midnight shift, we were wide-awake, gay and expectant. The radio on the ship blared the celebrations in Chungking; the news of the offered surrender was established fact. The surrender offer was made known first through *Domei*, the Japanese papers, and then officially to the U.S. and England via Switzerland, and via Sweden to China and Russia. However, at this moment, the war is not over.

The Japanese offered to surrender unconditionally in accordance with the Potsdam Ultimatum, with the reservation that the Emperor retain his throne. This is the fly in the ointment. At this moment, this afternoon, all the leaders in the capitols of Japan's enemies are in conference considering this peace offer. From what I can gather from the broadcasts, it remains doubtful whether we shall accept the surrender unless it is unadulterated, complete surrender with no strings attached, even though the Emperor, we are told and I have read, is just a figurehead, a puppet, and personally didn't want the war. So far, our premature celebration has been mild; all ears are tuned to the latest official developments.

Two facts undoubtedly hastened the inevitable end: 1) the atomic bomb, another of which was dropped on Nagasaki destroying 30% of the city, and 2) the entry of Russia into the war the day before yesterday. At present, she is bombing, attacking and pushing ahead on the ground in Manchuria and Korea. Even if this surrender offer is spurned, it can only be a short time until the war comes to an end. The Japanese are disintegrating. No B-29s are flying today.

The radio informs us that more than half of our people hold the opinion that we should *not* accept this offer. Except for the fact that the Emperor's remaining in power allows the Japanese to "save face," in fact, keep some sort of national unity, I don't suppose his remaining on the throne makes much difference. A rejection may cause the Jap fanatics to make a stand and, although futile, would cost more American and more of our allies' lives. Anyway, by this time tomorrow we should know the official answer. It is still difficult to believe that, after so long, the end is so close.

Our high-point men are being transferred to other companies, which indicates that we will soon participate in another move.

August 12

This evening we still await the final and absolute surrender of Japan. Our country has acknowledged receiving the Japanese offer with the reservation concerning Hirohito. We have replied that the Emperor would be allowed his life, but that our military leaders will rule Japan. We also require that all POWs be immediately transported to directed ports in order to board our transports. We now anxiously await the answer from Japan. We all feel sure it will be: "We surrender."

Last night when the news of the Jap offer of surrender first reached us, there was a short blowing of train whistles and mild yelling in camp. However, we all remained skeptical that this was the real end, and we continue so, until definite word reaches us.

More and more everyday it seems this organization is scheduled for Japan, either as invasion or as occupation troops. It will happen soon, with the next taskforce. Yesterday our sizes were taken for clothes, including overcoats, and rumor has it that ODs will be issued to us. None of us will mind going too much if the war is over.

Today a large troopship with 5,000 aboard pulled in at the next dock. These troops came from Italy and have two years overseas and 60 to 75 points. It is disappointing to us that such troops should be coming this way, because they make it that more difficult for us to get back, we who have the same number of points. It does not seem logical to me to send these troops over here when there are so many with less than a year overseas—and so many still in the U.S.

Am reading *Point Counterpoint* by Aldous Huxley. Have to laugh every time I think of F. reading it, and becoming so aroused that he had to go out and have intercourse with a Filipino.

Well, we continue to wait—and perhaps it is only a matter of hours. In Manila last night MacArthur said to cheering soldiers in the streets that he hoped, from the bottom of his heart, "that this is the end." A million hearts, and more, are in perfect accord.

August 14

I was hoping that this notebook would end with news that the war is over—but it continues. The Russians are bombing and sweeping through Manchuria and Korea. We have been anxiously awaiting the word from Japan that would end it, but so far she has been absolutely silent since receiving our last answer. Now that the end is so near, we are all aroused to a new pitch of hate and want to see the Japs utterly smashed if they do not end it soon.

Harris, Williams, Demers, Dininny and Young were transferred to the 622nd and 612th Port Companies. They are our highest point men. We got, in return for Harris, an oldish fellow, one Joe Corriveau, a Frenchman. Seems like a good fellow, a Pfc who has 70 points. The colorful Harris (Pfc Harris) is gone. He turned out to be a pretty good fellow, these last three months. I can't say that I'll miss that voice and laugh, but I will miss his crazy ideas and liveliness. Zenovich, who wasn't selected, got a tough break with his 84 points. Amos Jones has 80 and Stahl 79, who are the remaining highest. Below that the men with high points begin to get plentiful.

Streptococcal infections have become epidemic in our company. Our dayroom and some hastily-erected tents are being used as isolation wards. About 25 men are down, one out of every nine men in the company, or two full work gangs. So far Hindmon is the only man our squad has lost, but he's almost recovered.

August 16

It's Over!! It's Over!! It's Over!!

Yesterday morning I awoke to find that the war is over. It happened at 8:05 A.M., and we found out about it shortly afterward. How often have men wished that they might wake one morning to find that it has all been a bad dream. The Jap delegates are first to fly themselves to Iwo Jima, and tomorrow they will be flown to Manila to sign the Articles of Peace.

There was only the mildest celebration here, because we have been expecting the end for three days. Only a few of the fellows got drunk; there was no unusual noise, but it was quite plain how happy we all were. Every man's thoughts immediately turned from the news to thoughts of home and how long it will be before we see it again. So far, our work schedule remains the same, and undoubtedly there remains plenty of work for us to do. We still may be part of the occupation forces that will go to Japan, but I believe it is doubtful. We all talk of home by January or February, and I do believe it will be by spring.

This afternoon as I sit in our new, luxurious dayroom, the South China Sea looks very blue and peaceful. The end of the war seems to have permeated even the elements and inanimate things of the world. There are the ships peacefully riding anchor, the warm sun brightening natural, rich colors. There has never been such a day for us in nearly four years— or, perhaps, in the history of the world.

August 16th, 1945.

It's Over!! It's Over!! It's Over!!

Yesterday morning I awoke to find that the war is over. It happened at 8:01 A.M. and we found out about it shortly afterward. How often have men wished that they might wake one morning to find that it has all been a bad dream. Tomorrow the Jap delegates are to be flown to Manila to sign the articles of peace. The Japs are to first fly themselves to Ie Shima the island where Pyle was killed. Here there was only the mildest kind of celebration. This especially because we had been expecting the end for 3 days. Only a few of the fellows got drunk, there was no unusual noise. But it was quite plain how happy we all were. Every man's thoughts immediately turned from the news to thoughts of home; and how long it will be before we see it again. So far our work schedule remains the same, and undoubtedly undoubtedly there remains plenty of work for us to do. We still may be part of the occupation forces that will go to Japan, but I believe it is doubtful. We all talk of home by January or February, and I do believe it will be by spring.

This afternoon as I sit in our new, luxurious day room. The South China Sea looks very blue and peaceful. The war being over seems to have permeated even the elements and inanimate things of the world. There are the ships riding anchor peacefully, the warm sun brightening nature's rich colors. There has never been such a day in nearly four years — or perhaps in the history of the world.

Diary page, Aug. 16, 1945, Luzon, Philippines.

7

Manila, Yokohama, and Home

—————— Aug. 19–Nov. 26, 1945 ——————

August 19

We leave for Manila tomorrow. We were alerted last night and are scheduled to leave here tomorrow night at six by train. This is not unexpected. There has been talk of moving for several weeks. Manila will be only a temporary stop where we will be staged for Japan or China. At least we will get a chance to see Manila before leaving the Philippines. I spent all day packing, with the usual problem of getting all my books in. None of us regrets leaving Base M, which has given us plenty of steady work and gets more GI daily.

Though the war is over, it is not yet official. Today the Japs are scheduled to be in Manila to sign the terms. This was supposed to have happened several days ago, but Hirohito asked for more time. The Japs still continue to fight on isolated fronts, where news of the war's end cannot be transmitted. Hirohito is going to send envoys to these fronts to order cease fighting, and he estimates that this will take one to two weeks. I read his speech to the people, and it did not sound like the speech of a man who has accepted utter defeat but more of a subtle explanation that time will prove Japan equal in technological advancement to the U.S. and the rest of the world. Several of his war-time cabinet members have been reinstated in the new cabinet. Anyway, as yet there is no so-called "V-J Day."

There has been considerable talk about demobilization, and the plan to discharge 5½ million troops in a year. We figure that we shall be home by March. Meanwhile, it looks certain that we will be temporary occupation troops somewhere soon. Not only will this be interesting and make the time go faster but, perhaps, get us home that much sooner.

Willard Dixon had a tough break yesterday. A tent pole slipped out of a sling at the top of the hatch. Point-first, it pierced his left hand. The result is that a bone was taken out of the hand, and that will shorten one of his fingers.

An order stating that all men over 38 are eligible for automatic discharge affects four of the men in the company: Joe, our replacement for Harris, Harty, Zenovich who has 84 points, and "Dry Balls" Russell, our 1st Sergeant who never knows anything. Scott, the youngest man in the outfit (he volunteered at 17), is awaiting an emergency furlough because his father is very ill. Little by little the old men of the company are leaving, and eventually there will be a complete turnover.

Lt. Pranke caught me on deck smoking for the second time a few nights ago. I had just come out on the midnight shift, was hazy, as one is at that hour, and completely forgot the new order about no smoking on deck. He told me he was going to break me, that I would be a private in the morning. I felt sure he would carry it through, especially after that talk about discipline he gave us last week and that famous remark, "I'm from a line outfit." About two hours later he called me up on the boat deck and informed me that he would not break me. We had a nice, friendly talk. That makes twice I've nearly lost my rating, though this time it would have been for a petty and unintentional offense. I did have a few nasty visions of KP though, but otherwise I was too disgusted to care. He didn't even know I was a non-com in his own platoon. But that is common ignorance among our officers, including the C.O.

August 22

I write this in Manila, where we arrived yesterday morning. We broke camp on the 20th, leaving the skeletons of bleached and blackened bamboo frames in what had been one of our best camp areas. We made huge bonfires out of the furniture and scrap lumber we had accumulated. We were all set to go by mid-afternoon and had several hours in which to lay around. We carried the usual equipment, except I was able to turn in my shovel before we left. No more foxholes or slit-trenches.

At about 5:30 P.M. we loaded into trucks and trailers and were transported to the station. We were crammed into cattle cars, 60 men into a car, or rather into a bare box on wheels with absolutely not a thing in it but us and our equipment. There wasn't even a broom to sweep the floor. We consoled ourselves with the thought that the only luck of the 244th was being missed by bombs. Anyway, there was plenty of air. The upper half of the box was open, but there was a tarp over the top. Before we left Sanchez's and Scott's girls came down to say goodbye, and Ralph's girl was so overcome she could do nothing but stare at him while the tears ran down her cheeks. Among the cattle in our car were Lt. O'Loughlin and Vierschilling, so things were quite lively. Stahl and I were first into our car. We got a corner where we were joined by O'Loughlin, Vierschilling, Adams, Hendricks, Heffle and Norvell.

Heffle and I usually end up travelling together, it seems. We spent quite a few hours standing and watching Luzon go by, including very green rice fields with natives working in them up to their waists in water. Some of the scenery was beautiful. (Before we left, we had also bid goodbye to Eriksen, whom we shall probably not see again, along with the other high-point men.) Towards dark the fellows got tired of standing and began sprawling on the floor, on and amongst packs, rifles, gas masks and cartridge belts. We had been issued three K-ration units and a can of water to a section.

Around 7:30 we pulled into Daguapan where we laid over for an hour. Fortunately we stopped by a little café and lodging house where Stahl knew two pretty girls. Both were home and so Stahl, O'Loughlin and I spent an entertaining hour in talking with them and sitting around the house waiting for the train to continue. Here we heard the news that the Jap envoys had arrived in Manila. A memorable feature of the house was the verandah in the rear that overlooked a quiet, shallow fishpond, silvery in the moonlight, and cooled by a fresh, gentle breeze. It was difficult to have to go back to that crowded, bare boxcar. But go we did at about 10:30, and then commenced one of the most miserable nights of travelling I've experienced in the army.

It was impossible to stretch out. Despite our cramped, grotesque positions on the floor amidst our equipment, our bodies became entangled. In our little corner at least six pair of legs lay interwoven on top one another. The whole scene of inert bodies, squeezed and crammed, reminded me of those atrocity pictures of bodies piled upon each other, only we were alive.

Softened by a blanket, my pack served as a pillow for Heffle and me. I kept getting Stahl's heels in the small of my back, and my own feet were lost in a tangle of bodies a few feet further down. I got little sleep, waking every few minutes with cramps in various parts of my body. I retreated as much as I could into my corner, making the best of it, my thoughts seasoned with various black epithets about the army. Some of the fellows managed to sleep several hours at a time. To accomplish this, I think they must have temporarily died.

We arrived in Manila early in the morning after nearly 200 miles of clacking tracks and a bumping, swaying car. It rained, of course. We marched into a big, leaky station, where our section was assigned to unload the two boxcars that carried our equipment. It was an easy detail: five hours waiting and an hour's work. We wandered out of the station and got our first real glimpse of Manila. We were in a section of the city called North Bay, with the famous Manila Chinatown only a few blocks away. About half-a-dozen of us went into a neat looking restaurant and spent 17 pesos on five sandwiches, one coffee, one cake. I paid 3½ pesos for a meagre egg sandwich and a three-bite slab of cake. The robbery of the prices was offset by the novelty of eating in a real restaurant, with silverware, tablecloths and waitresses. Later, we found these extremely high prices common in Manila.

About noon we were relieved, and we piled into trucks to go to our area. As we drove toward our camp we saw a bit of the city: large buildings, most with gaping shell and bullet holes, and the black marks of dead fires; streets piled with burned rubble, smashed cars. It was, in short, a city made gaunt by war. But it isn't a dead city, nor an entirely smashed one. Many of the partially-ruined buildings are utilized. There are all kinds of shops open, and a number of running civilian cars. The streets roar with army vehicles. There are many people about, and the Filipino women here have lighter complexions.

We arrived at our area which has warehouses with tin roofs and concrete floors. Though we are crowded, a foot on each side of our bunks, it's not bad. We have a regular kitchen, latrine and showers, and electricity. We've had a lot worse.

Last night I went out on pass to see the sights. I went to an army-run place called the Snack Bar, and drank three Coca-Colas, the first in two years except for the hospital, and they were real cold. I just stood there and relished them. They were stranger to the palate than the whiskey we had later on in the evening. The Snack Bar has bowling alleys, movies, and a basketball court. In town I saw the first WACs I've seen since being overseas. Manila is alive at night, especially to us who have been "in the sticks" for so long. I felt like a country rube walking along the streets. The city is well-lighted, and some of the massive buildings serve as busy offices and headquarters. At the Bar met Stahl, Langham, and Monroe; we walked around the town stopping at shops and at a few bars. The whiskey costs a peso a shot. There are many drunks. The women are more sophisticated and painted in Manila than elsewhere we have been. You can buy the late city editions on the streets, and there are several civilian movies. One called the Ideal is especially reminiscent of a typical movie at home. I felt less aware of army life last night than in many a month. There are many nightclubs with bands, and I saw one place that even had fluorescent lighting. Of course many fellows were interested in the numerous prostitutes. They are inexpensive compared with the cost of everything else. It all was exhilarating and exciting after so long.

We are camped in the old "walled city," across the Pasig River, where so much furious fighting took place, evident in the ruins. The original bridges are all out, but they have been repaired by the army. There are all kinds of outfits in the city, though it doesn't seem excessively crowded. The harbor is loaded with the ships for the forthcoming occupation. I hope this afternoon we shall be able to secure passes to see more of Manila.

The 16 Jap envoys, who were here and left yesterday, have arrived in Japan. That is a step closer to the final surrender. The local papers proclaim occupation will take place in 10 days. It does seem that it will only be a matter of a few days until we will be on our way. The strongest rumor has two of our companies going to Tokyo and two to Yokohama. The 496th Port Bn. is stationed right across the way, and I've seen a few faces I recognize, but I can't remember names after more than two years. So we all end up in the same place, though I believe our company has seen more of this war than any other port company, and will continue to do so.

It feels wonderful to be moving around in the midst of all this activity. Some of my happiest moments are when I travel.

August 24

The last two days have been a merry-go-round of immense fun. Night before last Jim Langham, Jack Havron, Monroe, Flynn, Heffle, Denison and I had dinner together for 51 pesos at a restaurant called Chungking. After that we went to a place named the 400 Club, a nightclub way up at the other end of Royal Avenue. We bought several bottles of whiskey and then proceeded to look for the place. It took us an hour-and-a-half to find it, and the driving rain and dark streets off Royal Avenue did not help. I was fairly familiar with Royal, having spent all that afternoon walking it from one end to the other, just taking in the smells of the city, the excitement, and looking at the incredible number of shops, bars and nightclubs.

The club had a good band, an indoor and outdoor dance floor, and a small patio. There are numerous women, mostly Filipino, some Spanish. In a few moments we had women at our table. I got the company I wanted in a Spanish girl named Virginia who spoke English well, is tallish, a good dancer, and 25. It felt strange to have a good-looking girl dance close and be mildly affectionate. We all had a roaring time. The prices were terrific, but we were having such a good time that the money didn't mean anything.

The girls get a soft drink about two inches high, and diluted at that, for which we shell out three pesos a glass. Virginia and I had quite interesting talks. She was surprised to learn my age (most people usually are) and remarked how old young Americans look these days. Perhaps we all have aged a great deal during the last 2½ years of knocking about. I notice that some of the other fellows look older.

All of us got pretty high. I knew everything I was doing, but the whole world was looking much improved after several hours at the 400 Club. The city closes up at 10:30, and our passes are only good until 11:00 P.M. We were fortunate the last two nights in getting rides almost to our warehouse door. Though I have never done any kind of heavy drinking, it can't be helped in this city. I never saw so much liquor. Fellows who have hardly touched a drop, like myself, have been high for the past few days. It is good to be able to release some of our long, pent-up, exuberant spirit. The night before last our group spent about 500 pesos and counted it well worthwhile. Last night we went to the same place, Flynn, Herb, Norm and I. Herb and Norm had the same women, Flynn and I just free-lanced. Virginia came right over to me when we got there, but about 20 minutes later she was with a big party across the floor and that was the last I saw of her. I didn't care much about that one way or the other, but Ron was pretty annoyed with the girl he thought he was to have tonight not wanting to stay with him. But, all in all, it was fun. We only bought one bottle, enough to last us the night, and so we did not spend so much. My bankroll at the moment is exactly 21 pesos. At the end of the evening Virginia told me that she had made a date for the party she joined because she wasn't sure I was coming back. Some of us plan to go back again tonight.

We spent some time in the Red Cross building yesterday in the center of town. The top floor is a dream, cool, quiet and full of air and sun and great overstuffed armchairs. In these one can really stretch out. Yesterday I sat in a really comfortable chair for the first time in two years. There is a PA system for the news and classical music. One is quite high up, in a relaxing atmosphere, and you can see the panorama of bustling and broken Manila. Already some of those long, jungle-ridden months seem a bit dim. The set-up here is much the same as we had in Sydney. We don't do anything, just wait for orders and go out on passes. Yesterday we turned in our old jungle packs, together with the remains of our jungle hammocks, and received a new pack that comes in two pieces with enough straps and catches to harness a set of mules.

I feel that our hard days are over. This coming Sunday our first occupation troops will land in the vicinity of Tokyo. MacArthur lands Monday following. I do not believe we shall leave for a number of days yet, now that it seems certain we are not to be among the initial occupation troops. The various landing sites and orders controlling Japs' actions upon the arrival of our forces have been specified. It seems unlikely that there will be any trouble. Every day more Jap forces are laying down their arms, and soon the final papers should be signed. Our four men 38 years or older are not going with us because their travel orders came through. I have met quite a few fellows in Manila from the ETO [*European theater of operations*].

August 26

I spent the night before last at the 400 Club with a big crowd. Virginia was with me about half the evening. That previous afternoon Heffle and I walked through the crowded streets and noisy markets of Chinatown. In walking the streets of foreign cities and absorbing all the activity in shops and of garrulous crowds, I was realizing an old dream. There was a whole symphony of smells. Every few yards a new one impinged itself upon the senses. There are numerous *caratellas*, small carriages drawn by small horses. This city has the most crossbred people imaginable. All the strains of the Orient seem to have mixed their blood here. I've seen some Chinese frocks and ivory carvings that I would love to buy, but they are difficult to send home and for me to meet their current prices. While we were walking, a cute little girl asked me for a few centavos. When I gave them to her, it seemed that every kid in a radius of two blocks had heard the money jingle. I felt like Gulliver with at least 20 kids pulling at my arm and yelling. If it weren't for Herb pulling on my other arm, I would have been swept away.

I've gotten to know my way around Manila. Yesterday Sanchez and I went over to see his Spanish friend, Luis Mandayeta, who lives on Arlaque Street, just to the right of Quezon Bridge. It turned out to be an interesting afternoon. We met 13 of the 14 that make up the family, which includes six girls and four boys. About half the family spoke English. They all spoke Spanish. We spent more than three hours there in a large, pleasant and airy room in which they live as refugees. We traded war experiences. They were an extremely well-to-do family, who owned a large house, cars, etc., and a sugar plantation in Los Negroes. Their house was destroyed in the fighting. They lost everything except what was on their backs, and during the Jap occupation they went to live in Manila. They had seen the "death march" and had helped the internees with food, water, cigarettes, up to six months ago when suddenly no more contact was allowed with them. Another new atrocity story that I heard was that the Japs would offer candy to the children, and when they approached would throw them live hand-grenades instead. We had the whole family around us a good part of the afternoon, and I really enjoyed the conversations.

What made the visit come off so well was Sanchez's ability to speak Spanish; he was able to entertain the Spanish-speaking part of the family while I handled the English. They were well-informed and vastly interested in all we had to say. It helped that I understood a little Spanish and could pull out an occasional phrase from the hazy depths of memory.

Sanchez and I stopped in a Catholic church on the way back to camp. I like the serenity of a church, an oasis of quiet in a noisy city. The church's religious significance has no effect on me, but the hush and soft lighting are soothing and restful. I do get a warm feeling seeing people at worship, though I am not moved to do so. The Spanish people here seem very devout and maintain many old customs which the Filipinos have adopted. There is something intriguing about religion; I think I would like to know more about it.

August 29

We are now on 24-hour alert. It seems certain that it's to be Japan; the C.O. informed us this morning that we will be occupation troops. Today our gas masks were taken up, and we were issued shelter-halves. Worked this afternoon at 43rd Division HQ—unloading trucks. Saw a bit more of the city including the Chinese cemetery, a place of weird mausoleums in definite Chinese style. Manila has been a pleasant and opportune rest, and we've all immensely enjoyed it. The hottest rumor has us headed for Kyushu, the southernmost island of Japan. [*Kyushu would have been our destination had the war not ended and had the Allies been required to invade Japan. The assault on Kyushu, code name "Olympic," was scheduled for November 1945. The 6th Army, to which we were attached, led by General Walter Krueger, would have invaded Japan with a force of 767,000 men. Estimated American dead and wounded were 268,000. Although we did not know these figures, I, along with the company old-timers, felt our luck had run out and we would be among the casualties. For a description of the invasion plans known as Operation Coronet, had the war continued, see Spector's account.*]

Today troops landed in Japan by plane in the Tokyo area. Twenty men were killed in a plane accident—a really tough break for those poor guys. We should pull out at any time. Meanwhile been spending my time relaxing in the Red Cross building, listening to music, seeing a few movies, and taking in Manila in general.

Letters from Mom and Dad today, first ones responding to the end of the war. Dad wrote a really fine letter, telling me about Mother's long vigil and concern for my safety. To make sure of its preservation I shall quote it here:

> Now I want to tell you something that has been on my mind for a long time. The subject is Mother. Never in all my life have I seen a person so devoted to a son as she was. From the day that you were inducted her every thought was of you. Her letter-writing to you was exacting, never a day went by that she didn't write to you. She would get out of bed at all hours of the night, and many a time I found her writing to you at two or three in the morning. When you requested something she wasn't happy until it was on its way. When she didn't get any mail from you for a long time it was very pitiful to see her suffer. Now that it is over she has become impatient as to when you will be home. I can't write all this to you as it should be written, but believe me anything fine that can be thought of a mother, you must think that way and always think that way because your mother deserves every respect that you can give her; she is that kind of person. I have not been able to put down on this paper exactly what I want to, but I think you get the general idea.

How well I have known all this in my heart. Dad's simple eloquence is a tribute that shall long live in both our hearts. Surely it has been Mom's constant letters, concern, fortitude and her thousands of silent prayers that have given me strength and emotional balance when I needed them. They have been a fine family, all of them. My heart is warmed this night as it has not been in many days. Surely I must prove myself worthy of such love and faith—the supreme trust and supreme gift that one person can endow upon another. What a wonderful day it will be when I see them all again—and I smile now as I write for the picture is plainly in mind. Someday, when I am reading this to Mom [*this never happened*], I will at this moment walk up to her and kiss her as I am so fondly doing now in my mind's eye.

August 31

Last night turned out to be one of the pleasantest in many months. It started off strangely. I had fallen asleep before lunch, and after I was awakened I thought I was having supper. Following the meal I rushed to get dressed and get a pass because I thought it was about 5:00 or 6:00

P.M. Because the day was very cloudy, it could easily seem that time. Before leaving the camp I saw Lt. Wenz, who just got out of the hospital here in Manila and was awaiting shipment to Mindanao to be C.O. of a colored port outfit. He was hurrying the process along. The Lt. was not looking well; he had that pasty look that many old-timers have over here. We talked, and he told me quite a bit about the Colonel which wasn't complimentary. It is true that the Colonel never did us much good. He is now back in the States while his battalion carries on. He is, as always, "right behind us." It was good to see the Lt. I left rather quickly because I thought it was evening, and I was anxious to get to town to attend one of the late shows.

Arriving at the Red Cross I noticed it said 1:50, but I figured something had happened to the clock, that it couldn't possibly be that time. I was walking toward the theaters when suddenly the sun burst through the overcast. The sudden, full light of mid-afternoon struck me like a blow, because I was psychologically set for the accumulating dusk. I looked up and there was the sun burning straight overhead. I felt completely dazed for at least a minute until I realized what had happened. It's very odd, how confused one's mind can become.

After spending some time at the Red Cross and attending a movie, I started back to camp about 7:00. It was really evening this time as I started across Quezon Bridge. I kept feeling all day that something unusual was going to happen, and so I was not surprised when, upon reaching the other end of the bridge and looking over the side toward the banks of the Pasig, I saw a woman with long, red hair sitting on a stone wall with her dog, and smoking while watching the sunset. A woman with red hair like that is automatically a beacon of interest in the countries I have been in. She looked youngish from a distance of about 75 yards, but her movements were those of a mature adult, so I could not be sure. Anyway, the picture of her sitting there, with that full head of red hair shining like a fiery sun in the fading day, along with the feeling of adventure that had haunted me all day, impelled me to go around the bridge and down to the river bank.

After sauntering down I stopped about 20 yards from where she was. While lighting a cigarette, I wondered how to make a decent approach. Fate, it seems, took a hand. It started to rain, and I walked toward the porch of the building where she seemed to be living, and because she was friendly, I found myself talking to a decidedly unusual-looking woman. Her thick, long, red hair was her most striking feature. Closer inspection revealed her delicate and thin features, and a face lined by time and experience. Every feature revealed that she had gone through an ordeal. Her eyes were very blue. She seemed about 50, perhaps a bit younger. Her body was thin and her skin very white. Well, it was not long before I learned a lot about her. She talked easily and gracefully. I was pleased to hear a cultured voice again. I nearly jumped with the joy of having polite conversation. Anyway, this lady (my poor memory for names upon first meeting serves me ill here) had been in the Islands eight years, three of them in the prison camp of Santo Tomás. Her native home is San Francisco, and I was sure she had attended a fine school somewhere.

It began to rain harder. She [*Mrs. Debyshire*] invited me into her apartment which took up about half the ground floor of a former telephone company building. She introduced me to her husband, an American businessman, quiet and rather pleasant, and to Mr. Hoskins who was another prize discovery of the evening. He is an Englishman in every pore, from his speech and manner to his ideas and humor. The lady's husband, I learned, was the former head of the telephone company in Manila, and the Englishman was in the gold mining business, one of the main Philippine industries. Hoskins was born here, but at an early age he went to England for his education. He was an infantry officer in the last war. He too had been a prisoner. His wife, I gathered, had died recently from heart disease, though he never admitted it in plain words. Soon the four of us were playing bridge and exchanging the small talk and pleasantries that can be managed between hands. The lady didn't play too good a game, and I secretly smiled when one time I saw perspiration become visible on her brow during a difficult bid. The two men ridiculed her in good spirit but a little unmercifully, and further flustered her already shaky knowledge of the game. I did my best to pull her out of any embarrassment she suffered.

The best part of the evening came after we had finished playing and settled down to some tea and cakes. It was pleasant to be served by a gracious woman, to have a napkin on my knees, and to have food passed around on plates. I guess I basked in the easy grace of cultured people, courtesy, good talk and alert minds, and drank it all in. I had ignored my thirst for sociability and civilized people these long months, because I knew that it couldn't be slaked.

It was apparent that the strength of character of these three people helped them to survive three years in a Jap prison camp. Yet in spite of the awful conditions, the starvation diet, the treachery and swinishness of the Japs, these three had not forgotten basic civilities. It takes heart and, yes, guts, to be people like that. I was interested in everything that happened during their internment. They told me about the 140 grams of rice mush a day, the death rate of eight prisoners a day from disease and malnutrition, the eating of dogs and cats, the Japs making the women and children stand for an hour for roll calls, their unmeasured meanness, the lack of food as the Japs began to lose the war in 1943, the escapes, the captures and subsequent punishments (beatings and water torture), the clandestine radio, the improvisations. Their bitterness against the Japs shone in their eyes. My lady's quiet voice urged the killing of thousands of Japs with more atomic bombs in the same tone that she used to ask if I would have another cup of tea. That quiet tone made her conviction even more forceful. The Englishman permitted himself a vehement "Swine!" and with such feeling that the one word was a book of anguish. It made me feel even more bitter than I have about this drawn-out surrender, about the Jap statements since the cessation of hostilities, and about our lack of forcefulness with a people whose basic reason and logic seem replaced by brutal and beastly instincts.

The Englishman was particularly interested in new tactics and weapons in comparison to WWI, about which he told me quite a bit. He too had suffered as a prisoner, but he was less inclined to speak of his experiences. They spoke about the killings that were endured, and the final brutality of the Japs in beheading members of the prisoners' executive council after the "Yanks" had invaded the Philippines. It is a tragedy that so many died during the last days before liberation. Hoskins spent a night in a ditch with his ill wife while the battle roared around them. What these last three years must mean to them all, and how bitter they must be.

They were interested in my experiences in the war and the army in general, and in knowing about rationing in the States, and about life there now. They had devoured all the latest magazines in order to catch up with the world again. Where the Japs are, time moves counterclockwise. They lost everything, their homes and all their possessions. But they seemed to be picking up the pieces and enjoying those "simple" luxuries of food and electric lights. Although both the food and the apartment were simple, they are luxuries in comparison to a prison camp. "Red" showed me around the flat as if she were giving me a tour of a really fine home. But that's all incidental to the feeling that these people gave me and what I learned about the Philippines and pre-war life here. The evening shines like a diamond as I turn its facets in my mind, and especially in comparison to these army days. After bidding them goodnight and expressing the hope of visiting them again, I also told them frankly that it had been one of the pleasantest evenings I've had in the last two years. As I walked back to camp, thinking about the evening and the discussions, the seeds of feelings sown during the conversation of the evening sprouted new ideas and made the long walk to camp seem but a moment.

The company is full of new men. The new names on the board and the new faces I see as I walk through the camp indicate that our outfit has a history. Most of these men have low points, though some have substantial service time. We have 19 men in our section now, but five are new men I've seen for the first time this morning.

Some new information has been published concerning discharge. As soon as MacArthur says he no longer needs combat men, the points we have earned since May 12th will be added, and a new critical score of 80 will be set. Men with 60 do not have to come overseas. If we get points only for overseas time it will give most of us 70 to 72 points, and a good many will be eligible for discharge. There may be additional points for the occupation of Japan. Anyway, all of us who originally composed this organization will be eligible the next time. Next spring begins to look more and more logical as our probable homecoming date.

We are still on 24-hour alert. Company D, headed for Shanghai, still waits to pull out. All of us are packed and could move in two hours. I packed some books in Redwine's locker that otherwise I would have had to abandon. Our new packs are comfortable. MacArthur is in Japan for the signing of the surrender on September 2nd. Korea is to be occupied September 7th. Could be us. Typhoid shots this afternoon.

September 2

Tonight finds me on C.Q., and with all these new men in the company, it is a job. Today at 10:35 A.M. the instrument of surrender was signed, and the war is officially over.

A load of mail from home brightened this rainy, gloomy day. I also got a letter from Pap who is now a civilian. He got out August 13th, a civilian the day before the Japanese surrendered. First he had a three week layover in Leyte, and then proceeded to the States via Hollandia, which took another three weeks, but he was out of the army in less than a week after he landed. Good old Pap; it was swell to hear from him. We are still awaiting movement orders, and it looks like we will be attached to the 43rd Division. Not official yet. Dropped by to see Mr. and Mrs. Debyshire, but they were taking a siesta so I did not disturb them. I left a carton of cigarettes. Mr. Hoskins saw me and invited me to come back again soon for a round of bridge.

September 8

We have been sailing for about 30 hours. Our destination is Tokyo Bay!

On Sept. 4th we received orders to move. After breaking camp, we shouldered our packs and usual equipment, minus a gas mask, and marched down to the ship at a nearby dock.

We had mail call that day, and I was pretty shocked to learn that Mark had been killed; Allan briefly informed me as if I knew about it already, and thus it was more of a shock. This news, coming some months after the close of the European war, made it unexpected. Poor Mark. How his mother must be suffering; I recall her well. He was married shortly before coming overseas too, and I remember Nancy, though I only met her a few times. He was a good fellow, and he is the first among my old friends who has been killed in the war. [*Allan and Mark were among my boyhood friends, three of whom were killed during World War II.*] It seems that I congratulated myself too soon in not having any of my friends hurt or killed. Mark has haunted my thoughts for the past few days and has resurrected many incidents of four and five years back.

We boarded our ship of moderate size about 8:30 P.M. The bustling dock was piled high with organizational equipment, and I saw lift-jitneys used for the first time in years. We boarded up a gangplank, for a change, and we were assigned a compartment deep in the hold of the ship. I was pleased to note immediately that it wasn't going to be a bad trip. The hold was clean, the ventilators in order, and there were drinking fountains with ice water. There are showers with fresh and hot water available, and a clean, roomy latrine. All this was luxury compared to other ships we've known. The bunks were the usual transport kind, and I drew the middle one among the five high, near the entrance to our compartment.

After an hour of stowing and hanging our equipment, we were assigned to load the ship at midnight. Stahl and I rounded up a crew of 10 men out of the 18 we have in our section now. Charley Norvell left the company with an appendicitis attack the morning before we left. He's had them for a long time, and when I saw him after a bad night a few days before leaving, he looked white and drawn. He was reluctant to go on sick call for fear of missing this trip. It is questionable whether we shall see him again. Men lost at this stage of the game take their service records with them. They can be assigned anywhere after release from the hospital. We left Colby and Gligo at San Fernando.

We pulled into mid-harbor the next afternoon where our convoy was beginning to shape up. The harbor is loaded with ships. We spent the next two days getting organized, and sweating out chow lines. They could be much worse; they're only 900 troops aboard. We are called out to chow by companies. We spent our time waiting to sail, reading and seeing movies at night. The officers' quarters are, as usual, really comfortable with mattresses, pillows, tables, chairs and other comforts and conveniences that have been foreign to us for so long. Travelling is rarely a hardship for them. The food is good, even excellent in comparison to past days. The crew is orderly, disciplined and efficient, the ship clean— all of which means a great deal to travelling troops. The compartments are fairly well-lighted, and except when the ventilation system is on the blink, as it was a few days ago, the hold remains comfortable and sleepable. Norm and I slept on deck the last night in the harbor, and it was good sleeping.

Yesterday morning our ship pulled out in convoy. It is not a large convoy, 21 ships carrying, I judge, about 15,000 to 18,000 troops. Various naval units escort us just as in wartime. It is a fast-moving convoy.

A short time after sailing, this announcement came over the PA system: "Now our next stop will be Tokyo Bay. Now our next stop will be Tokyo Bay." Norm and I looked at one another and cheered, as did many others aboard. Surely this is the last leg of our journey before starting home. But it wasn't only that thought that made us cheer. It was also the excitement of going to Japan as a victorious army, and that we had come the long road from Sydney up through New Guinea, through the Philippines, and survived to enter the very heart of the enemy. It's been a long road paved with hardship, blood and death, and it is salted with the perspiration of our labors. May it be a road that leads to a new world of peace and tolerance. That is the hope of many—but the faith of how many? Anyway, we are Japan-bound and should get there in about four or five more days. Having come this far I am glad I am going—and I'm pretty sure that this will be my last boat ride before the one that has San Francisco Bay as its destination.

We sailed out of Manila harbor and along Bataan Peninsula which looked solemn and mysterious wrapped in a filmy blue haze and sheltered under low clouds. At the tip of Bataan stood much-battered Corregidor. We passed the famous island about noon and could see its sides ripped raw by bombings and shellings. It was a beautiful picture when we passed there, Corregidor standing bright and detailed against the hazy blue of Bataan, while between us and the island a destroyer cut the blue sea, making it foamy white at the bow and kicking up a lacy white wake. It was beautiful. I shall remember that scene, and I thought of how the men who had once gallantly defended the little island should have liked to have seen our convoy sailing past and headed for Japan. I remember in high school following the battle of Bataan and the retreat to Corregidor—and here I was seeing it for myself on the way to Japan. It was a day filled with historical significance, and I believe many men felt it in, at least, some vague way.

In a few moments we report to sick bay for another shot. It is good to make a trip without the strain of alerts and attacks, although there is a regular blackout at night except for the running lights. There was a noisy anti-aircraft practice yesterday, but I think we have experienced our last real alert or raid.

September 15

My 21st birthday finds me sitting among the buildings and ruins of Yokohama.

During the trip we ran into some rough weather for about a day-and-a-half, skirting a storm. Otherwise, the trip was without unusual incident. I read six books: *Castaway; Not Too Narrow, Not Too Deep; Best Plays of 1944* and others. There were the usual routines of "sweating out" chow lines, sleeping and playing bridge. On the morning of the 13th I went on deck to find a slate-gray day and a fine rain. The weather, much to our delight and discomfort, was cold. This was Tokyo Bay, and our first glimpses of Japan were the gray-blue smudges that lay on the horizon between the breathing gray of the ocean and the blanket gray of the sky. Our paravanes (mine sweepers) were lowered over the side but shortly taken back aboard. About 10:00 A.M. we sighted a fleet of fishing boats lying off the port bow. I felt more than ever that keen anticipation when sighting the traces of a new land on the horizon. To me this is one of the most exciting moments in the world, "even more exciting than nude women," as I facetiously told Flynn and Denison.

We continued to sail deep into the bay and then we stopped. The peter boats were lowered over the side, and a Jap pilot taken aboard. He guided us through a series of breakwaters and lighthouses right up to the harbor docks. As we drew closer to the shore, we saw it was unlike any other we had seen in several years. There were large buildings, dock areas, cranes—in short, a true city lay spread before us, and it was Sakuragicho, the main port of Yokohama. The pilot's Japanese coming over the PA system made us all lend a curious ear. While sailing down the harbor, our eyes widened to see the overwhelming strength of our navy. There were numerous aircraft carriers, their huge but dim outlines silhouetted against the bleak day, squatting battleships, numerous cruisers and destroyers—a tremendous armada. In contrast lay the burnt and rusting hulls of a once-powerful Jap navy, now so utterly smashed.

After the usual delay in organization, we disembarked from our transport late in the afternoon. We had arrived. This was Japan, our final goal.

We assembled on the dock area and marched into a huge building that had belonged to the N.Y.K. Lines whose ships had once carried passengers all over the world. We arrived wearing our suntans and leggings. Five minutes after entering the building we were told to change into fatigues and prepare to work a ship. We reluctantly broke into perfectly made and balanced field packs. Five minutes later orders were rescinded; the ship would not be in until midnight. The army is still the army, Japan or not. Eventually we set up cots on the second floor of the building. We were fairly comfortable, despite the cold. (The cold I caught on the ship, aggravated by the cold weather here, developed into a bad head and throat cold with a persistent cough, which I have at present.) Thus we settled in and sprawled on our bunks—and that's how we invaded Japan. Better than landing on D + 1, as we had been scheduled to do before the atomic bombs were dropped.

Flynn, Miller, Hillsberg and I spent our first night in Japan not digging foxholes, or sleeping on the sand, but playing several hours of bridge. Half the section went to work with Stahl at midnight, and I was supposed to take the other half at 5:00 A.M., but fortunately that shift never materialized, and I was able to get a good night's sleep. It was a pleasant change from past invasions.

We awoke the next morning to pack immediately and to prepare to move. The first platoon moved out early to our assigned area. We were left behind to clean up the mess remaining from two meals of K rations and the asssorted trash that soldiers leave in their wake. (We laughed when we remembered joking about sweeping down the streets of Japan!) The morning also brought our first contact with Jap civilians. Four of them poked through the trash pile we made, collecting the numerous unopened rations, the usual waste of the American army. A crowd soon gathered around these four scavengers, and we viewed them with mixed feelings. I could not help thinking that is where they belong, on the trash pile, remembering the prisoners of Santo Tomás and other cruelties. However, to feel bitterness against poor individuals is like trying to hurt an elephant by making faces at him. I hope the proper action will be taken in the proper places. Condo, a replacement corporal, took one of the full gunny sacks of rations from one of the Japs. The Jap followed with an obsequious, toothy grin—the epitome of toothy grins—and Condo had him bowing before he returned the sack.

About 10:00 A.M. the next morning our platoon fell in and marched through the streets toward our camp area, and we got our first good look at Yokohama. It had alternate sections that were well-preserved or completely reduced to rubble. Everything that wasn't hit, bridges, tram lines, etc., was in good shape. However, you could see where a stick of bombs, fire or otherwise, had left a wake of utter destruction.

We marched through the town observing, and observed curiously by the Japanese population, among them former soldiers. Everyone seemed quite docile. We saw our first Japanese women, some dressed in multi-color kimonos, a few in dresses. The women seem mostly chunky, but not unattractive. Some of the men are good-looking and well-proportioned, though generally short—but some are like the caricatures of the Japs familiar to most Americans: toothy grins, black-rimmed, low-slung glasses, and a vacant look. On some street corners there are Japanese policemen, toy-like in black uniforms and leggings, capes and swords. Bicycles are common.

Our area is right in the heart of town, a solid block of rubble over which we have built this temporary camp. Around us are former bank buildings, and various impressive looking structures of three, four, five stories. They are all built in a box-like way. Many of the roofs have trees on them for the purpose of camouflaging guns. There are also car lines, and numerous trolley cars go rattling by, looking almost exactly like those at home. It's good to see a city again, though largely war-torn. Manila, or rather what is left of it, does not compare.

We spent the rest of the day moving rubble and building camp. By evening we had put up 21 squad tents, a mess hall tent, supply and orderly room tents, and dug a latrine. It was good going, and the C.O. said so at evening formation. There are 12 of our section in our tent. We strung lines and put up mosquito bars. In spite of the cool weather, the mosquitoes are numerous. The broken water main at the edge of the camp provides a continual flow of clear, cold water. By evening we were set up, washed, shaved—and we even had a hot meal of bully beef and lima beans. By dint of our good work we were allowed to leave camp to see what we could see, provided we were in proper uniform, carried our rifles, and were back by 10:00 P.M. Sol Miller, Ron, Norm and I left camp together just to scout around and get the feel of the place.

Some of the buildings were well-lighted, but for the most part the city is dark and dreary. We boarded one of the trams (they don't ask soldiers to pay), filled with Japs, and we rode awhile. The trams move right along. The people were more than a little apprehensive of us, especially when we handled our rifles. A loud laugh or voice seems to frighten them. Many smile toothily at us and seem anxious not to cause trouble or get in our way. After riding around for awhile, and finding out we were headed for the geisha house section, we retraced and went to the large railroad station. There we learned that trains leave for Tokyo every 10 minutes and take 45 minutes. We didn't have enough time to make this little jaunt so we decided to ride only to the next stop, which is Yokohama Station.

The trains are comfortable, about the size of our subway cars, and they move at a good clip. Everywhere we went we were the object of curious eyes. There were many Japanese soldiers, discharged and on their way home, and officers who looked aloof and bore their ignominy as well as possible. While aboard the train one Japanese struck up a conversation with me in excellent English. He told us that there was not much to see at night and that the best place to see was Tokyo during the daytime. I complimented him on his English and asked him where he had learned the language. He replied in NYC. He lived on 190th Street in Washington Heights! This really surprised me. He was surprised too when I informed him I lived 10 blocks away. "Ah, Dyckman Street," he said. It is a small world, and here this cliché is really appropriate. He is a dentist and had his office just off 42nd Street. He had returned to Japan in 1940 for a visit and had been caught here by the war—so he said. It was fascinating to have met him. During all the time I've been in the army, I've never met anyone from Washington Heights or Inwood. I had to come to Yokohama to find a Jap who lived there! I wanted to get his name and address, because he might be a useful contact, but we had arrived in the station and the other fellows wanted to get off. I was strongly tempted to stay on, but didn't. I knew I would regret it, and I am regretting it now.

Yokohama Station was dull and dreary, and there was nothing to see along the bare streets. We hardly left the station. Norm and I sold a pack of cigarettes for 10 yen. We later found out the standard price is 20, in Tokyo 30 yen. We got a couple of bows with this transaction. The exchange here is 15 yen to the dollar. We met a soldier who explained all this and exhibited a roll of yen notes from a day's transactions in Tokyo with cigarettes and rations. A carton sells for 300 or more yen. This soldier was in a repatriating team, processing Allied POWs and collecting atrocity data. He gave us a lot of information about his interesting work and helped us to get the feel of the place, which was the purpose of our wanderings. Then we returned to camp. Today, so far, we have done nothing except wait for orders. The C.O. told us that this is only a temporary camp, which none of us regrets hearing.

Most of the fellows are only interested in finding out about the geisha houses. It seems that most of them are temporarily closed, waiting for army inspection. Also the union or association to which the houses belong has ordered them closed for several days.

Lt. O'Loughlin got drunk with a lieutenant from another outfit, an old buddy, and he has been restricted to the area. He must sign in like any restricted EM, and he awaits action from Battalion Hdqtrs. He reports that Jap beer is excellent, which we learned on Biak.

I am anxious to visit Tokyo, and hope we can get out of camp this afternoon, but it is doubtful. Anyway I went to sleep last night excited by the prospect of new sights and experiences. The occupation has been so peaceful I can't see why large numbers of troops cannot be sent home soon, especially us old-timers with two or more years of overseas service. We are still getting used to being in the homeland of the enemy and the strangeness of having on all sides of us a people who have been our enemy for nearly four years. I've no doubt that the novelty will soon wear off.

Though everything is orderly now, we hear that the first occupation troops, among them sailors and marines, did considerable looting. The Japs bow, smile, and do their best to be peaceful. I'd like to meet that Jap from NY again and really find out things. Mail call!

September 19

Mail call brought 11 letters, including letters from Dale, Enid and Ginger. As yet I have only written home. Enid, typically, dedicated exactly one line of her letter to the end of the war. Ginger expects me home in two months!! Everything at home has been all right, with high elation over the ending of the war.

We have been working on the ships for the last two days, but not very hard. Our platoon has the midnight-to-eight shift, and it is indeed a long pull. It gets cold at night, and last night I wore two shirts under my raincoat. Night before we had a high wind, strong enough to whip an empty cargo net around me and the winches. When we got back to camp our tents were flapping like birds straining at leashes. One of the kitchen tents was already badly torn, and the insides of our tents were a mess.

There is talk of a recount of our point scores, giving us credit for time since May 12th to September 2nd. This will give me 69 or 70 points. Stahl has informed me that I am up for T-4 and Smitty will get my buck corporal job. I would prefer the T-4; I do not want a buck sergeant's rating. Having been a non-com for a year now, I know what a headache the job of section leader can be. Much better to have the three stripes without the headache. Stahl will probably be leaving shortly. Flynn and Skivington, two other buck corporals, are also up for T-4, so there will be quite a few new assistant section leaders. Charley apparently will not rejoin us.

I have managed to see more of the country. Two days ago Monroe, Norm, Ron and I went to see Tokyo. We all took cigarettes to sell at the rate of 30 yen per pack—which is $2.00 per. Sold eight packs and picked up a Jap-made pocket book for two packs. The people were hungry for them but even more hungry for food. A small piece of chocolate sells for 20 or 30 yen, and a K-ration for as much as 70. The Japanese seem to be the quickest crowd-forming people in the world, and they are extremely curious. If two or three soldiers stop to talk in a group for a few minutes, or if one exhibits a pack of cigs or something to eat, there is a ring of people five-deep around him in a moment. They all seem anxious to please, though 90% of them, and probably more, neither speak nor understand any English.

On the way to Tokyo via train, we could plainly see how completely the industrial back of Japan has been broken. All of the factories were blasted. All that usually remains of one is the fire-blackened chimney as tombstone to mark the place. Huge swaths of every city are completely burned out and reduced to a layer of rusting rubble.

Tokyo on Sunday is even more desolate than usual. It is a melancholy sight to see one of the huge and modern cities of the world war-torn and largely deserted. One feels uneasy, as if in the presence of the dead. A few people wander the streets hungrily and with wary eyes. Every other building is either partially or completely destroyed. The intact buildings have the same box-like structure as those that we first saw in Sakuragicho.

The streets of Tokyo are wide and there are some pretty parks. A number of streams cut through the city. We walked around for several hours, and every other street corner is a black market center. By far the most interesting sight we saw was the Emperor's grounds and, I think, his palace. The grounds are like a huge park, with rolling spacious lawns and neatly-arranged shrubbery. We were not allowed on the grounds, but they are easily seen from the outside. The main entrance has huge iron-grill gates. Set against the green hills was a pretty white house, with its black roof turned up at the edges. We supposed this to be the main building or palace. Surrounding the grounds is a high stone wall, and between that and the sidewalks of Tokyo is a wide and deep moat filled with various kinds of fish. Over the moat fly numerous delicate, small, white birds that swoop and wheel in the air. They spot a fish, make a vertical dive of 40 or 50 feet, and plunge into the water with a small, neat splash. They look exactly like miniature suicide planes. In the thin afternoon sun the palace and grounds had an aura of serenity and reverence. It is undeniably beautiful, and this atmosphere is enhanced by the Japanese who, when they pass the gates, remove their hats and bow in the direction of the palace. Many Japanese soldiers and some civilians lounged peacefully on the outer fringe of lawn and under trees on our side of the moat, and many Japs were hungrily eyeing the fat carp swimming in it.

We returned to Yokohama and spent that evening walking around its suburbs. The houses are neat with yellow, woven floors. The dress for many at night in their homes is a G-string for the men, nothing for the women from the waist up. Then an old Jap woman took us for a two-mile hike to a geisha house. The place, discreetly lighted, looked comfortable and immaculate. There was much glass and neat woodwork. The girls were intriguing and especially pretty with their high-piled black hair, small, neat, doll-like features, and colorful kimonos. They looked as if they would be interesting to be with. Some sailors already were there, and we were informed through an interpreter that an appointment must first be made. After a two-mile return hike, we missed the last car back to camp and had to walk another four miles. The air was brisk; Norm and I didn't mind.

Last night Stahl, Stewart, Adams, Hendricks and I went out to scout around. They knew a new section where there were many geisha houses and straight prostitutes. We got there quite late, and so most of the houses were occupied. We saw many women, some rather pretty. Two fellows finally met one Japanese girl in a blue kimono who took them into her place, which was lighted with an eerie green light and looked straight out of an adventure story. They both had intercourse with her for 50 yen each. If I ever decide to use one of these women, it will not be on a share-the-body basis. That is positively out. The area was intriguing, with the Japanese pattering around in dimly-lit houses, which threw their pale yellow gleams on the dark little streets. I walked back to camp alone, while the others waited several hours.

For the past few nights a shuttered house on a nearby corner has housed a few prostitutes. One fellow, a replacement in Stew's section, had one on the shower room floor. Last night they had one who went in for sex orgies, and this morning some of the fellows were washing penises that had been bitten! And incidentally, that water is so brutally cold, it takes one's breath away.

I have been considering going to a geisha house, but unless the conditions are as I would like them, I shall not. We few remaining virgins are having the same temptations and problems. The situation is humorous, hugely so in one sense—and quite serious from another.

[*The following entry was not in the diary itself, although it most certainly occurred as described here. I wrote it about six months after my discharge, in response to a college English class assignment.*]

September 21

The location of the 244th Port Company in the middle of the Yokohama financial district led to some remarkable events. To explain them I have to refer back to our days in the Philippines.

When the Japs had invaded the Philippines, they had brought with them an enormous supply of invasion money, officially called "occupational currency." The bills were of various size, colors and denominations, designated in pesos, printed in English. Each bill clearly stated that it was issued and backed by the Bank of Japan. This money became absolutely worthless with our invasion of the Philippines and could be had for the asking. I, along with many others, sent these bills home in letters as souvenirs.

Sam Owen, our stocky and swarthy cook, took to collecting large bundles of the Japanese invasion money, as we called it, and for reasons that were never clear to any of us, he half-filled a barracks bag with these bills. We all thought him a fool to be lugging around all this useless, worthless weight, though we supposed the bills might have some souvenir value back in the States.

About three days ago Sam came into our tent and pulled out a large wad of bills, rolled up like toilet paper, which proved to be perfectly negotiable Japanese brown and green yen now familiar to us. We all assumed he had been doing some heavy trading—after all, as a cook, he had easy access to supplies, but no. He explained that he had simply walked into one of the local banks and presented a wad of his Japanese invasion money from the Philippines at one of the counters, and asked for an exchange. Apparently a timid and intimidated bank clerk got the bank president, who spoke some English, and Sam, who is imposing in size and girth to begin with, pointed out that the bills he had were backed by the Bank of Japan, as plainly stated on each piece of money. The bank president authorized an exchange of local yen for invasion money yen on a one-to-one basis. Sam exchanged about $300 worth, and he managed to keep his jubilation under control while he signed for the money, at the request of the bank president, and pocketed the cash.

Sam made a deal with us. He would give those who would exchange the invasion money a certain sum, which he would record, and after each of us made an exchange, he would split the sum 50/50. He warned us that we might have to sign a paper when we made the exchange, as he had done.

Off we went in two's and three's to the various banks in the area to make our exchanges. The inside of the bank I went to was much like a

U.S. bank, except there were no individual stations, just a long counter. It went much as Sam described. A bank official was called who examined our money and authorized the exchange, and then presented us with a growing list of familiar names which we signed. Then we returned to Sam, who sat on his cot amidst piles of money like a caricature of a plutocrat, and we gave him his 50%. The news quickly spread, and Sam had practically the whole company wanting to get in on the deal.

That evening, to celebrate our sudden wealth, about 10 of us went into Tokyo and walked into a fancy hotel. We explained that we wanted a good dinner served, with plenty of saki and beer. About an hour later we were all seated on the floor around a low table, while four or five Japanese waitresses in kimonos, pattered in and out of the room bringing all manner of dishes, and mounds of rice, and trays full of saki and beer. The whole atmosphere was something like a college fraternity party— and of course some of the fellows got drunk and were loud and laughing, and sometimes ugly, on the train back. The Japs who were travelling late would not look at us and acted as if we did not exist. Our night out in Tokyo had not been very expensive, and we still had plenty of money left the next day. Sam's supply had dwindled, though.

The following day, when the banks opened, even more of the fellows in the company had Sam's invasion money in their pockets, but few were successful in making the exchange. It seems that one of the bank presidents had phoned General MacArthur's headquarters and inquired if the Jap banks were obliged to exchange Jap yens for Philippine invasion money. The answer, of course, was "no"—and our enterprise ground to a quick halt as the word spread from bank to bank.

The next morning, about 5:00 A.M., we were surprised to hear the blast of a whistle and the voice of the 1st Sergeant rousting us up, announcing a company formation. It was damp and cold, and there was still ground fog swirling between the rows of tents and in the surrounding Yokohama streets. We knew something was up.

After we had formed up, the Captain came out of his tent, flanked by the Lieutenants, and behind them was a line of Japanese, formally dressed in striped pants and long-tailed coats, and high hats. It was clear what this company call was all about, and we sheepishly grinned at each other.

"Men," said the Captain, "these men have come to see me with a complaint. It seems some of you have been cashing in on the invasion money issued by the Japanese government for use by its military in the Philippines. Now this man," he said, indicating the Jap nearest to him, "has phoned General MacArthur's HQ in Tokyo and was told the Philippine money is worthless and should not have been exchanged. These men have brought me the lists of names of those who made money exchanges, and the amount each was given. I am going to read these names, and I expect each of you to return the money.

"As I read off the names," continued the Captain, "I want each man to step forward: Clark Gable, Jimmy Stewart, Bob Hope, Mickey Mouse . . ."

An incipient giggle started in the ranks, gathered volume as the Captain continued to read the names we had signed, and finally crested into hysterical laughter. The Captain tried to keep as straight a face as he could manage, while the Japs looked at each other in surprise, and then dismay. "I'm sorry," said the Captain to them, "none of these names are of men in my company." The Japs walked away, fading into the ground fog, while we staggered about in uncontrollable laughter.

[*As I later discovered in a back issue of the English language newspaper,* The Nippon Times, *published in Tokyo on September 17, 1945, the use of occupation currency was "strictly banned." Apparently this edict, announced by the Finance Ministry of the Imperial Japanese Government, had not yet been widely disseminated during the early days of the occupation.*]

September 26

The company is on edge—and has good reason. Yesterday, which marked our two years overseas, an order came through stating that all men with 70 points and over will be in a disposition center by October 1st!! This morning 18 of our men with 80 or more points left for such a center. The majority of us have 73 now, having received credit for the southern Philippines (we sailed by at an opportune time) and six more points of overseas credit.

Today we unloaded navy transports which brought in the 97th, 85th and 78th Divisions (the ones who wrote to the President protesting their shipment overseas again). This evening all men with 60 points and more in the 43rd Division and 1st Cavalry are boarding to go home. Need it be written how they felt? They all carried either Jap sabers, or Jap small arms or rifles as going away presents. Pretty fine. We are all now convinced of the nearness of our own repatriation, probably well before Thanksgiving. Hallelujah! Can this be real? After waiting for so long it hardly seems possible. Yet, how can it be very long?

Meanwhile, the order concerning us has been unofficially confirmed by all our officers: 162 men and two officers, the Old Man and Pranke, will be eligible. All the men, including me, are as nervous as cats. These days now move by with miserable slowness, and we have really been sweating them out.

Because of this recent order, what was a great disappointment to me now seems trivial. I was to make T-4, but Charley Norvell returned and I lost out. Then with Stahl leaving, I was to become section leader which calls for buck sergeant. With Henehan platoon sergeant, and Lt. Pranke not liking me much, nor me him, Skivington was given the section. This opened up ratings in other sections and blocked ours. Skivvy has been a corporal longer than I have, and an acting section leader longer, but it is a bitter pill to take for I have worked hard to get ahead. As I have seen plenty of times before, it takes more than work to get promoted. Stahl's utter obsequiousness in this matter, his lack of guts, so disgusted me that I could not stand to have him talk to me during the last few days he was here. When Lt. Pranke approached him about Skivvy, he said without a murmur of opposition that he was going home, and washed his hands of the whole matter. He was pleased with himself for avoiding an argument and preserving his rating and skin up to the last moment. This gutless exhibition was the straw that broke the back of my tolerance for his attitudes. I hoped I wouldn't see him again. We did not say goodbye. I've hardly ever felt so let down in my life. Though my hard work has taught me a great deal and benefited me in various ways, as far as advancement goes it has been for naught. There was just too much stacked against me. So I am still corporal, but what difference now with home a few weeks away—and to return in good health and stable mind. I would have written all this last night except that I had one of my infrequent attacks of chills and fever for about 12 hours. Haven't been taking enough atabrine. I took three atabrine last night and awoke feeling better this morning, well enough to go to work for eight hours. But I am tired of ships, ships, and more ships. But there is an end in sight.

During the past days I have been to Tokyo several times, and I've visited the Emperor's grounds, having been allowed into them. At the Hotel Marunouchi, a place out of a spy novel, I spent a few interesting evenings before dinner in conversation with members of the pre-war Italian Embassy. I learned quite a bit from them about the Japanese and the war from the enemies' side because they were here through the entire thing. I was amused by the little Italian boys and girls speaking English with a perfect British accent. The Italians are anxious to return home, to a very blasted Italy I imagine. One fellow, with clipped moustache, monocle and faultless dress was the epitome of the diplomat in appearance and manner. His knowledge of English was extensive though rusty.

Tonight I shall write home about these new developments. I am almost tempted not to because there have been so many disappointments in army life. If something goes wrong this time, it will break the heart and spirit of 164 men. The company only has 38 men who are not eligible. As for me, I am both calm and nervous, calm that at last the end of this life is in sight, on edge because things go wrong so easily in the army. A few days more will tell the story, and what long days they are going to be.

September 30

We are still waiting like wound-up springs for our release to a disposition center or ship. Rumor has us slightly delayed because a colored outfit was found to have more points than we do. It still looks as if we'll leave early next month. I am anxious to see if points will be dropped by October 1st, as General Marshall said they would two weeks ago. It will feel a lot better to know definitely that we are eligible. This waiting has been very hard on all the men, and none is reluctant to tell you. Have written home, and to Dale informing them that this would be my last letter to them while I am in the army. I told Dale to answer to my home address.

I shall have to start giving some thought to the future, and yet I find it almost impossible to settle my mind to anything until I am in the tranquillity of home—and have gotten in some living.

October 1

Today the points were to be dropped to 70, but it hasn't happened yet. There was news today that the 43rd Division was the first returning unit from the Pacific. The next division, the 31st, is scheduled to leave at the end of this month. I hope we shall not have to wait that long. I will feel a lot happier when we are eligible by an official drop in the score.

Have been buying a number of kimonos, and having fun finding and then bargaining for them.

Last night Ron and I went to a reconditioned theater in Yokohama. We once again saw Lanny Ross, this time in his last overseas army performance. It was a good show and like a sentimental reunion when he led us in songs that reminded us of our days way back in southern New Guinea. He still has a good voice, but he's a good deal grayer now. The MC told us he had 173 points. I know he has been overseas longer than we have by a few months. Ross is a major now, well-deserved for all his entertainment of troops during these past two to three years. True to army style, the power failed during his last song. He finished it with a dead mike and in the beam of GI flashlights.

This morning we heard a smooth-voiced radio announcer tell us about the various steps in our discharge processing. We stood around listening to it like a bunch of poor boys being told about the rich boys' Christmas.

October 7

Last week the points were officially dropped to 70 for discharge which makes me eligible. We are automatically declared "non-essential," and await transportation. This last week has seemed extra long. I have seen quite a number of men boarding ships with 70 points or more. It is only a matter of days until our orders finally come through. The army is clearing the disposition centers here now. Perhaps we will be among the next batch.

A few days ago nine of our men shipped out. They are over 35 and had at least two years service. Among them were some of the original men of the outfit. My old friend "Cuz" Adams was among them, and he was the saddest fellow for a soldier going home that I have yet seen. He deeply regretted leaving so many good friends behind; he badly wanted to return with the rest of the company. He also left with a case of piles, because he feared he would be hospitalized if he reported it to the medics. Among those who left were Lewis King, Henehan and some of the replacements. Poor Rooney missed it by having only 23 months in service. Capt. Reinhardt also left. After being in command for 18 months, he did not even say goodbye to the men.

Last night we took influenza shots. Besides a sore arm, my legs and back ache which didn't make handling 300 to 400 pound boxes any fun last night. We are on the 3:00 P.M. to midnight shift now, and those nine hours are brutal. I'm afraid I've been in a sour mood, not toward other people, but just in general what with not feeling well, with the strain of waiting, with working long hours in miserable weather or through cold nights, with officers who continue to ride us to work hard, and with having to stand a 6:00 A.M. reveille after getting to bed past midnight. It is only the imminence of going home that keeps most of the old fellows going.

At lunch today we felt surfeited for the first time since our arrival in Japan. There was unlimited fresh chicken, and I had a mighty share of that. It felt good not to have any twinge of hunger. There is a rule now that we can't give our leftovers to the Jap kids and old women who wait patiently and hungrily with their tin cans to get what we don't eat. It is awful to see them watching food dumped into garbage cans and watching us with eager, pitiful faces. A little kid with hungry eyes and empty pail tears at my heart and spoils the meal I have eaten. I can hardly wait to get started home and away from this army life and all its spirit-decaying rules and boredom.

October 14

These last few days of clear weather have been a pleasant relief from the recent weeks of bad weather. Yesterday we were issued heavy under-clothing, socks and an OD shirt which came in handy, with more to come. The bad weather has held up everything, especially troop transports. We spent most of our time in bed to keep warm. Those rainy days passed wearily, our dark tents lit by a few candles. Half the time the fellows didn't know whether it was day or night. But now we are fairly comfort-able with more suitable clothing, wood floors, a built-up camp, better food, and not too much work. Two nights ago I froze through C.Q., the last one I will serve in the army, I hope. Spent a good part of that night wrapped in a blanket, reading and enjoying *The Citadel* by Cronin, and listening to Lt. Murphy and Lt. Walker tell tales about their promiscuous days. Murphy was always caught "by my girl."

Meanwhile we continue to wait for our ship. Now with the clearing weather ships are expected. The 35-year-old men still await transporta-tion at the Zama Academy (West Point of Japan). The *Stars and Stripes* said yesterday that 44,000 men will leave the Yokohama area in October, and that 267,000 men will return from the Pacific per month for the next three months. If we don't leave this month, despite our excellent chance, we shall surely ship out early next month. Embarkations remain unpre-dictable because of our limited transports, inevitable delays, and tem-porary set-ups at the disposition centers. Adding to our difficulties are the strikes at home, especially of longshoremen. These strikes create a chain of delaying circumstances—with overseas troops at the butt end as usual.

Our section has dwindled to 15 active men. Kolbet and Blessin are transferred to the service section, Thomas is supercargo, Sigley is in the hospital, and there are always two or three men on detail, all of which leaves us with a skimpy section. Now there is an order out to work all the men all the time. Each shift becomes more tedious to me. I could kick myself when I recall that I could be supply sergeant now had it not been for my loyalty to Stahl. Well, I'll learn eventually, I suppose.

Last night I had an unusual experience, unusual for me anyway. The results of it have mentally and emotionally affected me. It may be aptly entitled, "Reflections on a Geisha House."

Having heard so much about geisha girls and the houses, I became curious about them and wanted to visit one. Sancho took me to a house which was on "vacation" (which means you can do anything but have intercourse with the girls). That was a good set-up for me because I just wanted to satisfy my curiosity, and I would be spared the embarrassment of refusing to have intercourse with one of the girls. So after taking our cholera shots (which hurt later), we set off for Omoiri, one of the biggest geisha towns in the vicinity. It was dark when we got there, and after Sancho's fuzzy memory had unravelled the way, we arrived at a large, square building. We entered, and at the foot of some stairs we removed our shoes and went upstairs. There was a large room on the second floor in the middle of the building that looked something like *Esquire* pictures of a harem. It was a long, wide room, with high ceilings, well-lighted by oriental-style electric lamps. The floor was of yellow, woven matting, soft and clean, that gave comfortably to the feet. At one end of the room there was a stage. The building was large, and when I explored it later, I found numerous corridors and many similar rooms.

But for the room itself. One's first impression is of a riot of color. First one notices the splashed colors of the various kimonos, obis and haoris the girls wear. Most of these clothes are quite beautiful. Then one sees the vividly colored mats scattered over the floor. Next one becomes aware of the soldiers and sailors and girls in various recumbent positions on the mats. It's a rather pleasant though bawdy atmosphere. Some men just sit and talk to the girls, others lie down with them, others lie under a cover with them, and some simply roam around. Each little group or couple is oblivious to everyone else.

Sancho knew one of the girls from his earlier visit. Soon he was talking with her, and I with a rather cute girl called Hanako. To her I was immediately a "nice boy." We managed to converse through sign language and a smattering of Japanese and English. She told me she was 18. Naturally these are very easy women and will settle back on a mat as soon as you want to. I felt shy at first, and then later, with the first girl in my arms since leaving Australia two years ago, I felt strange. She was a pleasant-looking girl, small and compact, and wore a colorful kimono. Sancho's girl was taller, very full-bodied. I wasn't as much interested in the girl as I was observing what went on in that place and getting its atmosphere. Some of the girls were passably pretty and all of them literally colorful. They wear make-up and perfume, preen a great deal, have good complexions, speak in cooing voices when addressing us but harshly among themselves, and seem clean except for the bottoms of their feet because most of them are barefoot.

There was some drinking going on, much beer. The drunken sailors gave a bawdy and raucous touch to the place. Despite the girls' ingratiating dispositions, coos and smiles, it wasn't difficult to see that they were hardened to the whole scene. It is only to be expected that under the veneer of pleasantries their trade exacts, they should be used to everything, with night after night of entertaining. Their bodies are playthings, and they have no objection to men handling them in any manner they please, and quite openly. Men of all rank were there including officers as high as major. One big lieutenant settled down with a girl for several hours in a kissing session that I have seldom seen equalled even back in the days of heavy petting parties. That's really what it was, a petting party on a grand scale. Men were chasing women, and then some were wrestling with them. As I remarked to a fellow next to us, "New Guinea was never like this."

Sanchez propositioned his girl and she was willing to go back to camp with him. Mine wanted to go back with me, though she told me 50 times not to tell Griffin (a new fellow in our outfit) because she learned that I knew him. I wasn't keen on this idea nor anxious to commence my sex life with a Japanese geisha girl, no matter how willing she was. I knew I wasn't going to take her to camp, and I told Sancho not to suggest that the four of us would go. Griffin showed up, and she took off with him, and so I was free for several hours just to loll, observe and enjoy what I saw.

It is difficult to capture my feelings, and the oddity of the position I found myself in, especially after such a long alienation from any kind of intimate relationship with women.

Hanako turned on the tears for Griffin, which neither he nor I understood. He has been seeing her often. I read about the history of the geisha and their ability to turn on tears as easily as a faucet. So she cried and was miserable for several hours, and then Griffin left. About 10 seconds after he said goodbye, she was by my side, and the redness and puffiness of her eyes completely vanished! Quite a stunt. She still wanted me to take her to camp to sleep with me, and here I saw my opportunity to get out of it easily. I feigned anger about Griffin, and, though I treated her kindly, I was adamant about not taking her back. She tried. Hotsu, Sancho's girl, tried, and then they brought in another girl to translate who explained to me, "No pom-pom—just sleep." Finally, Sanchez himself tried to change my mind. Sancho couldn't understand my refusing such a "wonderful opportunity," because in a few days "the same thing will cost plenty." Besides, he told me, the night before several of the fellows tried to get Hanako to go back with them, but she wouldn't. I guess she just took a liking to me or was in the mood. Anyway, at last she settled for letting her walk with me to Omoiri station—which she did.

At midnight we waited at the station for about a half-hour. There were a few Jap soldiers and civilians around. I felt sort of foolish standing with a Jap girl whose head came to my chest, but it was fun. The train came, and I said goodbye to her. She asked me to return today—rather tonight.

The three of us returned to camp. Hotsu climbed into Sancho's bed right across from mine. About 10 minutes later the creak of the bed, and their heavy breathing indicated they were in the frenzy of intercourse.

In the pitch black, I lay there listening to "two savages in bedlam," as Aldous Huxley wrote of intercourse. It was clear to me that all evening I was at the center of powerful and deeply conflicting emotions. On the one hand I felt a certain repulsion, disgust and indignation with what was happening in the cot next to mine, that it was, somehow, all wrong, and that if it were me having intercourse for the first time under these conditions, it would have destroyed something in me.

If I had decided on or forced myself into intercourse last night, I know that something would have been torn out of me. I cannot completely explain it. There was a barrier in my mind that was stronger, whatever it was, than any passion that I had felt. Why? I'm not sure. What reason do I have to be so moral? I've not been raised with such strictness as to make that a barrier. Then I was afraid I did not act because, as Enid once said of me, I took "a satisfaction in my own virtue while laughing at or looking down at others." Surely this cannot be true. Everything in my mind cried "wrong"—and I was powerless. Not afraid—but powerless. At least, so it seemed.

I fell asleep and did not stir until Skivvy woke us for reveille. Skivvy went to wake Sancho and grabbed the girl instead. I couldn't help but laugh because he was so surprised. He got annoyed and threatened to turn Sancho in if he didn't get Hotsu out quickly. He's been throwing threats around pretty often, and eventually they aren't going to do him any good as far as getting along with the men. He worries a great deal about getting home and protecting his rating, I suppose. Anyway, as we fall out for reveille, the girls who spent the night in our quarters, usually three or four of them, fall out on the other side and gather together in the cold gray dawn. It is both comical and pathetic.

All day today I have been strangely and obscurely bothered by the events of last night. I do not quite comprehend myself and the conflicting, myriad feelings of shyness, compassion, unreality and tension that I have felt all day.

October 22

Today we are more on edge than we have been for the past four weeks. Last night the disposition center was cleaned out, and the group of 35-year-old men are aboard a ship at south pier. This morning there are a number of transports already in and more expected during the coming two weeks. Rumors fly thick and fast that 70-point men will soon receive their orders. It's a cinch that it can't be much longer that we have to wait.

Yesterday we got about 40 replacements who are low-point men from the 542 Amphibious Engineers. Their unit is going home and these men have points in the 50s. Our section drew four of them, and so we are again up to strength at 18. Most of them seem to be Northerners and a pretty good bunch of fellows with about 12 to 14 months overseas. We are glad to see them augment our strength. Down on the docks during the past week we have mainly been supervising Jap labor. The fellows split the hold time up so that they are down there only an hour or so out of the whole shift, just sitting and watching. The Japs handle all the dock labor. It's a soft deal for us.

Mom writes that Bob Bernstein and Sylvan Jacobs visited her recently. Bob is considering making the sea his career. Sylvan is awaiting discharge on November 1st *at home.* He has 63 points. [*Bernstein and Jacobs were two close boyhood and high-school friends. Jacobs was wounded in Europe. Bernstein, indeed, went on to a career in the merchant marine after the war.*] Speaking of points, at the non-com meeting a few nights ago, Power informed us that the men who had 62 points on May 12th have gained another two points. That gives me 75. Good insurance in case of trouble over that last five we got.

The other day while shopping around Yokohama, I was astounded to come upon a crowd of American soldiers who were watching a nude Japanese girl standing on a street corner. I write "astounded" because the event was so incongruous. Yet there she was, disrobed of her few poor rags, a girl of about 18 or 19. A few fellows threw cigarettes at her, and then she calmly sat down on the sidewalk and pulled on her jeans. She was perfectly inscrutable during the performance. Her legs were badly scarred, and she had an ugly body. It was revolting, yet so odd I could not help but laugh at this impromptu nudity.

We have been issued additional OD and other heavy clothing, which we certainly need here. For the past few days it has been wet and cold; the chill knifes through tent and clothes.

October 24

This morning at a company meeting Lt. Murphy informed us that our orders were due within the next three days, and probably tomorrow. He asked the experienced fellows to maintain discipline and be "garrison soldiers" for the next few days in order to impress our replacements. This will be a novelty to us.

This afternoon we were told to turn in all our superfluous equipment by tomorrow, and that is welcome news. Early this evening our replacements rolled into camp with packs on their backs, helmets, rifles, etc. They certainly looked good to us for every one of them means a ticket home for one of us. There were about 120 of them. I spoke to several. The majority of them are Southern boys with about six months in the army, trained for the infantry. Of course they asked a million questions about everything from beer to women. Seeing them lined up for chow, and hungry, reminded us of the day we landed in Sydney and had that supper of one sardine and some soup. That was a century ago. Tomorrow they will undoubtedly hear about Gloucester and Biak!

Some of the officers and Sgt. Power have seen our orders. We should have them within the next 24 hours and be aboard ship by the end of this week, in four or five days. I may make it home by Thanksgiving after all. That would be wonderful! The fellows are happy tonight, but our departure, like the end of the war, comes after so many false starts and long anticipation that we take the news calmly and in stride. I'll only really feel assured that we are States-bound when that ship is cutting the water of the Pacific.

Our company finally was awarded the good conduct medal, most of the men getting it. Norm and I, desperadoes that we are, did not receive it because of that time we were picked up in Daguapan. What a farce!! Men who have committed all kind of offenses received it, but since an official complaint was lodged and therefore a record kept, we were eliminated. It proves the old saying, you only get punished for what you're caught doing, not for what you do—or as Lt. Wenz would say, the only crime in the army is getting caught. This penalty reminds me of the situation that busted Major Jollopo in *A Bell for Adano*. It's gotten under my skin, but what the devil, those are the breaks. [*As it turned out, we did receive the good conduct medal at the time of our discharges.*] Anyway that departure day is finally coming, and I'm in one piece, healthy—and, I think, sane enough. God, but it will be good to be home and with the family again. What else matters in comparison to that?

Last night we put in a 12-hour shift loading mail on the *Tennant*. Had charge of the gang. There is an excellent chance that was the last shift we shall ever have to pull on the ships.

I just asked myself how I feel tonight. I say calm. I try to realize that at long last we shall soon be taking the first step of the long voyage home. I imagine, though, that all of us will be experiencing some rather strange reactions during the next two months.

October 25

Orders came in tonight. We leave tomorrow morning. Lt. Murphy read the list of eligible men, and it was music to our ears. Everyone of us who is eligible is flying so high that Fujiyama is just another hill.

The day has finally arrived, and I may be able to make Thanksgiving at home at that. What else is there to say; all I have written before will have to serve to explain how I feel. No one sentence or paragraph would be adequate.

Wrote my last letters tonight to Mom, Enid and Edith. It will be wonderful to see everyone again. I'll be glad to be on our way; it has been brutally cold the last few days. I will not write any more now. Everything or anything I say seems inadequate.

October 27

Yesterday morning 150 of us, all the remaining old men of the outfit, left camp. Lt. Murphy gave us an expected farewell speech, and soon we were loading into trucks and ducks. While waiting, some of the geisha girls from Omoiri came to say goodbye to the fellows in camp, and among them was Hanako! She looked much more painted and less appealing in stark daylight. At any rate, I told her I was returning home. She grasped my hand and began to cry, the tears rolling copiously down her round cheeks. It's a thing she does easily, but it's the most sentimental send-off I've had in the army since leaving home.

In a little while we were waving goodbye to the few remaining old replacements, to the new ones, and to the camp itself. There weren't many or anybody, I believe, that sent any lingering glances back. After a cold, dusty, dirty ride, we arrived at Zama Military Camp which is now the 4th Replacement and Disposition Center. The camp is about 20 miles from Yokohama and situated on a plateau amidst high mountains that surround us on all sides. They are massive and barren, with wispy bits of white clouds floating around the ridges. It's cool here, and at night it's cold. Zama was the West Point of Japan. It has spacious grounds for drill, and the buildings are barrack-like, long and wide, and alike.

We were assigned to one of these barracks shortly after arriving. It proved to be a large building, with a concrete floor, and built of heavy, bolted timbers. The building is separated into sections by sliding doors. There are about 400 soldiers in each section. The rows of cots are lined up side by side. These are good facilities. The food has not been anything to rave about, but no one complains very much about any discomfort.

This morning we began our processing. We handed in excess clothing and had our service records checked in an interview. We were assigned to separation centers. Mine is Fort Dix as it is for men from NYC. Fort Knox is the one for nearly all upstate New York men. The other fellows were assigned to their respective nearest separation points. So it seems that I shall end my army career at the place where I started it, Fort Dix.

Now I have a souvenir Jap rifle to clean up—and I thought my rifle-cleaning days were over. We await transportation—air, if any is available, which is highly doubtful. There are about 4,000 men in the camp. Those here longest came in five days ago. So chances look pretty bright for starting home soon. I am still getting used to the idea.

November 2

Have spent the last week waiting patiently, reading, playing bridge with Seth, Ron and Mark [*Emanuel Mark, a late replacement*]. The days are long and cool, the nights long and cold. Sometimes we must sound like an old soldiers' home. Because we are all veterans of at least two years, we discuss New Guinea and the other places and campaigns in the way people might discuss a mutually-known city in the States.

I was ill for three days with a bad cold which finally resulted in a miserable night of chills and fever, a combination of the cold and perhaps a touch of malaria. An abrupt change in weather has several times made me react with malaria symptoms, as it has many other fellows. I am getting used to the cool weather, but it was hard to take for awhile. I broke up my illness with large doses of atabrine, aspirin and cold tablets.

The troops slowly move out. Three days ago all the fellows scheduled for Fort Dix (about 35 in the company) were alerted, but nothing happened. Since then the whole 260th Replacement Co. has been on the alert; small groups of them have been moving out. About 15 of our men, all Southerners, will move out tonight. These are among the advance parties for two ships, and we hope to be among the main body going on them. The Americal Division started loading four days ahead of schedule, and those troops are taking a good portion of the shipping, probably

Arthur Monroe (l.) and Sy Kahn, awaiting embarkation from Zama after service as occupying troops in Yokohama, Japan, October 1945.

affecting us. All day today and yesterday long lists of names have been called (they sound like the Fordham University football line-up), and here and there an answering "Yooo" means that a man in this particular barracks has been named. It should only be a few days until we are aboard some ship. My hope to return by Thanksgiving is just about nullified.

I've gotten to know Manny Mark from Brooklyn and Alvin Berchin from Upper Bronx better while waiting in Zama. Both are Jewish lads and recent additions to the company. Al is an extrovert, good-natured, raucous, and fun. He can tell a good story. Mark is a fellow who will give you the "shirt off his back." However, he has hammered at me about construction work, riveting, and a fellow named Roy, whom he idolizes, until I have been driven to the border of exasperation. For several days he talked for hours about labor complaints, about Roy, about his dislike of the army, his former company and its deceased captain, to the point where it became painful to listen, even though much of what he told me was interesting. He has either realized that I have reached my limit in listening or else he is all talked out. He has done me several favors. His main virtue is to give of himself, but he doesn't know when to quit. I can't be hammered at too long by anyone. I still like to have a lot of time to myself.

I have not spent much time thinking about the future except to anticipate a vacation after I return home. I know I should be trying to make more definite plans, but somehow I can't. It is difficult to think about as I face returning (which is paradoxical), and somehow I feel it will not much affect what is going to happen anyway.

Each day I anticipate my return, especially with Mom's letters continuing to reach me, revealing her own anticipations that ring with nervousness, pleasure and anxiety. How good it will be to see them all and to be home! Of course there is still a long voyage to make, but it looks as if I will be fortunate enough to return in time for the Christmas holidays. I know anytime will not be too late for those waiting.

November 4

At 3:00 A.M. on the morning of the 3rd, we were woken and told to prepare to move. It was cold and damp, but no one complained at the discomfort, knowing what this move meant. Our names were called off; I am in the Fort Dix group—Group 26. After our barracks bags were hastily inspected (all we had to do was open the tops) and various papers were collected, we stood in long lines for several hours, chilled while we watched a gray, cold dawn. During this time we built fires on Zama's fields, fed with planks from the Jap barracks, around which we huddled and drew some warmth. At about 5:15 trucks arrived and took us to a troop train. I had a tough time lugging all my equipment: a heavy duffle bag, a field-pack carrier bag, a telephone bag filled with my diaries and miscellaneous equipment—and a Japanese rifle. I pulled the muscles in both arms and both shoulders, but made it aboard in place. Maggie [*Romeo Magnotti*], Micky [*Michael Cancilla*], Ron [*Flynn*] and I, all buck corporals and assigned to Ft. Dix, stayed together. During the moves we caught sight of familiar company faces here and there. We are all split up into our separation center groups now, though we are all on the same ship.

It took over four hours to cover the 20 miles from Zama to Yokohama, an exasperating trip of frequent stops and waits and switch-backs. I got my first good look at Mt. Fujiyama while on the train. It was an impressive sight. The mountain is a perfect cone shape with an immaculate head of white snow towering into the sky. Indeed it lives up to its importance. A ring of clouds surrounded the summit, adding to the mountain's detached impressiveness. It seemed as if the volcano was aware of its greatness and beauty, loftily looking down at other huge, but lesser mountains paying homage in their drab green and gray dress.

At noon we finally unloaded from the train near south pier. We had a half-hour wait and then were trucked the short distance to the pier. Finally the moment came when an officer read off the list of names. We yelled answers to our own, shouldered our bags, and climbed that long, last gangplank. My stuff weighed on me terribly, but I loved every step of it. Micky, who only carried a light duffle, shouldered my rifle for me, otherwise I don't know if I would have gotten all my stuff aboard. The name of this magic carpet we boarded is *Sea Runner.*

The rest of the day was surprisingly efficient. We were immediately assigned to bunks, and I found myself in the lower hold, right up in the bow. These were the miserable standard bunks, but the compartment is clean and roomy—and how I welcome that room. Ron is in the next bunk. It's a wonderfully comfortable ship, with a large, white-tiled latrine. We have only two big meals a day, but they have been good. There is a mess hall and, wonder of wonders, tables *and seats.* Everything is so clean and efficient that this trip home should not be hard to take. By evening I was all set up and quite happy to be aboard. Mark, Ron and I, after a hearty meal at 6:00 P.M.—for we had not eaten for 24 hours—sat on deck, smoked and talked. We all felt good to be alive, and I said so. But I also felt a pang for those men who will lie forever on those islands, and in the depths of New Guinea, who have already been dimmed in our thoughts, and forgotten by much of the world. Yes, how fortunate and good to be alive and to be on our way home.

To top the evening off splendidly, I received two well-timed packages and five letters. Packages were from home and contained canvas shoes, which are comfortable wearing instead of combat boots, and a timely, fairly bursting box of candy.

Two letters were from home. One had a clipping in it showing the Ft. Dix separation center. It said one out of every five soldiers was discharged from there. Mom's hope, that one of these letters would be the last, is coming true. It's beautiful the way everything is working out.

Got a letter from Stahl who is a civilian now. He hoped that my "plight and situation" worked out satisfactorily. Took him 10 days to get home, six days in Stoneman, flew to Newark—then to the Gap—and discharged October 22nd.

The ship is refueling out in the bay. Soon we will leave Japan, probably tonight or even this afternoon. The great, white, decapitated head of Fuji floating in the mists will fade in the distance, as will my overseas life, as each passing inch, yard, mile brings me closer to home.

We are taking the northern route to Seattle, and I anticipate it will be cold this time of year. The trip is expected to take 10 to 15 days, depending on wind and weather.

Spent this morning discarding several books. I felt as if I were destroying a part of myself. They have been old, faithful friends, and I have carried them far. However, I must disembark with a lighter load or else I shall have extreme difficulty. These books make up a good part of the load I carry. I could not bring myself to part with *Cock on the Ridge,* because it is good poetry and from Miss Sophian, nor the little book of "Composers" which Enid's mother sent me. I still have half my books left, and those I will get home with me one way or another. And now to keep busy for the rest of this trip, reading, sleeping, playing bridge and living in the wonderful aura of anticipation of home.

November 16

At this moment I am sitting in the telephone building of Vancouver Barracks, waiting for my call home to come through.

Our trip from Japan was long but not unpleasant. We made about 400 miles on good days. During the roughest day of the storm we ran into, we only made 210. Leaving Japan we sailed north, skirting the Aleutian Islands by only 250 miles, running into storms on the way. The weather was bitter cold, the seas gray and rough, and a loud and mournful wind whistled through the rigging. For three days the only time we went on deck was returning to our hold after meals. The ship heavily rocked and pitched, and sometimes she would shudder as if she were some wallowing animal receiving mortal blows, or some fish fighting a hook.

When we first hit the storm area and the first wave broke over the side, water poured into the hatch from a loose hatchcover. At the same time the ship shuddered as if she had hit something solid. This combination created an image in our minds that we had struck something and were leaking. Everyone dashed for his life preserver, but a moment later we were feeling a little foolish. That was the beginning of the roughest sea I have ever sailed. I was slightly ill a few times, but for the most part I took it rather well. Many of the fellows really suffered, especially Muscles and Blanco. I spent my spare time playing bridge with Seth, Mark and Ron, and reading *War and Peace*—a marvelous book with some fascinating ideas on history. Meanwhile the sea roared through sunless, gloomy, moaning days. I was glad when we got away from the Aleutians and into calmer seas and warmer weather. That also meant sleep. For three nights the pitching and rolling of the ship made sleep impossible in No. 1 hold.

While we were at sea, our destination was changed from Seattle to Portland. And so, after uneventful days filled with talk of home and food, etc., on the morning of the 15th we reached the Columbia Basin and proceeded up the Columbia River. Once we started inland, a general feeling of tension grew. Our suppressed exuberance seemed to churn the entire ship. The green and gold hills on both banks of the river were fascinating to eyes that had not seen a change in season for so long. The evergreens, actually austere and green, seemed lush and rich, while other trees trimmed the hills in gold.

Here and there on the banks of the ———— [*At this point, my writing was interrupted by my phone call home.*]

I have just finished talking to the family. I was so excited I don't know if I can remember half of what I said, but it was utterly wonderful—how can one really describe these feelings?

Babs answered the phone as she was the only one at home. She started to cry, and all she could say for a whole minute was, "It's so wonderful to hear your voice"—over and over. Finally I told her where I was, and that I had a kimono for her, and other little bits of information that flew in and out of my head. She sounded so grown up. Then while we were talking, both of us wonderfully excited, I heard her call, "Mom, it's Sy," and then Mother's voice asked how I was, and then she said that she was too excited to talk and that Dad would talk to me. He sounded calm and the same as ever, but I bet he actually wasn't so calm. He asked me a lot of questions, how I was, where I was, how long it would take me to get home. And then he told me the surprising news that they had just returned from Bermuda!! It looks like all of us are coming home from overseas! (I just finished telling Ron and Mark about the call, which relieves some of the tension. Mark just finished his call. The calls make you feel a little drunk and giddy.) Dad kept wanting to send me a railroad ticket, and I had to keep telling him that I was still in the army and that it was impossible. When I told him I would be home about December 1st, he wanted to know what was holding me back. And then he said, "Now that you've come this far—be careful." What a marvellous break that they got home just when they did. Two minutes later would have been too late. One can not put a price on the value of that five-minute phone call. And how that time flew!! Right now I feel that I'm glowing. I can just picture the post-call reaction at home. What a wonderful moment to be alive.

To get back to the Columbia River—and with considerable effort. There were picturesque hunters' shacks on the banks in small clearings. Sometimes we passed a sawmill, or a tug pulling a load of logs, or a farmhouse which nudged its way into the hills, or a fishing point.

And then it began to rain. I gratefully stood in it and watched the banks slip by for several hours. Toward early evening we approached the lighted and large Portland docks at the end of our 85-mile trip up the river. The decks were jammed with troops as we nudged our way into the berth. Norm and I were lucky, right on the rail amidships. As we drew close there was terrific tension. Everyone was abnormally quiet, and talking in whispers though not aware of it. As we drew closer we could distinguish people on the docks—and then suddenly, like the storm that follows the calm, the ship broke into the wild antics of a seething, half-hysterical mob whose roar grew with each passing moment. On the docks, held back by MPs, were all kinds of beautiful girls, civilian, WAC, Red Cross, all smiling and waving—and there were some middle-aged mothers and old men, and youngish women with children. It was a bedlam.

Amidst the joking, laughing, and screaming some of the people on the dock recognized their sons or husbands. Everybody yelled at each other, back and forth, from dock to ship. Then, there was a giant roar as the heaving lines were caught on the dock. The girls looked like dreams, American women, in American clothes, talking our own language!! A cameraman, standing on the dock in front of Norm and me took a flash photo. It was fast growing dark. The fellows started throwing things to the girls on the dock: cigarettes, Jap flags, bayonet holders, anything that came to hand.

After awhile, the troops were persuaded to get below and clear the decks. We were jammed below, but it was only a short time before

"Group 26" was called over the PA to disembark. I got my bag from on deck where we had piled them that morning, shouldered it, and with a boost onto the gangplank, crossed from the ship to the United States!

We filed into a clean, well-lit warehouse. The Red Cross girls met us there with milk, newspapers, apples, coffee—and their lovely selves. Every woman looked like a queen to us. In a moment we had all downed half-quarts of milk, and what a taste that revived. The taste of milk was like silk on our palates. We then piled into trucks driven by trim WACs. And were they fast on the comebacks with the inevitable soldiers' cracks. We were all roaring with good humor, excitement, and the pleasure of talking to American girls again. Some fellows started dancing with them in the warehouse. The repartee was fast and furious and fun.

We drove 10 miles at a fast clip to Vancouver Barracks, marvelling at the neon signs, the advertisements, the stores bursting with goods. We made jokes about this "beachhead." A "Dine and Dance" sign, flashing with red neon lights, seemed an arrow pointing to Heaven. It took our breath away to see towns so wonderfully whole, intact and healthy. The stocked window cases, new cars, people, drive-in stands, lighted windows, civilians—the richness of America burst in our faces from the first moment we left the troopship—that link from Hell to Heaven.

Upon arrival in camp we were assigned barracks. Ron and I got a double-decker. It had springs and mattresses, and the orderly room gave us a mattress cover and comforter. We dashed over to the latrine, and in 10 minutes Mark and I were taking steaming hot showers. Immediately afterwards, we were directed to a movie house where we were greeted by the Port Commander who told us that we would leave here in a few days, that we would pull no details, and then gave us a list of the comforts that are here and that had us writhing with anticipation. All this was greeted with cheers. His address was followed by an extremely good USO show. After that Mark, Ron and I went to the taproom, a treasure house of items we used to dream about. There were all kinds of ice cream, sodas, cakes, and huge, foamy pitchers of beer. This place was roaring with excited men. We demolished plenty of popcorn, and the beer kept coming by in bigger and bigger pitchers. We then went to the very comfortable service club, with its armchairs, library, games, records, etc., and there we got cold cokes through the magic of the nickel machine.

Sleeping last night was like lying on a cloud. It was torture to have to get up this morning off that soft bed and from under that comforter. But as recompense there was milk for breakfast, fresh eggs, cereal, etc., in unlimited quantities and tasting as breakfast never did overseas. While going to breakfast we bought morning papers, and there on the back page was the picture that the photographer had taken with Norm and me right in front of the multitude on the *Sea Runner*. It's a pretty good picture of me. All the fellows in the outfit recognized us and told me about it. That was a thrill.

Dinner was the steak dinner we were told about, and I must describe this meal. It contained all the ingredients we had missed for so long. First, two large pieces of tender steak, lettuce and tomatoes, fresh peas, corn, bread and butter, milk, french fries, ice cream and fresh strawberries. On the table were trays of fresh fruit—pears, apples, oranges—and my long-dreamed-of grapes. Ron and I couldn't say anything. Every once in awhile we would look up from our eating and just grin foolishly at one another.

Besides eating three immense meals today, and in addition several milk shakes, pie a la mode, more ice cream, etc.—so much that I could not swallow a crumb at this moment, I also sent a package home of all my letters and books, and bought a wristwatch in the PX. [*The wristwatch still runs, but the letters and books, so long saved and carried with great difficulty, never arrived. The diaries, however, never left my possession.*]

We are just barely beginning to get used to the wonders of this place. One can't possibly realize the richness of America unless it can be seen in comparison with the rest of this war-torn world. America is bursting with luxury, everything about it reflects this, the people, even the sidewalks. Everything is superlative and luxurious. There has been no war here, and thank goodness for that. And, of course, how good it is to be back among the people of my own country.

All the fellows are split up into various barracks, according to their prospective separation centers. We are scheduled to leave here tomorrow or the next day, and I do hope it's that soon. Especially after that memorable phone call home, there seems no limit to my anticipation. But meanwhile we are treated with kid gloves and like kings—and it's not hard to take.

November 23

My army career is fast coming to a close with each passing mile that this rocking, bouncing train covers. This marks the third day of our journey from the West Coast to our destination, Ft. Dix.

The stay at Vancouver was extremely pleasant, and we spent those five days there sleeping late and comfortably, taking passes into town at night, and eating haphazardly at all hours of all foods. I refreshed long dormant tastes with such things as oysters, salads, fruits, sodas, milk, ice cream, chow mein, pies, etc. Mark, Ron and I spent a good deal of time together, though one day Herbeck went into Portland with us. The first pass we had in the States took us into Vancouver and later Portland via easy hitchhiking. It was an incomparable thrill to see an American city lit up, blazing in neon, the stores, each a minor wonder in itself, and the people energetic and healthy.

There was such an abundance of places and activities that we could, at first, only walk the streets, gape, and feel absolutely wonderful and transported to a new world. Going into a civilian clothing store was great fun. The variety of clothes to wear, of colors and styles, made a pleasing sight to these eyes long inured to drab green. We went bowling, to movies, ate and ate—and then ate, and even went to a USO dance where we all danced. We broke into the ways of American life again. I found one rather pleasant girl (who turned out to be the president of the club) and spent most of the evening with her. Later a gang of us went out for sodas after the dance. That Alaskan waitress who looked and acted like Ann Sothern was great fun. It was like old times.

It was not easy for us to talk or act civilly. We all had to keep a sharp check on our language, and sometimes were awkward gaps in the conversation. But on the whole, people were more than civil to us, and, best of all, the army left us completely alone. In a few days we were wearing our ribbons and overseas stripes (I have twice sewed on the stripes in the wrong spot) and began really feeling like returnees. This short period of time gave us the chance to convert from our rough army life and ways to the more careful manner and luxurious life of civilians. We have not found it a difficult problem (so far), but at times we are awkward, feel strange and estranged, and stand amazed.

One thing marred these few days. Early one evening in Portland, after I came out of a movie, I had a familiar attack of chills and fever, along with pain in the small of the back, the fatigue, and all the rest of it. I left Mark and Ron early and proceeded back to camp. I was quite tired by the time I had walked as far as the USO in Vancouver from the bus stop, and I still had ¾'s hour walk to go. So I stopped at the USO to recover a bit from the attack, and I also gave myself the pleasure of playing Schubert's "Unfinished," the first classical music I've heard in many months. The sound was poor, as was the atmosphere for Schubert, but I enjoyed hearing it again.

Returning to the barracks after a dark, chilly walk, I was informed that we were to leave the next night at 11:00 P.M. The next day found me recovered and living in anticipation of making this last big trip. Of course we did not leave at 11:00. At 2:30 A.M. the trucks came, we loaded up and were quickly driven to a waiting train. The cars were Pullmans, invitingly made up with new, crisp, white sheets and pillows, and by 4:00 A.M.

Mark, Ron and I were gratefully in bed. At 5:10 A.M. we started this last big lap of our long voyage home. We didn't get up till noon, though I slept fitfully.

It has been tiring riding on the train, mainly because I experienced another attack yesterday, a severe one, of extreme chills and, later, fever. This one lasted about six hours and then abated by degrees throughout the night and into the next morning. Whether or not these are malaria attacks I do not know, though they may well be. Then, it might be that jaundice acting up. The backache and almost complete exhaustion are particularly annoying because they continue after the chills and fever abate. I shall try to find out what I have at Dix.

Right now we have completed more than half our trip cross-country. We are about 100 miles from Minneapolis, our next stop. After spending nearly a day crossing Washington, we cut across Idaho, Montana, North Dakota and Minnesota. Travelling an extreme northern route, we are, at points, only short distances from the Canadian border, but we have now turned south.

The country we have seen is desolate and drab for the most part, and one state looks much like another. There is nothing but huge expanses of wasteland or farmlands shrouded in winter frost and gloom. The thin layer of snow and morning frost make a novel sight; the weather is quite cold. Last night it was only 10 above zero. These cars are well-heated, and so we have not really experienced the cold, only seen it through the double panes of glass. It looks uncomfortable. Soon we will reach territory more familiar to our eyes. We are all East Coast fellows on the train, from New York City or other parts of the State. Our speed has been irregular. During our frequent stops we manage to augment our meals with hasty purchases. We pour from the train as if we were making a beachhead. Anyway, we have a supply of oranges, cakes, and I even bought a mince pie because it was Thanksgiving and I couldn't get any other except pumpkin. I don't really like pumpkin or mince. Skivvy came around with some "Thanksgiving cheer" in a bottle, looking for fellows in our outfit who are on the train. There are about 45 of us. Next stop at Minny we shall try to get milk and cokes.

I have been able to occupy some of these long hours reading *Moby Dick* by Melville, and enjoying it when I can concentrate. It is a wonderful feeling knowing each jounce is one less and brings us closer to a discharge from the army and to home. I still can't sleep two in a bed, and I had an uncomfortable night last night with only three hours of fitful sleep. Tomorrow I get the top bunk again; that will be a relief. That should be the last night of this trip, I hope.

Another few weeks, days rather, and this shall all be behind me. Roll on you barren hills, faster and faster.

November 26

Tonight I wait for my name to be placed upon the roster which will start my processing for discharge. How long I have waited to write these words.

The trip on the train, immediately after my last entry, proved to be very uncomfortable. I was ill with a severe malaria attack. I was taken with the symptomatic chills, fever, fatigue, pain and nausea. It became so bad that Mark called a doctor who examined me and pronounced "malaria." I stayed in bed late mornings, ate little, took doses of atabrine. [*I remember that one morning an officer came to see me while I remained in bed. He said that I was too ill to continue the trip, and that at the next stop close to an army hospital, I would be taken off the train. I gripped the sides of the berth and said, "Sir, I am going home. You will have to blast me out of this bed." He nodded, turned and left, and I heard nothing more. I was absolutely determined that nothing, no one would delay my return home.*] I remained ill enough to warrant calling an ambulance to meet me at Fort Dix. However, fortunately, the malaria attack subsided the day we arrived at Dix, and I was able to walk under my own power and to carry my gear, not without some difficulty.

We were put through a fast reception of turning in gear and service records. Then we were transported to those familiar barracks that so long ago looked so bare and now seemed luxurious. I phoned home last night and spoke to Mom and Dad, telling them I would be back by Friday, discharged and a civilian. It was, without saying, wonderful to talk to them. They want to meet me at Penn Station when I get in.

So we spend our time simply waiting for that final roster posting and processing to begin. Blanco, Mark, and Ron Flynn have already been posted. At any rate, it should only be a matter of four more days at the most. They will be long ones.

Epilogue

Following my discharge from the U.S. Army on November 28, 1945, barracks bag on my shoulder for the last time, and a souvenir Japanese rifle over the other shoulder, I boarded the train for the short ride to Pennsylvania Station in Manhattan. Soon after my arrival I caught sight of my parents and sister, who were peering into the crowd and waiting for me. The long dream of my return began to transform into reality. After our effusive embraces, my father drove us up Riverside Drive, along the Hudson River, to our apartment in upper Manhattan, in Inwood. I recall that during much of the drive I was silent, marveling at the overwhelming solidity of New York. It was early evening and the city seemed festooned with lights, and then, close to home, I saw the George Washington Bridge spanning the dark river with a bracelet of light. Among familiar sights, with my family around me, I knew I was home; but the strangeness and alienation I felt, and that I expected would pass, never did.

Good as it was to be home, I soon found out that just as I had outgrown my old civilian clothes, I had also outgrown the past. Having no clothes that fit me, and until I could purchase a new wardrobe, I continued to wear my beribboned uniform, with its hash marks for overseas service up the left sleeve. My fourteen-year-old sister looked at me in awe; my parents were circumspect and tentative as they observed their transformed son, who sometimes went to bed at 8 P.M. with malaria's chills and fevers, who started and crouched at sudden sounds, who anxiously looked skyward at the sound of passing planes, and who, when not silent, picked his words carefully lest he step on a verbal land mine and explode the expletives and obscenities of army language.

My repatriation took a bizarre turn when, on several occasions, neighborhood people looked at me with startled expressions. It seems another soldier named S. Kahn, a Bronx resident, had been killed during the war, and some people assumed I was the casualty. Somehow this confusion of identity seemed appropriate to my feelings during those early days of transition to civilian life. I sometimes felt like a ghost of my former self in a distant life.

Foxhole Dream on Biak Materializes for Vets

Between Japanese air raids on lonely Biak Island of the South Pacific in June 1944, a couple of men of the Third Platoon, 244th Port Co., sat in their foxholes and thought it would be a good idea to have a reunion when the "war is over and we're out of this mess."

Their dreams were realized last night when 24 veterans of the platoon gathered with their wives and girl friends in the Rathskeller Room at Hotel Markeen for their first annual dinner.

While most of the veterans came from other cities, seven are from the Buffalo area. They are Robert C. Colby, Charles E. Herbeck and Andrew S. Monroe, all of Kenmore, and Andrew N. Denison, Andrew DiPirro, Theodore Dzielski and Herbert W. Hepple of Buffalo.

Each member of the group paid into a fund five guilders (about $2.50) each month while overseas. The money was sent to Mr. and Mrs. Charles Herbeck, Sr., 38 Victoria Ave., Kenmore, who banked the money. Last night the sum had reached $525.

The 24 members trained together in Pennsylvania and California, later serving overseas in Australia, on New Guinea, Biak and Luzon, and at Yokohama. During 26 months overseas they were subjected to 308 enemy air raids.

Newspaper account of the Buffalo, N.Y., reunion of the Third Platoon of the 244th Port Company, Aug. 31, 1946.

GREETINGS

★

Nope, not from the President this time, mates. We hope that this banquet will surpass the expectations that we all dreamed of on Biak Island where the idea originated. You will not be bored by after-dinner speakers as our program is very simple . . . eat, drink, dance and be merry. So let's get on the ball and have fun!

From banquet program.

Twenty of the twenty-four New York veterans attending the reunion banquet in Buffalo, N.Y., Aug. 31, 1946. Memory has disassociated some names and faces. From left to right, standing: 2d, Charles Fitch; 3d, Henry Sweeney; 5th, Arthur Beal; 6th, James Henehan; 7th, Charles Herbeck; 8th, Andrew DiPirro; 9th, Robert Colby. From left to right, seated: 2d, Ronald Flynn; 3d, James Illes; 5th, Arthur Monroe; 6th, Richard Tipple; 7th, Andrew Norman Denison; 8th, William Hyer; 9th, Sy Kahn; 10th, Raymond Gillis.

Sy Kahn (l.) and Norm Denison at the reunion of the 244th Port Company, Buffalo, N.Y., Aug. 31, 1946.

I found myself also out of touch with the immediate past. None of my army friends lived nearby, and I maintained contact only with Norm Denison. Eventually I was best man at his wedding. There was one reunion of 244th Company veterans held in Buffalo, New York, on August 31, 1946. The plans for it had begun on Biak Island, and those of us interested, mainly from New York State, and particularly Buffalo, had made monthly contributions during the war for that eventual celebration. Following that happy event, except for Denison, I had no further contact with survivors of the 244th. Several years later, Denison's marriage having gone asunder, as did so many postwar marriages, including my own, even Denison and I lost touch in the thickets of our civilian lives. Currently I know nothing about any soldier with whom I served, and sometimes I wonder how many are still alive. However, because of my recent work on my war diaries, they are all reenlivened in my mind, and I remember them as they were.

As for my small family whom I loved and who helped to sustain me during the war, and whose letters and image kept my dream of home alive, they were soon gone. From the moment of my return my mother became increasingly ill with the complications of diabetes. In June 1948, I hurried from my graduation ceremonies at the University of Pennsylvania in Philadelphia to my mother's bedside in a New York City hospital, as I had done so often during those undergraduate college years while her health had deteriorated in a dreadful downward spiral. I arrived within hours of the university ceremony to find her in a terminal coma. Early the next morning she died; she was forty-seven. Her mother, my only living grandparent, with whom I shared a deep affection, died a few years later; and then, within an even shorter time, my father died at age fifty-five. My sister, Barbara Kahn Mayes, shortly after our mother's death, went with her husband to live in Tucson, Arizona, where she continues to reside.

Among my friends before the war, and during it, I maintain contact only with two. More than likely it might have been three. Edith Herbst Demby, a young married teacher, who had been a close friend, died suddenly of spinal meningitis early in the 1950s. Carolyn Heilbrun continues an ever-expanding career as an eminent scholar, feminist, and author, following her distinguished tenure as professor of English at Columbia University. Dale Cook married in 1949, and she and her husband reside in New Zealand. After decades of silence, following the cessation of our correspondence in 1952, we again correspond, but we have not seen each other since the day I left Sydney, Australia, in 1943.

I make these closing comments on my World War II diaries on the evening of the fiftieth anniversary of the attack on Pearl Harbor. This morning I watched the televised tributes and ceremonies that took place on the memorial that spans the battleship *Arizona*'s sunken hull, and I was particularly moved by the fact that three or four times each minute a drop of oil seeps to the surface from the *Arizona,* and by the image of those droplets spreading on the water's surface in a sheen of rainbow colors. It seems to me that the war itself, although concluded forty-six years ago, has not ended. Characteristically, returning soldiers kept silent about their experiences, though some retailed to their friends and family amusing or comic incidents and stories. Also, we were anxious to recover and to get on with our civilian lives. But like the *Arizona* sunk in Pearl Harbor's shallow water, the war remained just below the surface of our minds, and for its veterans continues to release the droplets of flashback and memory.

The war jarred and altered every American life. My diary, long ignored, offers some record of how and why that happened. If there are other diaries, as well there may be, I hope they too will surface to amplify the record and to display the colors of who we were, what we experienced, and who we became.

Appendix

495th PORT BATTALION
APO 4759, c/o Postmaster
San Francisco, California

27 August 1943

This letter was received by me and I am sure that all men in the battalion would like to have a copy of it.

LESTER R. DORFMAN
Warrant Officer (jg), USA,
Special Services Officer.

UNSUNG HEROES
by
Pfc. Thomas Haynes
245th Port Co.

Out of this war-torn nation comes an outfit whose future destiny may challenge the chapters of history in ages to come. This outfit, still in its infancy, is known as the Port Battalion.

When this great nation of ours was confronted with the task of defending global peace, she also was forced to place able-bodied manpower on foreign soil. This in turn led to one dynamic answer—war. When war did strike its deadly blow, men and materials were sent to the defense of helpless, unprepared allies.

Today, as the conflict is at its climax, more materials have to be sent every day to far-flung corners of the world. This is where Port Battalions play their most important role. Men from all walks of life start their new vocation with vigorous effort to first, become soldiers and second, to become skilled and capable of loading and discharging ships loaded with vital materials at ports abroad.

These same men are taught the Army's Ten Commandments in addition to their technical fields. Hard hours of drilling, hiking, and learning to defend themselves, is but a minor detail compared to future accomplishments. Hence, when basic training is completed the men of the Port Battalion are taken to a port where they learn winch operating, longshoremanship, and in general the complete fundamentals of loading a ship properly.

A great majority of the American public knows little of the enterprises that are a constant burden to these men. Unsung in their acts of patriotism and glory, their slogan is cherished among their outfits, namely, "The Supplies Must Get Thru Regardless of How or What the Cost of Human Annihilation." Oftimes they are sent to foreign outposts unaware of what difficulties and obstacles are ahead of them, but in true American fashion they land as pioneers, and work day and night until their destined port is their home. Here happy and content they feed the life-line of the Armies. This same life-line that brought devastation and humility to great nations and world conquerors. This life-line is based on one title and title alone—Supply. Without supplies the power of a mighty nation could and would collapse in a short time.

But then the inevitable question arises. "Who are these men? Are they trained to do this work, or has it been their life's occupation?"

No, they were men who were formerly clerks, salesmen, students, businessmen or laborers. But by constant training they were taught how to handle cargo with the utmost facility.

Prior to the inauguration of the Port Battalion men who were unskilled and incapable handled the cargo, and most times there were casualties and heavy losses of equipment. Today though, by the great genius of far superior brains, there came forth the Port Battalions to meet and correct the errors of their forbears. Hence, when ships are to be loaded or discharged today, there is a skill and workmanship uncompared to former times. We do not condemn or criticize these men before us, because we understand the fact that they were not trained in that line. The training and connection with a Port Battalion leaves us no alternative but to believe that it is one of the greatest ideas of modern warfare and rapid transit service.

One point that comes to our mind is, "What happens when actual bombing or combat comes?" This question was also answered by our officers. When actual bombing or strafing comes our way: we are to meet it with the same calmness and coolness as we would on the field of battle.

Under fire we might lose some men, but our teaching enables us to think fast, therefore preventing a heavier list of casualties.

So in an untiring and undying tribute to the officers and enlisted men we uphold the creed of the Port Battalions and what it stands for.

Someday, somewhere, whether it be in San Francisco, Chicago, or New York, the gold and crimson banner of the 495th Port Bn. will wave with a wreath of glory for the mission she will complete after the war clouds of this nation will drift into peaceful oblivion.

Unsung, least heard of, but loyal to the colors and banner she serves, we salute you—Port Battalions.

Note: Copies of this hyperbolic letter were distributed to the 495th Port Battalion shortly before the outfit embarked for overseas duty. As might be guessed, the reaction to the letter was mixed, but it is an example of the rhetoric, emotion and patriotism often characteristic of those times. As for us, the full reality of the war was still thousands of miles beyond the western horizon, and that reality was to prove quite different from that suggested by the letter.

THE LORD'S PRAYER   THE TEN COMMANDMENTS

(Translated from the English into the tongue of the natives of New Guinea, Pidgin English)

PRAYER BILONG BIG MASTER

Fader ubilong mipella
Ustopalong Heaven,
All hearem talk about U.
Kingdom bilong U I kum
Along ground allsame along Heaven.
Give mipella Kai Kai alongday
Forgive wrong bilong mipella
Allsame mi forgive wrong alone nothapella.
Take along us not to wrongdo
Mipella folla U away from wrong
Upella bilong Kingdom cum
Same power. Same Glory
Allsame now. Allsame Time.   Amen.

COMMANDMENTS MIPELLA DO

1. Man I got onepella God, Ino got nothapella God
2. Man Ino try make nothapella God
3. Man Ino swear
4. Man I keep No. 1 day, No. 1 day bilong Big Master
5. Man I good along. Fader, good along mimma
6. Man Ino kill
7. Man Ino take Mary bilong nothaman
8. Man Ino steal
9. Man Ino lie along nothapella. I talk tru all time
10. Man I see good something bilong notha man, Ino wantim alltime.

Presented at Services, Sunday, 20 February 1944, by Chaplain Walter D. Owen, 495th Port Battalion.

Note: Because of the great number of languages and dialects spoken by the Melanesians, the natives of New Guinea and its offshore islands, prewar missionaries and white traders devised Pidgin English as a common language. This language not only facilitated communication between foreigners and New Guinea natives but also among the local tribes. Pidgin English was not, of course, "the tongue of the natives" in any indigenous sense. Tribes had their own languages. In any case, few American soldiers knew, or had reason to learn and use, Pidgin.

FRONT LINES

PHILIPPINES ARE INVADED

Friday, 20 October [1944], 10 AM
—Three years after the fall of Corrigedor the greatest amphibious task force in the Southwest Pacific landed once again on Philippine soil. The forces were reported as having driven 750 yards inland in the face of mortar opposition. It was reported that all beaches have been secured and that the third and fourth waves have gone ashore. The landing was made on Leyte, 340 miles from Manila. The land operation was supported by bombers and naval warships.

An eye-witness account to the *New York Times* by war correspondent Frank Gluckhorn stated that the American flag was once again on Philippine soil as wave after wave of experienced Southwest Pacific jungle fighters made their landing on Leyte, which is above Mindanao and above [sic] Luzon.

A convoy of more that 1500 vessels of every description left Dutch New Guinea Friday, October 13. They hovered in the vicinity of the central Philippines for three days during which time carrier-based planes pounded targets in the Philippines. The troops landed without opposition. They advanced inland toward the airdrome in 15 minutes. The troops progressed under heavy mortar bombardment. It was reported that by nightfall more troops will have landed on Leyte Island than on D-Day in Europe. The Philippines have been under heavy bombardment for 14 days; while the great task force waited in the vicinity of the central Philippines for a favorable [change] in the weather. A task force carried the cream of American troops ashore.

GENERAL MacARTHUR WITH TASK FORCE

General MacArthur came personally with the task force aboard the cruiser Nashville. He was accompanied by Sergio Osmena, president of the Philippines. General MacArthur said, "American forces are on Philippine soil once again." He told the Filipinos that the force came dedicated to the task of destroying enemy control "over your lives. At my side," he said, "is Sergio Osmena." He called upon a supreme effort by the Filipinos to let the enemy know that an enraged populace faced them from within as well as a force from without.

Note: Although our company did not participate in the initial invasion of the Philippines on Leyte, news of this action was received with jubilation. The Leyte landing marked the culmination of the long drive back from Australia and New Guinea to retake the Philippines. Three months later the 244th sailed into Lingayen Gulf and participated in the D-day landing on Luzon. Manila, Bataan, and Corregidor to the south would eventually fall.

CONFIDENTIAL

FIELD ORDERS	)	
	:	244th Port Company
NUMBER 1	)	APO 159
		25 December 1944

MISSION:

a. This unit is attached to the 543d EB & SR for operations in the objective area. The mission of this unit is to furnish labor and supervisory personnel for unloading of LCT's, LCM's, LSM's, and self-propelled barges.

DEFENSE PLAN:

a. The 244th Port Company under the 543d EB & SR is responsible for beach and dump defense and will furnish necessary air sentinels to assure timely warning of imminent air attack.

b. All personnel will dig foxholes with overhead cover at the first opportunity and will sleep therein until instructions are issued to the contrary. The construction of such foxholes will not interfere with the jobs to be done.

c. Work will not cease at the sounding of RED ALERT, but will continue until the beach is actually attacked. Work on the ships will never cease except to seek individual protection against direct attack.

d. Work will cease to defend against ground attack only on the order of the Shore Party CO, except that in an emergency, the CO of this unit will take the necessary action for defense.

e. All personnel will have their individual weapons readily available at all times.

f. A shell will not be kept in the chamber of any piece unless hostile action is unquestionably imminent. There will be no firing or throwing of grenades except against a positively identified enemy. BE SURE BEFORE YOU FIRE AT NIGHT ESPECIALLY. STAY IN YOUR FOXHOLE AT NIGHT, FOR YOU MIGHT BE TAKEN FOR A JAP.

g. On order of the Shore Commander, necessary men for line combat will be drawn from the company.

ALERTS:

a. Navy:
Flash Red: Air attack imminent. (Corresponds to Army Red Alert)
Flash Blue: Air attack probable. (Corresponds to Army Yellow Alert)
Flash White: All Clear. (Corresponds to Army All Clear)

b. Army:
Normal: No enemy or unidentified targets.
Yellow: Unidentified aircraft twenty (20) minutes from defended area.
Red: Enemy or unidentified aircraft ten (10) minutes from defended area.

WARNINGS:

Yellow Alert: No alert will be sounded.
Red Alert: Selected Bofers guns will alert adjacent units by firing three (3) rounds at one second intervals. This warning will be spread by three (3) short blasts of sirens or Klaxons. NO MAN IN THIS UNIT WILL USE A FIREARM TO SOUND THIS ALARM.
All Clear: Selected Bofers guns will fire one (1) round to indicate "All Clear." Within the company area one long blast on a whistle will indicate "All Clear." NO MAN WILL DISCHARGE A FIREARM TO SOUND "ALL CLEAR."

FIRE CONTROL:

The men in this unit will not fire upon hostile aircraft except when the unit is in the immediate vicinity of a low strafing attack. At this time extreme care must be taken that ground installations and personnel are not hit. UNDER NO CIRCUMSTANCES WILL MEN FIRE AT PLANES WHEN IN THE VICINITY OF AAA DEFENSES.

PASSIVE DEFENSE:

a. All men will take maximum advantage of cover, dispersion, and camouflage.
b. Foxholes and slit trenches, with overhead cover, will be dug to protect personnel from aerial bombs and falling flak.

UNIFORM:

1. CLOTHING FOR VOYAGE:
The uniform for embarkation and the voyage will be cotton khaki. The uniform, HBT, impregnated, carried in the jungle pack during the voyage, will be worn upon debarkation. After changing to HBT the cotton uniform will be placed in the jungle pack. Jungle packs of sections will be tied together and placed in a unit dump in the bivouac area, where guards will be posted. Leggins need not be worn after embarking upon the ship, but till further orders the uniform will be worn properly, with sleeves rolled DOWN, and all buttons buttoned. Section leaders will be held responsible for the carrying out of all orders for the men in their sections.
2. ON PERSON:
Uniform, HBT, impregnated
Carbine
Gas Mask
1 protective cover   )

1 tube protective ointment) Carried in Gas Mask Cover.
1 eye shield   )
Helmet, steel with liner
Shoes, Service
Leggins
Belt, pistol, with filled ammo pouches.
Canteen, with cup (Filled with water)
Knife, hunting (if desired)
Kit, first aid, jungle
Packet, first aid
Flashlight (if issued or desired)
Machete
Tool, entrenching (shovel or pick)

IN JUNGLE PACK:

1 Poncho or raincoat
1 Food bag
1 pair socks, impregnated
2 pair socks, at least
1 Uniform, HBT impregnated
3 Handkerchiefs
1 Pair shoes or jungle boots
1 Bath towel
Underwear
1 Mess kit complete
Toilet Articles
Writing material
Cigarettes and smoking tobacco
Gloves, working
1 Protective Cover

IN JUNGLE HAMMOCK:

Flotation bladder
Blankets

NOTE: Take sufficient clothing to last you for at least a month, for it is not expected that our duffle bags will arrive much before S + 18. Soap will be issued for washing clothing.

CHEMICAL WARFARE:

Gas masks will bear the name and serial number of the owner. Upon receipt of orders from the Division Commander, gas masks will be collected and kept in the company supply till needed.

Each individual will land equipped with a waterproofed gas mask which will remain waterproofed until required to be worn. The hose clamp will be removed as soon as the possibility of immersion in water is past.

SANITATION AND HYGIENE:

Keeping clean is going to be a bit difficult for the first few days, however, from aerial photos of the area we are going into, there are sufficient rivers from which to obtain water to wash. Each man will be expected to keep his body and clothing as clean as possible. No man will grow a beard, but will shave daily. Remember those fox-holes are kind of crowded sometimes, and you might get scratched on somebody's whiskers.

The water supply at our destination will not be safe for drinking till chlorinated. The 6th Division has experienced engineers chlorinating water, so the chlorine is not noticeable. So play safe, and drink only water that has been chlorinated.

Malaria regulations will be stringent and fully enforced. The uniform will be worn properly. If you still don't know how to wear it properly, see your section sergeant. Leggins will be worn at all times on shore.

Typhus is very prevailant [sic] in the area we are to occupy. Impregnated clothing will be in your possession so use it. The impregnation solution consists of a mixture containing G.I. soap, so be sure and wear at least undershorts. Typhus fatalities are very high, so take all precautions available.

ROBERT O. REINHARDT,
Captain, TC, Commanding

Note: These field orders were distributed to the men while waiting at Sansapor, New Guinea, to board a convoy ship for the invasion of Luzon in the Philippines.

CARGO CONTROL SECTION
SHORE PARTY
543d ENGINEER BOAT & SHORE REGIMENT

CONFIDENTIAL

22 December 1944
A. P. O. 159

SUBJECT : Labor Detail Plan (FAR SHORE)
TO : Commanding Officers 294th Port Co., 244th Port Co., APO 159

1. The plan for organization of labor details, and the manner in which they report, of far shore S day is outlined below:

Off in charge	NCO		Slot Detail	Orgn
Capt Jackson	Cpl Hambley	W	1 Off:1 NCO:50 EM	294th Port
Capt Long	Sgt Herbert	O	1 Off:1 NCO:50 EM	294th Port
Capt Knight	Sgt Fisek	S	1 Off:1 NCO:45 EM	244th Port
Lt Arden	Sgt Stacey	P	1 Off:1 NCO:45 EM	244th Port
Lt Huntoon	Sgt Munyer	K	1 Off:1 NCO:50 EM	294th Port
Lt Usoskin	Cpl Patrick	C	1 Off:1 NCO:45 EM	244th Port
Lt Trentacoste	S/Sgt Kearnes	L	1 Off:1 NCO:45 EM	244th Port

2. Details will be organized as shown above. All details will be organized and assigned before departure from near shore, and every individual will be unquestionably familiar with projected location and relative position, Officer and NCO in charge, of the slot at which his detail is to work.

3. When organizations reach the beach at the far shore, they will proceed under company direction to their assigned bivouac area. There they will drop all equipment immediately, and proceed under direction of Officers in charge of details to Cargo Control CP, where they will report either to Capt. Rodgers, Lt Martin, or M/Sgt Stewart. From here details will be dispatched to their slots. If for any reason, either of the three of these individuals cannot be located, report direct to their assigned slot, and inform Officer in charge that they are reporting direct.

4. a. When details report to slots they will be furnished with rations and water, arms details will not return to bivouac area, nor be released for any purpose except by O in C.

   b. Do not quit work for air raids unless told to do so by O in C or O in C detail.

DISTR: 1 Ea Indiv 294th, 244th Port Co.

2 Ea Orgn concerned
1 Ea S/T Off.

PAUL B. RODGERS, Jr.
Captain, CE
Adm Off

WHEN FIRST REPORTING, DETAILS WILL REPORT TO CARGO CONTROL CP _____

TO Captain Rodgers, or Lt. Martin, M/Sgt. Stewart, in the order named. If you cannot locate either of these individuals at CP then you are to report direct to the slot to which you are assigned. However, all of these individuals will be present unless they have become casualties, so look thoroughly for them at CP2 before proceeding to your slot.

BE SURE YOU KNOW YOUR JOB

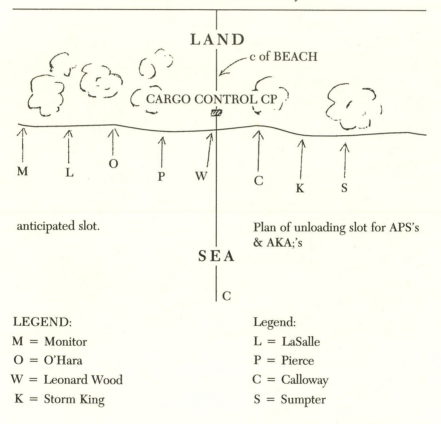

LAND

c of BEACH

CARGO CONTROL CP

M   L   O   P   W   C   K   S

anticipated slot.

Plan of unloading slot for APS's & AKA;'s

SEA

C

LEGEND:

M = Monitor

O = O'Hara

W = Leonard Wood

K = Storm King

Legend:

L = LaSalle

P = Pierce

C = Calloway

S = Sumpter

Note: These orders and plans were shared by company officers with noncommissioned officers in preparation for the D-day landing on Luzon, January 9, 1945. During the actual landing, I was in charge of "Boat Team 9," a unit of seventeen men.

Published Weekly by the 373rd Port Battalion TC 1 July, 1945

244TH NEWS

Now it can be told! At last the censorship restrictions have been lifted on what can be said about personal experiences 'South of the Equator'. Result: The volumes of outgoing mail have reached an all time high . . . Most of the boys can write a novel on the rugged Cape Gloucester campaign. When and if they run out of New Britain palaver they can fall back on 'Bloody Biak' or even Aitape. . . . All the reenforcements can talk about is the voyage of the Sea Star (though I don't see why). According to them that liquid safari was rougher than Gloucester or Biak combined (true, how true). Our worthy censor won't need scissors to go through this new crop of mail, a shovel will be more in order. . . . Homeward bound are our four "high point" men, Joss Joslyn, Mike Hudaick, Pete Peterson, and Leo Walsh. Joss had 97 points, while the others had 98 each. The point system is off to a good start. . . . Also heading for the States is George Milligan. George is over the 40 year age limit now set for automatic discharge. Don't worry if you don't go home right away on the point system. After you hit the 40 year mark the Army can't hold you for more than 90 days (O Yea)! . . . Spoked by Red Glasgow, the Birmingham Bullet, the fast 244th basketball quintet is now clicking smoothly in practice sessions. The boys are primed to top any and all competition in Base M. . . . Al Berchin, the Bronx pundit, is now on detached service in Manila. . . . Ed Odom's section is very quiet and peaceful these days. From "Buffalo" Hudaick, just before he left us last week, came this famous last word, 'REST!'

Pfc Sol Miller, Reporter for the 244th

Note: In this weekly bulletin, news of each company was shared. The column dealing with the 244th is of particular interest because the replacements mentioned indicate the vacancies created by our ongoing casualties, and because of the specific reference to my foxhole buddy and friend, George Milligan, whose forty years qualified him for replacement.

Foxhole Dream on Biak Materializes for Vets

Between Japanese air raids on lonely Biak Island of the South Pacific in June 1944, a couple of men of the Third Platoon, 244th Port Co., sat in their foxholes and thought it would be a good idea to have a reunion when the "war is over and we're out of this mess."

Their dreams were realized last night when 24 veterans of the platoon gathered with their wives and girl friends in the Rathskeller Room at Hotel Markeen for their first annual dinner.

While most of the veterans came from other cities, seven are from the Buffalo area. They are Robert C. Colby, Charles E. Herbeck and Andrew S. Monroe, all of Kenmore, and Andrew N. Denison, Andrew DiPirro, Theodore Dzielski and Herbert W. Heffle of Buffalo.

Each member of the group paid into a fund five guilders (about $2.50) each month while overseas. The money was sent to Mr. and Mrs. Charles Herbeck, Sr., 38 Victoria Ave., Kenmore, who banked the money. Last night the sum had reached $525.

The 24 members trained together in Pennsylvania and California, later serving overseas in Australia, on New Guinea, Biak and Luzon, and at Yokohama. During 26 months overseas they were subjected to 308 enemy air raids. [*Buffalo Courier-Express* Sunday, Sept. 1, 1946]

GREETINGS

Nope, not from the President this time, mates. We hope
that this banquet will surpass the expectations that we all
dreamed of on Biak Island where the idea originated. You
will not be bored by after-dinner speakers as our program is
very simple . . . eat, drink, dance, and be merry. So let's get
on the ball and have fun!

Note: This occasion marked the first and only reunion of veterans of the 3d platoon, 244th Port Company. That evening, after the festivities, I experienced a severe attack of malaria's chills and fevers which vividly recalled my years in the South Pacific. After about three more years of these intermittent symptoms, the attacks ceased.

Index

Some names in the index are incomplete and sometimes lack designation of rank. These men are listed as "EM" (enlisted man). In these cases, the diary and military archival rosters fail to give complete information, and memory, unfortunately, after fifty years cannot with accuracy recall full names and rank.

Professor Emeritus Sy M. Kahn earned his Ph.D. in American and English Literature at the University of Wisconsin in 1957. After thirty-seven years of teaching at various colleges and universities, both in the United States and Europe, including twenty-three years as professor of English and drama at the University of the Pacific, he was awarded the Order of the Pacific, the university's highest academic honor. At this time the Fulbright Commission cited Professor Kahn as a "sensitive and judicious American" for advancing international understanding during his tenure as professor of American literature with four Fulbright grants to universities in Greece, Poland, Austria, and Portugal.

Dr. Kahn is the author of six books of poetry, editor of a book of essays and of a selection of poems by Harry Crosby, and has published thirty-seven scholarly articles in literary journals, encyclopedias, and books of literary criticism. He has written two produced plays and has directed more than three hundred and fifty plays for academic, civic, and commercial theatres. For his work as a poet and as a director, he has received various awards.

Since his retirement from Pacific, Dr. Kahn has been a guest professor at universities in Wales and in Germany, and he coontinues to direct plays, to lecture, and to write.